Managing and Leasing Commercial Properties

Practice, Strategies, and Forms

Volume I

THE REAL ESTATE PRACTICE LIBRARY: REAL ESTATE DEVELOPMENT

Managing and Leasing Commercial Properties

Practice, Strategies, and Forms

Volume I

ALAN A. ALEXANDER, CPM, CSM, CRE

RICHARD F. MUHLEBACH, CPM, CSM, CRE, RPA

JOHN WILEY & SONS, INC.

New York • Chichester • Brisbane • Toronto • Singapore

SUBSCRIPTION NOTICE

Library of Congress Cataloging-in-Publication Data

Alexander, Alan A.
   Managing and leasing commercial properties : practice, strategies,
and forms / Alan A. Alexander, Richard F. Muhlebach. — 2nd ed.
       p.   cm. — (Real estate practices library)
   Rev. and consolidated ed. of the earlier works, c1990 and c1991,
with the same title.
   Includes index.
   ISBN 0-471-30656-8 (cloth : set; available only as a set). — ISBN
0-471-30658-4 (cloth : v. 1). — ISBN 0-471-30659-2 (cloth : v. 2)
   1. Real estate management—United States. 2. Commercial
buildings—United States—Management. 3. Commercial leases—United
States. 4. Building leases—United States. 5. Commercial leases-
-United States—Forms. 6. Building leases—United States—Forms.
I. Muhlebach, Richard F., 1943–   . II. Title. III. Series.
HD1394.5.U6A37   1994
333.33'8—dc20   93-23316

Printed in the United States of America

10 9 8 7 6 5 4 3 2 1

To my loving wife and partner, Jeanne,
whose dedication, love, and support
make endeavors such as this book possible.

A. A. A.

To my parents, Frank and Flora,
who instilled in me the work ethic
to be a property manager.
To my children, Kathy and Eric,
who have shared the life of a property manager.
And especially to my loving wife, Maria,
who, for over 25 years, has always been
with me when I needed her.

R. F. M.

Preface

M*anaging and Leasing Commercial Properties* addresses the number one issue in property management in the 1990s—enhancing value. This book provides practical and successful techniques for a proactive approach to managing, marketing, and leasing commercial properties. This is not a book on the theory of property management; it is a practical, hands-on approach. The reader, whether a property manager, asset manager, portfolio manager, leasing agent, developer, or investor will be able to immediately implement management, marketing, and leasing techniques after reading the relevant chapters. The information is provided in a logical sequence that takes the reader through the process of managing and leasing a commercial property.

A major portion of *Managing and Leasing Commercial Properties* is devoted to marketing and leasing. Greater opportunities exist to enhance value by increasing the property's income than by reducing expenses. The chapters on leasing explain how to develop, implement, and administer an effective leasing program.

Management techniques common to the management of every type of commercial property are discussed in chapters on budgeting, maintenance management, and emergency procedures.

Specific management techniques for shopping centers, office buildings, and industrial properties are discussed in three chapters.

A history of commercial property management and the state of the industry is reviewed in the opening chapter. This is followed by a chapter reviewing the operations of a property management company.

This book was written as a day-by-day, hands-on guide that the real estate manager, whether a property manager, asset manager, or leasing agent, will return to time and again to find answers, proactive management and leasing approaches, and useful forms. In addition, the book offers the philosophy that managing the real estate asset is a profession that involves managing and successfully dealing with people rather than managing brick and mortar, steel, and concrete. Following this approach to managing real estate assets, all transactions must be good for everyone involved for the property to be successful.

ALAN A. ALEXANDER
RICHARD F. MUHLEBACH

San Francisco, CA.
Bellevue, WA.
October, 1993

Acknowledgments

A special acknowledgment to Karin Grice and Angelia Humphery for their invaluable assistance in the preparation of this book.

The authors are grateful for the knowledge and insight they gained through their association with Robert Parks, TRF Pacific; Robert Bearson, Advisors to Business Management; John D. Lusk, The Lusk Company; Alan Levy, Tishman International Companies; Harry Newman, Newman Properties; Stephen Roger, Aldrich Eastman and Waltch, Inc.; William Stites, Schwabe, Williamson, Ferguson and Burdel; Tom Jackson, Hall-Conway-Jackson; Richard J. Gamba, Citicorp Investment Bank; and William Steele, American Building Maintenance.

A special debt of gratitude is owed to the Institute of Real Estate Management, the International Council of Shopping Centers, and the Building Owners and Managers Association for their excellent educational programs and outstanding publications that have played an important role in formulating the management philosophy of both of the authors.

A.A.A.
R.F.M.

About the Authors

ALAN A. ALEXANDER, CPM, CSM, CRE, is senior vice president of Woodmont Managements, Inc., Belmont, California, which specializes in the managing, leasing, developing, and consulting of income-producing properties. Currently the firm's projects include office buildings, apartment complexes, and shopping centers. Prior to merging with Woodmont Managements, he was president of Alexander Consultants, a full service management company—with a specialization in commercial properties. He has provided problem-solving consultation on properties throughout the United States. He is the former senior vice-president of Fox & Carskadon Management Corporation with responsibilities for a portfolio of properties worth in excess of $100 million dollars in four western states. As director of leasing for Fox & Carskadon Financial, Mr. Alexander was responsible for the leasing of all shopping centers owned by the company throughout the United States. Mr. Alexander is on the national faculty of the Institute of Real Estate Management and is a frequent speaker at the International Council of Shopping Center Programs. He has been the moderator and speaker for over 200 seminars on developing and management and leasing of shopping centers and small office buildings for the Northwest Center for Professional Education. He is the author of several articles published in the Journal of Property Management and is a contributing author of the book *Managing the Shopping Center* published by the Institute of Real Estate Management. Mr. Alexander was inducted into the Academy of Authors of the Institute of Real Estate Management in February 1984. He is the past president of the San Francisco Bay Area Chapter of the Institute of Real Estate Management.

In 1992 he received the Distinguished Service Award for educational service to The International Council of Shopping Centers.

Richard F. Muhlebach, CPM®, CSM, CRE, RPA is president of TRF Management Corporation, Bellevue, Washington. TRF Management Corporation is responsible for the management and leasing of shopping centers, office buildings, medical buildings, and industrial park space in the Northwest and Alaska.

Mr. Muhlebach has over 20 years experience in managing, leasing, and developing and rehabing commercial buildings. Previously he served as vice president for Tishman West Management Corporation and was the general manager of The City, a 2-million square foot, mixed-use development in Orange County, California. He was responsible for converting a distressed open regional center into a successful enclosed mall. He also supervised the management of several high-rise office buildings in Los Angeles.

Previously, Mr. Muhlebach served as vice president and director of property management of the Lusk Company, a major residential and commercial developer in Irvine, California. He has managed and leased neighborhood centers to multi-level regional malls, low- to high-rise office buildings, medical buildings, industrial parks, commercial and residential condominiums, and major residential developments. He has been responsible for the management and leasing of properties located from San Diego County to Fairbanks, Alaska, and rural communities such as Eagle River, Alaska, to major metropolitan cities such as Los Angeles.

Mr. Muhlebach is a senior instructor for the Institute of Real Estate Management (IREM) and an instructor for the International Council of Shopping Centers (ICSC), the Building Owners and Managers Association (BOMA), and he teaches real estate management and leasing at the University of Washington. He is a frequent lecturer in Singapore and has served as a real estate consultant and as an expert witness.

He is co-author of the three book series, *Managing and Leasing Commercial Properties*, published by John Wiley & Sons, *Shopping Center Management* published by the Institute of Real Estate Management and *Shopping Center Tenant Relations* published by the International Council of Shopping Centers. As author of over 50 articles on real estate, he has been published in the *Journal of Property Management, Shopping Center World, National Mall Monitor, Journal of Real Estate Development, Real Estate Finance, Real Estate Today, Commercial Investment Real Estate Journal, National Real Estate Investor, Buildings,* and journals in Asia. He has twice received the *Journal of Property Management's* "Article of the Year" Award. He is a member of the *Journal's* Academy of Authors. Mr. Muhlebach has also served on the editorial review boards for four of IREM's books—*Principles of Real Estate Management, Leasing Retail Properties, Recycling: Successful Strategies for Residential and Commercial*

Properties, and *Before Disaster Strikes*—along with *Managing and Leasing Residential Properties* published by John Wiley & Sons.

Mr. Muhlebach is a Certified Property Manager®, Certified Shopping Center Manager, Counselor of Real Estate, and a Real Property Administrator.

Contents

One

Introduction

§ 1.1 HISTORY OF COMMERCIAL PROPERTY MANAGEMENT

Property management has evolved during the twentieth century from a role of caretaker to a profession with responsibility for creating or enhancing value in real estate.

At the turn of the century, property management was limited primarily to rent collection and maintenance. The property manager's role did not change significantly until after World War II, when vacancies reached a level of concern to property owners. At that point, the manager's responsibilities were expanded to include renting and leasing.

Historically, property management was not considered a leading position in real estate. That changed in the early 1970s, when REITs (Real Estate Investment Trusts) and syndications became the popular method of purchasing income-producing real estate. These arrangements were initially very successful, and within a few years the real estate market was glutted with them. In their competition to purchase property, many REITs and syndicators overpaid for properties and miscalculated their income and expense projections. Thousands of properties across the country were foreclosed. Banks and other institutions became owners of scores of problem properties. These lenders looked to property managers for merchandising, leasing, and renting expertise to assist in turning around their distressed properties. Property management was no longer perceived as a secondary position.

The commercial real estate market continued to improve in the mid to late 1970s. This was one of the best times in the history of the shopping center industry. Although the office building market had been weak during the mid seventies, by the end of the decade vacancies were down to 1% or 2% in several metropolitan areas. Industrial development, especially

1

high-tech developments, also flourished during the late 1970s. During this period, the property manager's role was focusing on management, operations, and energy conservation.

A short review of commercial real estate in the 1980s and early 1990s indicates what the commercial property management profession, commercial property management firms, and commercial property managers can expect in the mid- and late 1990s.

(a) OFFICE BUILDING INDUSTRY

The office building industry entered the 1980s following a down market during the mid and late 1970s. Class A office building rental rates which nationally were in the $6 to $12 per square foot per year range in the mid-1970s doubled, tripled, and even quadrupled in many cities in the early 1980s. Vacancy rates that were high in most areas of the country for the second half of the 1970s dropped to below 4 percent nationally in 1980. Many areas of the country as diversified as Anchorage, San Francisco, and Washington, DC, experienced vacancy rates below 2 percent.

During the first two years of the 1980s, construction cranes became a common sight in every major city and throughout the suburbs. Real estate journals extolled the wisdom of developing and investing in office buildings, and every commercial developer wanted to build them, . . . and many did. Office buildings became the preferred investment property type for institutional investors.

The office building boom lasted only a few years, and by 1983 the country was glutted with vacant office space. Construction continued at a rapid pace, however, because of the 3- to 7-year lead time to develop and bring on line a mid- to high-rise office building.

A development takes on a life of its own and frequently the developer cannot or will not stop its progress. Halting a project early in its development stage can have severe consequences to the developer. Land purchases, guaranteed land loans, pre-development costs, architectural fees, are commitments developers can't avoid. In addition development and other fees are often essential to the continued operation of the development firm. Many developers took a chance by continuing the development process when the market was already over-built, hoping that the market would turn by the time their office building was ready for occupancy. These buildings added to an already over-built market.

Vacancy rates in the mid 1980s exceeded 10 percent in most areas. Many cities, especially those in oil-producing states, experienced vacancy rates from 25 to 35 percent. When the price of oil plummeted from over $30 per barrel to less than $10 per barrel, vacancies skyrocketed in Houston, Dallas, Denver, and several other cities in Texas, Oklahoma, Louisiana, Alaska, and other states dependent on oil production.

In 1986, Dallas had in excess of 25 million square feet of office space vacant, while Houston's vacant office space exceeded 44 million square feet. In many cities, effective rental rates dropped to pre-1980 levels. Rental rates in Anchorage for class A office space dropped from $2.35 per square foot per month to less than $1.00 per square foot per month. Elaborate over-standard improvements and extensive free rent were common concessions. Many landlords offered one year's free rent on a three- or five-year lease for a half or full floor tenants.

During the early 1980s, interest rates reached their highest in history, and developers, unable to obtain acceptable financing terms, joint-ventured their office building development with institutions and other investors. Often institutions would either make a below-market interest loan for an equity position or a share of the property's cash flow, or they would contribute all of the cash to develop the building for a major share of the equity. In addition, they would receive a preferred return and sometimes a guaranteed return for the first few years of the project. When the office building didn't lease at pro forma rates and by lease-up projections, and extensive over-standard tenant improvements were given to most tenants, cash calls were required to support the building's operating expenses and/or debt service.

Developers' income comes from development fees, cash flow from buildings, and the equity in properties that is converted to cash through a sale. Development fees were dramatically reduced due to limited development opportunities. Few properties had positive cash flow or equity. Many office building developers found themselves with limited funds, a large overhead, and cash calls they were unable to fund.

Many developers were unable to contribute their share of the cash call and their ownership of the building was either reduced, eliminated, or they just walked away from their building entirely. This was a quiet and private form of foreclosure. Often, the public was unaware that the developer, who received the publicity for developing the office building and who may even have had the company's name on it, had lost the building.

The second half of the 1980s saw lenders requiring preleasing commitments, vacancy rates in the 15 to 22 percent range, effective rental rates a third to a half of the rates of the early 1980s, and institutions shying away from office building investments.

In 1990, the vacancy factor nationally was just under 20 percent. In 1991, office building vacancy rates began slowly diminishing, rental rates gradually increasing, and concessions being reduced. Rental rates, however, are still substantially below the rates necessary to support new development activities. Performance in the office portfolios will only recover as rents improve and that will take several years with no speculative development.[1] Limited construction activities through the first half of the 1990s will bring the office building market back in equilibrium in

---

[1] *Emerging Trends in Real Estate 1991*, prepared by Real Estate Research Corporation and underwritten by Equitable Real Estate Investment Management.

the end of this decade, just as the limited construction of the mid- and late 1970s was one of the factors that created a strong office building market in the early 1980s.

(b) INDUSTRIAL PROPERTY INDUSTRY

In the 1980s the industrial real estate market was over-built in most areas of the country. While the situation was serious, the problems were not as severe as those of the office building markets. This market entered the 1990s with a slow recovery. Coldwell Banker's 1990 survey of industrial buildings in excess of 100,000 square feet shows a vacancy rate of 6.9 percent. This report indicates that more than 70 percent of the available space in these buildings is nonmanufacturing space.

The supply and demand balance remained fairly stable for the first few years of the nineties. According to both the Coldwell Banker index (for buildings of at least 100,000 square feet) and the Grubb & Ellis survey (buildings 25,000 square feet and over), there has been little change in vacancy rates from 1986 and 1991. Warehouse/distribution space will remain the keystone of industrial property investments. Transportation hubs will be the most popular locations. Flex space is still in oversupply throughout the United States.[2]

Just like the office building market, a slowing of construction activity from the mid-1980s to the mid-1990s will bring the market to an equilibrium between supply and demand. During the last half of the 1980s, industrial properties outperformed office buildings. During the early 1990s, industrial properties were one of the preferred choices of investors.

(c) SHOPPING CENTER INDUSTRY

The shopping center industry's experience was quite different from that of the office building industry from the mid-1970s through the end of the 1980s. Unlike the office building market, the 1970s was a boom time for shopping centers. Development was at an all-time high, and more regional malls and strip centers were developed than at any other prior time in our country's history.

Then in 1981, the market took a dramatic turn when the country entered into a recession and interest rates climbed to 18 percent and above. These two events were devastating to the retailing industry. Not only were sales sluggish as a result of the recession, but retailers' cash flow was negatively impacted when they financed their inventory at unheard of high interest rates. The combination of the recession and high

---

[2] David Weisel, "The Outlook for Industrial Real Estate," *Commercial Investment Real Estate Journal*, Fall 1990.

interest rates dramatically slowed the formation of new retail businesses and the expansion of existing retailers.

The result was a significant reduction of demand for small shop space in strip shopping centers. In addition, the early 1980s had the highest number of business failures since the Great Depression. Strip center rental rates were either flat or reduced throughout the early and mid-1980s in most communities around the country. Landlords offered rent relief to struggling retail tenants. They believed that partial rent and an operating business was better than another vacancy.

Regional malls fared much better since the majority of their merchants are credit-worthy national or regional tenants. In addition, most regional and super-regional malls have a well-established customer base and limited competition. Few malls were severely affected by the recession and high interest rates. The demand for additional regional malls, however, was limited because most areas of the country were adequately served by existing regional malls. Most of the activity in regional mall development was either expansion and/or remodeling of existing centers.

By the mid- to late 1980s, the shopping center industry improved. Shopping centers, especially regional malls, became the prime real estate investment choice of institutions and pension funds. Commercial developers looked to shopping center development to replace their office building and industry property development activities. One indication of this renewed interest was the significant increase in attendance in the late 1980s at the International Council of Shopping Center's annual conventions in Las Vegas.

With most commercial developers interested in shopping center development, the industry became overbuilt. "Clearly, the shopping center market resembles the office market of two years ago, when it was on the verge of collapse," maintains David Shulman, who directs real estate research at Salomon Brothers Inc. "It will take a couple of years to work off the excess space."[3]

The shopping center market is mixed as it enters the 1990s, not just by geographical regions but within markets. "The nationwide vacancy rate for shopping centers, according to the ICSC, was 10.6 percent in 1989, almost unchanged from 10.5 percent in 1988. The region encompassing Texas, Oklahoma, Louisiana, and Arkansas fared the worse, with a 20.8 percent vacancy rate, while the California, Oregon, and Washington region was the healthiest, at 5.5 percent."[4]

The November 1990 issue of *Monitor* reported the national average vacancy rate to be 15.9 percent for downtown retail properties, 12.3 percent for strip centers, and 6.5 percent for enclosed malls. A good

---

[3] Mitchell Pacelle, "Mall Developers Face Severe Credit Pinch," *The Wall Street Journal*, November 13, 1990.

[4] *Ibid.*

example of the diversity of the shopping center market in the early nineties was on the West Coast. Southern California was fairly strong, while the Seattle area had pockets of strengths and weaknesses. Anchorage is still reeling from an over-built strip shopping center market, while rental rates are a third to a half of what they were in the early 1980s.

Seattle is a good example of a region with a varied shopping center market although the economy in the Pacific Northwest, and especially Seattle, was strong entering the 1990s. Some Seattle neighborhoods were over-built and rental rates for strip shopping centers had been flat for the past five years, ranging from $8 to $12 per square foot per year. In other neighborhoods, such as Bellevue, the market was and still is strong with little available space and rental rates ranging from $16 to $22 per square foot per year.

In downtown Seattle's retail core—an area of three to four square blocks—rental rates for storefront shops ranged from $35 to $45 per square foot per year. Yet retail space outside the core area ranged from $12 to $27 per square foot per year. Regional malls in the greater Seattle area have very low vacancy rates and rental rates ranged between $25 and $40 per square foot, but only one or two regional malls will be developed in Western Washington in the 1990s. Seattle is typical of what many areas of the country will experience. Successful shopping center development in the early 1990s in Seattle occurred in selected pocket areas. A good site, developed with the right anchor tenants may be just a few blocks from existing shopping centers that are suffering from flat rental rates and high vacancies.

One of the primary criteria for success for a strip shopping center is location. Shopping centers developed on secondary sites have problems competing in a soft economy and over-built markets. Next, the shopping center must have the right anchor tenants and tenant mix for the trade area. The layout of the shopping center must provide each space with good visibility, traffic flow, and access.

The size and configuration of the shop space must meet the needs of the retailers and not be based on the developer's goal of maximizing the amount of gross leasable area (GLA) on the site. Most retailers downsized in the late 1970s and early 1980s. Strip shopping center shop space in excess of 2,000 square feet had limited potential uses. Seattle, like many areas throughout the country, will have limited new retail development, and those shopping centers that are built will be based on the above criteria. Few regional malls will be developed throughout the 1990s. Shopping center development in the early 1990s was at a slower pace than the mid- and late 1980s.

A dark cloud looming over the shopping center industry was the recession the country entered in late 1990 and continued through most of 1992. The 1981 recession dramatically impacted retail sales. This was a major cause of the slowdown of the growth of retail stores. The 1991 census of U.S. Shopping Centers conducted by the *Monitor*, a leading shopping center industry publication stated:

> This year's census suggests that shopping center developers are taking the threats to heart. Where 2,210 new centers opened in 1989 (a 10.3 percent rise over 1988), this year 153 fewer opened, a decline of 7.2 percent.
> Moreover, square footage of GLA grew 7 percent while sales increased only 6.2 percent. The result was a decline in average annual sales per square foot of GLA, to $160.90 from $162.02 the year before. Only 19 states saw average sales per square foot increase, while 31 experienced decreases.[5]

All retail properties, from super-regional malls to specialty centers, will be tested in the 1990s. Slower economic growth, changing demographics, and turmoil among retailers (especially department stores) are the key issues.[6] In the early 1990s, category killers, warehouse stores, supermarkets expanding to 50,000 square feet and greater and the power center threaten the traditional strip center and the local retailer. The trend for retailers to downsize was reversed with retailers building large stores to dominate a product line.

(d) COMMERCIAL DEVELOPMENT

The impetus of commercial real estate activity is development. The development of a building activates all the real estate disciplines. A land broker sells the property to the developer. The developer's project manager and support staff take the project from conception through grand opening. A mortgage broker and loan officer arrange the financing. Architects, consultants, general contractor, and subcontractors are hired to design and build the project. Leasing agents are retained to market the building and negotiate the lease terms. Corporate real estate managers represent major tenants in lease negotiations. A property manager develops and implements the building's management plan. An investment broker sells the building. An asset manager is assigned to maximize the return on the newly acquired investment. All of the aforementioned disciplines are dependent to one degree or another on the amount of ongoing development activity. When development activity slows, each of these real estate professionals and related disciplines are negatively affected.

As described earlier, commercial real estate is over-built in most areas throughout the country leaving relatively few premier sites available. In addition, environmental issues, especially properties containing wetlands, are an impediment to development. Environmental concerns

---

[5] Robert E. O'Neill, "Planning Ahead for 1991," *Monitor*, November 1990.

[6] *Emerging Trends in Real Estate 1991*, prepared by Real Estate Research Corporation and underwritten by Equitable Real Estate Investment Management.

will delay and sometimes prohibit the development. The wetlands issue is of such concern on a national and local level that the Urban Land Institute has developed a two-day seminar titled "Wetlands and Real Estate Development."

Obtaining financing for a new development is another hurdle. "Effects of the savings and loan crisis are being felt nationwide, either directly through a general dearth of loans from thrifts or indirectly as commercial banks, insurance companies, and other institutional lenders scrutinize their loan portfolios and lending practices. The pool of available loan money is 'much tighter than a year ago' simply because there are 'fewer sources of money,' says Jonathan A. Rosen, a partner with Sonneblick-Goldman, New York."[7]

Lenders are more conservative than in the past, and they have tightened lending requirements. Lenders now evaluate a borrower's entire portfolio and not just the property that is being considered for the loan. The lender's evaluation will include an analysis of the credit of the building's tenants, environmental issues, the impact the neighborhood and the competition has on the property, along with supply and demand. The lenders are going back to basics and using good lending practices.

No longer can a developer obtain 100 percent financing. Developers are required to put equity in their deals. Traditionally, developers have not had to put their dollars in the deal and are not accustomed to putting their money into the development process. For most proposed developments, 50 to 70 percent financing is all a lender will allow the developer. Many developers will need substantial equity partners. The marginal developers will be out of business. The positive effect is fewer projects will be developed and those that are developed will have a high probability of succeeding.

With an over-built market, investors are reluctant to provide the 30 to 50 percent equity necessary for the developer to obtain financing of a proposed project. Many developers who survived the 1980s entered the 1990s cash poor and/or with properties that have negative cash flow.

All of these factors, primarily the over-built market, have resulted in fewer development opportunities in the early 1990s. Most developers have prepared for the turbulent 1990s by redefining their market, downsizing their operations, and exploring opportunities to create additional profit centers. Reflecting their optimism, developers are referring to their adjustment to the market not as downsizing but in a positive term—rightsizing.

Many developers became merchant builders in the late eighties and first few years of the nineties by preselling their development to generate operating capital. Some developers are using the talents of their

---

[7] David Wagman, "Recession Worries Close Lending Spigots," *Shopping Center World*, October 1990.

construction staff to offer construction management services and/or general contractor's services to the community. Another potential profit center is expanding the property management department. A developer offering fee property management services has an excellent potential for covering part of the development firm's overhead and/or generating a profit. The entry into third party fee property management is, however, charged with potential problems.

(e) THE 1990s

Early in the 1990s, most metropolitan areas were still overbuilt in most commercial property types. The office building market continued to suffer from the record development activities that occurred during the first half of the 1980s. Adding to the problem of excessive supply of office space from the 1980s was the downsizing, or "rightsizing" of hundreds of firms and the merger and consolidation of several financial institutions. Firms downsized primarily for one of two reasons: The recession caused them to lay off people or technology enabled firms to operate with fewer people. One example of downsizing with new technology is the manufacturing industry. Airplane and automotive manufacturers can produce the same number of planes and automobiles with fewer people. Every business is impacted by technology. Office tenants need less file storage space when they convert the content of file folders in metal cabinets to computer files. Retailers and manufacturers are employing just-in-time delivery systems. Through computerized inventory control, suppliers deliver merchandise and supplies only when they are needed. Many tenants no longer need large storage areas for inventory that will not be needed for weeks or months.

The fiscal crises of the late 1980s have had a lasting impact on commercial property markets. One of the fallouts of the savings & loan and banking crisis is the closure and mergers of hundreds of financial institutions. In the northwest, when the two largest banks merged, tens of thousands of square feet of office sublease space were placed on an already overbuilt market.

The shopping center market is also overbuilt and some areas have seen anchor mall tenants close. Some of the nation's most prominent department stores filed for bankruptcy. Most of these bankruptcies were the result of excessive debt caused by leveraged buyouts. During the bankruptcy proceedings, some chain department stores closed their nonperforming stores, leaving malls with empty anchor tenant space. However, by 1993, most of the department store chains that filed Chapter 11 petitions were coming out of bankruptcy.

In many areas of the country, rents continue to decline and concessions have increased. There are few areas where rents can support new development. Most experts predict that the office building market will remain overbuilt during the remaining years of the 1990s. One might say that 20 years of office building development occurred between 1980 and 1982.

Since shopping centers are location-dependent, there will always be a need for new shopping centers to follow the path of residential growth, though new development opportunities will be limited during the mid- and late 1990s. New and expanding retailing concepts (e.g. value-oriented tenants and category killers) will generate the need for some development activity, such as power and outlet centers.

Industrial and high-tech properties are experiencing some of the challenges of the office building industry and some of the unique development opportunities of the shopping center industry. Most areas are overbuilt, yet new, high-tech industries and technological innovations will create development activity.

During a soft market, every developer is optimistic that he or she can find a site and develop a building that is "right" and will lease up well. As long as financing is available, developers will find what they believe is a "niche market or area" in which to build. Unfortunately, for most developers obtaining financing and equity funds is more difficult than finding prospective tenants for a new development.

In the early and mid-1990s, the credit crunch was the primary reason why few projects were developed. Banks and other types of financial institutions had excessive nonperforming real estate portfolios. Many lenders not only foreclosed on properties, but had loans on properties where, even though the loan payment was current, the value of the property was less than the balance on the loan. Many lenders either stopped or greatly reduced the amount of loans for new commercial developments and for the purchase of existing commercial properties. Most developers could not meet the qualifications of the limited numbers of commercial loans available. Lenders required significant pre-leasing to creditworthy tenants and a low loan-to-value ratio. During the 1970s and most of the 1980s, loans were typically 90 to 100 percent of the cost to develop a project. Thus, a $10 million commercial development would require equity of $1 million or less. Often the developer would be able to finance the entire development cost by showing that the project would be worth considerably more than the loan when it was completed and leased. In contrast, during the early and mid-1990s, banks offering commercial loans were loaning only 60 to 70 percent of the development cost. The same $10 million commercial project would require $3 to $4 million dollars of equity. Since few developers have millions of dollars in reserve, not only did they have problems obtaining a loan, but they also had to find joint venture partners who would provide the substantial equity. The combination of scarce commercial loans, high equity requirements, and an overbuilt market with depressed rents just about eliminated all commercial development in the early and mid-1990s.

One of the casualties of the real estate crisis of the early nineties is a lost generation of entrepreneurial developers. Developers are the engine of commercial real estate. Their activities propagate other real estate activities. When developers are developing, loan officers are making loans, architects have buildings to design, contractors and construction workers have buildings to build, appraisers are valuating proposed developments, leasing agents have new and exciting products to move, investment brokers have sales opportunities, investors have greater investment choices, and property managers have additional buildings to manage. When developmental activity slows down or comes to a halt, all of the real estate professions and related industries are severely impacted. Since 1991, the construction crane has been an endangered species in most areas of the country.

Although the commercial real estate industry has experienced its worst period since the Great Depression of 1929, in the early and mid-1990s, the remaining portion of the decade should improve. The supply-and-demand equation will come close to equilibrium with limited commercial construction activity by the end of the 1990s. As vacancies decrease, rents will increase while concessions will decline. New buildings will be developed because of a need for space, not a need for tax write-offs. The saying in commercial real estate in 1990 was "stay alive 'til ninety-five"; the saying in the mid-1990s is "find something to do 'til 2002."

Though every segment of the commercial real estate industry has been impacted by the depressed real estate market, the property management industry has fared considerably better than all of the other commercial real estate professions. Though there have been numerous new property management companies formed during the past few years, and a shifting of properties from one property management company to another, the industry did not have a major downsizing.

(f) CONCLUSION

It has been said that the 1990s will be a time when the commercial real estate industry pays for its excesses of the 1980s. The industry is downsizing or rightsizing. The industry will need a recovery in effective rents before there is an appreciable increase in development activity. With limited development activities, it is safe to say that in the early 1990s the industry had too many developers, project managers, loan officers, leasing agents, and construction managers.

After the Tax Reform Act of 1986, syndicators were all but put out of business. In the late 1980s, developers started to be impacted by the reduction in development activities. In 1990, loan officers felt the result of fewer development projects. In 1991, leasing agents and brokers were impacted by fewer new projects and a gradual reduction in vacant space in some areas. New development activities almost ceased due to the credit crunch. Property management and asset management may be the only commercial real estate disciplines that do not experience a reduction in their number of professionals. As long as the inventory of income-producing properties remains the same, there will be a need for the same number of property managers and asset managers.

The inventory of commercial buildings will continue to increase, though slightly, through the 1990s. Developers and investors are viewing property management in a different light, and this will cause significant changes in the property management industry. These changes will impact property management firms and property managers.

§ 1.2   NEW BREED OF OWNERS

In the early 1980s, it was virtually impossible for developers to obtain traditional financing for a project. Obtaining 100 percent, 90 percent, or even 80 percent financing at interest rates below 10 percent was impossible. To continue to operate and build projects, developers either participated in joint ventures with an institution that provided most or all of the funds to develop the project, or they obtained a loan at an interest rate below market and provided the lender with a percentage of the equity and/or cash flow and appreciation of the property.

Property managers who worked for developers now also reported to the developer's institutional partner. When the office building market was overbuilt in the mid-1980s and rents were 25 percent or more below pro forma, many institutional partners became sole owners of buildings. If the developers were unable to contribute their share of the cash call to support the building's deficits, their equity positions were reduced. In many cases, the developer's position was eliminated, although the developer continued to manage and lease the project. This is the primary reason why relatively few foreclosures of medium to large commercial buildings occurred in the mid to late 1980s.

Syndication was again popular in the 1980s, and property managers were again managing property for syndicators. However, the Tax Reform Act of 1986 reduced the tax benefits of owning properties, and many syndicators were unable to continue to obtain funds from investors who were seeking tax benefits. Many syndicators dramatically reduced their real estate purchases.

Pension funds and insurance companies were another major player in commercial real estate during the 1980s. By the late 1980s, these institutions became the major purchasers of medium to large commercial projects. Their objectives in purchasing real estate differed somewhat from the developers' or syndicators' objectives. Pension funds and other institutions are typically long-term investors. They are not fee-driven buyers. Their analysis of the property for purchase, called due diligence, is typically intense, thorough, and sophisticated. They are purchasing property for its potential yield. Yield has two components—cash flow and the appreciation of the property. Institutional buyers are looking to enhance the value of the property they purchase.

After the properties are purchased, the institutions assign them to an asset manager. The asset manager is responsible for a portfolio of properties and complements the responsibilities of the property manager. The eight generic functions of asset management are (1) acquisition, (2) selection and supervision of the property management company, (3) performance monitoring/control, (4) retenanting/rehabilitation, (5) peripheral development, (6) refinancing, (7) restructuring ownership, and (8) disposition.[8]

By the early 1990s, the supply of commercial space slowed because of limited new construction. At the same time, the demand for space continued to drop in many areas of the country. There were three main effects from this imbalance in the supply and demand for space; (1) rents dropped below most buildings' pro forma rents; (2) concessions increased to entice tenants to move out of other buildings; and (3) vacancy rates continued to climb into the low double-digit range. Up until the mid-1980s, a building's stabilized occupancy was considered 95 percent; in the early 1980s, developers and leasing agents talked of a 90 percent stabilization rate. By the mid-1990s, the number was lowered by some developers and investors to 85 percent occupancy. The lowering of some real estate professionals' opinion of the stabilized occupancy rate was a reflection of not only the current occupancy rate but also of the concern and anticipation that these rates would not significantly improve throughout the mid-nineties. There was also concern that in some areas of the country the office building market would not improve during the remainder of this decade.

Many building owners who acquired their properties during the 1990s and who did not have deep pockets (and few developers and private investors did) found themselves negotiating with the building's lender to restructure the property's mortgage. Thousands of building owners were in default of their mortgage. Most of the defaults were classified as monetary defaults—the building owner was unable to continue to pay the monthly mortgage. Some building owners were in non-monetary default of their mortgage. Several actions can cause non-monetary default, such as (1) failure to pay the property's real estate taxes, (2) the building's ownership or the general partner filing for bankruptcy protection, or (3) the building's debt coverage ratio dropping below an acceptable

---

[8] Real Estate Research Corporation, *The Key to Profitable Real Estate Investment: Asset Management* (1985).

agreed upon ratio. The building's owner and the lender usually tried to negotiate or "work out" the problem with the mortgage default. The lender might agree to a cash flow mortgage, where all the net operating income (NOI) is applied to the mortgage payment. A second option is a moratorium of the debt service (loan or mortgage payment) for a specific period. A third option is an interest rate reduction, where the interest rate on the loan would be lowered to an agreed rate or tied to a financial index. In each of these options, the difference between the original mortgage payment and the new negotiated mortgage payment would often be added to the balance of the loan. Another option would be debt forgiveness. In any of these negotiated "work outs," the lender may ask for a percentage of the profits when the building is sold as consideration for their restructuring the loan. When the building owner was unable to "work out" the loan, the lender usually acquired the property by a deed in lieu of foreclosure or foreclosed on the property. During the foreclosure proceedings, the lender usually petitions the courts for a court-appointed receiver to manage the property until either the lender acquired title to the property or a "work out" agreement was reached.

Hundreds of banks and savings & loans (thrifts) acquired ownership of thousands of properties by foreclosing on nonperforming loans. These properties were placed in the banks or savings & loans' Real Estate Owned (REO), also known as Other Real Estate Owned (OREO), departments for management and disposition. The lenders' goals were to dispose of the property at the highest price possible, as soon as possible.

While banks and savings & loans were foreclosing on properties, hundreds of these institutions were in financial trouble. Nonperforming real estate loans were one of the major contributors of the banks and savings & loans' problems. When the Office of Comptroller of the Currency (OCC) closed failed banks, they turned the management and resolution of the institutions to the Federal Deposit Insurance Corporation (FDIC). The Office of Thrift Supervisor (OTS) oversaw the savings & loans. They turned over a failed savings & loan to the Resolution Trust Corporation (RTC) for management and resolution. The FDIC and RTC were responsible for the liquidation of the assets, including foreclosed properties, and of failed banks and savings & loans. These properties were sold through auction, bulk sales, or individual property sales. Many real estate investors and developers were unable to participate in bidding and acquiring these properties for lack of equity and of the ability to finance the properties. A term coined during the late 1980s, "cash is king," described the requirements to purchase most of the troubled assets. The majority of the troubled real estate assets or distressed properties were being purchased below replacement cost. The purchasers had the financial sources and real estate entrepreneurial skills necessary to hold these properties while increasing their value.

This scenario of what has happened with troubled real estate properties describes the three generations of commercial property owners during the early- to mid-1990s. The first property owner was the developer or investor who acquired the property in the 1980s. The lender was the second property owner through foreclosure. The new investor was the third owner of the property during this relatively short period.

Property management firms have dealt with three generations of property owners in a relatively short period. Such a rapid change of ownership resulted in turmoil for many property management firms. Frequent change of property ownership causes frequent changing of property management firms that must be hired to manage the property. Many owners have either managed the property themselves or have brought in a property management firm they prefer over the property's existing property management company.

Property management accounts are usually acquired when a property is developed or when the ownership changes. Third generation owners are likely to retain ownership of their properties for at least three to five years until the property regains value. There will be fewer developers and fewer financial institutions seeking the services of property management firms during the mid-1990s as (1) foreclosed properties are sold off, (2) some insurance companies assume the management of their properties, and (3) the private investor re-emerges.

§ 1.3 PROPERTY MANAGERS OF THE 1990s

The goals and objectives of institutional owners, combined with their reliance on the property manager to achieve their goals, have changed the manager's role. Property managers are expected to enhance value. They must understand how their responsibilities effect the property's net operating income and thus effect its value.

Property management has become more proactive than reactive. The successful manager anticipates problems and opportunities and responds in advance to control the situation.

Management today is complex, and the astute property manager must have a multitude of skills and abilities. A typical week's activity will bring the manager in touch with legal problems, maintenance situations, marketing and leasing activities, human relations problems, construction needs, accounting problems, and a host of other diverse but interrelated activities. Many tenants are sophisticated business people, and the commercial property manager often interacts with some of the top talent in the business community. When tenants decide to open a store in a shopping center or lease space in a high rise, they are making a major financial commitment to the success of their business and that of the building. As a result, it is not uncommon for a prospective tenant to inquire into the capabilities of the building's management and even into the qualifications of a specific manager.

The property manager responsible for the direct management of the property is accountable on a daily basis for enhancing the property's value. Most property managers of the 1990s will be working either directly for the institutions as fee managers or employees, a developer who is expanding its property management department or company by soliciting third party fee management or investors who have elected to manage their own properties or traditional fee management companies.

§ 1.4   PROPERTY MANAGEMENT INDUSTRY TRENDS IN THE 1990s

The challenges for the commercial real estate industry during the 1990s will cause major changes in the property management industry. The property management industry had always been relatively immune to real estate recessions. However, this recession is different: While the inventory of available buildings to manage is not growing, the industry is also not shrinking. This fundamental market shift will cause a major shake-up that will impact property management for years to come.

The changes that are emerging during the turbulent 1990s include: (1) the market for fee property management services is shrinking; (2) developers are soliciting third party (other owners' properties) property management; (3) several institutional property owners and private investors are now managing their own properties; (4) property management employment opportunities are shifting; (5) there is a growing trend for property management firms to merge, form networking associations, and purchase one another; (6) the only growth area has become managing distressed or troubled properties; (7) Real Estate Investment Trusts (REIT) are increasing the ownership of properties and many REITs will manage their properties; and (8) the main competitors of many property management firms are their own clients.

The greatest challenge and fear for owners and operators of fee property management firms is first on this list: the shrinking of the universe of properties available for third party management. The inventory of the number of commercial buildings is not declining but it is not growing either. Developers are not adding to this inventory by developing new buildings due to (1) overbuilt markets, (2) rents below the levels needed to justify new buildings, and (3) the credit crunch. In addition, hundreds of property owners have exercised their rights to cancel their property management contracts with 30- to 60-day notice and are managing the properties themselves. The combination of limited or no new product along with existing product being removed from the market caused the number of properties that are available for fee management to shrink.

Developers are soliciting other owners' properties to manage. Traditionally, most medium- to large-size commercial developers managed their properties, while small developers awarded the management of their properties to fee (third party) property management companies. When developers are not building projects, they are not earning development fees. Their other primary sources of income are cash flow from existing successful buildings and from the sale of successful properties. For many developers in the 1990s, the income from these three sources is either significantly reduced or non-existent. Many developers are either soliciting the management of other owners' properties and/or have taken their properties away from third party management firms and are managing their properties themselves. In §§ 2.3 and 2.5 we discuss a developer starting a property management company or department.

The third change is that major property owners, such as insurance companies, are creating subsidiary property management companies and are selecting their most profitable properties to manage. Insurance companies usually own major office buildings, malls, and industrial properties. These insurance firms had either entered into a joint venture partnership with the developer of the property or had purchased the properties from the developer. In both situations, it was common for the insurance company to use the developer's property management firm to continue to manage and lease the property. In the early- to mid-1990s, a few of the insurance companies canceled or didn't renew the property management contracts on many of their properties. They awarded the property management contracts to their new subsidiary property management company. These property management firms usually retain the existing on-site management, administrative and maintenance staff, and pick up where the prior property management firm left off. These firms can "cherry pick" which properties to manage and can leave the marginally profitable properties to the existing property management firm. After they have selected the best properties to manage, some will solicit other owners' properties to manage.

Many small investors are beginning to manage their properties "in-house." The reason these and other firms are going to in-house management is to generate income that was lost or reduced from their real estate or other business activities.

The fourth change is the shifting of employment opportunities in the property management industry. The employment opportunities have shifted from third party property management firms to either developers who are expanding the existing property management department of companies, or to institutional property owners and investors who are managing their owner properties and opportunities in a bank's real estate owned (REO) department. Some of the developers are not hiring property managers but promoting administrative personnel into property management positions. In some areas of the country, property managers will have few employment opportunities because many of the firms that are taking their properties in-house to manage will assign the management responsibility to existing staff.

The fifth change is the trend for property management firms to merge, network, or purchase one another. Some property management executives believe that through rapid growth they can position themselves as a major player in the industry and can operate more efficiently and cost effectively. They offer a property owner, usually an institutional owner, their ability to manage properties in several states. They believe the property owner would rather deal with one firm with one accounting reporting format, and interface with one property management executive if things go wrong, rather than deal with several firms with different computerized accounting reports and several executive property managers. Other property management executives believe that property management is a localized, hands-on business. They wonder if the large firms will become top-heavy with executives' big salaries, benefits, and support staff. The jury is still out on the success of this trend; it will be the late 1990s before we'll know if bigger is better or smaller is smarter.

The sixth trend is the proliferation of distressed properties. In many areas of the country, managing, leasing, and selling troubled properties is the only growth area in commercial real estate. Property managers are serving as court-appointed receivers and are managing foreclosed properties for banks, other institutions and the Resolution Trust Corporation (RTC). In some states, such as Texas and California, managing troubled properties is a new segment of the property management industry, while in other states, such as Washington, few commercial properties have been foreclosed and the RTC's activity is limited.

The seventh change is the re-emergence of Real Estate Investment Trusts (REITs). Once again REITs have become a viable and popular means of purchasing and financing real estate. Many national and local developers are using their portfolio of properties to form REITs. Some developers will use part of the capital they raise purchasing additional properties. Until 1986, REITs could not manage their own properties. Many REITs will manage their properties thus further reducing the number of properties available for third-party management.

The eighth change is the most frightening challenge. Fee property management firms' number one competitor is their clients. Many property management firms lost portfolio size in the early and mid-1990s. The loss of many of their management accounts was attributed to property owners deciding to manage their own properties. This trend will continue for many property owners until the income that can be earned from other real estate activities, such as development, syndications, and other real estate activities once again far exceeds the income earned from property management.

The good news for the property management industry is that it has not significantly downsized. There will always be a need for property managers.

§ 1.5 PROFESSIONAL ORGANIZATIONS

Managing a property is no different from running a business. Both entail accounting, financial analysis, financing, marketing and sales (leasing), public relations, people skills, maintenance, real estate and business law, and handling the unexpected. No one can be an expert in all these areas. Fortunately, the commercial property management industry is served by three professional organizations. These organizations trace their history to the early years of property management. They conduct research, present educational programs, publish periodicals and textbooks, hold local and national meetings, lobby on a local and national level, award professional designations, and serve their members and the real estate industry on a local and national level.

(a) INSTITUTE OF REAL ESTATE MANAGEMENT

The Institute of Real Estate Management (IREM), an affiliate of the National Association of REALTORS®, was founded in 1933. IREM awards the Certified Property Manager (CPM®) designation to managers who have distinguished themselves in experience, education, and ethical conduct. All CPM® members must abide by a code of ethics established by the Institute of Real Estate Management. Those violating the code are subject to revocation of their designation. To qualify for the CPM® designation, a candidate must successfully complete an intense series of IREM courses.[9]

IREM offers the most complete real estate education program in the industry. Its 300 series of courses are week-long programs that provide the foundation for a solid property management education. Each course focuses on a specific property type—apartments, office buildings, shopping centers, or government-assisted housing, providing an in-depth examination of management techniques for that particular property.

IREM's 400 course, Managing Real Estate as an Investment, is designed for property managers involved in fiscal policy decisions for investment real estate. The course also discusses the management plan.

The 500 course, Problem Solving and Decision Making for Property Managers, teaches students to identify problems that affect a property's performance and to formulate viable solutions.

---

[9] Institute of Real Estate Management, *Your Real Estate Investment Deserves a Certified Property Manager* (1989).

Course 701, Managing the Management Office, teaches the latest techniques in the operation of a successful management office. Course 702, Advanced Management Practices and Techniques, is designed for executives who want to sharpen their management and human relations skills.

IREM publishes a comprehensive line of professional books, monographs, cassette tapes, and a leading property management periodical, *The Journal of Property Management.*

In 1945, the Institute set standards under which certain firms could be recognized as Accredited Management Organizations (AMO). Holders of the AMO designation have met IREM's standards of education, experience, integrity, and fiscal stability.[10]

There are approximately 100 local IREM chapters in the United States and Canada. Each conducts monthly meetings, provides miniseminars, and serves the interests of the property management profession.

IREM's national headquarters are located at 430 N. Michigan Avenue, Chicago, IL 60611 (312/329-6000).

(b) INTERNATIONAL COUNCIL OF SHOPPING CENTERS

The International Council of Shopping Centers (ICSC) was formed in 1956 to serve the shopping center industry. ICSC awards three professional designations, CSM (Certified Shopping Center Manager), CMD (Certified Marketing Director), and CLS (Certified Leasing Specialist).

The objectives of the CSM program are to:

1. Establish and advance high standards in shopping center management. A CSM must be able to manage all types and sizes of shopping centers, in a wide range of geographical locations.
2. Recognize managers who meet these professional standards.
3. Encourage others to train for careers in shopping center management.
4. Establish and maintain educational standards for the profession.[11]

The first CSM exam was administered in May 1964. It is a written examination that covers operation and construction, leasing, accounting and record keeping, finance, center retailing and merchandising, promotions, community relations, insurance, and law. Initially, the testing process consisted of an eight-hour essay exam followed the next day with a one- to two-hour interview. This format was changed in 1980 to an all-day written multiple-choice exam.

---

[10] A. Downs, *Principles of Real Estate Management*, p. 18 (1987).

[11] International Council of Shopping Centers, *CSM, CMD Directory* (1987).

The Certified Marketing Director (CMD) program, formerly the Accredited Shopping Center Promotion Director (ASPD) program, was initiated by ICSC in 1971.

The objectives of the CMD program are to:

1. Establish high professional standards in the marketing activities of shopping centers. A CMD must be able to direct the marketing and promotion efforts of all types and sizes of shopping centers in a wide range of geographical locations.

2. Give industry wide recognition to marketing/promotion directors who achieve professional standing.

3. Establish educational standards for the profession.

4. Encourage others to train for careers in shopping center marketing.[12]

The CMD examination is a multiple-choice written test that covers the marketing plan, product development/center merchandising, retailing/store merchandising, media planning, public relations, and administration.

ICSC offers extensive educational programs at the regional and national level. The School of Professional Development is a week-long session offering courses on development, finance, leasing, management, design and construction, and marketing. Idea Exchanges are one-, two- and three-day seminars on specialized topics that are offered throughout the country. The annual convention, held in May, is a week-long program featuring speakers, a trade show, exhibits, and a leasing mall. At the leasing mall developers, brokers, and retailers meet to make business deals. The Council also offers several one-week courses on shopping center management, advanced shopping center management, marketing, and promotions. ICSC publishes books, technical reports, legal reports, and other specialized bulletins as well as checklists designed for use in the field.

Senior Designations

As of 1993, ICSC has adopted a program to recognize existing CSMs and CMDs for a Senior designation. The stated objective is to "Encourage the ongoing education and professional development of shopping center managers and marketing directors who have achieved their initial designations." The Senior level status will be conferred on those members who can demonstrate an active level of participating in the areas of Education, Service, and Professional Recognition within the

---

[12] International Council of Shopping Centers, *CSM, CMD Directory* (1987).

industry. The Senior level designation will be valid for three years and will require that the recipient requalify every three years thereafter.

The CLS designation is new in 1993 with the first test scheduled for October 1994. The new designation is designed to recognize the leasing specialist in the shopping center industry. The qualificataions will include a requirement of at least four years of active full-time experience in shopping center leasing and/or completion of the ICSC leasing and Advance Leasing Certificate programs, or completion of the ICSC Advance Leasing Certificate Program with related work experience, or completion of the ICSC Advanced Leasing Certificate Program and the successful completion of 30 hours of instruction of college level courses or real estate continuing education courses at an approved institution of higher education or other recognized provider. Proof of a real estate license in good standing in any state or province can be used for part of the qualifications.

Once the designation has been achieved, the recipient will be required to participate in a continuing education program in order to retain the designation.

The International Council of Shopping Centers is located at 665 Fifth Avenue, New York, NY 10022 (212/421-8181).

(c) BUILDING OWNERS AND MANAGERS ASSOCIATION

In 1907, a group of 75 office building managers formed the National Association of Building Owners and Managers, later known as the Building Owners and Managers Association (BOMA). They held their first convention in Chicago in 1908. The program for this inaugural event included such topics as ventilation, economy in electric lighting, varnishes, cleaning problems, and division of costs of services in buildings—topics that are still discussed today. This convention was the first time commercial property managers met nationally to share ideas and exchange information.

In 1920, the association published the industry's first major research report on office building operating expenses, the annual *Experience Exchange Report* (EER). The EER analyzes the income and expenses of more than 3,000 office buildings across the United States and Canada, providing a standard of performance comparison for all office buildings. The report is the leading reference guide for building operation.[13]

BOMA monthly publishes *Skylines*, the only periodical devoted to the office building industry. BOMA International has published several books on office building management and leasing, including *Office Building Lease Manual, Leasing Concepts, Standard Method of Floor Measurements*, and *A Guide to Commercial Property Management*.

[13] BOMA International, *Forging the Future of the Office Building Industry* (n.d.).

Through its educational arm, the Building Owners and Managers Institute International, BOMA provides college-level courses leading to the professional designations of Real Property Administrator (RPA), Systems Maintenance Technician (SMT), and Systems Maintenance Administrator (SMA). The courses are taught locally in the United States and Canada and are also available through home study.

The RPA program consists of eight advanced education courses that cover building design, operation, maintenance, finance and investment, administration, insurance, legal concepts, and leasing.

Through a separate eight-course curriculum, the SMT and SMA programs provide hands-on courses detailing the operation and maintenance of building systems, building design, energy management, and employee supervision.[14]

BOMA has a chapter in every major metropolitan area and in many smaller cities as well. These chapters hold monthly meetings, lobby on behalf of the industry, and conduct miniseminars. BOMA also holds an annual convention and office building show. BOMA's national headquarters are located at 1201 New York Ave. NW, Suite 300, Washington, DC 20005 (202/289-7000).

§ 1.6   PROFESSIONAL DESIGNATIONS

The real estate industry is placing greater emphasis on professional designations. Today many institutional decision makers hold professional designations, and they are familiar with the stringent requirements for becoming a CPM®, CSM, or RPA. It is not uncommon for an asset manager to request that the property manager hold one of the aforementioned designations. Similarly, lenders and institutional owners often want to know about the qualifications of the property manager before becoming involved with a management company. They know that the quality of management will make the difference between a property that is operated as a first-class property and one that has chronic problems. They also know the importance of the property manager in enhancing value. An owner will want a CSM or CPM® to manage its mall and an RPA or CPM® to manage its office building or industrial property.

Professional designations offer tremendous benefits to the property manager. The recognition that professional designations brings places the property manager in an elite group of professionals in the real estate community. The educational requirements to obtain the designations give the manager the knowledge and practical skills needed to succeed.

There are also financial benefits to be gained by holding a valued professional designation. The Huntress Real Estate Executive Search Firm

---

[14] *Ibid.*

in Kansas City did a survey of all its placements and found that when the only difference between candidates was a professional designation, people with designations usually obtained a starting salary 10% to 15% higher than those without them.

§ 1.7   ABOUT THIS BOOK

Managing and Leasing Commercial Properties discusses property management with a view to enhancing value. The book offers a hands-on approach to the management, operations, and leasing of commercial properties. It addresses the daily problems of the property manager and suggests answers. Where appropriate, the text mentions management and leasing strategies that have not been successful to keep the reader from repeating the mistakes of others.

The introduction reviews the history of property management, how the responsibilities of the commercial property manager have evolved, and what is expected of property managers in the 1990s. Because no single individual can acquire the knowledge to stay at the cutting edge of the industry by him- or herself, this chapter has reviewed the services offered by professional organizations in commercial property management and explained the value of three leading property management designations.

Chapter 2 discusses how to start a commercial property management company, identify its market niche, and administrate the company.

Chapter 3 on income and expense analysis reviews the methods in developing a property's month-to-month cash flow projection.

Chapters 4, 5, and 6 review the three commercial property types—shopping centers, office buildings, and industrial properties—and the responsibilities the property manager will face with each on a daily basis.

Chapters 7 and 8 are step-by-step guides to developing and implementing a marketing and leasing program. All areas of marketing and leasing are discussed: working with the brokerage community, finding tenants, analyzing deals, reviewing the leases for each property type, re-leasing, and lease renewal. These chapters take the reader through the process in conducting a market survey and determining market rates for a building.

Once a lease is executed, the property manager must administer it. Chapter 9 reviews the procedures in administrating the obligations of the tenants and the landlord.

Properties can be maintained in a crisis intervention manner or under a maintenance management program. Chapter 10 outlines a step-by-step method for creating a maintenance management program, and discusses specific maintenance tasks and the maintenance agreement.

Property managers will handle multiple emergencies, from natural disasters such as earthquakes, hurricanes, and tornadoes, to man-made disasters such as fires, bomb threats, and assaults. Chapter 11 discusses how to establish and implement emergency procedures.

Chapter 12 on reports to owners establishes a reporting format that keeps the property owner aware of the activities of the property, the market conditions, financial forecasts, and potential opportunities and problems.

Chapter 13 discusses the challenges of managing properties in different times while Chapter 14 is a collection of forms and procedures that are useful in several different areas of property management.

This book was written to help property managers immediately implement the principles and techniques of effective commercial property management in their daily activities. This is not a book on theory, but a hands-on book that explains state-of-the-art techniques for managing and leasing commercial properties.

§ 1.8 CONCLUSION

Commercial property management is a challenging and rewarding career open to all. There is nothing that a property manager does that cannot be performed equally well by either gender, and age is no barrier at all; the selection factors are ability, knowledge, and judgment—in other words, professionalism. Commercial property management is both satisfying and frustrating. There are many rules and yet there are none. Because we are dealing with many personalities, we need to amend rules, change approaches, and rethink procedures to satisfy the various occupants and users of our properties.

This book hopes to convey two important principles that are important for the successful property manager of the 1990s: one, property managers are hired to enhance the value of a property and, two, property managers do not manage brick and mortar and steel and concrete, they manage people.

This book is not meant to replace the fine educational programs of the Institute of Real Estate Management, The International Council of Shopping Centers, The Building Owners and Managers Association, or other active property management organizations. Rather, it is meant to be a guide to principles and practices that have been successful over the years. It is hoped that this book will provide direct answers to many of the day-to-day problems that property managers face and, more importantly, that it will provide a strong base of understanding of commercial property management and leasing that will guide the property manager to proper decisions well beyond the scope of the book itself.

Two

The Property Management Company

§ 2.1 INTRODUCTION

The principles property managers use to operate a property and enhance its value are the same principles needed to operate a successful company or department. The property management company is a service business that seeks to generate profits and enhance the value of the company. The primary responsibilities of the person who heads a property management company are business development, personnel management, and establishing and monitoring policies and procedures. This chapter reviews the concepts used in developing a market, establishing a property management company, and marketing the company.

The products a property management company has to offer are time and expertise. They are provided by the company's personnel and are reflected in its operating expenses. The single largest operating expense, usually ranging from 60 to 67 percent of the operating budget, is payroll costs. This chapter also discusses staffing, position responsibilities, and personnel issues.

§ 2.2 MARKETS TO SERVE

Every business must develop its market niche to be competitive and successful. In the retailing industry, a small retailer cannot compete

with Macys or JC Penney by carrying every product line found in a giant department store. It isn't possible or necessary for the small retailer
to carry every product a potential customer needs. It makes more sense
to try to be the best in one or a limited product line or specialty. The
merchant can develop an area of expertise and offer a depth of merchandise selection and service that even the giants cannot offer. The
store becomes known as the best source for a particular product or service. This philosophy has helped many small businesses succeed in the
competitive retailing industry.

Most property management firms are small businesses. These en-
trepreneurs are competing with each other, with the regional and national full-service brokerage firms, and with developers who have entered
the property management business. The small- to medium-size property
management firm can be competitive and successful in the real estate industry by copying the philosophy of the successful small retailer and developing its own market niche. Property management is a specialty
within the real estate industry. Within this specialty are subspecialties—
property types and special services. The property management firm develops an expertise in one or more of these areas—its market niche.

There are four interrelated criteria to consider in developing a market niche: property type, level of service, geographic area, and property
ownership. Each must be analyzed as to the availability of product, the
company's interests, the expertise of the staff, the competition, the cost
to do business, and the profit potential.

(a) PROPERTY TYPE

Most property management firms operate in metropolitan areas in
which various types of property exist. This allows the firm to specialize
in the management and leasing of one or two particular types of property. Firms in rural areas have limited opportunities in any one property
type and often manage a combination of property types.

Most property management firms specialize in either residential or
commercial management. Commercial properties include office buildings, industrial properties, and shopping centers. The subtypes are garden, mid-, and high-rise office buildings; medical buildings; freestanding
industrial buildings; multitenant industrial parks; strip, neighborhood,
community, and specialty centers; and regional malls. Each subtype requires a distinct expertise, and commercial property management firms
must decide in which type they will specialize.

When developing a market niche, the property manager must determine which properties are available for fee management. Most large
commercial buildings, such as high-rise office buildings and regional
malls, are managed by the owner. Every major developer has an in-
house property management division, and many regional and national

syndicators have their own property management companies. In the early 1990s, major insurance companies formed subsidiary property management companies to manage their large properties.

When an institution purchases a large commercial property, it frequently looks to the developer with whom it has a relationship to manage its acquisition unless it has its own property management company. When a property is purchased from a developer with guaranteed rents for a period (e.g., one to three years), the developer retains the management of the property at least through the guaranteed period.

The opportunities for most third-party property management companies are in managing small- to medium-size commercial properties of up to 300,000 square feet. It is virtually impossible for smaller firms to acquire the management of large commercial properties. The few opportunities that exist are in smaller communities where it is not cost-effective for the owner to manage the property.

Most commercial property management firms will develop an expertise in one or more subproperty types. In today's competitive market, it is very difficult to cross over to another property type without previous experience. For instance, a firm that specializes in the management of suburban low- and mid-rise office buildings can extend its services to industrial properties or shopping centers, but it is difficult to develop the same level of expertise for all three property types. Likewise, apartment building managers with many years of experience may have a difficult time breaking into commercial property management. On the other hand, a client with whom a position of trust has been built may ask a manager to cross over and manage another type of property.

Institutional owners and other absentee owners look for a company with a specific area of expertise to manage their $5 million to $50 million investment. The owner will look not only at the company's reputation, but at the competence of the manager who will be responsible for the property. Professional designations—the RPA (Real Property Administrator) for office buildings, the CSM (Certified Shopping Center Manager) for shopping centers, and the CPM (Certified Property Manager) for all types of properties—are evidence that a manager is experienced and has received specialized training.

Once the firm has selected a type of property to specialize in, it can select the level of service, the geographical area, and the clientele it wishes to serve.

(b) LEVEL OF SERVICE

The field of property management offers different levels of services, depending upon the expertise of the firm, the needs of the owner, and, ultimately, the level of service a company wishes to provide. All owners do not need the same level of service. A property owner who lives a few miles from the property, who knows the area and has no partners to report to, may prefer a basic level of service with a lower management fee. However, an absentee institutional owner who is representing an investment fund or a pension fund may prefer a more complete level of service.

A company that tries to offer different levels of service will become known as the lowest common denominator of services. The owners and directors of the company must determine what level of service it will provide and develop and market the company to that level.

(c) GEOGRAPHIC AREA

The third criterion in developing a market niche is targeting which geographic area to serve. The area can range from a limited two-mile downtown radius to an entire state or region. The management company should analyze its existing portfolio, the company's personnel and capabilities, its cost to do business, management opportunities, and competition in determining its areas of service.

The property type will partially dictate the area to serve. A firm specializing in the management of neighborhood and community shopping centers will manage in the suburbs and in several counties. A firm specializing in the management of older mid-rise office buildings will manage in the downtown area.

Next, the size and capabilities of the staff must be considered. A firm with only two property managers does not have the resources to effectively and profitably manage a portfolio of properties located over a wide area. The cost of doing business increases as the properties are farther away from the office and from one another. The cost is measured in direct expenses and travel time.

If there are sufficient opportunities to manage properties in another county or state, the profit potential may justify expanding a management company's geographic area of service. Or a valued client might request that a firm manage one of its properties outside the firm's normal geographic service area, and the company might move into the new area to preserve the relationship with the client. However, managing one large neighborhood shopping center that is several hundred miles from the main office is seldom cost-effective or profitable.

The level of competition is another factor to consider when determining which areas to serve. A company might turn a profit if it can fill a void in a portion of a state that has few professional commercial property management firms. Conversely, venturing into a highly competitive area may prove to be unprofitable and a poor use of the company's most valuable resource—its personnel's time.

(d) PROPERTY OWNERSHIP

A property management company must identify its clients and develop the company to meet their needs. For instance, institutional owners require extensive financial reporting using their accounting reporting format, while a local owner will probably accept the property management firm's basic reporting format. The experience and abilities of the person assigned to manage the property must match the needs of the owner. A sophisticated owner may not interact well with an entry-level property manager.

Analyzing these four criteria will enable a company to identify, establish, and market its services. The final result will be a well-defined market niche around which the company can be built and promoted.

§ 2.3   STARTING A PROPERTY MANAGEMENT DEPARTMENT OR COMPANY FOR A DEVELOPER

The real estate market is cyclical. From the late 1980s through the mid-1990s, the commercial real estate market was overbuilt. Until the market turns, developers must reposition themselves to survive. Those developers who survive the first half of the 1990s will not only be positioned for the upturn in the market but will have fewer competitors since many developers will have left the field.

For many developers, repositioning includes offering third-party property management services. Virtually every national developer and many regional and local developers are offering or are contemplating offering and creating a fee property management department. This is an excellent opportunity to generate additional income; however, it is not as simple as it appears to enter the business of managing properties for others. This section will discuss the advantages the developer has in starting a property management company, what adjustments the developer must make to be successful, and some of the challenges in creating and operating a successful fee property management company.

First, most developers are well-positioned to start a property management company. Their property management division or existing company is managing a portfolio of properties that is an excellent base for establishing a third-party fee management company. If the fees they charge the properties they own are market fees, their property management department is probably operating at either breakeven or a profit. The key to their profitability is charging market fees. Developers who offer their property management services at a low fee to attract investors in their developments will not earn a profit.

Many developers have institutional joint venture partners who own and regularly purchase properties. These partners, who are usually located out of state, are a prime source of property management business. Developers with multiple offices can provide market coverage within a region. Most developers have strong broker relationships that can facilitate the leasing of a client's property. Institutional partners have clear investment goals and objectives—something developers understand. Developers have national contacts and strong relationships with most of the players in the real estate community. Developers can offer a wide range of services including construction management, rehabilitation, refinancing, and lease supervision. A strong advantage for most developers is their understanding of the real estate development and investment process along with their entrepreneurial outlook. They are by nature proactive people. Their perspective includes seeking unique leasing opportunities, and even a change of use for the property.

There are adjustments and challenges that developers must consider when venturing into the fee property management business. The first adjustment is an attitude change. When development activities are booming, property management is often relegated to a secondary position in the firm. When property management services are offered to a third party, the property management department or company must be given equal status to the other departments in the company and not be considered a "back room" operation.

Developing a property management department or company is similar to starting a property management company. First, a market niche must be identified and developed. The initial market niche for the developer's property management company is the property type it develops. The market niche can easily be expanded, as explained later in the chapter.

The next step in developing the property management company is to determine the staffing needs. Although it is usually best to promote someone internally, a developer may not have a person with property management expertise on staff. The new property management company must start with expertise. Credibility is established not by a company's name or affiliation with an existing company but by the level of service it provides.

An experienced property manager is needed to develop the company. If the initial portfolio of properties is small—less than 10 small properties or 8 medium-size properties—the director of property management, with the assistance of an administrative assistant, will be responsible for managing them. When the portfolio is more than 9 or 10 small properties or 7 or 8 medium-size properties, additional property managers will be needed. Whether the next property manager hired will be an experienced manager, an entry-level manager, or someone promoted from an administrative position within the company will depend on the size of the portfolio, budget constraints, the level of service provided, and the amount of time the director of property management can devote to training.

An adequate support staff is needed to back up the property manager and to handle the accounting responsibilities. Ideally, the property management company will not share clerical and bookkeeping personnel with the developer. When the work of both companies is assigned to one person, the developer's work takes priority. A professional commercial property management company cannot be developed if it is treated as a second-class entity.

If the property management company is handling properties not owned by the developer, these properties must be given first priority. Every property owner wants to believe that his or her property is the only one the company manages. The company should work to give this impression.

It is best to have the management company's accounting department separate from the developer's accounting department. At first this may not be possible, but once the property management company needs at least one full-time bookkeeper, that person should report solely to the director of property management. It is possible for the controller of the developer's accounting department to oversee the property management company's accounting department, but the property management company should have its own accounting department as soon as its size justifies the separation.

Another adjustment is realizing that the developer must check with the property owner or asset manager for approval on over-budget expenditures and lease terms that are not within the leasing guidelines. Basically, developers are accustomed to "calling the shots" on their properties, but as property managers, they must operate within the policies and procedures of the property owner.

If the property management company is to be profitable, it must charge market fees for all the properties it manages, including the developer's properties. Many developers will offer a lower property management fee as part of the negotiations with a joint venture partner and then wonder why the property management company is not profitable.

It usually takes 6 to 18 months before a property management company starts to show a profit. The developer must be able to endure the start-up costs. The size of the portfolio managed and whether or not the fees are at market rates are major factors in determining when the company becomes profitable.

One of the most misunderstood issues in property management is whether the developer's property management company must have a corporate real estate broker's license and property managers with real estate licenses. If the property management company is a separate company from the development company, many states will require that the company must be licensed. If a property management department is established as part of the development company, the developer may need to be licensed only if property management services are provided for properties not owned by the developer in the name of the development company.

In most states, a real estate license is required when managing properties for others, and may even be required when managing properties owned by the developer. If the developer is a general or limited partner in a project owned by the partnership, a real estate license probably will be required because the property management department is not managing a property owned by the development company but one owned by the partnership. The best way to avoid this problem is to have a corporate real estate license for the developer's property management company and have all property managers licensed. The real estate laws of the state where the company operates should be checked. There are differences in many states' licensing laws.

Do not enter the property management business only as a way to survive the downturn in the market. Such reasoning would become evident to potential and existing clients. Property owners want to know that their property management firm is committed to its industry and to the long-term potential of their property. Developers must demonstrate the seriousness of their commitment by pledging resources, state of the art equipment, personnel, and especially the right attitude to the new property management venture. The developer must understand that property management is one of the most competitive types of businesses—the service business.

The developer's name and reputation may obtain a few property management accounts, but the name alone will not keep these accounts. Only professional service will. Every client wants to believe that his or her property is the only property the company manages. This can only be accomplished with the "right" attitude and property staffing. An experienced property manager will need to be assigned to the position of director of property management. Promoting an inexperienced administrative assistant to be the company's property manager is not showing a commitment to professionalism.

Developers must be certain that there is no conflict of interest with the leasing and management of their properties and the properties they are soliciting for management. Many developers do not have an in-house leasing staff, and this may need to be overcome. The developer can either sell the benefits of using exclusive brokers or hire a leasing agent.

The advantages to developing a fee property management company far outweigh the potential problems. Entering into the property management business, however, is like entering into any other type of business. The right attitude and sound business practices are essential to success.

A property management company will not salvage a developer, but it will provide additional revenue and cover some of the developer's overhead. Property management can also open the door to other services such as leasing, construction management and possibly generate development opportunities.

§ 2.4 MANAGING PROPERTIES IN-HOUSE

Real estate investors are confronted with a situation similar to developers—fewer deals. Fewer deals or fewer investment opportunities are the result of difficulty in obtaining financing, increased equity requirements, and fewer benefits to the ownership of real estate than pre-1986. Investors must generate income to continue to operate, and providing property management services for their own properties is a potential profit center. The reason for this is the same as for developers soliciting third-party fee management—to generate additional income and cover some of the investment company's overhead.

The first consideration when contemplating providing in-house property management services is whether the investor has a portfolio sufficient in size to create a property management division. A rule of thumb is a minimum of 300,000 square feet of commercial space could generate sufficient fees to support a property manager, a part-time secretary, and a part-time bookkeeper.

It is best for the investor to wait until he or she has a sufficient portfolio to support an experienced staff rather than to assign the rent collection and limited property management duties to clerical or administrative personnel. After reading this book, you will recognize that there is considerably more to managing a property and enhancing its value than collecting the rents and sweeping the parking lot.

All of the principles outlined for a developer seeking third-party management business (§ 2.3) apply to developing an in-house property management department. The important considerations are attitude and commitment.

If an administrative person is assigned the responsibility of managing a small portfolio of properties, that person must be placed on a fast track to acquire all the knowledge of property management and leasing. Many community colleges offer property management classes. The Institute of Real Estate Management (IREM), International Council of Shopping Centers (ICSC), and Building Owners and Managers Association (BOMA) offer excellent one-week seminars for entry level and experienced property managers. IREM and BOMA have chapters throughout the country and attendance at their meetings is the best place to network in property management. Each of these professional associations mentioned has extensive publications on office building, shopping center, and industrial park property management and leasing.

One caution, however. Property management is not a part-time career and must be treated with professionalism.

There are opportunities to generate additional income with an investor developing an in-house property management department, but with every opportunity for success is a corresponding opportunity to fail if the endeavor isn't approached professionally.

§ 2.5 STARTING A FEE MANAGEMENT COMPANY

Starting a fee property management company has challenges that are not faced when starting a management company for a developer. Starting a business without any properties to manage can place financial as well as mental strain on the new entrepreneur.

A start-up fee management company is invariably a very small organization. It is likely to consist of an owner/property manager and a secretary, or possibly two partners, a bookkeeper, and a secretary. The main initial challenge is developing the business and convincing potential clients that the firm has the expertise and depth of management to operate the properties efficiently.

One of the most critical concerns in starting a company is also the most difficult to determine—the aptitude for self-employment. It is possible to be an excellent property manager as an employee but not do well working alone. Once the manager becomes self-employed, the duties expand well beyond day-to-day property management activities. Now there is a company to run as well as properties to manage. This entails business development, employee relations, accounting supervision, governmental reporting, cash flow management, and a host of other responsibilities that have little to do with property management but a great deal to do with business management.

The form of the business structure is also important. Most small management companies start out as proprietorships. While there are many advantages to incorporation, there are also many drawbacks, and it is commonly held that the individual property manager receives limited liability protection through incorporation. Depending on the income level of the owner of the company, there may be some advantages to incorporation from a tax point of view that are not normally available to the individual. Partnerships allow managers to share the load, but they also make one partner liable for the acts of the other.

All of the steps outlined in § 2.3 are necessary in starting a fee management company. The manager must take the lead in organizing the office. Before the doors of the new company open, policies and procedures, an accounting system, forms, and reporting formats must be in place.

It is critical for the small entrepreneur to decide what type of properties the company will handle because many owners look for experience in a particular property type. The temptation will be strong to be a generalist and take on all types of properties, thereby increasing the potential client base and the management portfolio. However, today's commercial property market is so complex that it is much better to specialize and become recognized in one specific area of property management.

A second important decision concerns the area to be served. A small company cannot effectively cover a large geographic area, and yet a manager may have to target a larger area just to have sufficient product to support the new business.

Before leaving a lucrative job for the uncertain area of self-employment in fee management, the property manager should analyze past and present contacts to determine if these are likely future clients. Great care must be taken, however, in contacting clients of the present employer as there may be ethical and legal issues involved. If the property manager has been in contact with many property owners and has been active in professional associations and civic activities, there probably are a sufficient number of potential clients to start a company. Since this is a very subjective decision, it is important to be honest in evaluating one's situation. An error in judgment can be very costly to the entrepreneur.

Business development is typically a slow process in commercial properties. The management of small apartment projects can change hands rather quickly, but medium and large commercial projects seldom switch management without careful thought and planning. Therefore, the property manager should devote time to some form of business development each day. Once contact has been established with a potential client, the manager should keep the contact active. It is not unusual for six months or more to lapse from the initial discussion on a new commercial account to the actual start of the management contract. Property managers cannot wait until they lose one management contract before they start looking for a new one.

When a property owner selects a management company, he or she is hiring not a company, but an individual. Therefore, owners of property management firms must market themselves. The successful property manager has a reputation for honesty, integrity, knowledge of the market, proven results, and product knowledge. That reputation is generally the vehicle for new business. It is important that the property manager let owners know about the new company. There are several ways to do so.

1. Personal Contact. The most effective tool the property management company has is personal contact. The property manager can target a specific building or group of buildings, obtain the owners' names from tax records, mail them a brochure, and follow up with a phone call to set a meeting. Tracking a property's sale with a follow-up letter to the buyer can also be effective. Attending ICSC, IREM, or BOMA meetings where property owners or asset managers are likely to be present is another excellent way to make contacts. Very little in commercial real estate happens quickly, so after contacting an institution and discussing the company's services the property manager should keep in touch in an effort to build a relationship.

2. Identifying Property Ownership. One of the most effective approaches to developing property management accounts is to use tax records to identify the owners of commercial properties. It usually takes a fair amount of time to see results with this approach. When calling potential clients the talents and abilities of the new firm should be presented in a positive way, but the existing property management company should not be criticized. After all, the property owner may be managing the property.

3. Publishing and Speaking. Writing articles for trade journals can be an effective strategy, especially if reprints are mailed to a select list of prospective clients, followed with a phone call. Being a panelist or guest speaker at professional association's meetings is excellent exposure and allows people to get to know the manager over a period of time.

4. Referrals. Referrals are one of the most effective entrees the property manager can have. Current clients can be a great help if they are aware that the manager is looking for business.

5. Press Releases. Any time the property manager accomplishes anything newsworthy, a press release should be distributed. News items can include taking on new business, negotiating a significant lease, obtaining a professional designation, or hiring a new staff member.

6. Civic Activities. Civic activities give a return to the community that supports the property manager. They also put the property manager in touch with other civic leaders, who are often good business contacts.

7. Advertising. Advertising in local newspapers and mass media is not very effective. The owners of a multimillion dollar property are not likely to place their assets in the hands of an unknown manager based on an ad. A recurring ad may help establish a presence in the marketplace, but generally personal contact is necessary.

8. Brochure. A professionally designed brochure can be an excellent introduction to new clients. It can convey the image of success by indicating years of experience, specific credentials, and properties currently under management. A brochure should be followed up with personal contact.

Most fee management companies in the United States are relatively small in size and are able to concentrate on specific markets while providing a good living for the owner. On the other hand, commercial property management deals with very large investments, complex buildings, and sophisticated owners. This is not an area for the neophyte to jump into hoping to grow with the situation.

§ 2.6 MANAGEMENT FEES

(a) ESTABLISHING THE MANAGEMENT FEE

Property managers often have difficulty establishing what management and other fees to propose when submitting a management proposal. There are several factors to consider. In the majority of management proposals, the company's primary objective is to generate a profit for the property management company or department. However, there are times when other reasons for acquiring a management account take precedent over generating a profit for managing the property. This situation usually occurs when income or a profit can be generated from other activities that is greater than the income or profit earned by managing the property.

A brokerage firm may offer a management fee at or below cost to acquire the leasing and sales listing. The potential commission earned from leasing and/or selling the property will far exceed the profits generated from managing the property. The brokerage firm may believe that controlling the property is more important than the management fee. This approach can have an adverse effect on the profitability, and sometimes viability, of the firm's property management department, who generally have internal goals to meet.

The property may be distressed and part of an existing client's portfolio, and the property owner requests a favorable fee. When a property management company enters a new geographical area or wants to manage a property type that is new to the company, they may use discounted fees. To acquire these properties and establish credibility in these areas, the property management company may propose a fee below its typical charge. A development company may offer its property management services at a lower fee as part of the negotiations with a joint venture partner. New property management companies may offer a very attractive fee to increase their portfolio size.

The executive property manager in each of these situations may be caught between meeting the primary objective of the company and generating a profit for the property management company or division. By cost accounting the income and expense and arriving at the anticipated profit or loss to manage a property, the executive property manager can confidently address what will happen when management fees are prepared for any of the reasons just discussed. Though the vast majority of property management proposals are intended to generate a profit for the management company, it is important to review all the possible scenarios for submitting a management proposal and develop the appropriate management fee.

The first issue to consider is the *purpose* for acquiring the management of the subject property. Then, the executive property manager must know the cost to manage the subject property.

This cost is made up of fixed and variable expenses. The fixed expenses include the general and administrative (G&A) expenses to operate the company, whether or not additional properties are added to the company's management portfolio. Variable expenses are primarily those expenses that would not be incurred if the property management firm did not take on the management of property under consideration.

The first variable cost is the cost of the property manager assigned to manage the subject property. Will the property require an experienced property manager or an entry-level property manager? Will the property require additional management time to resolve maintenance, leasing, or tenant problems?

The next cost is the accounting and support staff involvement. The property management company's controller and the executive property manager should meet with the potential client to review the accounting and reporting requirements. Private investors and developers will usually accept the property management company's standard accounting and reporting format. Institutional owners will require their own chart of accounts, accounting format, and time schedules. The time it takes for the accounting department to meet the requirements for some institutional owners can be twice the time required to prepare their standard accounting reports.

Another variable is the involvement of the property manager's assistant, secretary, or clerical staff. Extraordinary expenses including travel to visit the subject properties or meet with property owners, and special reports are additional cost variables to consider.

The cost to manage the property takes into consideration each of the fixed and variable expenses. A profit is added to these costs to arrive at the proposed management fee. What should the profit be? Unfortunately, the answer is not simple. There is no standard profit margin for property management services. The profit margin is based on several factors, the foremost being the competition and the complexity of the management assignment.

The exceptional expertise needed to resolve a property's problems justifies a higher profit margin. The problem may be in marketing, renovation, or tenant relations, and only a few professionals may be experienced or equipped to handle the challenge. This is no different than going to a medical specialist who charges more than a general practitioner. Exhibit 2.1 contains a sample form used to cost account and calculate a proposed management fee.

Property management is a highly competitive service business. Since all service companies do not provide the same services, a property management firm must develop a market niche that includes its standard level of service. If a company's market niche is to provide a high level of commercial property management service primarily to institutional owners, it will not be able to meet or beat the fee proposed by a property management company that provides only basic

EXHIBIT 2.1

Management Account Income and Expense Analysis Form

Income
- Fixed Income
  - Management fee .... $_____
  - Other income .... $_____
    - Total anticipated .... $_____

- Variable Income
  - Commissions .... $_____
  - TI supervision .... $_____
  - Additional management fee .... $_____
    (Based on higher than anticipated
    occupancy in building)
  - Other income .... $_____
    - Total potential .... $_____

Expenses
- Fixed Expenses
  - Payroll cost .... $_____
  - Rent .... $_____
  - General and Administrative .... $_____
  - Equipment .... $_____
  - Insurance .... $_____
  - Other expense .... $_____
    - Total Fixed Expenses .... $_____

- Variable Expenses
  - Property management payroll cost .... $_____
  - Administrative staff payroll cost .... $_____
  - Accounting staff payroll cost .... $_____
  - Travel expense .... $_____
  - Office expense .... $_____
  - Other expense .... $_____
    - Total Variable Expenses .... $_____

TOTAL FIXED AND VARIABLE EXPENSES $_____

Profit from anticipated income $_____

Profit from anticipated and potential income $_____

services A property management firm should base its fee on its level of service. As in any business, a property management firm will not get—and should not get—all of the projects it bids for. If it does, its bid structure may be too low. A property management company should, however, be concerned if it is not awarded the management of a property because the property owner didn't believe the company could handle the account or that there were more qualified property management firms.

After developing several management proposals, the executive property manager will have a sense of how many projects each property manager can effectively handle, what amount of extra time is required for most special assignments, and the cost to operate the company. It is tempting to use a rule of thumb number or percentage when determining a management fee. A cost analysis, however, should be prepared for *each* management proposal.

Most management fees are a percentage of the base or gross income collected versus a minimum fee. The minimum fee protects against a large number of vacancies or major lease concessions, such as free rent, that impact the property's income stream.

If the commercial property requires an on-site management staff, the decision must be made whether the property management company will pay for the on-site management staff out of its management fee or if this cost will be billed directly to the property. There are advantages and disadvantages to both approaches. When the cost of the on-site staff is an expense of the property, the executive property manager can more accurately estimate the cost to manage the property and to control the firm's cost to manage the property. The property owner is aware of the actual cost to operate the on-site office and can better estimate if the property management company's fee is fair.

Some property owners prefer that the fee is inclusive of all costs including the on-site staff. They believe this will allow them better control of their management cost.

A property management firm may prefer including the cost of the on-site staff in its minimum fee when it assigns additional management accounts to the on-site staff. This often occurs when a commercial property isn't large enough or the property's income isn't adequate to support an on-site staff. If the executive property manager can assign additional properties for management to the staff, the on-site staff can be economically justified by all parties.

Property management fees are a steady and predictable source of income to pay the company's operating expenses and generate some profit, but the greatest profit opportunities usually come from leasing and brokerage activities.

Other potential sources of income are tenant improvement supervision and a payroll charge or fee for handling the payroll for the on-site maintenance personnel. The payroll fee is a percentage of payroll cost. This fee covers the additional time to handle the maintenance personnel payroll functions, and since the maintenance personnel all become employees of the property management company, unemployment or worker's compensation claims will go against the property management firm's credits. An alternative is to include this cost in the management fee.

Tenant improvement (TI) supervision is a fee charged for supervising the TI construction. If the property management firm is licensed to serve as a general contractor, it can act as and receive the general contractor's fees. Most property management firms are not general contractors; however, they often are asked by the property owner to coordinate the TI work among the tenant, space planner, general contractor, and property owner. A fee, usually a percentage of the construction cost, is paid to the property management firm for its involvement in the TI work.

Most property owners recognize the important role the property manager plays in increasing the property's cash flow and enhancing its value. Some owners are willing to share these increases with the property management firm and are beginning to offer incentive fees.

The incentive fee can take many forms, limited only by the imagination of the people negotiating the management agreement. Typical incentive fees include: an increase in the commission rate when exceeding a leasing goal; percentage of the savings of a budgeted major repair or renovation; percentage of the increase of the net operating income (NOI) above a budgeted amount; a portion of the percentage rents paid by retail tenants; and a percentage of the savings in budgeted operating expense.

The basic property management fee, which is generally a percentage of the income collected, is a form of an incentive fee. The more income collected, the higher the property management fee. Incentive fees recognize an extraordinary effort, a unique expertise, or are a reward for performing well on a problem property or in a difficult situation.

(b) MANAGEMENT FEE ANALYSIS

Determining (1) the cost to manage a property and (2) the profit potential from managing and possibly leasing the property can be estimated by using a complex analysis or as a shot in the dark. The executive property manager should know the basic fixed cost to operate the property management company, with or without adding or subtracting management accounts.

To arrive at the cost to manage a property, the executive property manager needs to calculate the variable cost to manage the subject property. Exhibit 2.2 provides for a segregation of fixed and variable costs. This form also provides for known and potential management fees.

When figuring the fixed and variable expenses, there will be some costs that could be included in either expense category. Most of these

EXHIBIT 2.2

Property Management Company's Operating Expenses Form

I.   Personnel - Salary and Benefits

    A.   Salaries   Percentage of total budget

A.	Salaries			Percentage of total budget
	1. Accounting	$_____		_____%
	2. Administrative and clerical	$_____		_____%
	3. Property manager	$_____		_____%
	4. Executive	$_____		_____%
	Salaries subtotal		$_____	_____%
B.	Payroll costs			
	1. Accounting	$_____		_____%
	2. Administrative and clerical	$_____		_____%
	3. Property manager	$_____		_____%
	4. Executive	$_____		_____%
	Payroll costs subtotal		$_____	_____%
C.	Employee Benefits			
	1. Accounting	$_____		_____%
	2. Administrative and clerical	$_____		_____%
	3. Property manager	$_____		_____%
	4. Executive	$_____		_____%
	Benefits subtotal		$_____	_____%
	Total salary and benefits cost		$_____	_____%

II.   Personnel Expense

A.	Dues	$_____		_____%
B.	Travel	$_____		_____%
C.	Education	$_____		_____%
D.	Auto allowance	$_____		_____%
	Total personnel expense		$_____	_____%

III.   Office Expense

A.	Licenses and fees	$_____		_____%
B.	Postage	$_____		_____%
C.	Rent	$_____		_____%
D.	Supplies	$_____		_____%
E.	Other	$_____		_____%
	Total office expense		$_____	_____%

EXHIBIT 2.2 *(Continued)*

IV.	Administrative Expense			
	A. Audit	$_____		_____
	B. Insurance	$_____		_____
	C. Legal	$_____		_____%
	D. Other	$_____		_____%
	Total administrative expense		$_____	_____%
V.	Equipment expense			
	A. Lease payments	$_____		_____%
	B. Maintenance	$_____		_____%
	C. Other	$_____		_____%
	Total equipment expense		$_____	_____%
VI.	Marketing			
	A. Advertising	$_____		_____%
	B. Brochures	$_____		_____%
	C. Entertainment	$_____		_____%
	Total marketing expense		$_____	_____%
	TOTAL OPERATING EXPENSE		$_____	_____%
VII.	Reserve for _____		$_____	_____%
VIII.	Profit		$_____	_____%
	GRAND TOTAL OPERATING EXPENSE AND PROFIT		$_____	_____%

Divide the total operating expense by the number of square feet of commercial properties managed or by units of 1,000 or 10,000 square feet managed to determine the cost to manage a property or commercial properties on a per square foot, or any predetermined unit (i.e., cost to manage every 10,000 square feet of commercial property.) This number doesn't include incentive program, such as bonuses, or a profit margin. Dividing the unit of management by the grand total provides the cost to manage a property by unit size when a profit and bonuses are factored in.

costs will be insignificant compared to the other expenses. The important fact is that these expenses are identified and included in either the fixed or variable costs.

Some fixed costs do not depend on the size of the management portfolio. For instance, they include payroll costs for the executive property manager, his or her secretary, the receptionist, and the controller. Other fixed costs include rent for the office space, equipment costs (computer, copier, postage meter, etc.), insurance (auto, errors and omissions, liability, etc.), general and administrative (G&A) (supplies, telephone, licenses, etc.), and miscellaneous expenses. These five categories can be expanded for detailed cost accounting.

The variable expenses are those expenses directly related to managing the property. The primary expense is the payroll cost—the pro rata cost of the property manager and the administrative and accounting staff. The executive property manager along with the property manager assigned to the property must estimate the percentage of the time he or she and the support staff will spend each month on the property. The time the staff spends managing the property will be significantly greater during the first two months of the management account than during the balance of its term. This is the most important consideration since employee compensation consumes by far the greatest portion of the cost to manage a property. Other costs that can be attributed to a management account are travel expenses, direct office expenses (such as long distance telephone calls), telecopier and air express costs, and a miscellaneous category of other expenses.

The other element in analyzing whether a property will be profitable to manage and what management fee to propose is the known or anticipated income and any potential income from fees. The known or anticipated income is either the base management fee or the management fee as a percentage of the income when the building's income stream can be fairly accurately estimated. Unless the building is in a lease-up stage, the property manager can estimate with a high degree of accuracy the property's income during the first few years of the management agreement's term. Other known income components can include remodeling fees, tenant improvement supervision fees, and payroll fees.

Additional potential income is from lease or sales commissions, TI supervision, and other income. The potential income depends on several variables, some or all of which the property manager has only limited or no control over.

Caution is advised when discussing the potential lease commission income with a property owner. Sometimes property owners either have an unrealistic perception of market conditions, the position of their property in the market, or the amount of space that can be leased in a given period, or they may use the potential leasing commission as a carrot to entice the property management firm to manage the property for a lower management fee.

(c) COMMISSION INCOME

Commission fees are an important income component for most commercial property management firms. Many small- and medium-sized firms will discover that their management fees cover the company's operating expenses, but the majority of the firm's profits are derived from commissions earned by leasing and/or sales activities. Commission income can be the difference between a profitable or unprofitable year. Some firm's year-end bonuses or incentive programs are funded either directly or indirectly by the commissions earned.

Commercial property management firms should maximize their opportunities to earn commission income. The commission opportunities from leasing activities can produce a steady and somewhat predictable income stream.

Another reason to develop an aggressive leasing program is that the time spent leasing earns greater income than the profit earned from the management fee for a proportionate amount of time spent managing the property. For instance, the management fee for one year for managing a 60,000 to 80,000-square-foot shopping center will probably range from $30,000 to $45,000 while the commission earned for one lease of 2,000 square feet for five years can range from $5,000 to $10,000. A management fee for a 50,000-square-foot office building can range from $20,000 to $40,000 while one lease for 6,000 square feet for five years can earn a commission between $12,000 and $30,000. Leasing multiple spaces can earn commissions in excess of the management fee.

Another and more striking comparison is found when analyzing the profits from a management account as compared to the income earned from leasing activities. Using the example of the office building, if the property management firm's profit margin were 12 percent, the profit from managing the building would be between $2,400 and $4,800. The commission earned from just one 6,000-square-foot lease is 2 to 12 times the management fee profit, yet the time spent managing the office building for one year far exceeds the average time devoted to completing a lease deal.

Once the decision is made to either offer leasing services or to become more aggressive in leasing activities, the executive property manager needs to evaluate the firm's approach to leasing. Issues to consider include whether the firm is positioned to assume leasing responsibilities or to expand its leasing efforts; which types of property to lease and where; what commission rates to charge; who will be responsible for leasing; whether to split the commission with the property manager, and, if so, what formula to use.

When determining if a commercial property management firm is positioned to assume leasing responsibilities, two questions must be asked: (1) Do the property managers have expertise in leasing and if not, how do they become trained? (2) Do the property managers have sufficient time to lease a property or properties? Most firms will answer yes to both of these questions.

If the property managers do not have time for leasing activities, an analysis should be made of the impact on the company if its management portfolio is reduced and the property manager devotes time to leasing activities. Another consideration would be to hire more administrative help to assist the property manager in daily management tasks, thus allowing more time for leasing. A third alternative is to hire a full-time leasing agent.

The second issue to consider in soliciting a leasing assignment is what type of properties, what geographic location, and which specific properties should the property management firm lease. The property owner's goal is to lease the property as quickly as possible at market rates. The property management firm should have this objective as one of its primary goals for the property.

Some properties' leasing requirements cannot be met effectively by the property management firm. A property may have too many vacancies for a property manager to spend sufficient time away from his or her management duties to be effective in leasing the property. In this case, the executive property manager should recommend a firm with full-time leasing agents and request retention of the lease renewals.

Another reason for not handling the leasing of a property is that it may be too far from the property management office. In either case, the property owner will appreciate the executive property manager's honesty in recommending another leasing agent. This open and honest approach will help build credibility in the property management firm.

The next consideration is the commission rate proposal. Commissions are negotiable and are based on several factors:

- The difficulty of the leasing assignment
- Market conditions
- The size of the space(s) being leased
- The length of the lease
- The gross or net rental income from the tenant
- The expertise of the person leasing the property
- The property management firm's cost of doing business
- What the market will bear

- Whether the potential commission justifies the amount of time required to lease the vacancies
- What the property owner believes is fair compensation for the service received.

A very important decision is who will be assigned the leasing responsibilities. Some property management firms have full-time leasing agents, while others assign property managers to lease space. Property managers have varying levels of leasing expertise, and a challenging leasing assignment may require more than one property manager to lease the property.

The final consideration is how, if at all, the commission earned will be shared with the property manager. The common commission split for leasing agents with no base salary is either a 50/50 split or a 50/50 split with the leasing agent receiving an increased percentage of the split as his or her volume of leasing activities is increased.

Property managers receive a salary and other benefits, usually including a bonus. Because of these expenses of the property management company, the split may be other than 50/50. For instance, the property manager may receive 20 or 30 percent of the commission earned by the property management firm. Another approach is to pay a year-end incentive based on the total commission earned. Whatever the arrangement, it should be an incentive for leasing success, especially since commission income is an important component in the property management firm's profitability.

If the commission split is less than 50/50, an incentive commission may be added to the commission formula. The commission split can become greater for the property manager when he or she leases more than a pre-determined square footage of space. For instance, the commission split is 30/70 for the first 20,000 square feet leased, 40/60 for the next 20,000 square feet leased, 50/50 for the next 10,000 square feet leased, and 60/40 for all additional space leased. Another approach is to increase the split from 30/70 to 50/50 or greater once the share of the commissions earned by the company equals the property manager's salary and payroll costs.

Another incentive program is to set leasing goals for each property manager and when his or her goal is exceeded, the commission split is increased. For instance, the commission split provides the property manager with 30 percent of the commission, but when the leasing goal is surpassed all future commissions are split 50/50.

Most commercial property management firms seldom have the opportunity to sell a property, and unless a sales listing is obtained, it is best not to budget sales commission income. When most property management firms sell a property, the commission earned is unanticipated and represents a significant portion of the firm's income.

(d) MANAGEMENT FEE CALCULATION

Calculating the management fee on commercial properties can be a rather complicated process. It is not unusual for some owners to have very special requirements in arriving at the final fee for a given property.

While the most common form of management fee is a percentage of the gross income against a minimum monthly fee, there are many variations.

Some management fees are calculated on the rental income only and exclude any common area billbacks or reimbursements of any sort. There are fees that are computed on one percentage rate up to a given amount and then on a lower percentage rate above that figure.

In some situations, the income is shown on an accrual basis but the management fees are based on a cash basis; therefore, the income must be adjusted prior to calculating the fees.

The use of a management fee calculation form (Exhibit 2.3) will show both the accounting supervisor and the client exactly how the fee was calculated, making it much easier to ascertain that the final fee is accurate and in accordance with the agreements. The figures used to calculate the fees must be traceable to the operating statements with explanations for any differences.

§ 2.7 TRACKING MANAGEMENT ACCOUNT LEADS AND PROPOSALS

The executive property manager needs to develop a system to track management account leads and management account proposals (Exhibit 2.4). These forms enable the executive property manager to keep a log that tracks the progress of the property management firm's activities in acquiring property management accounts. These forms should be reviewed at least weekly to ensure that all possible action to obtain these accounts is being taken. Periodically, a summary can be prepared of the results of leads and proposals. It is especially helpful to know why proposals were not accepted. This will indicate actual or perceived weaknesses within the company. The executive property manager can then develop a plan to alleviate the company's actual weaknesses. Alternately, the manager will realize that the company cannot successfully compete in a specific area.

§ 2.8 COMPANY EXPANSION

What size should our company be? Can we become more profitable if we grow, or will we just have more problems? Both questions are frequently pondered by owners and directors of property management firms. Expanding a company provides for potential increased profits, additional

EXHIBIT 2.3

Management Fee Calculation Form

For the Period From: _____ To: _____

Property Name _____   Prepared by (Firm Name): _____

                                   Contact Name & Phone No.: _____

Property Location _____   Reviewed by: _____

                                   Approved by: _____

Basis for Fee:			
Base Rent	$		
Percentage Rent			
Utility Reimbursements			
Real Estate Tax Escalation			
CAM			
Parking			
Other: Explain in Detail			
Total Fee Basis			
Fee Percentage	×	%	
Fee Earned This Period (Percentage or Fixed Fee)			
Total Fee Due Manager			
Deduct: Fee Paid This Period			
Balance Due Manager (End of Period)		$	

EXHIBIT 2.4

Management Account Proposals and Leads
(Use one form for leads and another for proposals)

1st Contact	Property Owner	Property	Action	Comments/ Results

recognition, a more stable base of operations, increased company expertise, and personal gratification. However, if the expansion is not planned,
it can easily become a disruptive force within the company and a financial burden.

The first step in expanding a company is to develop a three- to five-year
growth strategy that focuses on expanding the company's market niche.
Once the direction for expansion has been determined, a plan is developed
to accommodate the changes to the operations of the company. Expanding a company's management portfolio will impact its space requirements; clerical, administrative and management staffing; computer
capacity; equipment requirements; and operating expenses. The owner
and the director of property management must be willing to commit time
to the expansion effort.

The first consideration is to decide in which area the company should
grow. Should the growth be within the present market niche, or should
the market niche be expanded? Should the growth extend to providing
services in addition to property management (e.g., leasing, consulting,
brokerage, or appraisals)?

The most likely expansion is to broaden the property type managed in
the present market niche. First consider the property types that have
considerable crossover of responsibilities and expertise. A company specializing in suburban office buildings can consider expanding into industrial properties. There is less crossover of responsibilities and expertise
between office buildings and shopping centers. The least amount of
crossover is between residential and commercial properties.

Broadening the company's portfolio of property types may require
modifying the management and accounting reports. For instance, shopping centers require a detailed analysis of each tenant's sales and a different approach to tenant's bill-back charges. The most drastic changes
to the reporting program would be adding residential properties to a
commercial property management company, or vice versa. The manager
can learn about various types of property by studying this book and the
suggested reference materials, by attending property management and
leasing seminars, and by joining professional organizations that represent different property types.

Another growth strategy is to expand the geographic area in which the
company operates. In many areas it is possible to expand by increasing
the sphere of operation. For instance, in southern California, a company
could expand from Los Angeles County to Orange County to Riverside
County to San Diego County. In other areas, expansion may require giant
geographical leaps. For instance, a company in the Seattle area could expand east across the Cascade Mountains to eastern Washington, south to
Portland and, in a major move, north to Anchorage, Alaska. A move of this
magnitude would require either developing a program for managing
properties from afar, discussed later in this chapter, or incurring the

expense to open a branch office. In any event, expansion into another state may require obtaining a real estate license in that state. An analysis of the market and competition would tell a company whether there were sufficient opportunities to enter the market without having any management accounts in the new area.

An immediate means of entry into another area is by purchasing a local property management company. The regional or national brokerage firms and developers who are operating in several areas can bring their property management division into an area to support an established brokerage or development operation.

A more long-term expansion strategy is to broaden the client base. A firm that specializes in managing for local owners and developers may expand its client base to institutional owners. Institutional owners tend to be more sophisticated and demanding. They might visit the property manager less frequently because they are usually absentee owners, but their reporting requirements are more extensive, especially accounting reports. In addition, they usually have a larger real estate staff with a broad range of experience.

A major consideration when expanding a company is staffing the three levels—executive or supervisory, property managers, and administrative support. The first consideration is whether additional properties can be managed without additional personnel. Since most property management companies operate near or at maximum capacity, it is unlikely that more than one or two additional properties can be added without additional staff. During a growth period, a company adapts from being understaffed when a few additional properties are added to the management portfolio to being slightly over staffed when employees are hired after a few more properties are added, to being adequately staffed when another one or two properties are added. If the company continues to expand, this cycle will start over again.

The existing executive or supervisory staff can usually handle the growth. If the growth is an expansion into a new property type—for instance, a shopping center—a new supervisory position can be created when the portfolio justifies it. One consideration: If the expansion is geographic, will a property management supervisor be needed for a branch office?

The most difficult decision is to determine how growth will effect the property management staff. The company must decide if it has the expertise to expand into another property type. If not, a property manager will probably need to be hired to market the new property division. A company cannot always afford to hire experienced managers, but if only entry-level managers are hired, the company becomes a school for property managers. If the company is amply staffed with experienced managers, it might consider hiring an entry-level person who would be assigned to one of the experienced managers. If the most recent hiring has been entry-level managers, an experienced manager may be needed to provide a depth of experience.

Care must be used when determining which level of experience is needed in the new property manager. The level of service a company has established can greatly deteriorate if the expertise and experience are not maintained at the same level for each property type.

Increasing the portfolio will require added clerical, administrative, and accounting staff. The management level staff will work harder and longer during a period of growth until a new manager is added. However, it is unrealistic to expect clerical, administrative, and accounting staff to work longer hours over an extended period of time. There is a maximum amount of work that the staff can produce in a normal work week. Fortunately, it is possible to hire part-time and temporary personnel.

§ 2.9 MANAGING NEW ACCOUNTS

The addition of a new account is an exciting event for the management company because it represents a transfer of trust from the owner to the manager. However, it can be a confusing time for tenants. The property manager must act immediately to show the owner his or her expertise and to assure the tenants that their property is being managed by a professional manager and a professional company. The manager must take time to evaluate the property and to establish management systems and procedures. Although the ideal situation is to receive a thirty-day advance notice, the company should be prepared to assume the management of a property on a day's notice. If a new account is assumed in a haphazard manner, the ongoing management will always be flawed. It can take from one week to three months of intense effort to get a commercial property fully on-line and reasonably understood by the property manager and the administrative staff. This is a critical period, for the firm will never get a second chance to make a first impression on the property owner and the tenants.

There are six areas that need to be addressed when assuming the management of an office building or industrial property, and a seventh to consider when assuming the management of a shopping center. The seven areas are: property ownership, property operations, tenants, administration, leasing, tenant improvements and, for shopping centers, the merchants' association/marketing fund.

The property manager and the firm's controller should meet with the owner or asset manager to discuss the owner's goals and objectives for the property. The property manager can then develop the management plan. A management agreement must be executed between the parties before the company assumes management responsibilities. The most immediate items of agreement are the management company's spending authority, the type of financial and management reports and their due dates, and the names of the owner's representatives. The property manager should also establish the frequency of meeting with the owner.

Leasing responsibilities must be established during the meeting with the property owner. What are the parameters for leasing? What are the minimum rental rates, the minimum and maximum square footage, and the tenant allowance package that the property manager can offer a prospective tenant without the owner's prior approval? Who will prepare and pay for the marketing materials? If the management company's lease form is to be used, the property owner should review and give written approval. If the property management company will not handle leasing, what will its responsibilities be in interfacing with the leasing agent? If the property manager is responsible for supervising the leasing agent, will a commission override be paid to the property management company?

The next area of concern is construction. Who will handle the tenant's improvements? Will the property manager act as a general contractor, supervise the general contractor, or have no direct construction responsibility? If the property manager will be responsible for bidding, contracting, and supervising construction, a list of at least three contractors should be approved by the owner. If unit pricing is used, the property manager must bid each item for unit pricing. A space planner needs to be selected for office buildings and industrial properties. Construction plans should be obtained.

Administrative responsibilities start with knowing the owner's required accounting format and due dates. Prior years' and the current year's budget and tenant billings, list of delinquencies, and invoices not paid should be transferred to the property manager. The leases must be summarized with a report of lease restrictions, such as first right of refusal, exclusives, right of cancellation, options, and expiration date.

The manager must arrange for a thorough property inspection. This is an opportunity to prepare an inventory of equipment and a map showing all shutoffs and electrical panels. A project data book (discussed in § 2.24) is prepared for the property. Having completed the inspection, the manager then obtains the property's construction plans and a list of the general contractors and subcontractors who built the project. All maintenance contracts are summarized. If there are on-site personnel, employment records are obtained. The property management staff is immediately familiarized with the property. A tenant kit and emergency procedures are developed.

The property manager visits with each tenant as soon as possible, but first the owner sends each tenant a letter introducing the new manager and informing the tenants where to send their rental payments. If tenants have any complaints, this is the time to find out. It is better to hear all complaints immediately and respond to them than to have disgruntled tenants.

If the new property is a shopping center, the manager must find out his or her responsibilities regarding the merchants' association or marketing fund. What is the budget? When does the organization meet? What activities are planned? Who coordinates the activities? Who are the officers of the merchants' association?

The two new account checklists shown in Exhibits 2.5 and 2.6 are effective tools for ensuring that everything is done properly and in logical sequence.

These forms guide the property manager through the details of assuming the management of a new account. The forms are used to track critical information as well as delegate the specific responsibility for each area of information. The "corporate" section deals with obtaining the signed contracts and making sure they are distributed to appropriate departments and/or individuals. The "branch" portion of the form outlines the information that must be gathered and indicates persons and/or companies to be notified. The interface with the accounting department is a critical step as it will be processing financial information and paying bills and must have complete and accurate information on the new property.

EXHIBIT 2.5

New Account Checklist

Commercial Property

Project Name _____ Date of Commencement of Management _____

Property Manager _____

Management's Office _____ Property Owner _____

In order to establish a new property management account, the cooperation of management, accounting, personnel, and payroll departments is necessary to insure a smooth transition into our system.

A checklist for the establishment of a property management account will be initiated by the property manager to whom the account is assigned.

After all the required departments have completed their functions, a copy of the checklist will be sent to the director of property management for filing in the property's permanent records, with a copy retained in the files of the property manager.

		Initials	Date Completed
I.	*Administrative*		
	A. Execute management agreement.	_____	_____
	B. Send copies of signed contract to regional manager/branch office.	_____	_____
	C. Inform accounting department of new account/management fee information.	_____	_____
	D. Obtain current operating budgets for preceding and current year.	_____	_____
	E. Send form letters to tenants including request for new insurance certificates.	_____	_____
	F. Send form letters to suppliers/vendors.	_____	_____
II.	*Property Data*		
	A. Record lot sizes.	_____	_____
	B. Show type of construction.	_____	_____
	C. Obtain set of "as-built" plans.	_____	_____
	D. Compile all manufacturer's information regarding facilities and amenities (e.g., heating, air-conditioning, fire sprinkler systems) and originals of all warranties that apply to all mechanical equipment.	_____	_____
	E. Obtain inventory of personal property.	_____	_____
	F. Complete project insurance changeover.	_____	_____
	G. Obtain keys to vacant space.	_____	_____

EXHIBIT 2.5 *(Continued)*

	Initials	Date Completed

H. Obtain master keys (office building).	————	————
I. Record location of shutoffs, timers, etc.	————	————

III. *Income Data*

A. Record information regarding all lessees, including name/phone number of tenant contract and billing address if different from premises.	————	————
B. Show unit sizes (square footage).	————	————
C. Compile monthly rental (rent roll).	————	————
D. Record rental due dates.	————	————
E. Compile current list of delinquencies.	————	————
F. Obtain copies of all leases and pertinent information.	————	————
G. Obtain insurance certificates.	————	————
H. List current vacancies.	————	————
I. Compile prospective tenant list.	————	————
J. Show other income (CAM, escalation, % rent, utilities, parking lot, etc.).	————	————
K. Total past year's gross sales for tenants.	————	————

IV. *Operating Expense Data*

A. Obtain copy of current and all past tax bills.	————	————
B. Obtain copy of most recent licenses and tax changes.	————	————
C. List all outstanding bills on hand with special instructions as to payment.	————	————
D. Obtain copies of most recent annual operating statements at least as far back as earliest base year for escalation.	————	————
E. Obtain copies of prior tenant escalations bills.	————	————
F. Obtain copies of previous sales reports.	————	————
G. Establish supplier list.	————	————

V. *Operations* (Expenses billed back to tenants)

A. Record salaries, payroll taxes, etc. for on-site maintenance personnel.	————	————
B. List on-site office expenses.	————	————
C. Purchase on-site furniture and/or supplies.	————	————
D. Record vehicle/mileage allowance (on-site vehicle registration, license, insurance).	————	————
E. Obtain original copies of all agreements with each contractor, monthly charge, and address/phone number.	————	————
1. Elevator	————	————
2. Escalator	————	————

EXHIBIT 2.5 *(Continued)*

	Initials	Date Completed
3. Janitorial	_____	_____
4. Landscaping	_____	_____
5. Music	_____	_____
6. HVAC	_____	_____
7. Parking lot sweeper	_____	_____
8. Snow removal	_____	_____
9. Sprinkler contractor	_____	_____
10. Pest control	_____	_____
11. Equipment maintenance contractor	_____	_____
12. Tenant improvement contractor	_____	_____
13. _____	_____	_____

F. Obtain copies of all certificates of insurance from the property's contractors   _____   _____

G. List service companies and suppliers, including names/addresses/phone numbers.

1. Plumber	_____	_____
2. Electrician	_____	_____
3. Roofer	_____	_____
4. Utility repairs	_____	_____
5. Parking lot repairs	_____	_____
6. Painter	_____	_____
7. _____	_____	_____

VI. *Accounting*

A. Assign project number and notify property manager.   _____   _____

B. Set up bank account.   _____   _____

C. Prepare bank cards, signatures.   _____   _____

D. Order checks, deposit slips, endorsement stamps.   _____   _____

E. Enter management fee information on computer.   _____   _____

F. Establish type of operating statement that owner requests.   _____   _____

G. List security deposits being held (how held: cash, savings account, etc.).   _____   _____

H. Set up loan payment information.   _____   _____

I. Set up supplier list.   _____   _____

J. Verify ledger card.   _____   _____

K. Obtain copies of any audits performed on tenants in past years.   _____   _____

L. Obtain owner's federal tax ID number.   _____   _____

M. Summarize leases.   _____   _____

VII. *Payroll/Personnel Departments*

A. Set up employees on payroll.   _____   _____

B. Set up employee permanent files.   _____   _____

EXHIBIT 2.5 *(Continued)*

		Initials	Date Completed
	C. Set up employees on group insurance.	————	————
	D. Provide employees with benefit handbook.	————	————
	E. Establish time card procedures for on site personnel.	————	————
VIII.	*Emergency Procedures*		
	A. Analyze property's security needs.	————	————
	B. Review property's security program.	————	————
	C. Develop emergency procedures plan.	————	————
	D. Develop emergency procedures handbook for property management staff.	————	————
	E. Develop emergency procedures handbook for tenants.	————	————
	F. Notify police and fire departments of property manager's name and phone number.	————	————
	G. Walk the project.	————	————
	H. Conduct practice emergency response with management staff.	————	————
	I. Conduct practice emergency response with tenants.	————	————
	J. Review emergency procedures handbook with tenants.	————	————
	K. Conduct building evacuations.	————	————
	L. Notify answering service of whom to call after hours and in emergency.	————	————
IX.	*Construction*		
	A. Obtain as-built plans.	————	————
	B. Hire a space planner (office and industrial properties).	————	————
	C. Develop list of contractors to bid.	————	————
	D. Obtain list of general contractor and subcontractors who built project.	————	————
X.	*Miscellaneous*		
	A. List any pending litigation regarding property.	————	————
	B. List owner's insurance agent.	————	————
	C. List owner's attorney.	————	————
	D. List owner's accountant.	————	————
	E. Obtain copy of property sign criteria.	————	————
	F. Conduct energy audit.	————	————
	G. Review tax assessment.	————	————

EXHIBIT 2.6

New Account Checklist Form
Shopping Centers

Date of commencement
Project name _____   _____ of management _____ _____

Property manager/branch assigned _____

In order to establish a new property management account, the cooperation of Corporate, Branch, Accounting, Personnel and Payroll departments is necessary to insure a smooth transition into our system.

A checklist for the establishment of a property management account will be initiated by the Property Manager to whom the account is assigned.

After all required departments have completed their functions, a copy of the checklist will be sent to the Corporate office for filing in the property's permanent records, with a copy retained in the files in the Branch office.

	Initials	*Date Completed*
A. *Corporate*		
1. Contract approval	_____	_____
2. Copies of signed contract to Regional manager/Branch office.	_____	_____
3. Copies of signed contract to corporate office.	_____	_____
4. Inform Accounting Department of new account/management fee information.	_____	_____
B. *Branch*		
1. Obtain operating budgets for preceding and current year.	_____	_____
2. Send form letters to tenants including request for new insurance certificates naming.	_____	_____
3. Send form letters to suppliers/vendors.	_____	_____
II. Property Data		
1. Lot sizes.	_____	_____
2. Type of construction	_____	_____
3. Set of "as built plans."	_____	_____
4. All manufactures information regarding facilities and amenities (i.e., heating, air conditioning, fire sprinkler systems, etc., and also originals of all warranties which apply to all mechanical equipment).	_____	_____

EXHIBIT 2.6 (Continued)

	Initials	Date Completed
5. Inventory of personal property.		
6. Project insurance change over.		

III. Income data

	Initials	Date Completed
1. Names of all lessees (Tenant master file). Include name and phone number of tenant contact and billing address where different from premises.		
2. Unit sizes (square footage).		
3. Monthly rental (Rent roll). Obtain copy of last rental invoices if possible.		
4. Rental due dates.		
5. Current list of delinquencies.		
6. Copies of all leases or rental agreements and pertinent correspondence with Lessees.		
7. Obtain copies of insurance certificates from each tenant.		
8. List of current vacancies.		
9. List of current Lessees on notice.		
10. Prospective tenant list.		
11. Set up ledger cards (Branch office bookkeeper).		
12. Other income.		
13. Gross sales reports for tenants for past year.		

IV. Operating expense data

	Initials	Date Completed
1. Copy of current and all past tax bills.		
2. Copies of most recent licenses and other tax changes.		
3. List of all outstanding bills on hand, special instructions as to payment of these bills.		
4. Copies of most recent annual operating statements, at least as far back as earliest Base Year for escalation.		
5. Copies of last tenant escalation bills.		
6. Copies of previous sales reports.		
7. Establish supplier list (To accounting).		

EXHIBIT 2.6 *(Continued)*

	Initials	*Date Completed*
V. Common area expense data (Expenses being billed back to tenants).		
1. Salaries, payroll taxes, etc.	_____	_____
2. Office expenses.	_____	_____
3. Vehicle/mileage allowance (on-site vehicle registration, license, insurance).	_____	_____
4. Original copies of all agreements with each contractor and their monthly charge.		
Names/addresses/telephone number of contractor.		
1. Landscaper	_____	_____
2. Pest control	_____	_____
3. Equipment maintenance contractor	_____	_____
4. Tenant improvement contractor	_____	_____
4a. Copies of all certificates of insurance for current project contractors.	_____	_____
5. Service companies and suppliers. Names/address/telephone numbers.		
1. Plumbers	_____	_____
2. Electricians	_____	_____
3. Roofers	_____	_____
4. Utility repairs	_____	_____
5. Parking lot repairs	_____	_____
6. Parking lot sweeper	_____	_____
VI. Payroll information		
1. Prepare employee envelope-file ('To accounting).		
Application, employment agreement, bond, W-4, group insurance card, new employee checlist, personnel status change.	_____	_____
2. Set up time card procedures on site if applicable (First day).	_____	_____
C. *Accounting*		
1. Assign project number and notify property manager of same.	_____	_____
2. Set up bank account.	_____	_____
3. Prepare bank cards, signatures.	_____	_____
4. Order checks, deposit slips, endorsement stamps.	_____	_____

EXHIBIT 2.6 *(Continued)*

	Initials	*Date Completed*
5. Set up management fee information for computer.	_____	_____
6. Establish type of operating statement owner requests.	_____	_____
7. List of security deposits behind held, show how held, (Cash, savings acct., etc.).	_____	_____
8. Loan payment information set up.	_____	_____
9. Set up supplier list.	_____	_____
10. Verify ledger card set up at Branch level.	_____	_____
11. Obtain copies of any audits done on tenants in past years.	_____	_____

D. *Payroll/personnel departments*

1. Envelope-files from Branch office received _____.	_____	_____
2. Set up employees for payroll purposes.	_____	_____
3. Set up employee permanent files.	_____	_____
4. Set up employees on group insurance plan.	_____	_____
5. Notify Branch office that employees are set up on payroll, etc.	_____	_____

E. *Merchants' Association/Marketing Fund*

1. Merchants' Association By-Laws.	_____	_____
2. Marketing fund or Merchants' Association lease requirements.	_____	_____
3. Property owner's dues.	_____	_____
4. List of tenant's dues.	_____	_____
5. Merchants' Association Board of Directors.	_____	_____
6. Annual budget.	_____	_____
7. Date and place of the meetings.	_____	_____

F. *Miscellaneous*

1. List any pending litigation regarding the property.	_____	_____
2. Review project security.	_____	_____

§ 2.10   TERMINATING A PROPERTY MANAGEMENT ACCOUNT

An account can be terminated for any number of reasons. The property may have been sold, and the new owner will manage it in house, or the owner may have accepted a lower management bid from a competitor. A property management company might give up an account if it is not profitable or if there is a philosophical difference between the manager and the property owner or its representative. Regardless of the reason, termination is no less important than taking over a new account.

The management transition should be orderly and complete. A sloppy termination can expose the property manager and the company to criticism, tarnish their reputation, sever a relationship, and even cause legal action. The areas that the owner is most concerned with are the accounting records, leases, and the transfer of funds. The accounting department will play a major role in the transfer of a management account. It is not unusual for extra compensation to be charged for a takeover or termination of a management account. This often occurs when an extraordinary account of time is needed to organize a property in disarray or to assist the new manager assuming the account.

The checklist in Exhibit 2.7 can help to ensure that all administrative, accounting, and personnel issues are handled properly when a management account is terminated. The form should be maintained active until all items have been completed.

EXHIBIT 2.7

Termination of a Property Management Account Checklist

Date of Termination

Project Name _____ of Contract _____

Project Number _____ Project Type _____

Date Notice Is Given to Owner_____ Received from Owner _____

Property Manager/Branch _____

A complete and efficient transfer of a property management account requires the cooperation of the property manger, accounting, and personnel/payroll departments. The procedure to be followed and functions performed by each department are listed below:

A checklist for the termination of a property management account will be completed by the property manager for every account to be terminated.

The completed checklist that has been initialed and dated as each procedure is accomplished will be placed in the permanent account files.

After the accounting department has completed Section II, it will forward its completed copy to the office headquarters for review and filing in the property's permanent records, retaining one copy for the property file in the accounting department.

When notice for termination of a property management account is given to the property manager by an owner, it will be necessary for all departments to expedite these procedures. The property management agreement requires 30 days' notice, but is the exception rather than the rule to receive a full 30 day's notice. When notification is received, the property manager should immediately review the property management agreement for any special clauses regarding termination.

	Initial	Date Completed
I. *Administrative*		
A. Property manager receives notice of cancellation of account by owner.	_____	_____
B. Property manager notifies by telephone:		
Branch manager	_____	_____
Regional manager	_____	_____
Accounting/Controller	_____	_____
President	_____	_____
C. Property manager prepares backup memorandum with pertinent information and sends to:		
Controller	_____	_____
President	_____	_____
Regional manager	_____	_____
Payroll department	_____	_____

EXHIBIT 2.7 *(Continued)*

	Initial	Date Completed

D. Property manager shall prepare a form letter and send to all suppliers and vendors. Copies of these form letters shall be sent to existing owner, branch office file, on-site manager (if applicable). This letter shall accomplish the following:

   1. Establish final date responsible for debts incurred as managing agent. _____ _____

   2. Request final billing and/or disbursement, to close account. _____ _____

   3. Provide new ownership contact if available. _____ _____

   4. Follow up letters to utility companies with a phone call to identify meter reading date and respective billings. _____ _____

E. Conduct a personal review with project's employees to determine whether employees will be terminated or retained and transferred to another project. The following will then be accomplished:

   1. Send a form letter as a follow-up to the personal interview to all project employees notifying them of their employment status. Send copies to owner of project and payroll department. _____ _____

   2. Obtain final time cards from all employees and forward to payroll department. _____ _____

   3. Prepare cover letter identifying status of each employee and forward to payroll department along with appropriate personnel status change forms, which are to include: _____ _____

     a) Total salary due through termination date

     b) Settlement of vacation time due

     c) Incentive commission due

F. Property manager or owner will prepare a form letter to the tenants regarding termination of management. This letter should contain information concerning future rent checks. Send copy of letter(s) to owner. _____ _____

G. Update personal property inventory list and provide to management office files and owner. _____ _____

EXHIBIT 2.7 *(Continued)*

	Initial	Date Completed

H. Remove from the project site all supplies, etc. that have not been paid for by the project. _____ _____

I. Notify local police and fire departments that property manager will no longer be responsible for the property. Provide specific date of termination. _____ _____

J. Notify answering service (office/project) of change in management and specific date of termination. _____ _____

K. For purposes of proration, property manager shall have information available to be able to coordinate final accounting of payables and receivables, which would include: _____ _____

   1. Receivables _____ _____

      a) Rent collected

        (1) Base rents

        (2) Percentage rents

      b) Prepaid rents collected

      c) Deposits collected (for security or keys)

      d) Other income collected

        (1) Utility reimbursements (as part of tenant rebilling process)

        (2) Vending machine income

        (3) Tax bill-back reimbursements (as part of tenant rebilling process)

        (4) CAM reimbursements (as part of tenant rebilling process)

        (5) Insurance reimbursements (as part of tenant rebilling process)

        (6) Increased operating cost reimbursements (as part of tenant rebilling process)

   2. Payables _____ _____

      a) Prepaid utility accounts

      b) Prepaid service accounts

      c) Unpaid bills

      d) Prepaid operating permits

L. Property manager shall meet with on-site manager to accomplish the following: _____ _____

   1. Reconcile petty cash fund.

   2. Determine mileage reimbursement due.

EXHIBIT 2.7 *(Continued)*

	Initial	Date Completed
3. Define outstanding physical problems.		
4. Review inventory.		
5. Determine tenant prospects in process.		
6. Determine any tenants that may be leaving in the near future.		
M. Return policies and procedures manuals.	_____	_____
N. Property manager shall meet with new operator on project to turn over information. Property manager must receive a written receipt for:	_____	_____
1. All personal property as shown on original physical inventory		
2. All pertinent on-site records		
a) Leases		
b) Tenant correspondence		
c) CAM records		
d) Tax bill-back records		
e) Insurance bill-back records		
f) Tenant sales records		
g) All operating permits		
h) Copies of current contracts		
i) Tenant roster		
3. Project keys	_____	_____
4. Listing of paid deposits held and being transferred, prepaid rents, and delinquent rents	_____	_____
II. *Accounting*		
A. Property manager gives notification that the account is to be terminated.	_____	_____
B. Determine the cash balance, if any, for the account versus bills on hand.	_____	_____
C. Discuss with prospective property manager any unpaid bills in the system. If there is insufficient cash in the account, the property manager is to provide a written priority list indicating which bills are to be paid.	_____	_____
D. Consider audit fees and payments due for:	_____	_____
1. Property management fee	_____	_____
2. Payroll charges	_____	_____
3. Leasing commissions	_____	_____
E. Verify deposits to be transferred.	_____	_____
F. Resolve petty cash on hand.	_____	_____
G. Arrange project audit by member of accounting department.	_____	_____

EXHIBIT 2.7 *(Continued)*

		Initial	Date Completed
H.	Notify new owner or owner's agent in writing of any loan payments or other normal recurring payments.	_____	_____
I.	Ascertain disposition of rental checks received after termination date.	_____	_____
J.	Ascertain disposition of any unpaid bills still in system or received after date of termination.	_____	_____
K.	If new owner will agree in writing to assume full liability for bills, bank charges, and any bad checks, close the account approximately ten (10) working days after the last day of the month. Maximum time to close would be fifty (50) days after termination of contract.	_____	_____
L.	Prepare the final statement of the account and submit to the new owner or agent.	_____	_____

III. *Personnel/Payroll*

A.	Upon receipt of employee status change, process transfer or termination of employees.	_____	_____
B.	If termination date is other than a normal payday, prepare special paychecks immediately.	_____	_____
C.	Mail or deliver final checks to property manager.	_____	_____

IV. *Miscellaneous*

A.	Send copy of this checklist, when completed, to the director of property management.	_____	_____
B.	Obtain signoff from owner or representative upon termination that the above has been done.	_____	_____

§ 2.11 STAFFING AND ORGANIZATION

Like other service industries, property management covers a broad spectrum of services ranging from rent collection, simple accounting, and responding to maintenance problems to providing sophisticated financial reports, developing a maintenance management plan, implementing a tenant retention program, developing and implementing a comprehensive marketing and leasing program, and rehabbing a property. It is necessary to develop the company's policies and procedures and to staff the company for its particular level of service.

(a) STAFFING CRITERIA

A number of variables interact in making decisions about the size of the staff, its level of experience, and the property manager's workload.

The first consideration are the needs of the property owner. Those who live or work near their properties and assume some of the management functions usually do not need a high level of service, but absentee owners such as institutions may want full property management service. Because these owners often report to investors, they may need an annual management plan, monthly management and inspection reports, close tenant relations, an aggressive marketing and leasing program, and construction coordination. They are relying on the manager to enhance the property's value.

It is wise to consider the accounting requirements of the property owner and of the property management company when making staffing decisions. Most institutional owners, pension fund advisors, and asset managers require sophisticated reports, while a private investor is usually satisfied with the management firm's basic accounting reports.

The level of staffing in a property management company also depends on the company's philosophy regarding the level of service needed for its market niche. If a company has established itself as a firm specializing in medium-sized commercial properties with a high level of service, each manager will handle fewer properties and have assistance from the support staff. If the company's niche is a low to medium level of service for smaller commercial properties, the level of service will be correspondingly less. A related issue is the experience of the staff, especially the property managers. An experienced manager can handle more properties than a novice.

By their nature, some types of properties require more management time. For example, shopping centers require more time than office buildings; office buildings need more time than industrial properties; and older properties usually require more maintenance supervision than newer properties. Problem properties also require additional management time and expertise. The problems may be in leasing, rent collections, maintenance, or insufficient cash available to operate the property.

The location of the property is another variable in determining the manager's workload. Time spent in traveling to the property reduces the amount of time available to manage the property. Properties that are more than a two-hour drive away or that must be reached by air transportation require additional travel time for each visit.

The number and type of tenants in a property also affect the manager's workload. The more tenants, the more time required by the accounting department for tenant billing, adjustments, and percentage rent adjustments. More tenants also require more of the property manager's time. A shopping center with a merchants' association or marketing fund will require more management time than one without these organizations.

The property manager can manage more properties if he or she has backup support. Secretarial and administrative support frees the property manager from routine clerical and troubleshooting duties. The accounting department can provide the manager with reports and a full range of accounting services.

There are no hard and fast rules about the number of properties an experienced manager with backup support can handle, but a guideline for a medium level of service is 8 to 12 properties in the 50,000 square feet to 150,000 square feet range and 5 to 7 properties at a high level of service. Seven 150,000 square feet properties would require more time than seven 50,000 square feet properties. This assumes that none of these buildings require an on-site manager. Most on-site managers for large office buildings or malls have limited, if any, time to manage additional smaller properties.

The size of the on-site staff depends primarily on the size of the building. The manager of an enclosed community mall frequently serves as the marketing director and is responsible for re-leasing with the support of a secretary or administrative assistant. The regional and superregional mall will be staffed with from three to five management and administrative people. In larger malls, a manager, possibly an assistant manager, a marketing director, possibly an assistant marketing director, and a secretary will provide the basic staffing. These malls will frequently have a security chief and a maintenance supervisor.

Mid-rise and large low-rise office buildings are staffed with a manager and secretary; the high-rise office building will often add an assistant manager. The maintenance staff will include building engineers and day porters. If the property management company's accounting is decentralized, a bookkeeper will be included with the on-site administrative staff.

(b) ON-SITE MAINTENANCE STAFF

Neighborhood Centers   Few neighborhood centers can justify a full-time on-site maintenance person. An alternative is to have a part-time maintenance person on site who is responsible for cleaning the common area, landscape maintenance such as mowing or fertilizing, cleaning vacancies, changing filters in the HVAC units, and other minor maintenance duties. Pruning and spraying of plants should be handled by experts. The advantage to having an on-site maintenance person is immediate response to calls. Also, the common area will be cleaner with regular attention.

Community Malls   Community enclosed malls are usually staffed with a working maintenance supervisor and a maintenance person. The janitorial service for the common areas can be in house or contracted. The supervisor oversees all contracts and performs some maintenance tasks. Major HVAC maintenance should be contracted, filter changes and limited preventive maintenance inspections can be handled by the maintenance staff. Routine maintenance is the responsibility of the on-site maintenance staff.

Regional and Super-regional Malls   The larger malls can justify management-level supervisors in maintenance, operations, and security. These malls generally have an operations manager and a security chief. The operations manager hires the maintenance crew, and the security chief hires and directs the security force. If the security is contracted, the mall's manager or assistant manager will work with the security company, and the security chief's position will be eliminated.

Mid- and High-Rise Office Buildings   Many high-rise office buildings will hire an in-house building engineering staff. In these cases, the lead maintenance person is usually the building's chief engineer. The number of engineers depends upon the size of the building. A building that contracts all mechanical maintenance will have a working maintenance supervisor in lieu of a building engineer. Day porters are scheduled to keep the lobby and common areas clean while the building is open whether or not the building is staffed with engineers or a maintenance supervisor.

Multitenant Industrial Properties   Large multitenant industrial properties operate somewhat like community mall. They are staffed with a manager and a secretary. The manager may be responsible for the tenant improvement work, or a tenant improvement coordinator may be on site. Since maintenance is usually limited to common areas, an on-site maintenance supervisor is seldom needed.

§ 2.12   HIRING PROPERTY MANAGERS

Property managers are the heart of the management company. The owner or supervisor can develop an effective marketing program, establish state-of-the-art policies and procedures, and develop a capable support and accounting staff, but if the property managers cannot implement the programs, the company will not succeed.

Several factors must be considered when hiring a property manager: the manager's duties; number of other property managers and their level of experience; size and type of portfolio under management; the type of property ownership; and the compensation program. When all of these factors are considered, the decision can be made whether to hire an experienced or an entry-level property manager. If a company has an experienced staff of property managers, an entry-level property manager may be hired to manage the smaller properties or serve as an on-site assistant manager. On the other hand, if a property management company has only a few experienced property managers and is taking on a portfolio of properties owned by a sophisticated owner, it may prefer to have a seasoned manager.

The company has several excellent sources to choose from in locating a property manager. Most local chapters of IREM and BOMA publish monthly member newsletters and will accept notices of positions available. IREM publishes a national newsletter, *CPM Aspects,* which has an employment section. Finding an executive-level property manager may require the use of a search firm that specializes in the real estate industry. Active participation in the three major commercial property management organizations—BOMA, ICSC, and IREM—is a good way to become aware of the property managers in the area and their expertise.

Entry-level positions can be filled by looking in house for administrative assistants or bookkeepers with management potential or by hiring people in related fields or college graduates. Some military positions are similar to property management positions, so retired military personnel are good candidates. Qualifications for a competent property manager include:

- Ability to handle a crisis
- Ability to handle several tasks at once
- Ability to return to one task when interrupted by another
- Ability to work with numbers
- Excellent people skills
- Self-motivated
- Team player
- Good business sense
- Understands legal terms in contracts and leases
- Sales skills
- Creativity
- Willing to be on call after hours
- Trustworthy and of high integrity
- Quick study.

(a) RESPONSIBILITIES OF THE COMMERCIAL PROPERTY MANAGER

The general responsibilities of a commercial property manager for shopping centers, office buildings, or industrial properties are similar, but those responsibilities must be tailored to the requirements of the building, the property owner, and the structure of the property management company.

A general list of duties and responsibilities for commercial property managers follows:

1. Collect rents
   (a) Deposit rent (on-site manager only)
   (b) Report deposit slips (on-site manager only)
   (c) Complete tenant computerized ledger file or manual card (on-site manager only)
   (d) Delinquency follow-up
2. Obtain sales reports from retail tenants
   (a) Collect tenants' sales reports
   (b) Record tenants' sales (on-site manager only)
   (c) Follow up on missing reports
   (d) Analyze the sales reports
   (e) Prepare and distribute mall's monthly sales reports
3. Conduct retail tenant audits
   (a) Contact tenants regarding audit
   (b) Evaluate audit
   (c) Meet with tenant and auditor for audit review
4. Analyze store's sales, inventory levels, and store's operations
5. Prepare and distribute monthly management report
6. Prepare and distribute annual management plan
7. Report all insurance claims
8. Conduct monthly inspections and follow up on maintenance problems
9. Assist with litigation
   (a) Work with the property's attorney
   (b) Follow up on all litigation
   (c) Prepare and distribute litigation report
10. Develop and supervise maintenance management program
11. Coordinate security program
    (a) Assess the need for a security program
    (b) Develop and supervise security program

      (c)   Review daily security reports (properties with on-site security)

      (d)   Review store opening and closing reports (on-site mall manager)

12. Promote positive community relations

13. Approve expenditures

      (a)   Approve invoices

      (b)   Forward invoices to payables

      (c)   Review tax assessments

14. Monitor budget vs. actual reports

      (a)   Report on vacancies

      (b)   Meet with maintenance staff

15. Hire, train, supervise, and terminate administrative staff

16. Develop emergency procedures

      (a)   Instruct the staff on emergency procedures

      (b)   Conduct tenant training sessions

17. Coordinate leasing activity

      (a)   Conduct market survey

      (b)   Develop rent schedule

      (c)   Maintain a state-of-the-art lease form

      (d)   Negotiate leases and renewals

      (e)   Develop and implement leasing plan

      (f)   Analyze tenant mix periodically

18. Monitor tenant's insurance requirement per the lease

19. Develop and implement a marketing program

      (a)   Install on-site signage

      (b)   Develop marketing material

      (c)   Keep brokers aware of the property

      (d)   Build rapport with the brokerage community

20. Develop a risk management program

21. Evaluate real estate tax assessments and coordinate appeal of assessed valuation

22. Develop a tenant retention program

23. Analyze rehabs and modernization possibilities

24. Supervise tenant improvements

25. Develop a public relations programs

26. Establish and maintain a rapport with the property owner

27. Develop and implement a tenant retention program

(b) RESPONSIBILITIES OF THE SHOPPING CENTER MANAGER

Shopping center management includes the previously mentioned responsibilities as well as responsibilities unique to managing a retail property. These include:

1. Manage community room
    (a) Market the rooms to the community
    (b) Schedule use
    (c) Distribute rules and regulations
    (d) Have agreement signed
    (e) Collect deposits (include self-addressed, stamped return envelope)
    (f) Inspect room after use and coordinate cleanup
2. Communicate with merchants
    (a) Visit merchants monthly
    (b) Prepare monthly newsletter
    (c) Prepare and review the tenant kit with the merchants
3. Participate in merchants' association/marketing fund
    (a) Attend member meetings
    (b) Attend board of director's meetings
4. Coordinate tenant services
    (a) Co-sponsor seminars with police on how to prevent shoplifting and credit card fraud
    (b) Coordinate retailing consultant service.

(c) RESPONSIBILITIES OF THE MALL MARKETING DIRECTOR

1. Conduct periodic market research
2. Prepare annual advertising, marketing, and promotions calendar
3. Develop annual budget
4. Implement advertising, marketing, public relations, and promotions program
5. Maintain rapport with the media
6. Review and approve invoices
7. Develop and operate accounting system
8. Visit periodically with merchants
9. Maintain close working relationship with manager of major stores

10. Participate in merchants' association/marketing fund meetings
    (a) Prepare agenda for general membership meetings and board meetings
    (b) Provide meeting notice for membership and board meetings
11. Adhere to the bylaws or rules and regulations of the marketing fund or merchants' association
12. Develop a public relations program
13. Hire, train, administrate, and supervise staff.

(d) RESPONSIBILITIES OF THE ADMINISTRATIVE ASSISTANT

The administrative assistant assists the property manager in the day-to-day management of the properties. Duties include:

1. Provide administrative support for leasing and marketing projects
    (a) Prepare leases
    (b) Review leases submitted by brokers
    (c) Prepare commission statements
    (d) Prepare mailings to brokers and prospective tenants
2. Compile insurance records
    (a) Obtain tenant's insurance certificate
    (b) Obtain contractor's insurance certificate
3. Coordinate maintenance
    (a) Expedite all maintenance calls
    (b) Periodically inspect the property
    (c) Provide emergency backup for after-hours calls
4. Maintain control of keys to vacancies
5. Perform all secretarial duties for the property manager
6. Prepare monthly management report and annual management plan for distribution
7. Establish and maintain tenant files
8. Obtain estoppel from tenants
9. Maintain project data book

(e) RESPONSIBILITIES OF THE ACCOUNTING PERSONNEL

1. Input property manager's income and expenses projections
2. Calculate base rent income based on lease-up predictions from property manager
3. Calculate tenant pass-through charges subject to the terms of each tenant's lease

4. Code accounts payable for projects to appropriate account numbers in the chart of accounts, and communicate with property manager regarding questionable coding

5. Deposit daily cash receipts from tenants

6. Record tenant sales reports

7. Reconcile bank statements

8. Type accounts payable checks

9. Summarize leases

10. Calculate consumer price index (CPI) increases

11. Track tenant's base rent step-up increases and CPI increases

12. Prepare and mail tenant rent invoices monthly

13. Calculate and compare year-end adjustments to actual expenditures for estimated tenant charges

14. File copies of accounts payable vendor checks

15. Calculate payments made to vendors for preparation of 1099 filing with IRS

16. Maintain general ledgers

17. Prepare budget vs. actual expenditures, income statements, balance sheets, expenditure journals, sales reports

18. Respond to tenant inquiries regarding accounts receivable amount disputes

19. Compile schedules and documentation for owner's auditors, state payroll tax auditors, state revenue auditor, federal income tax auditors, and state real estate licensing auditors

20. Prepare payroll checks and file payroll tax reports.

§ 2.13 OFFICE ADMINISTRATION

Whether a company is small or large, it is important to define roles. Property management activities involve considerable overlap among, for example, accounting, leasing, and management. If these areas are not clearly defined, some duties could be overlooked, or conflicts could occur. Clear job descriptions provide guidance, and an organizational chart clarifies the company's staff structure.

Regardless of the size of the administrative staff, the same high standards should apply. Office equipment should be in good working order, files should be maintained in impeccable condition for maximum access, all documents leaving the office should be letter perfect, and visitors to the office should be treated warmly and efficiently. In short, the same care that the staff gives to the management of its properties should be given to daily office functions.

The executive understands that a collaborative atmosphere among staff members generates greater productivity. Even tedious filing or typing becomes a means to achieving a more successful company to which everyone can contribute. This team spirit, exhibited by clear and honest communication, strong conflict-management skills, and problem-solving models, takes time to develop but is well worth the effort.

§ 2.14   REAL ESTATE LICENSING REQUIREMENTS

In most states, a real estate license is required to manage or lease commercial properties in almost every situation. This includes collecting rents. A company must be licensed to manage or lease properties owned by others. The company must have an individual who serves as the company's designated real estate broker, and each property manager must have either a salesperson's or a broker's license. When a company or person manages or leases a property without a required real estate license, the state can issue a cease and desist order and immediately stop their activity. A real estate license is not required to manage one's own properties, however, or to manage properties as an employee of the property owner.

There are some gray areas that may cause misunderstanding. For instance, if the Smith Development Company develops an office building owned by Broadway Office Building Partnership, of which Smith is a general partner, an employee of Smith Development Company would need to be licensed to manage or lease the property owned by Broadway Office Building Partnership. The property manager is an employee of Smith Development Company, not of Broadway Office Building Partnership. In this situation, Smith Development Company would need a designated real estate broker, and the property manager would need a real estate license to manage or lease the office building.

Another gray area in some states is whether a syndicator must be licensed to manage the properties syndicated. Some states have held that the manager must be licensed or have the same percentage of ownership as the general partner. While it is not a requirement in every state, it bears looking into if a syndicator plans to manage the property it syndicates.

Real estate laws are fairly similar from state to state, but there are variances. Prudent managers will check the licensing requirements for every state in which they operate.

§ 2.15   INSURANCE

The executive in charge of the management company should annually review the company's insurance coverage with its insurance agent. The types and limits of coverage will depend upon the philosophy of the company, the state the company does business in, and clients' requirements.

A listing of insurance coverage for property management includes: errors and omissions, fidelity bond, broad form money and securities bond, valuable papers and records, office personal property, comprehensive general liability, automobile liability, employer non-ownership automobile liability, data processing equipment, workers' compensation, and employee benefits (e.g., health, dental, life, disability). An excellent reference source defining insurance coverage is *Coverages Applicable* by Roy C. McCormick, The Rough Notes Co., Inc., 1981. The Institute of Real Estate Management offers its members a source to apply for errors and omissions insurance.

Property owners find that insurance consultants and brokers can be of great help in making final insurance decisions. The property manager, too, should be involved in the decision-making process, but unless trained as an insurance expert, the property manager should give advice sparingly. In the final analysis, only property owners can say how much risk they are willing to assume.

The property manager can be helpful in analyzing leases. It is not uncommon, for instance, for pad or outlot tenants to be required to provide their own fire and extended coverage insurance, a fact that can be missed by the insurance carrier and resulting in double premiums on that portion of the property. Usually, all commercial leases require the tenant to carry liability insurance and name the landlord as additional named insured. If this clause is in effect and properly administered, it will often result in reduced liability premiums for the property owner. The same consideration applies to contractors that work on the property.

With the aid of legal counsel, the property manager can assist in suggesting property lease language to protect the landlord against claims.

Most leases will have mutual subrogation clauses. This means that neither party—landlord or tenant—will try to collect from the other for any loss for which they are insured. For instance, the landlord's building and the tenant's fixtures may burn in the same fire. If the tenant carries fire insurance on his fixtures and if there is a mutual subrogation clause, the tenant would look to its own insurance carrier for recovery and not the landlord.

Such items as Ansul systems or similar systems for restaurants are very helpful and required in many communities. If a tenant is operating a game parlor, the lease may require that it provide security at its own cost. The property manager should evaluate each new use and provide protective language, with the help of an attorney, to be sure that the landlord's exposure is not increased.

The property manager can help with the insurance program by keeping the property in top condition and eliminating hazards. Common hazards include bird's nests in signs and other electrical outlets, open electrical connections in light poles, electrical panels and sidewalk outlets, speed bumps that are not properly marked, potholes in the parking lot, poor directional signs in the parking lot, missing stop signs, landscaping that blocks the driver's vision, poorly lighted public areas, badly cracked sidewalks, changes in grade without warnings, stairs without handrails, water continually dripping on walkways, and electrical cords on the sidewalk or hanging low over walks.

Many insurance companies conduct safety audits of the property and notify the owners of action they believe is prudent. In past years, these notices were in the form of a request; today they are likely to be a requirement of continued coverage and carry a deadline for implementation.

Insurance companies are paying close attention to the agreements between the landlord, tenants, property manager, and contractors to determine whether liability may be passed on to the property manager and/or the contractor. They have always had this right, but in the past the building owner's insurance would take care of the problem and little attention was paid to the coverage and culpability of the property manager or contractor. This is good news for building owners, but can easily put the property manager in the middle, and if he or she has not handled the situation properly, the property manager could very well wind up being held liable.

In a recent shopping center liability suit, a woman claimed to have fallen over a speed bump. The insurance company investigated and found that all of the speed bumps had been painted several years ago, but, for some reason, the bump in question had not been painted. In the final settlement, the center owner's insurance paid one-half of the claim, the property manager's insurance paid one-fourth, and the company that painted the speed bumps paid one-fourth. The property manager was held partially liable because he had contracted for the work, but he did not have a written agreement with the contractor and did not follow up to see that the job was performed properly.

Insurance coverage in a commercial property is intended to protect many interests: the building owner, the economic value of the property, employees of the owner, tenants, the property management company, contractors, lenders, the merchants' association or marketing fund, if one exists, and the public. A review of the insurance that should be carried by the parties involved in a commercial property follows.

(a) COMMERCIAL PROPERTY OWNER'S INSURANCE

All Risk Fire Insurance   This policy covers the building for fire and several other risks, but generally excludes flood, mud, water and landslide, earthquakes, and sewer break-up. These coverages can usually be added by endorsement for an additional fee. Vandalism and malicious mischief can also be added by an endorsement. The policies will usually be written for the replacement value of the property and, because of the increase in premiums over the last several years, will often be written with fairly substantial deductibles.

If an owner has several properties, they can be covered under a blanket policy and generally do so for a substantial savings due to the spread of risk. A management company can also arrange to combine properties under its control and gain a considerable benefit in reduced premiums for the property owners. The property manager may be liable, however, if the coverages were allowed to lapse or if the policies did not cover what the owners expected them to.

In earthquake areas, it is a major decision whether or not the owner will carry earthquake coverage. As an example, an $11,000,000 California shopping center near a fault line would require a premium of $14,000 annually with a deductible of $10,000. The property owner must decide how much of that risk he is willing to underwrite and how much he is willing to spend to cover the possibility of a devastating loss.

When tenants are covered by the landlord's fire and extended coverage policy, care must be taken as to how the deductible is handled with the tenants. A $10,000 deductible on this type of policy means that the tenant is not covered for anything but the largest of claims. The tenant should be made aware of that so it can, if desired, cover the deductible with other insurance or at least be aware of the exposure.

Sometimes it is prudent to obtain an endorsement for demolition insurance. Often the fire and extended coverage policy does not cover the cost of removing the damaged portion of the building from the land.

Liability Coverage   The owner of the property will carry liability coverage for the entire property including the common areas. Frequently, major tenant's leases will specify a minimum level of coverage, the tenant will participate in the cost of that policy and will be an additional named insured. In a recent shopping center case, a major tenant refused to pay its share of premiums of a liability policy with upper limits beyond the stated amounts in the agreements. The center owner carried $15,000,000 in liability, and the tenant's lease specified $7,000,000 and agreed to pay his share of premiums of the lower figure only.

Boiler and Machinery Insurance   This covers the engines, pumps, motors, compressors, gears, and so on, and is most commonly applied to air conditioning compressors and electrical cabinets.

Plate Glass Insurance   In general, the owner of a shopping center has very little need for plate glass insurance. The tenant's lease will usually make the tenant responsible for its own glass either by indicating it must insure the glass or self-insure and replace the glass if necessary.

Loss of Rents   This coverage protects the property owner in case of a large fire or other disaster and provides the rental income replacement to make the mortgage payment and pay ongoing costs while the property is being restored. Often major tenants will pay their share of the fire and extended coverage insurance, but not the loss of rents, as they believe rents solely benefit the landlord.

(b) TENANT'S INSURANCE

The standard commercial lease today will require the tenant to carry certain types of insurance for the tenant's protection but also for the protection of the landlord.

Fire and Extended Coverage—Stock, Fixtures, and Improvements Should there be a fire or other disaster at the property, the property owner wants the tenant to reopen the business. If the tenant does not have insurance, it may not have the personal resources to reopen. A clause requiring fire and extended coverage on fixtures and tenant improvements has been common in shopping center and industrial leases for some time and is now becoming common in office buildings as well. Often there will be a dispute as to whose insurance policy should cover a specific loss. It is a good idea to let the landlord's and the tenant's insurance companies— the experts—decide the areas of responsibility.

Liability Insurance   The typical commercial lease today will call for the tenant to carry $1,000,000 combined limit liability insurance naming the landlord and possibly the landlord's property management firm as an additional or named insured. This policy protects the tenant and provides protection to the landlord and the property management firm when included as additional or named insured who would likely be sued in any case involving the tenant. Some owners will reduce the level of coverage if the tenant's use is not considered to be risky. Often, owners will allow financially strong tenants to self-insure for many of the coverages listed here, but there are only a few tenants nationally that are strong enough financially to self-insure for liability coverage.

Plate Glass Insurance   Major tenants and national chain stores in shopping centers will self-insure for glass breakage since they understand the risk and can handle the cost. The small shop tenant generally does not have the resources to replace a large plate glass window if it is broken, and the astute landlord requires the tenant to carry plate glass insurance for their mutual benefit. One shopping center in California covers all plate glass under the landlord's policy and bills it back as a common area item, thereby reducing the cost to all parties involved.

Boiler and Machinery Insurance   Most shopping center and industrial property tenant leases state that the tenant is responsible for the care and maintenance of the air conditioning system and therefore should carry boiler and machinery insurance.

Workers' Compensation   If the building or building owner has any employees, not outside contractors, the owner will be required in most states to carry a workers' compensation policy. This policy covers employees in case of injury in a job-related situation and is generally available from private carriers or from the state.

(c) PROPERTY MANAGER'S INSURANCE

Property management firms must also take precautions to protect themselves and those they deal with by having adequate insurance. The most common coverages are discussed next.

Liability   The typical limits are between $1,000,000 and $5,000,000. The policy will cover the owner of the property as an additional named insured and usually does not have a deductible. Large institutions often will require higher limits of liability and will share in the cost of the higher premiums.

Errors and Omissions   This policy covers the property management firm in case of mistakes. For instance, if the property manager forgets to pay the premium on an insurance policy, it lapses, and subsequently there is a loss, the errors and omissions policy would cover the claim. Errors and omissions coverage is difficult to obtain and is expensive. Many carriers will not cover property management companies for errors and omissions (E&O). The Institute of Real Estate Management, however, has an arrangement with an insurance firm that offers E&O insurance to its members. As an example, in 1992 a company managing approximately 25 properties pays a premium of $17,000 for $1 million in coverage with a $25,000 deductible.

Fidelity Bond   Most clients require that a property manager carry a fidelity bond that protects the property owner from loss due to theft or misappropriation by the employees of the property management firm. This coverage is based on the total amount of risk; the limit is usually set by the client.

If the property management firm is operating as a proprietor, it may be unable to obtain a fidelity bond as the insurance companies feel the property manager is insuring himself. A good solution to the problem is for the client to take out the policy on the property management firm or property manager and have the property management firm reimburse him for the premiums.

Nonowned Automobile Liability   Because employees will use their cars in conducting business on behalf of the property management company, most firms carry liability for nonowned automobiles. Should the employee become involved in an accident while carrying out company business, the property management firm would be covered.

Workers' Compensation   The property management firm must carry workers' compensation mandated by most states. This coverage will protect the employee in the event of a job-related accident.

(d) CONTRACTOR'S INSURANCE

In addition to the landlord, tenant, and property management firm, contractors should also be insured. The property manager should require a written contract for all outside work that spells out exactly what is to be done and requires the contractor to provide evidence of the following coverages naming both the property owner and the property management company as additional or named insured.

The following coverages are evidenced by a certificate of insurance provided by the contractor to the property manager or property owner. In most cases, there is no extra charge to the contractor for this certificate, but if there is a charge the contractor will likely pass it along to the property owner or property manager.

Liability   At least $1 million in coverage. For contractors used on a regular basis, the certificate can be kept on hand and automatically renewed each year.

Automobile Liability   Most contractors come on the property in vehicles. They should be provided evidence of proper insurance coverage.

Workers' Compensation   This coverage is the same for the contractors as it is for the property owner and the property manager. It is not likely that a contractor's employee would sue the building owner or property management firm in case of injury, but evidence of the proper insurance can provide a level of protection.

Fidelity Bond   A bond is appropriate for contractors such as air conditioner repair technicians or janitors that work inside the tenant's premises.

(e)   INSURANCE ADMINISTRATION

In general, the property manager is responsible for the insurance administration even if he or she does not place the insurance. The property manager should have copies of all property owner policies along with the name, address, and phone number of the insurance representative who will handle any claims. Most insurance companies issue a directive on how to report a claim and that information should be kept in a secure place in the property manager's office so the procedure can be followed in case of loss. A summary of the policies should be kept on hand showing what coverage the owner has and any deductibles that may apply. A tickler file should be maintained showing the policy expiration dates.

Any incident that could lead to an insurance claim should be reported to the insurance company. Even if the owner makes a payment on an incident, the insurance company can provide advice and guidance. The property manager should not make a small payment outside of the insurance company since the claimant may have a greater settlement in mind and will use the original small payment as an admission of guilt.

For the contractor's and tenant's insurance requirements, the property manager should keep a tickler file showing the coverage and expiration dates. Thirty days prior to the expiration date, the insured should be notified that coverage is about to expire and an updated certificate is required. Often, a tenant will not understand, or will ignore, the lease requirements, and it is best to have the name of the tenant's insurance carrier on file and work directly with that carrier if the tenant does not respond properly. If a contractor or tenant refuses to provide coverage as requested, the manager should contact the owner's carrier for further instructions. The owner's carrier may want to provide interim coverage in the case of fire insurance or may be helpful in obtaining the necessary coverage from the tenant.

Insurance plays an important role in the operation of commercial properties today. It is incumbent on all property managers to be aware of the need for adequate insurance as well as the need for specific procedures to insure that complete coverage is in place and that the program is being properly administered.

§ 2.16   USING AN ATTORNEY

One of the frustrating aspects of property management today is the proliferation of lawsuits. The relationship between landlord, tenant, and manager is a complex one. The owner of the property and the fee manager may have differing legal positions in a particular situation and could well become adversaries as the facts of a case unfold. Additionally, the public is an important part of commercial projects, and this increases legal exposure.

It is incumbent upon the property owner and the property manager to be properly insured for liability in the event something goes wrong. They should have access to good legal advice in the preparation of leases, contracts, agreements, procedures, and even approach. No attorney can guarantee that a client will not be sued, but a good attorney can provide safeguards and planning that will minimize the exposure. Representative attorneys should be named early to be available on a consulting basis. Attorneys should be selected for their knowledge and experience in the area in question. Bankruptcy, for instance, is a complex field, so the property manager would be better off with an attorney who specializes in that area. Another specialized area is employee relations, which have become a key issue in many industries.

One positive side of our current litigious society is that property owners and property managers are generally aware of the potential problems of lawsuits and make extra effort to maintain good relationships and negotiate harder to resolve disputes out of court.

§ 2.17   MANAGING PROPERTIES FROM AFAR

Properties that are at least a few hours drive from the property management office and that have no on-site manager present many potential problems that must be carefully evaluated before a management proposal is submitted and a management plan developed. Who will supervise the maintenance program? How will emergencies be handled? Can a rapport with the tenants be maintained? How can the property manager be aware of what is happening in the community? Will the owner trust that the property is receiving sufficient attention? All of these concerns are eliminated with an on-site manager; however, most small and medium-sized commercial properties do not have on-site managers.

Generally, if a property is more than a two-hour drive from the manager's office, it is considered to be managed from afar. When a property is at this distance or greater, the manager probably will not be able to respond quickly to problems that arise, and a plan must be developed to address the above-mentioned concerns.

Routine maintenance and emergencies must be handled by a person in the area or on site. In some cases, a tenant can be hired to be the eyes and ears of the property manager. A real estate office in the building would be a likely candidate to assume this responsibility.

An alternative is to hire a part-time working maintenance supervisor. This person could be a maintenance contractor, a construction worker, or a retired person. Duties would include supervising the maintenance contractor, conducting periodic inspections, responding to maintenance calls and emergencies, cleaning the parking lot, and arranging for snow removal. This person could also let prospective tenants into a space when the leasing agent is not in the area. A maintenance contractor in the area can be hired to handle emergencies and to visit the property periodically.

The use of a full- or part-time working maintenance supervisor is an expense of the common area/escalation budget, landlord's budget, or both. The lease will determine if the supervisory time is a cost of the common area/escalation expense or the owner's nonreimbursable expenses. If the cost is not passed on to the tenant according to the lease, then the management agreement will determine if the cost of this person is a property management company expense or a property owner's expense. It could be the property management company's expense if these duties are normally performed by the property manager.

The property manager can develop a rapport with tenants by scheduling periodic visits to the property and spending a brief time with each tenant. Tenants should be introduced to the local maintenance person and given his or her phone number. The maintenance person must be equipped with a beeper and be accessible to both tenants and manager.

It is difficult but necessary to be aware of community activities and how they affect the property. The property manager can do this by subscribing to the local newspaper or joining the local chamber of commerce or board of realtors. The latter will provide information on local business concerns and an opportunity to attend board meetings. Periodic luncheon meetings with community leaders and regular meetings with the maintenance supervisor will provide worthwhile information about the property and community

To assure that the property owner receives satisfactory attention, the property manager should meet with the owner and explain in detail how the property will be managed—for example, who will respond to maintenance problems and emergencies—and address all issues that may be of concern to the owner.

An alternative to the program outlined above is joint management with either a commercial or residential property management company in the area. This company would perform on-site management. Its responsibilities might also include collecting rent and working with tenants, thus requiring the lead property manager to spend less time at the property. The property manager in this case works with the owner and maintains responsibility for accounting, budgeting, monthly and annual management reports, tenant relationships, and business decisions. Of course, the management fee must be competitive and split in a fair formula between the two companies.

When establishing a management fee for properties that are at a distance from the property management office, several expenses should be included. Travel costs will be higher if air travel and lodging are necessary. Even a two-hour drive to a property is time that could be used more productively. Entertaining community leaders and maintaining membership in business organizations are two other costs. The maintenance supervisor may be a cost of the property management company, charged to the project, or a shared expense. One additional cost is sharing the fee with another property management company.

There are numerous opportunities to manage properties from afar. These opportunities are usually found in the smaller community where professional commercial property management is limited or where a relationship is established with a property owner who prefers the services of a particular company over a local firm. Managing properties from afar is an effective means for a property management company to increase its portfolio size and profitability, but care must be taken in establishing the management procedures, analyzing additional costs, and establishing a fee that is fair to both the property owner and the property management company.

§ 2.18 INCENTIVE PROGRAMS

Incentive programs are designed to reward employees for achieving a goal, to acknowledge outstanding performance, to motivate people, to express appreciation, and to promote team spirit within the staff. Each incentive program should be analyzed to determine if it meets the intended goal, is perceived as fair, and is cost-effective. These programs can take many forms including:

- *Commissions.* A commission is the major incentive for leasing. Leasing agents who are not paid a salary are usually paid 50 percent or more of the commission paid to their broker. Property managers who are paid a salary must devote most of their time to managing the properties, but they will still have time to handle leasing and renewals. Since commission income often is the majority of the profit margin earned by a commercial property management company, a property manager who is motivated to lease space has a positive impact on the company's profits. A 20 to 35 percent share of the commission for new leases and renewals in addition to a base salary is an effective incentive program for managers. The percentage can be increased as additional space is leased.

- *Bonus for Acquiring Management Accounts.* A property management company's growth is dependent upon acquiring new accounts, so many companies offer their property managers an incentive to add properties to the company's portfolio. A common incentive is a bonus consisting of all or a portion of the first month's management fee. This incentive can also be offered to leasing agents or sales brokers in the community if they refer a management account to the company.

- *Equity Interest in Properties.* This is a common incentive program for upper management and executive positions in development firms. A small ownership position is given in a property being developed or syndicated.

- *Awards for Achieving Professional Designations.* A professional designation enhances both the individual's and the company's reputation in the industry. The company can acknowledge the property manager's achievement by sending out press releases; featuring the individual in the company newsletter; distributing a memo to all employees; marking the occasion with an in-house celebration; or presenting a gift such as a restaurant pass, a weekend getaway, or cash.

- *Awards for Performance and Meeting Goals.* A small monetary award or gift certificate can be given in recognition of individual accomplishments or for goals that have been met by a group. For example, a Pacific Northwest property management firm gives employees a gift certificate from a restaurant for sending out monthly management reports on time for all the properties for three consecutive months. Since preparing a monthly management report is a team effort, everyone works together to be on time with his or her portion of the report.

- *Annual Bonus.* A year-end bonus, sometimes referred to as the Christmas bonus, is an excellent way to reward the property manager along with the administrative and clerical staff for their work during the year. The bonus should be based on the company's profits and the individual's performance. One caution: If the same amount is given each year regardless of these two criteria, it will be perceived as an additional paycheck and not as an earned bonus.

- *Gifts of Appreciation.* Recognizing birthdays or employment anniversary dates is another opportunity to reward staff members. An informal get-together for coffee and presentation of a gift certificate or a congratulatory card is appropriate on an employee's anniversary. A management firm in the Northwest has a cake each month for all birthdays in that month. Employees are taken to lunch and given a $50 gift certificate to a department store on their employment anniversary.

- *Communication.* Because property management is a people-oriented business, good communication between and within departments is essential in promoting teamwork. Staff members need to feel that they are valued and appreciated not only by receiving external rewards, but by the goodwill of their coworkers. One way to foster cooperation and allow people to express themselves is to sponsor regular staff or department luncheons. Here staff members can discuss business concerns informally, brainstorm, and share suggestions while enjoying each other's company at a meal. Another opportunity is to take each department out to a monthly or quarterly lunch to review departmental operations. The lunch can be at or near one of the properties managed so the staff can visit the property. Another way to foster better communication and a positive team spirit is to schedule social events throughout the year so that staff members and their families can meet as friends and enjoy one another away from the office. A committee can organize events ranging from river rafting, to a Halloween costume party, to a summer picnic, to a family night, to a formal Christmas dinner.

Countless books have been written on team building, motivation, conflict management, and overall human relations. Since organizational goals are more likely to be met when people feel they are valued members of the company, property managers should learn to use the people management skills found in these resources.

§ 2.19 EVALUATING AND SELECTING A PROPERTY MANAGEMENT FIRM

There are several important factors that need to be taken into consideration when choosing a property management firm. It is essential to examine each relevant issue in turn.

(a) FINANCIAL REPORTING

Often the asset manager's first concern is the property management firm's ability to report the property's management and financial activities in the asset manager's format and deliver the report on a timely basis. Each asset manager depends on the property management firm for most of the information he or she needs to report on. With multiple property management firms reporting, the asset manager requires a standardized form using a particular chart of accounts. The asset manager will want to (1) know what software the property management uses, (2) determine whether the property manager can do accrual accounting, (3) review the firm's budgets, (4) understand the property management firm's budgeting process, (5) know who does the budgets, (6) be familiar with how the accountant interfaces with the property manager, and (7) know who does billings and collections.

The asset manager will want to know that the person in charge of the accounting department has a strong financial background and experience. Some asset managers will visit the property management firm's accounting department. The location of the accounting department, its furniture, equipment, and layout can provide an insight into the importance the property management firm places on the accounting function. If the accounting department is cramped and disorderly, then the property management firm may not understand the importance of the accounting and reporting requirements of the institutional owner.

One asset manager states that he asks the property manager that he is interviewing if he can see a copy of an arrearage report from one of the properties the firm manages. How long it takes for the property manager to find the report is an indication of the importance the property manager places on collecting delinquent rent. The property manager must understand the importance of financial reports, and his or her attitude should be, "In what format do you want the financial reports and when do you want them?"

(b) PROPERTY MANAGEMENT FIRM'S EXPERTISE

A major concern to the asset manager is what types of properties the property management firm manages. What is the size of the firm's portfolio and what proportion of the portfolio is each property type? Next, the asset manager will want to review the firm's client list which gives an indication of whether the property management firm is set up to meet the needs of institutional investors. A list of the properties managed in another indication of the firm's expertise and will also reveal any possible conflicts of interest. The asset manager will interview the property manager, the controller, and the director of property management. If the director of property management doesn't meet the asset manager or attend the interview and explanation process, the asset manager will question the firm's commitment to managing the asset manager's property. The asset manager will want one point of contact with the firm. This person needs to know the market conditions, understand the financial report along with good property management practices and principles.

(c)   MARKETING AND LEASING

The asset manager will expect the property managers to have knowledge of the market. Whether or not the property management firm will be responsible for marketing and leasing the property, property managers should be knowledgeable of the deals in the market. They should know each building's asking and deal-making rates, concessions, and vacancy rates per building. They should be familiar with the absorption rate and general level of leasing activity. When the property management firm is responsible for the leasing, the asset manager will interview the person leasing the property.

The leasing agent will be asked questions on the issues mentioned earlier. The leasing agent will be expected to provide projected rental rates (pricing each space individually), suggested concession package and tenant improvement allowance, along with an estimate of how long it will take to lease the building or individual spaces. The asset manager will want to know which properties are competition to the subject building.

The leasing agent should be prepared to describe a complete marketing and leasing program. The asset manager will want to know if the leasing agent has or is presently leasing similar properties and if any of the properties he or she is leasing presents a possible conflict of interest with the asset manager's property. The asset manager expects a proactive marketing and leasing approach. This includes the leasing agent being able to negotiate a deal within the parameters provided by the asset manager without constantly calling the asset manager for advice.

(d)   BUILDING TOUR

The asset manager will want to tour buildings in the property management firm's portfolio that are similar to the asset manager's building. The asset manager will be checking the building's common and public areas, observing the building's curbside appeal, signage, and, in particular, leasing signs, and the condition of vacant spaces. The asset manager will also observe whether or not the tenants recognize and acknowledge the property manager.

(e)   ADDITIONAL CONCERNS

The asset manager also wants to know if the person assigned to the property has any of the three commercial property management designations that are respected in the industry—CPM, Certified Property Manager, CSM, Certified Shopping Center Manager, and RPA, Real Property Administrator. A property manager who holds one or a combination of these designations has shown a commitment to knowledge and professionalism. A property management firm that encourages and supports its property managers' pursuit of professional designations demonstrates a vital interest in providing top quality services to its clients.

Some asset managers will check to see if the property management firm is an Accredited Management Organization (AMO). This designation is awarded by the Institute of Real Estate Management to firms that are thoroughly reviewed and meet strict criteria for professional standards and financial stability. An asset manager unfamiliar with the area will often look first for a property management firm with the AMO designation.

One asset manager stated that he observes the condition and amenities of the property management office. Is the office neat and organized? Does the office space configuration encourage effective communication? This may be a clue to how the property managers go about managing their portfolio or properties. He also looks at what is on the walls and counters. Is there an attractive display of membership certificates, pictures of properties, or artwork? Is the office warm and inviting? Property management is a people business, and understanding people is important to the success of a property manager.

When the property manager understands the needs of the asset manager, he or she is able to design a management and marketing program geared to these needs. This will enhance the property management firm's ability to acquire management accounts.

§ 2.20   ASSET MANAGEMENT

The asset management segment of the real estate investment industry is also impacted by the downturn in development and commercial real estate. Many of the small to medium-sized real estate advisory firms have cut back their staff resulting in a larger portfolio for their asset managers. Many of the major insurance companies are experiencing difficulties. Some of these firms' asset management divisions have had a hiring freeze and their asset managers' portfolios are likely to increase. Many asset management firms' ratio of assets to asset managers will increase. The increased responsibilities for many asset managers make it even more important for the property manager to understand and meet the needs of asset managers.

Property managers must be cognizant of the workload of the asset manager they work for. They need to be aware of special reports required of the asset manager, understand the asset manager's major concerns, and, above all, produce all financial and other reports required by the asset manager on a timely basis. These items can also be translated into how an asset manager evaluates and selects a property management firm. A survey of asset managers revealed a general consensus of the following criteria to evaluate and select property management firms. Developers who are exploring expansion of their property management departments into the fee management business, should review these criteria and compare them to how their property management department presently operates.

§ 2.21   THE PROPERTY MANAGEMENT FIRM

Though the property management industry is not downsizing (or right-sizing) as most of the other disciplines in commercial real estate, property management firms and property managers will be impacted by the state of the industry and what is happening to developers and investors. In the first half of the 1990s, the number of properties available for fee management decreased in many areas. Many investors removed their properties from the fee managers and manage the properties themselves.

In addition, property management firms are now competing with well-known regional and national developers for property management business. Local property management firms need not be afraid of the competition but must re-analyze the firm's market niche and determine if it remains competitive in meeting the needs of their clients. As discussed earlier, developers have both strengths and weaknesses in competing for fee management business. The property management firm should analyze the strengths and weaknesses of the developers in their areas and position themselves to compete effectively with the developers.

Many property management firms are finding they must devote more time to marketing their services. For instance, in the past a property management firm would lose one property a year and gain three or four, now the same firm is finding it is losing two to three properties a year, primarily to property owners taking their property in-house management.

One distinct advantage to the property management industry of developers entering into the fee management business is their impact on management fees. Developers are accustomed to earning large fees, and they are not likely to submit low fees in their management proposals. Most local property management firms will have a lower overhead than will developers and can compete on a fee basis.

When bidding on a management account, the property management firm should price its fees based on the value of its services. It doesn't make sense to price services at a breakeven just to acquire a management account. A property management firm should never be ashamed of its fees or upset if it loses an account to another firm because that firm's fees were substantially lower. If the level of service is priced correctly, the property management firm cannot and does not want to compete on price alone with a firm offering a substantially lower fee. A property owner who selects a property management firm solely on the basis of a low fee may not be content with the corresponding lower level of service and eventually will become dissatisfied with the firm. A property management firm should be concerned only if it loses out on a management bid because the property owner or asset manager believed the firm was not qualified on a basis of expertise or experience.

Some property management firms are tempted to provide two levels of service, believing that a lower level of service will compete with firms offering a lower bid. In reality, however, if two levels of service are offered, the property management firm will become known for its lowest level of service and its image and reputation will suffer.

When a property management firm re-analyzes its position in the market, the analysis will include which additional services can be added to increase additional sources of income or profit centers. The potential for the greatest additional income is sales, followed by leasing. Other potential sources of income are tenant improvement supervision, rehabilitation supervision, and consulting. Increasing the firm's geographical area of service and managing other types of properties are also potential avenues for increasing management fees.

Real estate is an incentive-driven industry. Developers get incentive from their potential to earn profits from a development; brokers and leasing agents have potential to earn big commissions; and mortgage bankers can earn substantial fees. Even property management is incentive-driven since management fees are usually a percentage of the collected rents.

Since the base of a property management firm's income is from management fees, the firm should consider offering its staff and the brokerage community an incentive for being the procuring cause or for providing a lead that results in a management account. For instance, the incentive amount for procuring an account could be the first month's management fee minus any on-site management costs.

For example, if the property management firm's fee for a mid-rise office building was $15,000 per month and the firm paid out $9,000 per month for the on-site staff, the incentive fee would be $6,000. If the firm's fee for managing a strip center with no on-site management was $2,500 per month, the incentive fee would be $2,500. This will motivate staff members to be aggressive in marketing the firm's services.

Staff members can also be encouraged to bring names and addresses of properties to the director of property management for follow-up. For instance, if a company bookkeeper became aware of a new building, he or she could inform the director of property management who would pursue the lead. If the firm acquired that management account, a finder's fee would be paid to the bookkeeper. Since the bookkeeper did not play a part in acquiring the management of the property, this incentive is less than the amount paid to a person who was the procuring cause. For example, the finder's fee could be 15 percent of the first month's fee. In the first example cited, the finder's fee would be $900. If the property was the strip center with a fee of $2,500 a month, the finder's fee would be $375. This is a significant amount for a finder's fee. Such a program motivates each person in the firm to be aware of potential properties for the firm to manage. One caution: The director of property management must check to see that the state real estate laws allow finder's fees for persons without a real estate license.

§ 2.22   PROCEDURE MANUAL

Property managers need considerable autonomy to be effective. Their wide range of responsibilities and the amount of time spent away from the office preclude constant supervision. Many of them work in branch offices or as on-site managers for a large commercial property with limited supervision.

In this autonomous structure, specific guidelines are needed to ensure that the manager operates within the framework of the company's policies and procedures. Property owners, too, have specific guidelines, which might include the length of maintenance contracts, rent collection, evictions, and leasing terms. The management company can develop a manual covering the policies and procedures of each property owner and those of the management company.

The procedure manual also details how each department functions and how all departments interact with one another. The manual may be used as a marketing tool when the property management company submits a proposal. It gives the owner, especially an institutional owner, a model of efficiency that inspires confidence in the company.

No two procedure manuals are alike because each is tailored to the philosophy and operation of the management company and to the type of properties manages. Exhibit 2.8 is a sample outline that can serve as a basis for a property management company's procedure manual.

§ 2.23   THE MANAGEMENT AGREEMENT

The management agreement is the basis for the relationship between the property management firm and the property owner or advisor. The agreement will establish the company's duties, authority, and compensation. This agreement must be carefully prepared and negotiated. A poorly drafted agreement can result in misunderstandings and eventually a

EXHIBIT 2.8

Procedure Manual Outline

SECTION I.   MANAGEMENT AGREEMENTS

Each management agreement is summarized into the following sections:

Property description: Address, square footage, and major tenants

Ownership: Name, address, and phone number of the ownership and its representative

Management agreement terms: Length, commencement and expiration date, cancellation rights, management fees, other fees including who pays for on-site personnel

Leasing: Leasing agent, commission schedule, and parameters within which a lease can be negotiated without the owner's approval

Expenditure limits: The amount of nonbudgeted maintenance and equipment expenditures allowed without owner's approval

Reports: List of the type and frequency of the narrative and accounting reports. Date reports are due. Name and Address of those who will receive the reports.

Operating account: Minimum balance required by the bank in owner's operating account

Insurance: Insurance requirements and policy limits for the property and for the management company

Legal counsel: The approved attorney

SECTION II.   GENERAL OFFICE POLICIES AND PROCEDURES

Explains office procedures and policies.

II-A1	Main office management personnel
II-A2	Branch office personnel
II-A3	New employees
II-A4	Terminating employees
II-A4a	Authority for personnel action
II-A5	Pay periods
II-A6	Time cards
II-A7	Office hours
II-A8	Vacations
II-A9	Illness
II-A10	Holidays
II-A11	Absence other than illness
II-A12	Medical, disability, and life insurance
II-B	Postage meter and mail
II-C	Office supplies
II-D	Automobile accidents
II-E	Expense reports
II-F	Petty cash vouchers
II-G	Filing system

EXHIBIT 2.8 *(Continued)*

II-7   Travel arrangements
II-8   Continuing education

SECTION III.   PURCHASING POLICIES AND PROCEDURES

Explains methods for purchasing and approving invoices.

III-A   Chart of accounts
III-B   Vendor/contractors lists
III-C   Monetary approval limits
III-D   Nonbudget/over-budget expenses over $1,000
III-E1   Definition of documents
III-E2   Purchase order numbering system
III-E3   Purchase order, blanket purchase order, confirmation of
            purchase order
III-E4   Instructions for preparing purchase order, blanket purchase
            order, confirmation of purchase order
III-F   Change order
III-G   Check request
III-H   Extra vendor work request
III-I   Capital expense
III-J1   Tenant extra order
III-J2   Instructions for preparing tenant extra order
III-J3   Tenant extra order log sheet

SECTION IV.   MANAGEMENT COMPANY'S ACCOUNTING POLICIES AND PROCEDURES

Provides instructions to the accounting department and information to others
in the company about how the accounting department operates.

IV-A   Tenant invoices
IV-B1   Processing an invoice
IV-B1a   Code of approval stamp
IV-B2   Not to exceed purchase order
IV-B3   Fixed-price contract
IV-B4   Utility and telephone bills
IV-B5   Unit price contract
IV-B6   Travel and entertainment vouchers
IV-C   Abstracting of contracts and equipment
IV-D1   Petty cash accounts
IV-D2   Instructions for preparing petty cash accounts
IV-E   Building managers checking account
IV-F   Merchants' association accounting
IV-G   Material & labor releases

SECTION V.   LEASING POLICIES AND PROCEDURES

Outlines procedures for working with brokers to complete a deal and for
moving the tenant into the building.

V-A1   Recognition of outside broker's status
V-A2   Nonrecognition of outside broker's status

EXHIBIT 2.8 *(Continued)*

V-B	Owner approval procedure
V-C	Lease exclusive and conflicts
V-D1	Lease summary preparation
V-D2	Lease preparation
V-E	Lease addendum
V-F1	Lease, amendment of lease, assignment, assumption, and consent
V-F2	Sublease agreement
V-F3	Holdover and termination agreements
V-F4	Lease termination agreement
V-G	Tenant work prior to lease execution
V-H1	Space studies (office building and industrial properties)
V-H2	Working drawings
V-I1	Tenant move-in
V-I2	Instructions for preparing tenant move-in
V-I3	Storefront allowances
V-J1	Lease commissions
V-J2	Lease commissions statement
V-K1	Tenant move-out
V-K2	Instructions for preparing tenant move-out

SECTION VI.   BUILDING OPERATING POLICIES AND PROCEDURES

Explains daily operating policies and procedures.

VI-A1	New tenant
VI-A2	Tenant list
VI-A3	Vacating tenants
VI-B1	Delivery of notice
VI-B2	Notices to pay rent
VI-C	Notice of delinquency
VI-D	Enforcing late charges
VI-E	Delinquency charge assessment letter
VI-F	Notice of default in payment of rent
VI-G	Rent relief
VI-H	Notice of abandoning tenant
VI-I	Application of security deposit to rent
VI-J	Holidays
VI-K	Tenant name change
VI-L	Tenant construction
VI-M	Security
VI-N	Maintenance
VI-01	Public use of community hall
VI-02	Public use of community booth
VI-P1	Merchants' association bylaws
VI-P2	Promotional fund bylaws
VI-Q	Building keys
VI-R1	Tenant HVAC calls
VI-R2	Tenant HVAC maintenance service

EXHIBIT 2.8 *(Continued)*

VI-S	Tenant janitorial complaints
VI-T	Building's organizational chart
VI-U1	Mall community booth guidelines
VI-U2	Public use of shopping center
VI-V	Litigation report
VI-W	Advertising agency
VI-X1	Budget input form
VI-X2	Budget explanation form
VI-X3	Tenant roster
VI-X4	Tenant charges
VI-X5	Tenant common area and escalation calculations

SECTION VII. CONSTRUCTION POLICIES AND PROCEDURES

Explains how construction of tenant's improvements is handled.

VII-A1	Tenant improvement estimates
VII-A2	Tenant improvement budget
VII-B	Tenant extra order
VII-C	Contractor's insurance
VII-D	Tenant's contractor
VII-E	Contractor's work order
VII-F	Construction contractor's request for payment
VII-G	Notice to security
VII-H	Construction completion
VII-I	Unit prices
VII-J	Notice of nonresponsibility
VII-K	Notice of completion
VII-L	Stock depletion reporting

SECTION VIII. INSURANCE POLICIES AND PROCEDURES

Provides instruction and forms for landlord's, tenant's, and contractor's insurance requirements.

VIII-A	Insurance agent
VIII-B	Outline of coverage
VIII-C	Notifying insurance agent—various phases of development and construction (new projects)
VII-D	Notifying insurance agent—Personal property purchased or leased
VII-E	Notifying insurance agent—Increased construction cost
VIII-F1	Preparation of accident/damage report
VIII-F2	General guidelines for reporting an accident
VIII-F3	Automobile liability, public liability, and property damage accident reports
VIII-F4	Employee accident reports
VIII-F5	Reporting requirements
VIII-G	New tenant
VIII-H	Existing tenants

EXHIBIT 2.8 *(Continued)*

VIII-I   New service contractor
VIII-J   Existing service contractor
VIII-K   Promotional events

SECTION IX.   REPORTS

Lists accounting and narrative reports.

IX-A   Delinquency report
IX-B   Lease expiration and deferred conditions
IX-C   Tenant sales report
IX-D   Expenditure report
IX-E   Rent roll
IX-F   Market surveys
IX-G   Breakeven analysis
IX-H   Monthly rental report
IX-I   Manager's monthly report
IX-J   Comparative occupancy report
IX-K   Leasing prospects report
IX-L   Space available report
IX-M   Monthly building status report
IX-N   Annual management plan

SECTION X.   SAMPLE LETTERS AND FORMS

Provides sample letters and forms for property mangers and their assistants.

X-1   Recognition of broker's status
X-2   Nonrecognition of broker's status
X-3   Broker's agreement
X-4a   Tenant lease information
X-4b   Addendum tenant lease information
X-5   Letter of transmittal to tenant—Signature of document
X-6   Standard transmittal letter
X-7   Consent to alteration letter
X-8   Transmittal letter to tenant with signed documents
X-9   Substantial completion letter
X-10   Sublease agreement
X-11   Landlord's consent to sublease
X-12   Holdover agreement
X-13   Termination agreement
X-14   Transmittal letter—Executed documents
X-15   Authorization to proceed with improvements
X-16   Lease commission statement
X-17   Leasing commission transmittal letter
X-18   Tenant information and emergency procedures manual—Letter
X-19   Mall/lobby directory listing authorization
X-20   Emergency notification
X-21   Office building security card

EXHIBIT 2.8 *(Continued)*

X-22   Security pass
X-23   Door and floor directory sign order authorization
X-24   Memo to clean space
X-25   Notice of delinquency
X-26   Late charge warning letter
X-27   Notice of abandoning tenant
X 28   Notice applying security deposit to rent
X-29   Letter to tenant—Holiday hours
X-30   Letter to tenant   Name change
X-31   Daily security report
X-32   Theft/burglary report
X-33   Accident/injury/property damage report
X-34   Inspection report—Shopping center interior
X-35   Inspection report—Shopping center exterior
X-36   Inspection report—Office building and industrial property
X-37   Monthly activity report
X 38   License, release, and indemnity agreement—Short form
X-39   License, release, and indemnity agreement—Long form
X 40   Transmittal—Tenant improvement plans
X-40a   Tenant extra order
X-40b   Tenant extra order log sheet
X-41   Letter to contractor—Insurance requirements
X-42a   Insurance requirement letters—Request for certificate
X-43b   Insurance requirement letters   Notice of nonconformity to limits
X-43c   Insurance requirement letters—Notice of expiration
X-44   TV antenna/satellite disk agreement
X-45   Contractor's work order
X-46   Transmittal letter—Work order
X 47   Notice of nonresponsibility
X-48   Notice of completion
X-49a   Insurance requirements—Shopping center lease
X-49b   Insurance requirements—Office building lease
X-49c   Insurance requirements—Industrial property lease
X-50   Monthly delinquency report
X-51   Tenant sales analysis
X-52   Moving notices
X-53   Lease amendment letter agreement—Rent relief
X-54   Tenant improvements—Budget
X-55   Maintenance request (call slip)
X-56   Memo to cleaning company (complaint)
X-57   Notice of default letter (shopping center)
X-58   HVAC maintenance notification letter
X-59   Rent deferment agreement
X-60   HVAC calls
X-61   Janitorial calls
X-62   Litigation report
X-63   Authorization to proceed with working drawings
X-64   Letter to tenant—Preparation of working drawings

EXHIBIT 2.8 *(Continued)*

X-65	Transmittal letter to broker—Signature of agreement
X-66	Transmittal letter to broker—Signed documents
X-67	Management agreement summary
X-68	Letter to tenant—Holiday cleaning
X-69	Talent release
X-70	Animal grazing agreement
X-71	Budget input form
X-72	Budget explanation form
X-73	Tenant roster
X-74	Tenant charges
X-75	Tenant common area charge calculations
X-76a	Merchants' association bylaws
X-77	Lease termination agreement

termination of the relationship. The real estate law in many states requires the property management firm to have an executed management agreement. Violation of this law can subject the company to disciplinary action by the real estate commission.

The management agreement is a document that is continually evolving to meet the needs of property owners and property management firms. It is not uncommon for a property management firm to revise its management agreement every few years to address new issues in real estate and to clarify the property management firm's authority, responsibilities, and compensation. The management agreement covers five areas: responsibilities, authority, term, compensation, and exhibits.

Most institutional owners and pension fund advisors require that their management agreement be used. Because these agreements are usually one-sided, they should be reviewed carefully. Although these clients are not willing to negotiate their entire agreement, they will modify certain clauses. The following clauses should be given particular attention: indemnification; reports after the agreement is terminated; commission fees on co-brokered deals; the party responsible for paying for marketing brochures. The item that is usually nonnegotiable is the client's accounting reports. The property manager must carefully analyze the time to prepare these reports and factor this cost into the management fees.

One of the most important and potentially costly issues since the mid-1980s is hazardous waste. A property management firm needs to be protected against another party's illegal use or disposal of hazardous materials. Paragraph 15 of the following management agreement provides for the property owner to indemnify and defend the property management firm against cost and penalties imposed because of the tenant's or a third party's use or disposal of hazardous materials.

Equal employment opportunity is not a new issue but one that may need to be emphasized. Paragraph 16 states that the property management firm is an equal opportunity employer and that the property owner and management firm will not discriminate in leasing space.

Occasionally, a property owner is tempted to hire the property management firm's employees, especially the on-site staff. The property owner may terminate the management contract and hire the former property management firm's trained employee to manage the property. Paragraph 17 states that the owner will not hire the property management firm's employees for two years after the termination of the management agreement. If the property owner violates this agreement, the property management firm is entitled to a monetary award for damages.

Exhibit 2.9 is a sample commercial property management agreement that can be modified to meet the specific needs of the property owner and the property. A review of important points in this agreement follows:

- *Appointment of Manager (Section 1.1).* The property management company is appointed the exclusive managing and leasing agent for the property. The second paragraph states that the manager shall be paid a leasing commission as set forth in the commission schedule attached as Exhibit C. This provision also states that the owner will pay any taxes assessed on the management and leasing fees.

Leasing commissions are an important income source for commercial property management firms. This agreement assumes the property manager will be the leasing agent for the property. The property owner may prefer to use a brokerage firm as the exclusive leasing agent for the property. In this case, the reference to the manager serving as the exclusive agent, commission schedule, and the leasing services of the manager sections will be eliminated.

- *Office Space (Section 1.3).* If the property has an on-site property manager, office space is provided at no charge and the cost to operate the office is paid by the property owner.

- *Management Services of Manager (Section 2).* This section covers several issues. The manager acknowledges receiving certain books and records, personal property, service contacts, and so on, that are listed on Exhibit D (Section 2.1).

  This section states that the manager will operate the building with first class professional management (Section 2.2).

  The remaining provisions in this section outline the duties and responsibilities of the manager. Since this agreement was prepared as a generic commercial property management agreement, this section may need to be modified to meet the needs of a particular commercial building and/or property owner.

  The monies collected provision requires the property owner to maintain a minimum balance in the manager's operating account to pay operating and other expenses (Section 2.4a).

  The repair and maintenance provision allows the manager to spend up to an agreed-upon amount for non-budgeted items with the owner's prior approval (Section 2.4d).

  The equipment and supplies provision provides for a similar spending limit (Section 2.4e).

  The insurance provision states that the manager will acquire the property insurance at the request of the property owner and that the manager will not be responsible or held liable for determining the amount or type of insurance coverage (Section 2.4g).

  The personnel provision states that on-site maintenance personnel shall be employees of the manager, the cost and expenses of these personnel shall be borne by the property owner and they shall be bonded by a fidelity bond (Section 2.4h).

- *Authority of Manager (Section 3).* Most property owners are concerned about which property manager is appointed manager of the property. The owner may even request or insist that a particular property manager is selected to manage the property. Manager's Representative (Section 3.1) has a place for the property manager's name to be inserted. If at a later date the property is assigned to another property manager in the firm, the property owner has 14 days, after notice of the change, to approve or reject the selection of the new property manager.

- *Contract and Agreement.* This provision prohibits the manager from entering into the maintenance agreement for longer than one year unless it contains a 30-day cancellation provision. (Section 3.3)

- *Compensation for Management Services (Section 4).* In addition to the base management fee in Section 4.1a, this provision provides for several other fees, including a tenant improvement construction supervision fee (Section 4.2) and administration fee, which is a fee for providing the payroll service for on-site maintenance personnel (Section 4.3).

  The largest fee the property management firm could receive is a commission for selling the property. If the property management firm is qualified to market and sell the property, it should attempt to receive the exclusive right to sell the property. Section 4.4a provides for an exclusive brokerage fee. Often the property owner is not willing to give the property management firm the right to sell the property and select a brokerage firm. Even though the property management firm does not receive the broker fee for selling the property, the property manager will be asked to assist with the sale. Even potential purchasers will want a tour of the property, copies of prior monthly management reports, and copies of leases. When the property is in escrow, the property manager will be asked to obtain estoppels from each tenant. These are time-consuming activities that are not normal management duties. Section 4.4b, transaction fee provides the manager with a fee for performing these services.

  Additional fees in this section include a fee for supervising major maintenance work (Section 4.5) and a fee for assisting or securing a loan for the property (Section 4.6).

- *Accounting, Records and Reports (Section 6).* Each property management company has a standard accounting and reporting system, but for some owners, particularly institutional owners, it must be modified. This section states that the property management company will provide its standard accounting and reporting system and the dates the owners will be provided these reports. If the accounting reports vary from the property management company's standard reports, they should be explained in an addendum in the management agreement. The property management company is committed to providing an annual budget by a certain date. The owner has 30 days to request changes after which the property manager has the authority to operate the property based on this budget.

- *Term and Termination (Section 8).* This section addresses the length of the management contract, how it can be canceled, and whether the property management firm is entitled to a cancellation fee. This provision also provides for the property management firm's responsibilities to provide records when the management agreement expires (Section 8.4d).

- *Designated Agent: Notice (Section 10).* Many properties have multiple owners. The owner must appoint a representative who will provide direction for the property and have the authority to make decisions. This clause also provides for compensation if the property owner hires one of the manager's employees or terminates the agreement.

- *Hazardous Substance Indemnity (Section 15).* One of the most important and potentially costly issues since the mid-1980s is hazardous waste. A property management firm needs to be protected against another party's illegal use or disposal of hazardous materials. Section 15 of the management agreement provides for the property owner to indemnify and defend the property management firm against cost and penalties imposed because of the tenant's or a third party's use or disposal of hazardous materials.

- *Management Agreement Summary.* Each management agreement can be summarized for easy reference (Exhibit 2.10). Though the form is self-explanatory, the authority section deserves comment. This section outlines the authority the property manager has to enter into maintenance contracts and leases without obtaining the property owner's approval. For instance, the property manager may enter into a maintenance agreement without the property owner's approval if the agreement doesn't exceed one year, has a 30-day right of cancellation, and the aggregate fee is less than $50,000.

Some property owners will authorize the property management firm to negotiate a lease as long as certain lease terms are not exceeded. For instance, a property management firm may enter into or finalize a lease negotiation as long as the space being leased is less than 10,000 square feet, the rent is above $18 per square foot per year, no more than one month free rent for each two years of the lease is given, the minimum term is three years and the maximum term is five years, and the tenant allowance does not exceed $10 per square foot. This enables the property manager to complete negotiations without frequent calls to the property owner.

In 1988, the Institute of Real Estate Management developed a general management agreement with an accompanying booklet explaining each provision.

EXHIBIT 2.9

MANAGEMENT AGREEMENT

OWNER:

_____

MANAGER:

_____

EXHIBIT 2.9 *(Continued)*

TABLE OF CONTENTS

EXHIBIT 2.9 *(Continued)*

EXHIBIT 2.9 *(Continued)*

EXHIBITS

EXHIBIT A: Legal Description

EXHIBIT B: Schedule of Basic Documents

EXHIBIT C: Commission Schedule

EXHIBIT D: Service Contracts

EXHIBIT 2.9 *(Continued)*

MANAGEMENT AGREEMENT

THIS MANAGEMENT AGREEMENT (the "Agreement") is made and entered into as of this _____ day of _____, 19___, by and between _____, a _____ (the "Owner"), and _____, a corporation (the "Manager").

W I T N E S S E T H:

WHEREAS, the Owner is the owner or ground lessee of that certain real property commonly known as "_____" located in _____, _____ County, State of _____, as more fully set forth in the legal description thereof attached hereto and made a part hereof as "Exhibit A" (the "Property"), on which Property is located certain real property improvements, parking spaces, and related facilities (the "Buildings") which Property, Buildings, and any other improvements now or hereafter located thereon shall hereinafter be collectively referred to as the "Project"; and

WHEREAS, the Owner wishes to retain the services of the Manager as manager of the Project with responsibilities for managing, operating, maintaining, and servicing the Project as stated in this Agreement; and

WHEREAS, any easements, covenants, conditions, and restrictions with respect to the Project now in effect are as more fully set forth in the Schedule of Basic Documents attached hereto and made a part hereof as "Exhibit B" (all of the aforesaid documents, together with all amendments and modifications now or hereafter made thereto, hereinafter collectively called the "Basic Documents"); and

WHEREAS, the Manager is willing to perform such services with regard to the management, operation, maintenance, and servicing of the Project and the obligations of the Owner as stated herein;

NOW, THEREFORE, in consideration of the foregoing and of the full and faithful performance by the Manager of all the terms, conditions, and obligations imposed upon the Manager hereunder, the parties hereto agree as follows:

1.   APPOINTMENT OF MANAGER.

1.1   Appointment.

(a)   Manager.   The Owner hereby appoints the Manager as the exclusive manager and the exclusive leasing broker and agent of the Project with the responsibilities and upon the terms and conditions set forth herein, and the Manager, by its execution hereof, does hereby accept such appointment.

(b)   Commission Schedule.   The Manager shall be paid a leasing commission as set forth in the Commission Schedule attached hereto and

EXHIBIT 2.9 *(Continued)*

made a part hereof as "Exhibit C." It is understood and agreed that any and all sales, use, business and occupations tax, or other such taxes, charged or assessed against or attributable to the fees, costs and expenses charged by, or paid to, Manager shall be the obligation of Owner and shall be paid in full by the Owner.

    1.2   Tax Numbers.   The Manager's tax identification number is _____ . The Owner's tax identification number is _____ .

    1.3   Office Space.   If the Owner requires an on-site manager or administrative person for the Project, then the Owner shall provide rent-free office space in the Project to the Manager, which space shall be sufficient to accommodate the Manager, on-site manager and/or administrative person and its employees in the performance of its obligations hereunder. All of the costs and expenses of operating and maintaining such office space shall be paid for by Owner, which costs and expenses shall include but not be limited to providing adequate office furniture, equipment and supplies, heat, electricity and air conditioning, refuse removal and other utilities and other costs and expenses related to such office space.

    2.   MANAGEMENT SERVICES OF MANAGER.

    2.1   Orientation.

        (a)   General.   The Manager hereby acknowledges receipt of certain books and records with respect to the operation of the Project, personal property on the Project belonging to the Owner, and all service contracts relating to the maintenance and operation of the Project, all as more fully set forth in the schedule thereof attached hereto and made a part hereof as "Exhibit D."

        (b)   Itemized Receipt.   After the effective date of this Agreement, upon request by the Owner, the Manager shall prepare and submit to the Owner a complete list of all books and records of the Owner held by the Manager, a list of all service contracts, and a complete inventory of all personal property received by the Manager.

    2.2   Management of the Project.   The Manager shall devote its reasonable best efforts consonant with first-class professional management to serving the Owner as manager of the Project, and shall perform its duties hereunder in a diligent, careful, and vigilant manner so as to manage, operate, maintain, and service the Project as a first-class commercial property. The services of the manager hereunder are to be of a scope and quality not less than those generally performed by professional managers of other similar, first-class complexes and properties in the area. The Manager shall make available to the Owner the full benefit of the judgment, experience, and advice of the members of the Manager's organization and staff with respect to the policies to be pursued by the Owner in operating the Project, and will perform such services as may be reasonably requested by the Owner in operating, maintaining, servicing, improving, and leasing the Project.

EXHIBIT 2.9 *(Continued)*

2.3 Use and Maintenance of the Project. The Manager agrees not to knowingly permit the use of the Project for any purpose which might void any policy of insurance held by the Owner or which might render any loss insured thereunder uncollectible, or which would be in violation of any governmental restriction, statute, ordinance, rule, or regulation. It shall be the duty of the Manager at all times during the term of this Agreement to operate and maintain the Project according to the highest standards achievable consistent with the expressed plan of the Owner. The Manager shall use its best efforts to secure full compliance of all lessees and sublessees, concessionaires, and others in possession of all or any part of the Project with the terms and conditions of their respective leases, subleases, and/or concessionaire agreements; provided, that Manager is authorized to refund security deposits to each tenant as required under the respective leases. The Manager shall be expected to perform such other acts and deeds as are reasonable, necessary, and proper in the discharge of its duties under this Agreement.

2.4 Specific Duties of Manager. Without limiting the duties and obligations of the Manager under any other provisions of this Agreement, the Manager shall have the following duties and perform the following services to the extent that Manager is in possession of sufficient funds from the Project.

(a) Monies Collected. Collect all rent and other payments due from lessees, sublessees, concessionaires, and others in the Project and any other sums otherwise due the Owner with respect to the Project in the ordinary course of business. The Owner authorizes the Manager to request, demand, collect, receive, and receipt for all, such rent and other charges and to institute legal proceedings in the name of, and as an expense reimbursable by, the Owner for the collection thereof, and for the dispossession of lessees, sublessees, concessionaires, and other persons from the Project. Such expenses may include the engaging of counsel of the Owner's choice for any such matter. All monies collected by the Manager shall be forthwith deposited by Manager, at Owner's option (i) in a separate bank account or accounts established by the Manager in the Owner's name for such purpose, having such signatories, and in a bank approved by the Owner (the "Separate Account"), or (ii) in the Manager's agency account. Funds deposited in such Separate Account shall not be commingled with any funds of the Manager. Funds deposited in the Manager's agency account may be commingled with other funds in said agency account. The Owner shall maintain a minimum balance of $_____ in the Manager's Separate Account or Manager's Agency Account with respect to the Project to pay the expenses of the Project. If at any time, the balance of the Separate Account, or the Owner's portion of the Agency Account, falls below said sum, then the Owner shall immediately upon notice by Manager, deposit an amount in such account sufficient to restore said account balance, or Owner's portion thereof, to not less than the amount set forth above. In no event shall Manager be obligated to extend its own funds on behalf of Owner where the Special Account balance of the Owner's portion of the Manager's Agency Account falls below the above sum. The Manager shall be responsible for the collection, disbursement, handling, and holding of the monies collected to the extent that a normal, reasonable, and prudent

EXHIBIT 2.9 *(Continued)*

businessman would be responsible for such collection, disbursement, handling, and holding of monies.

(b)   Obligations Under Basic Documents.   To the extent that monies are available from the Project, to duly and punctually perform and comply with all of the obligations, terms, and conditions required to be performed or complied with by the Owner under the Basic Documents relating to management, operation, maintenance, and servicing of the Project, including without limitation, the timely payment of all sums required to be paid thereunder, all to the end that the Owner's interest in the Project and its interests as Landlord under the leases shall be preserved and no default chargeable to the Owner shall occur under the Basic Documents. After disbursement of all funds specified herein or in any other provision of this Agreement, and after establishing a reasonable cash reserve in an amount mutually determined by Owner and Manager, any balance remaining at the time each monthly report is forwarded to the Owner (as described in Section 6.2) during the term of this Agreement shall be disbursed or transferred to the Owner or to such other person as directed from time to time by the Owner.

(c)   Taxes and Insurance.   Duly and punctually pay on behalf of the Owner all real estate taxes, assessments, and insurance premiums payable in respect of the Project or any part thereof, such to be paid prior to the time that any insurance policy would lapse due to nonpayment of the premium and prior to the time any penalties or interest would accrue upon any real estate taxes or assessments (except such interest as may accrue on an assessment payable on an installment basis which the Owner has elected to pay on an installment basis).

(d)   Repairs and Maintenance.   To the extent that monies are available from operation of the Project, to make all repairs and perform all maintenance on the Buildings, appurtenances, and grounds of the Project as required to be made by the Owner under the Basic Documents and in accordance with standards acceptable to the Owner. For any individual item of repair or replacement, the non-budgeted expenses incurred shall not exceed the sum of $_____ unless specifically authorized in advance by the Owner, excepting, however, that emergency repairs immediately necessary for the preservation and safety of the Project or danger to life or property may be made by the Manager without the prior approval of the Owner; provided, that immediately after such emergency repairs, the Manager shall send the Owner a report of any repairs so made.

(e)   Equipment and Supplies.   Make all arrangements for the furnishing to the Project of utility, maintenance, and other services, and for the acquisition of equipment and supplies as necessary for the management, operation, maintenance, and servicing of the Project, as required of the Owner under the Basic Documents; provided, however, the non-budgeted purchase of any single piece of equipment or order of supplies in excess of $_____ shall not be made without the written consent of the Owner.

EXHIBIT 2.9 *(Continued)*

(f) Tax Assessments. Keep the Owner informed of any change in the amount of real or personal property assessments or taxes relating to the Project, and recommend, from time to time, the advisability of contesting either the validity or the amount thereof.

(g) Insurance Coverage. If requested by the Owner, to cause to be placed and kept in force all forms of insurance required by law, or any mortgage secured by all or any part of the Project, to protect the Owner or any mortgagee, including, but not limited to, public liability insurance, fire and extended coverage insurance, burglary and theft insurance, and boiler insurance. All insurance coverage shall be placed with such companies, in such amounts, and with such beneficial interest appearing therein as shall be acceptable to the Owner and otherwise be in conformity with the requirements of the Basic Documents or any mortgage covering the Project, and, anything herein to the contrary notwithstanding, it is understood and agreed that the Manager shall have no responsibility, obligation, or liability for determining the amount or type of insurance which is required with respect to the Project. Should the Owner elect to place such insurance coverage directly, the Owner shall provide the Manager with a duplicate copy of the original policy, and the Manager shall thereafter keep such insurance in force. The Manager shall promptly investigate and make a full, timely, written report to the applicable insurance company, with a copy to the Owner, as to all accidents, claims, or damage relating to the ownership, operation, and maintenance of the Project, any damage or destruction to the Project, and the estimated cost of repair thereof, and shall prepare any and all reports required by any insurance company in connection therewith. All such reports shall be filed timely with the insurance company as required under the terms of the insurance policy involved. The Manager shall have no right to settle, compromise, or otherwise dispose of any claims, demands, or liabilities, whether or not covered by insurance, without the prior, written consent of the Owner. The Owner shall name Manager as an additional named insured on the Owner's insurance policy or policies carried by Owner with respect to the Property and/or Buildings.

(h) Personnel. Employ such on-site maintenance personnel on behalf of the Owner as necessary in order to maintain the Project in a first-class condition. All such on-site maintenance persons shall be employees of the Manager. The costs and expenses of such employees shall be borne by the Owner, which expenses shall include, but not be limited to, salary, payroll expenses, withholding taxes, automobile allowances, and Manager's standard employee benefits. Any employees, whether employed by the Owner or Manager, who handle or who are responsible for funds belonging to the Owner, shall be bonded by a fidelity bond in an amount of not less than $500,000.00.

(i) Other Services. Perform all other services necessary to comply with the provisions of this Agreement or as may be agreed to be provided by Manager. If the Manager provides any services to the Owner or any lessees or sublessees of the Project which are not provided for in this Agreement and for which a separate charge is made, then such separate charge shall be

EXHIBIT 2.9 *(Continued)*

retained for the account of the Manager, all as more fully set forth below; provided, that Manager shall notify Owner prior to providing such special services to any lessee or sublessee; and, provided, further, that any special fees payable by Owner for such special services shall be subject to the mutual agreement of Owner and Manager.

2.5   Additional Services.

(a)   **Additional Lessee Services.**   Should the Manager provide any services to lessees or sublessees which are not customary services or services not required hereunder ("Additional Lessee Services"), then a separate charge for such Additional Lessee Services shall be made to the lessee or sublessees receiving such Additional Lessee Services and the separate charge shall be paid to and retained by the Manager for its own account, and the Owner shall have no interest therein. The Manager shall pay all costs incurred in providing such Additional Lessee Services. All amounts received by the Manager from Additional Lessee Services shall be excluded from Gross Rental Receipts for purposes of the calculation of the Management Fee in accordance with Section 4 below.

(b)   **Additional Owner Services.**   Should the Manager provide any services to the Owner which are not customary services or services not required hereunder, such as, but not limited to, services related to a rehabilitation, remodeling, repair, or reconstruction of the Project or major tenant construction ("Additional Owner Services"), then a separate charge for such Additional Owner Services shall be negotiated between Owner and Manager before such services are performed by Manager.

(c)   **Money Management.**   Owner gives Manager authority to invest any sums which come into possession of Manager by reason of this Agreement and the Manager's actions. Manager will be limited to invest funds in money market savings accounts which are federally insured. Any such investment will be at Owner's sole risk, and Manager assumes no obligation or responsibility with respect to such investment. All interest earned on the investments shall be credited to the Owner's account. Manager shall receive an administrative fee of ten percent (10%) of all interest or other sums earned by reason of such investments. Any applicable sales tax on the fee will be paid by Owner.

2.6   Concessions Income.   Any income received by the Manager from vending or other coin-operated machines or concessions ("Concessions Income") shall be delivered to and retained by the Owner for its own account, and the Owner shall pay all costs in connection with Concessions Income. The Manager shall receive a Management Fee on all concession income as more specifically set forth below.

2.7   Compliance With Laws.   The Owner shall fully comply with all statutes, ordinances, rules, and regulations governing the Project and the business conducted therein; provided, that at Manager's election, the Manager may take such action as may be necessary to comply with any and all statutes, rules, regulations, ordinances, orders, or requirements affecting the

EXHIBIT 2.9 *(Continued)*

Project, promulgated by a federal, state, county, or municipal authority having jurisdiction thereover, and all applicable orders of the Board of Fire Underwriters or other similar bodies. Notwithstanding any voluntary action taken by Manager on behalf of Owner, the Manager shall be released from any responsibility in connection with any statute, ordinance, rule, or regulation pertaining to the Project or the business conducted thereof, and Owner assumes full and complete responsibility for compliance therewith and for the payment of any and all penalties, taxes, impositions, and fines resulting from a failure to comply with such statutes, ordinances, rules, and regulations.

2.8   **Notices.** All notices from any mortgagee, ground lessor, or other party to any of the Basic Documents given pursuant thereto or pertaining thereto and all notices from any governmental or official entity shall be forthwith delivered to the Owner by the Manager.

2.9   **Waiver and Indemnification.**

    (a)   **Waiver.** It is understood and agreed that Manager makes no representations or warranties with respect to the profitability of the Property.

    (b)   **Indemnification.**

        (1)   Subject to the provisions of Section 2.9(c) below, the Owner shall indemnify, defend, and hold Manager harmless from and against all suits in connection with the Property and from liability for damage to personal property and injury to or death of any person, except suits, damage, injury, or death arising through the gross negligence or willful acts of the Manager. Owner shall carry at its own expense public liability and elevator liability (if elevators are part of the equipment on the Property) naming Owner and Manager, which insurance shall be adequate to protect their respective interests, and shall be in such form, substance, content, and amounts reasonably acceptable to Manager, and to furnish Manager certificates evidencing such insurance. Unless Owner shall provide such insurance and furnish such certificate within sixty (60) days from the date of this Agreement, the Manager may, but shall not be obligated to, place said insurance, and charge the cost thereof to the account of the Owner. All such insurance policies shall provide that the Manager shall receive not less than thirty (30) days' written notice prior to cancellation of the policy.

        (2)   Subject to the provisions of Section 2.9(c) below, the Owner shall indemnify, defend, and save the Manager harmless from all claims, investigations, and suits, or from actions or failures to act of the Owner, with respect to any alleged or actual violation of state or federal labor laws, it being expressly agreed and understood that as between the Owner and the Manager, however, it shall be the responsibility of the Manager to comply with all applicable state or federal labor laws. The Owner's obligation under this Section 2.9(b) shall include the payment of all settlements, judgments, damages, liquidated damages, penalties, forfeitures, back pay awards, court costs, litigation expense, and attorney's fees.

EXHIBIT 2.9 *(Continued)*

(3)   Subject to the provisions of Section 2.9(c) below, the Owner shall pay all expenses incurred by the Manager, including, but not limited to, reasonable attorneys' fees and Manager's costs and time in connection with any claim, proceeding, or suit involving an alleged violation by the Manager or the Owner, or both, of any law pertaining to fair employment, fair credit reporting, environmental protection, rent control, taxes, or fair housing, including, but not limited to, any law prohibiting, or making illegal, discrimination on the basis of race, sex, creed, color, religion, national origin, or mental or physical handicap; provided, however, that the Owner shall not be responsible to the Manager for any such expenses in the event the Manager is finally adjudicated to have personally, and not in a representative capacity, violated any such law. Nothing contained herein shall obligate the Manager to employ counsel to represent the Owner in any such proceeding or suit, and the Owner may elect to employ counsel to represent the Owner in any such proceeding or suit. The Owner also agrees to pay reasonable expenses (or an apportioned amount of such expenses where other employers of Manager also benefit from the expenditure) incurred by the Manager in obtaining legal advice regarding compliance with any law affecting the Property or activities related thereto.

3.   AUTHORITY OF MANAGER.

3.1   Manager's Representative.   The Manager's initial representative shall be _____ (hereinafter referred to as the "Representative"). All employees of the Manager, including the Representative, shall be authorized to act as the Owner's agents. The Manager reserves the right to appoint a substitute representative who shall be acceptable to the Owner; provided, that the Owner shall have fourteen (14) days from receipt of written notice of such substitute representative within which to approve or reject said substitute representative. A failure or refusal to approve or reject said substitute representative within said time shall be deemed approval.

3.2   Execution of Contracts.   Subject to the provisions of Section 3.3 below, the Manager shall execute all contracts, agreements, and other documents and may undertake action necessary in the performance of its obligations for the maintenance of the Project as an agent of the Owner, as follows and as may be appropriate:

(PROJECT NAME)   (PROJECT OWNER),

By Its Agent: _____

_____   By Its Agent:

By: _____   _____
     (Designation of
      Corporate Office)   By: _____
                                              (Designation of
  or   Corporate Office)

EXHIBIT 2.9 *(Continued)*

3.3   Contracts and Agreements.   The Manager shall not execute and enter into and bind the Owner with respect to any contract or agreement having a term in excess of one (1) year, unless said contract or agreement contains a thirty (30) day cancellation provision, without the prior written consent of the Owner, including, but not limited to, contracts and agreements on behalf of the Owner for the management, operation, maintenance, and servicing of the Project; and the acquisition of utility, maintenance, or other services; or the furnishing of services to lessees or sublessees in the Project; and in the case of casualty, breakdown in machinery, or other similar emergency, if, in the reasonable opinion of the Manager, emergency action prior to written approval is necessary to prevent additional damage, or loss of life, or personal injury, or a greater total expenditure, or to protect the Project from damage, or prevent a default on the part of the Owner as landlord under leases or the Basic Documents, then such action shall be taken only in concert with prompt notification by the Manager to the Owner.

3.4   Use of Name.   The Owner authorizes the Manager to use the names "_____" and "_____" in the performance of its obligations hereunder and for the purposes of identification and advertising.

4.   COMPENSATION FOR MANAGEMENT SERVICES.

4.1   Management Fee.

(a)   Management Fee.   Owner shall pay Manager as compensation for the management services rendered hereunder an amount (the "Management Fee") equal to (a) _____ percent (____%) of the "Gross Rental Receipts" collected; or (b) a minimum fee of $_____ per month, whichever is greater. The Management Fee for a particular month shall be paid on or before the last day of the month.

(b)   Definition of Gross Rental Receipts.   The term "Gross Rental Receipts" as used herein shall mean and include all gross receipts (but not any sums which, under normal accounting practice, are attributable to capital) derived from the operation of the Project, including, without limitation, all rent, percentage rent, concessions income, income from lessees' reimbursement of real estate taxes, insurance and building Operating Expenses, and other sums and charges received from lessees, including payments from lessees and sublessees made in consideration of the cancellation, surrender, or modification of any lease, or made by reason of any default thereunder, or the application of security deposits upon defaults or toward the repair of any damage to the Project; provided, however, that Gross Rental Receipts shall not include sums paid to the Manager for Additional Services, or any security or other deposits.

4.2   Tenant Improvement Construction Supervision Fee.   The Manager shall receive and retain for its own account, in addition to and not in substitution for its Management Fee, a fee (the "Supervision Fee") equal to _____ percent (____%) of the cost of constructing tenant improvements and other construction activities from time to time on the Project. The Supervision Fee shall cover Manager's services in the supervision of the

EXHIBIT 2.9 *(Continued)*

construction of such tenant improvements by the lessee's or Owner's general contractor, as the case may be. Said Supervision Fee shall be paid in one lump sum or in equal monthly installments as may be mutually agreed by Owner and Manager.

      4.3   Administrative Fee. In addition to its Management Fee and any other fees payable to Manager under this Agreement, a fee (the "Administrative Fee") equal to _____ percent (___%) of the gross salary or salaries paid to on-site maintenance personnel and janitors shall be paid to Manager, which Administrative Fee shall cover the administrative payroll costs and expenses for such on-site maintenance personnel.

      4.4   Brokerage Fees.

          (a)   Exclusive Brokerage Fee. The Manager is appointed as the Owner's exclusive real estate broker and representative for the sale of all or any part of the Project. Upon the sale of all or any part of the Project, and in addition to its Management Fee and any other fees payable to Manager under this Agreement, the Owner shall pay to Manager a fee (the "Exclusive Brokerage Fee") in cash at the closing of the sale of the Project, or any part thereof, which Exclusive Brokerage Fee shall equal _____ percent (___%) of the gross sales price and/or consideration paid or payable with respect to the Project, or portion thereof, sold by the Owner.

          (b)   Transaction Fee. In the event the Manager is not appointed as the Owner's exclusive real estate broker and representative for the sale of the Project, or any part thereof, then it is understood that Owner will require Manager to perform and provide special and extraordinary services with respect to the sale of the Project or portion thereof. In such event, and in addition to its Management Fee or any other fees payable to Manager under this Agreement, the Owner shall pay to Manager a fee (the "Transaction Fee") equal to _____ percent (___%) of the gross sales price of the Project or portion thereof being sold, which Transaction Fee shall cover the Manager's extraordinary expenses incurred in performing and providing the special and extraordinary services necessary to assist in the sale of the Project or portion thereof.

          (c)   Definition. For the purposes hereof, the term "sale" or "sold" shall mean a transfer of the Owner's title and/or interest in the Property or part thereof, whether by deed, real estate contract, option agreement, conditional sales contract, ground lease or otherwise.

      4.5   Major Maintenance Supervision Fee. In addition to the Management Fee and other fees and compensation due the Manager under this Agreement, the Manager shall be paid a fee (the "Major Maintenance Supervision Fee") for the supervision of the installation and completion of major items of repair or maintenance. For the purposes hereof, the term "major items of repair or maintenance" shall mean maintenance or repairs which, individually or in a series of similar events or items of maintenance or repairs, cost $_____ or more for labor, materials, taxes and other expenses with respect thereto. The

EXHIBIT 2.9 *(Continued)*

Major Maintenance Supervision Fee shall equal ___ percent (___ %) of the total cost of the particular major item of repair or maintenance and shall be paid in one lump sum within ten (10) days after substantial completion of the particular major item of repair or maintenance, or upon such other basis as Manager and Owner may mutually agree upon.

4.6   Loan Coordination Fee.   In addition to the Management Fee and other fees and compensation due Manager under this Agreement, the Manager shall be paid a fee (the "Loan Coordination Fee") for the procurement and/or coordination of all construction, interim and/or permanent loans applicable to all or any part of the Property, Buildings or Project. The Loan Coordination Fee shall equal one quarter (¼) of one percent (1%) of the total principal amount of the particular loan and shall be paid upon the closing of the particular loan. For the purposes hereof, the term "closing of the particular loan" shall mean the date on which the documents securing repayment of the particular loan are recorded and/or filed, or if no such recording or filing occurs, the date on which the Owner becomes legally obligated to repay the particular loan. For the purposes hereof, the term "loan" shall mean increases to existing loans and refinances thereof.

4.7   Sales Tax.   It is understood and agreed that any and all sales, use, business and occupations tax or other such taxes (with the exception of Manager's income taxes) charged or assessed against, or attributable to, the fees, costs or expenses charged by, or paid to, Manager under this Agreement shall be the obligation of the Owner and shall be paid in full by the Owner.

5.   LEASING SERVICES OF THE MANAGER.

5.1   Brokers.   It is understood and agreed that the Manager is the exclusive leasing broker and agent for the Project; provided that the Manager may engage other brokers to assist Manager in leasing space in the Project (which brokers may be employees of Manager or an affiliated or related company), and otherwise supervise leasing arrangements for the Project, and shall share in any brokerage fees payable with respect to such leasing arrangements.

5.2   Right to Approve.   Owner retains the right in its sole discretion to approve the terms, conditions, and form of any proposed lease and to approve any prospective tenant.

6.   ACCOUNTING, RECORDS, REPORTS.

6.1   Records.   The Manager shall maintain its standard comprehensive system of office records, books, and accounts which shall belong to the Owner. The Owner and others designated by the Owner shall have at all times access to such records, accounts, and books and to all vouchers, files, and all other material pertaining to the Project and this Agreement, all of which the Manager agrees to keep safe, available, and separate from any records not having to do with the Project.

6.2   Monthly Reports.   On or before the _____ day of each month during the term of this Agreement, the Manager shall deliver to the Owner

EXHIBIT 2.9 *(Continued)*

(i) a Profit and Loss Statement representing the income collected and payment of operating expenses for the property, (ii) a capital expenditure journal, (iii) an operating expense journal, (iv) a delinquency report for the preceding calendar month, and (v) a tenant sales report, where applicable. The Manager shall use the Manager's standard chart of accounts and budgeting format in preparing the foregoing. The Manager shall not be responsible for providing the following schedules: interest accruals, depreciation or amortization of real or intangible assets, or any other duty not provided by standard property management accounting.

6.3   Annual Budgets.

(a)   Delivery of Budget. No later than _____ of each year, the Manager shall deliver to the Owner a statement setting forth in detail the estimated receipts and the estimated amounts required to be expended, on a cash basis, during the next succeeding calendar year, by the Manager in the performance of its duties hereunder, including, without limitation, the amount of real estate taxes, assessments, insurance premiums, and maintenance and other expenses relating to the Project operations. The Manager shall further provide such other financial information as is reasonably requested by the Owner. The Manager will cooperate with and give reasonable assistance to any independent public accountant retained by the Owner to examine such statements or other records pertaining to the Project.

(b)   Approval. Within thirty (30) days of receipt of the above named statement, the Owner shall either approve the same or provide the Manager with written notice setting forth those items which are unacceptable to Owner or advising Manager as to what additional information is required. Failure to provide such notice to Manager within said thirty (30) day period shall be deemed approval of the statement by Owner. Upon such approval, or in the event Owner shall fail to provide notice to Manager as set forth above, the Manager shall be authorized to operate and manage the Project in accordance with the budget provided to Owner for approval.

6.4   Employment Laws. Manager shall comply with all laws relating to the employment by the Manager of its employees.

6.5   Tax Reports. The Manager shall have no responsibility for the preparation or submission of any federal, state, or local tax report or return on behalf of the Owner.

6.6   Disbursements. The Manager shall have the option, as more fully set forth in Section 2.4(a) above, to deposit funds in a Separate Account or to commingle the Owner's funds in the Manager's agency account.

7.   EXPENSES.

7.1   Expense of Owner. All obligations or expenses incurred hereunder, including, but not limited to, on-site maintenance personnel and wages, payroll costs, and employee benefits with respect thereto, shall be for the account of, on behalf of, and at the expense of the Owner. The Owner shall not be obligated to reimburse the Manager for the Manager's home office

EXHIBIT 2.9 *(Continued)*

expenses for general office equipment or office supplies or telephone service of the Manager; for any overhead expense of the Manager incurred in its home office, for any salaries of any executives or supervisory personnel of the Manager, for any salaries or wages allocable to time spent on matters other than the Project, or for any salaries, wages, and expenses for any personnel other than personnel working at the Project site or with respect to the Project.

7.2 Reimbursement for Expenses. Any payments made by the Manager in the performance of its duties and obligations under this Agreement shall be made solely out of such funds as the Manager may from time to time hold for the account of Owner or as may be provided by the Owner. The Owner shall give adequate advance written notice to the Manager if the Owner desires that the Manager make payment, out of the proceeds from the Property, of mortgage indebtedness; general taxes; special assessments, or fire, steam boiler, or any other insurance premiums. In no event shall the Manager be required to advance its own funds in Payment of any such indebtedness, taxes, assessments, or premiums.

8. TERM AND TERMINATION.

    8.1 Term. Subject to the provisions of Section 8.2 below, this Agreement is for a term of _____ (___) years commencing on _____, 19___ (the "Commencement Date"), and terminating at midnight on _____, 19___ (the "Termination Date"). This Agreement shall continue on a month-to-month basis after said Termination Date unless terminated in accordance with Section 8.2 or 8.3 below.

    8.2 Termination for Cause by Owner. The Owner may at all times during the term of this Agreement and any extension thereof, and upon not less than thirty (30) days' prior written notice to the Manager, terminate this Agreement; provided, that in the event such right of termination is exercised during the initial term of this Agreement, then the Owner shall pay to Manager, on or before the effective date of termination of this Agreement, an amount equal to thirty-three and one-third percent (33-1/3%) of the remaining unpaid management fees for the balance of the initial term of the Agreement.

    8.3 Termination by Manager. The Manager may terminate this Agreement upon not less than thirty (30) days' prior written notice to Owner.

    8.4 Manager's Obligations After Termination. Upon the termination of this Agreement as provided above, the Manager shall:

    (a) Deliver Records. Deliver to the Owner, or such other person or persons designated by the Owner, copies of all books and records of the Project and all funds in the possession of the Manager belonging to the Owner or received by the Manager pursuant to the terms of this Agreement or of any of the Basic Documents, and

    (b) Assignment. Assign, transfer, or convey to such person or persons all service contracts and personal property relating to or used in the operation and maintenance of the Project, except any personal

EXHIBIT 2.9 *(Continued)*

Property which was paid for and is owned by the Manager. The Manager shall at its cost and expense remove all signs that it may have placed at the Project indicating that it is the manager of same, and replace and restore any damage resulting therefrom.

(c) **Termination of Obligations: Right to Compensation.** Upon any termination pursuant to this Section 8, the obligations of the parties hereto shall cease as of the date specified in the notice of termination, provided that the Manager shall comply with the applicable provisions hereof, and, provided further, that Manager shall be entitled to receive any and all compensation which may be due the Manager hereunder at the time of such termination or expiration. Such compensation shall include the Management Fee set forth in Section 4.1, 4.4 above prorated to the date of termination, together with brokerage fees due Manager for leasing activities through the date of termination. In order to compute the brokerage fee due Manager, Manager shall deliver to Owner within thirty (30) days after the date of termination, a list of all prospective tenants contacted by Manager or other brokers and for which Manager is owed, or may be owed, all or some part of a leasing commission. Such list shall include the name, address, and telephone number of each such prospective tenant, together with all lease proposals and other pertinent information in Manager's possession relating to such prospective tenant. In the event Owner shall within one (1) year of the date of termination, enter into a lease for space in the Project with a prospective tenant set forth on the list of prospective tenants given by Manager to Owner, then and in such event Manager shall be paid a leasing fee equal to the fee which would have been paid Manager pursuant to the Commission Schedule had the lease with such tenant been entered into prior to the date of termination.

(d) **Final Accounting.** In the event the Owner has paid the Manager all sums due Manager hereunder, the Manager shall, within thirty (30) days of the date of expiration or termination of this Agreement, deliver to the Owner the following: (i) an accounting reflecting the balance of income and expenses of and from the Project to the date of termination or expiration of the Agreement; (ii) any balance of monies of the Owner then held by the Manager; and (iii) all leases, receipts for deposits, insurance policies, unpaid bills, correspondence, and other documents which are the property of Owner in the possession of the Manager. The Owner shall have fifteen (15) days from the date the Manager delivers the foregoing to Owner within which to deliver to the Manager a written statement approving the foregoing as (i) a correct accounting of the income and expenses of and from the Project, (ii) the correct balance of monies of the Owner then held by the Manager, and (iii) all leases, receipts for deposits, insurance policies, unpaid bills, correspondence, and other documents which are the property of the Owner with respect to the Project or setting forth in reasonable detail why such approval cannot be given, including any inaccuracy in said accounting. Upon receipt of said written approval, or upon the expiration of said fifteen (15) day period, in the event such approval is not given, the Manager shall be deemed to have fully performed all of its obligations under this Agreement and shall be fully released by Owner from any and all liability and obligation to Owner under this Agreement and the performance thereof by the Manager. The

EXHIBIT 2.9 *(Continued)*

Manager may retain copies or duplicates of all documents, accountings, leases, and other papers delivered to the Owner that are required to be maintained or retained under, or in order to comply with the law of the state in which the Property is situated and/or the state in which the Manager's offices are located.

9.   <u>NO AGENCY.</u>

The Manager shall be responsible for all of its employees or employees of any affiliate, the supervision of all persons performing services in connection with the performance of all of the Owner's obligations relating to the maintenance and operation of the Project, and for determining the manner and time of performance of all acts hereunder. Nothing herein contained shall be construed to establish the Manager as an employee of the Owner.

10.   <u>DESIGNATED AGENT; NOTICES.</u>

(a) <u>Owner's Designated Agent.</u> The Owner hereby designates _____ (the "Designated Agent"), whose mailing address is _____, as the agent of Owner to whom Manager may deliver or mail all notices required or desired to be given Owner hereunder and from whom Manager shall receive all consents, direction, decisions, and notices required or desired to be given by Owner hereunder, as set forth below. The delivery of notice or requests, correspondence, communication, consents, waivers, or other matters to such Designated Agent, whether in person or by mail as set forth herein, and/or the service of process upon such Designated Agent shall be conclusively deemed as delivery of the same and service of process upon Owner. The Designated Agent and/or office may be changed from time to time by the Owner upon not less than ten (10) days' prior written notice to the Manager.

(b) <u>Authority of Designated Agent.</u> All correspondence, communication, requests, notices, waivers, consents, direction, and other actions of the Owner shall be through the Designated Agent, and the Manager shall have the right to rely with acquittance upon any correspondence, communications, requests, notices, consents, directions, or other actions received from or demanded by the Designated Agent.

(c) <u>Notices.</u> Unless otherwise specifically provided, all notices, demands, statements, and communications required or desired to be given hereunder shall be in writing and shall be sent by registered or certified mail, if intended for the Owner, addressed to the Designated Agent at the Designated Agent's address set forth above, with a copy to:

_____

_____

_____

_____

EXHIBIT 2.9 *(Continued)*

and, if intended for the Manager, addressed to the Manager at:

_____

_____

_____

_____

or to such other address as shall from time to time have been designated by written notice by either party to the other party as herein provided.

11.   CAPTIONS; PLURAL INCLUDES THE SINGULAR.

The captions of the Agreement are inserted only for the purpose of convenient reference and do not define, limit, or prescribe the scope or intent of this Agreement or any part hereof. Words used herein shall include both the plural and singular and the male shall include the feminine and neuter genders.

12.   APPLICABLE LAW.

This Agreement shall be construed in accordance with the laws of the State in which the Property is situated.

13.   ENTIRE AGREEMENT.

This Agreement embodies the entire understanding of the parties, and there are no further agreements or understanding, written or oral, in effect between the parties relating to the subject matter hereof.

14.   MANAGER'S OBLIGATIONS UPON SALE OR FINANCE OF PROJECT.

It is understood that the Owner may sell, or obtain loans secured by, all or some part of the Property and/or Project. The Manager shall have no obligation to respond to or make any information, records, files or other data available to any third party except upon the prior written direction and authorization by Owner.

15.   HAZARDOUS SUBSTANCES INDEMNITY.

The Owner shall indemnify, defend and save Manager and Manager's respective officers, directors, shareholders and employees harmless from and against any and all of the costs (including attorneys' fees), penalties and charges assessed against or imposed upon Manager by reason of the Owner or any other third party keeping on or around the Project, whether prior or subsequent to the date of this Agreement, for use, disposal, treatment, generation, storage or sale any substances, wastes, or materials designated as, or containing components designated as hazardous, dangerous, toxic or harmful and/or which are subject to regulation by any federal, state or local law, regulation, statute or ordinance (collectively the "Hazardous Substances"). The Owner shall be exclusively liable for any clean-up, monitoring, reporting, civil

EXHIBIT 2.9 *(Continued)*

or criminal penalties, charges, fees or expenses (including attorneys' fees or costs) with respect to the Hazardous Substances, and Owner shall indemnify and defend Manager against the same.

16. EQUAL OPPORTUNITY.

It is understood and agreed that Manager is an equal opportunity and non-discriminatory employer. The Owner and Manager agree that there shall be no discrimination against or segregation of any person or group of persons on account of race, color, creed, religion, sex, age, or national origin in the lease, transfer, use, occupancy, or enjoyment of the Property, nor shall the Owner or Manager permit any discrimination or segregation with respect to the selection, location, number, use, or occupancy of tenants of space within the Property.

17. MANAGER'S EMPLOYEES.

Owner understands and agrees that the Manager has expended great amounts of time and effort in the selection, hiring, and training of its employees; and that the Manager's business, and the conduct thereof, is dependent to a large extent upon maintaining and retaining employees who have been trained by the Manager, and that the Manager faces extreme hardship and monetary loss whenever such employees leave its service. For the above-stated reasons, the Owner agrees that it shall not, directly or indirectly, during the term of this Agreement or for two (2) years after the expiration of the term of this Agreement, employ or solicit for employment, or otherwise engage, Manager's employees. Owner further agrees that the Manager shall be entitled to injunctive relief, monetary damages, or both, upon the Owner's violation or breach of the foregoing.

IN WITNESS WHEREOF, the parties hereto have executed this Agreement as of the day and year first above written.

OWNER: **MANAGER:**

_____

By:_____   _____

_____, President

EXHIBIT 2.10

Management Agreement Summary Form

Project No. _____

Project Name _____   Location _____
                                                  See Addendum ☐

OWNERS INFORMATION	
Owner(s):	Agreement Date:
Address:	Term:
	Commencement:
Phone:	Expiration:
Owner's Representative:	Cancellation Provision:
Leasing Agent	Owner:
Insurance Agent:	Manager:
Accountant:	Property Manager:
Miscellaneous:	Miscellaneous:

FEES	
Management Fees:	Lease Commissions:
%:	New:
Minimum:	
Other fees:	Renewal:
On-Site Office:	Options:
On-Site Employees:	
Misc:	Misc:

AUTHORITY	
Maintenance Contracts:	Leasing:
Maximum Term:	Maximum Sq. Ft.:
Maximum Amount:	Minimum Rent:
Cancellation:	Minimum Term:
Repairs Cost Max.:	Maximum Term:
Equipment Cost Max.:	TI Allowable:
Fidelity Bond:	Net Worth:
Insurance Responsibility:	Concessions:
Misc:	

ACCOUNTING			
Reports: Type	Date Due	Chart of Accounts:	
		Bank Account:	
		Audits:	

Prepared by_____   Date: _____   kg/masummry.frm 7/90

§ 2.24   THE PROJECT DATA BOOK

Every property generates a large quantity of information. Some of the information is used in the daily operations of the property, and some is used only occasionally or in an emergency. Information for the operation of the property needs to be summarized, compiled, and available for quick reference. This information is divided into two general areas: lease summaries (discussed in Chapter Eight on lease administration), and property information.

The property information is compiled and placed in a project data book (Exhibit 2.11). The book's first section contains general information such as the property's address, ownership, owner's representative, architect, general contractor, leasing agent, property management company, attorney, insurance agent, and accountant. Also included are the phone numbers for police, fire department, and utility companies.

The next section of the project data book consists of statistical data: number of acres, square footage, number of parking stalls, dates of construction commencement and completion, and the major tenants and their opening dates. A plot plan is marked with shutoff valves, lock boxes, and employee parking area.

Another section lists the square footage of each space or suite, the tenant's name and address, and the after-hours phone number of the tenant's manager. Additional information includes a list of vendors and contractors with business and after-hours phone numbers. If available, a similar directory of the original construction subcontractors is helpful.

It is important to keep the data book current. If the data are entered into a computer, the book can be revised and updated easily. A master copy of the project data books for all the properties managed by the company is kept in the manager's office for the staff's reference. Each on-site management office has a copy of the information for that property, and property managers keep copies of the project data book at their desk, in their car, and at home. Because many maintenance calls and emergencies occur after business hours, it is essential that property managers have the project data available wherever they are.

§ 2.25   TENANT IMPROVEMENTS

Tenant improvements can be as simple as laying new carpet in an office building or as complex as building a new restaurant on a shopping center pad or outlet. But whatever the scope, the completion of tenant improvements is an integral part of the manager's relationship with both landlord and tenant. Even if the manager does not have direct responsibility for them, tenant improvements that are not completed on time or according to plan will ultimately become a management problem. Overseeing

EXHIBIT 2.11
Project Data Book

Project No: 1234

LINCOLN PLAZA
Lincoln Way and Main Street
Redwood City, WA 90513

Owner:	Lincoln Plaza, a limited partnership 12400 SE Dolores Street Redwood City, WA 90513 Ronald Smith Manager Real Estate Investment Dept.	(123) 456-7811
Architect:	Smith and Jones 11 N. Elm Redwood City, WA 90513	(123) 567-8901
General Contractor:	Acme Construction PO Box 9889 Emporia, WA 90514	(123) 885-7824
Leasing:	Commercial Leasing Corporation Eric Muhlebach 1234 Broadway NE Redwood City, WA 90514	(123) 555-2241
Management:	Able Management Corporation Maria Rivera 4 N. Plaza Square Redwood City, WA 90514	(123) 456-0000
Attorney:	Kathy Muhlebach Thompson Building, Suite 450 Redwood City, WA 90514	(123) 555-8960
Insurance Agent:	North, Fuller, and Fry Thompson Building, Suite 222 Redwood City, WA 90514	(123) 555-0082
Accounting:	Lee Lloyd Associates 1464 S. Pine Street Redwood City, WA 90514	(123) 456-1040
Police Department:	Redwood City Police Station 411	Emergency: 911 Business: 555-1255
Fire Department:	Redwood City Fire District	Emergency: 911

EXHIBIT 2.11 *(Continued)*
Utilities

Water/Sewer:	Redwood City Water District No. 45 PO Box 78 Redwood City, WA 90514	555-8901
Gas:	Houston Natural Gas 11 Industrial Way Redwood City, WA 90514	555-0041
Electricity:	Redwood City Power and Light PO Box 667 Redwood City, WA 90514	555-3781

Statistical Data

Acres: 13.5
Square Feet: 148,702
Parking: 824
Construction Began: April 1980
Construction Completed: November 15, 1980
Opened: November 15, 1980
Major Tenants Open:

Ace Supermarket	November 15, 1980
SaveRite Drug Store	November 18, 1980
Redwood Hardware	April 1, 1981

EXHIBIT 2.11 *(Continued)*

Property Management Subsystem
Current Date 4/22/94   Project No.: 3033
Page No. 1   Project Data Report   Shoppers Plaza

Tenant	Sq. Ft.	Trade Name (1) Tenant Addr/(2) Pref Mail Address	Telephone Contact #s
A	35,875	Dave's Home Center #250 Mgr: Dave Davis (1) 1717 Lincoln Way Suite #A Redwood City, WA 99456	(301) 255-4678 (301) 255-2063 Emergency ( ) -
A-04	2,400	Vacant Mgr:	( ) - ( ) -
A-08	1,600	Beauty Supply Shop Mgr: Sara Burdell (1) 1731 Lincoln Way Redwood City, WA 99456	(301) 255-6508 (301) 458-2013 Emergency ( ) -
A-10	1,620	Quality Homes Realty Mgr: Fred Goodsen (1) 1782 Lincoln Way Redwood City, WA 99456	(301) 256-4062 (857) 236-5437 Emergency ( ) -
A-02	2,420	The Paint Bucket Mgr: Mark Langdon (1) 1783 Lincoln Way Redwood City, WA 99456	(301) 256-2910 (857) 236-1039 Emergency ( ) -
A-06	1,600	The Happy Hobby Shop Mgr: Nancy Young (1) 1784 Lincoln Way Redwood City, WA 99456	(301) 256-3042 (301) 236-2075 Emergency ( ) -
B	21,875	Redwood Drug Store Mgr: David Smith (1) 1790 Lincoln Way Redwood City, WA 99456	(301) 256-3924 (206) 876-5689 Emergency ( ) -
B-02	2,420	Humpty Dumpty Computer Store Mgr: Bob Mills (1) 1782 Lincoln Way Redwood City, WA 99456	(301) 256-9856 (301) 236-6809 Emergency ( ) -
B-10	1,400	The Shoe Box Mgr: Robyn Kildere (1) 1783 Lincoln Way Redwood City, WA 99456	(301) 256-1037 (301) 627-4052 Emergency ( ) -
B-12	1,400	Showtime Video House Mgr: Steve Stodsen (1) 1784 Lincoln Way Redwood City, WA 99456	(301) 327-8019 (857) 236-2145 Emergency ( ) -
B-14	3,600	Susie's Cards and Gifts Mgr: Susan Hopson	(301) 256-3291 (301) 256-4687

EXHIBIT 2.11 *(Continued)*

Tenant	Sq. Ft.	Trade Name (1) Tenant Addr/(2) Pref Mail Address	Telephone Contact #s

		(1) 1786 Lincoln Way
		     Redwood City, WA 99456
		(2) Bob Smith
		     1025 6th Avenue
		     Everett, WA 98203
			Emergency
			(206) 362-7891

B-16	2,080	The Sound System
		Mgr: Howard Hanson
		(1) 1786 Lincoln Way
		     Redwood City, WA 99456
		(2) 20922 NE 81st Street
		     Bothell, WA 98011
			(301) 256-9876
			(857) 236-0154
			Emergency
			(349) 746-5183

B-18	2,740	Quality Health Foods
		Mgr: James Ingalls
		(1) 1787 Lincoln Way
		     Redwood City, WA 99456
		(2) 14400 Elm Street
		     Centralia, WA 99934
			(301) 256-3768
			(301) 236-6929
			Emergency
			(406) 294-6024

B-19	2,400	Half Price Shoes Store Mgr: Fred Foster (1) 1788 Lincoln Way Redwood City, WA 99456	(301) 256-6942 (857) 468-5437 Emergency ( ) -

B-20	1,600	Jessica's Hair Designs
		Mgr: Jessica Giovanni
		(1) 1790 Lincoln Way
		     Redwood City, WA 99456
		(2) 4442 Naples Way
		     Woodinville, WA 98056
			(301) 256-2059
			(301) 248-3012
			Emergency
			(206) 641-9690

B-21	1,600	Carol's Children's Clothing
		Mgr: Carol Young
		(1) 1791 Lincoln Way
		     Redwood City, WA 99456
		(2) 1212 Elm Street
		     Centralia, WA 94657
			(301) 287-7066
			(857) 236-5437
			Emergency
			(602) 348-8023

C-01	43,851	Super Giant Market
		Mgr: Bruce Harrison
		(1) 1782 Lincoln Way
		     Redwood City, WA 99456
		(2) 4316 120th SE
		     Firndale, WA 96709
			(301) 246-4052
			(301) 246-5437
			Emergency
			(301-245-6290

C-02	1,132	Posies Flower House Mgr: Jan Johnson (1) 1783 Lincoln Way Redwood City, WA 99456	(301) 256-3448 (301) 236-5300 Emergency ( ) -
C-04	1,132	The Pasta Plaza Mgr: Fred Goodsen	(301) 256-4062 (857) 236-8023

EXHIBIT 2.11 *(Continued)*

Tenant	Sq. Ft.	Trade Name (1) Tenant Addr/(2) Pref Mail Address	Telephone Contact #s
		(1) 1784 Lincoln Way	Emergency
		Redwood City, WA 99456	( ) -
C-06	894	Sew & Sew Shoe Repair	(301) 256-4062
		Mgr: Sam Smith	(857) 236-5437
		(1) 1785 Lincoln Way	Emergency
		Redwood City, WA 99456	( ) -
C-08	894	Triple A Insurance	(301) 286-9734
		Mgr: Charles Simonson	(301) 246-1465
		(1) 1786 Lincoln Way	Emergency
		Redwood City, WA 99456	(301) 245-6290
		(2) 6489 124th SE	
		Oakdale, WA 98745	
C-10	894	Vacant	( ) -
			( ) -
			Emergency
			( ) -
C-11	43,851	Flower Fresh Dry Cleaners	(301) 346-2354
		Mgr: Robert Wilson	(301) 246-1587
		(1) 1788 Lincoln Way	Emergency
		Redwood City, WA 99456	(301) 245-6290
C-12	1,175	Redwood Chiropractic Clinic	(301) 278-3267
		Mgr: Dr. Charles Hurt	(301) 246-6598
		(1) 1787 Lincoln Way	Emergency
		Redwood City, WA 99456	(301) 245-6290
		(2) 8096 Elm Avenue	
		Rosewood, WA 98054	
Pad 1	2,875	Home Town Bank	(301) 246-7008
		Mgr: James Richards	(301) 246-3432
		(1) 1710 Lincoln Way	Emergency
		Redwood City, WA 99456	(301) 245-0554
		(2) 12276 Green Street	
		Redwood City, WA 99456	
Pad 2	3,550	The Pizza & Pasta Parlour	(301) 246-5454
		Mgr: Catello Pagano	(301) 246-8765
		(1) 1714 Lincoln Way	Emergency
		Redwood City, WA 99456	(301) 245-6290
		(2) 12256 Maple Street	
		Redwood City, WA 99456	
Pad 3	3,750	Down Home Dining Restaurant	(301) 246-8956
		Mgr: Daniel Denning	(301) 246-3446
		(1) 1716 Lincoln Way	Emergency
		Redwood City, WA 99456	(301) 245-7860
		(2) 12067 5th Avenue	
		Firndale, WA 96709	
	148,702	Total Project Sq. Ft.	
		End of Project	

EXHIBIT 2.11 *(Continued)*
LIST OF VENDORS

JANUARY 1994

Electrical:	Burke Electric 3511 W. Greenview Way Kennewick, WA 99336	John Brown (509) 746-5489 (509) 582-7113**
Fire Sprinklers:	Safety Fire Protection PO Box 1567 Pasco, WA 99301	Richard Young (509) 547-3478 (509) 735-5698**
Glass:	Associated Glass 18956 Highway 95 Lynnwood, WA 09456	Bill Kirk (206) 546-3456 (206) 778-2387**
HVAC:	Brown Controls 3006 Northup Way Bellevue, WA 98004	Fred Jones (304) 567-9823 (206) 454-1278**
Janitorial:	Young's Janitorial Service 1010 Elm Street Kirkland, WA 98033	Robert Young (206) 821-5496 (206) 823-6897**
Maintenance:	Columbia Maintenance, Inc. 120 S. Main, PO Box 345 Woodinville, WA 98076	Russ Goldstone (509) 734-6253 (509) 783-1674**
Pest Control:	Allsafe Pest Control 26th E. 2nd Avenue Redmond, WA 98056	Richard Buford (509) 582-4198**
Plumbing:	Paula's Plumbing 1346 SE 132nd Street Kirkland, WA 98034	Paula Stone (206) 823-2698 (206) 823-4587**
Roof:	Master Coatings Route 1, Box 34 Woodinville, WA 98056	Darrell Fox (509) 546-1219
Towing:	R & J Towing 1416 Gillespie Redmond, WA 98045	Greg A. Showalter (203) 454-6872

**Home Phone Number

LIST OF SUBCONTRACTORS

Acoustic Treatment:	Acoustical Design, Inc. 1194 Andover Park W Seattle, WA 98189	Walt Cramer (206) 575-1923
Caulking:	Stark's Caulking 3225 S. 276th Auburn, WA 98002	Debbie Stone (206) 854-8334

EXHIBIT 2.11 *(Continued)*
LIST OF SUBCONTRACTORS

Ceramic Tile:	Expert Tile Company 9632 Midvale Avenue S Seattle, WA 98104	Gary Grice (206) 525-4885
Concrete Pouring & Finishing:	Beeks Concrete Co. Route 2, Box 2945 Bellevue, WA 98004	Thom Thum (206) 454-6790
Dock Equipment:	Westcoast Handling Systems PO Box 8834 Redmond, WA 98056	Dan Thomas (203) 454-3465
Hollow Metal Doors & Frames:	Brennan Supply 14032 S.E. 132nd Street Redwood City, WA 98045	Mike Estes (509) 546-8723
Rolling Steel Door:	Steel Door Company 1300 Columbia Center Blvd. Firdale, WA 98456	Steve Stark (509) 745-2098
Sliding Hollow Metal Doors:	Steel Door Company 1300 Columbia Center Blvd. Firdale, WA 98456	Steve Stark (509) 745-2098
Electrical:	Westside Electric Co. 2121 North 38th Street Seattle, WA 98014	Bill Rauch (206) 632-3467
Flashing & Sheet Metal:	Foster Sheet Metal, Inc. PO Box 6148 Bellevue, WA 98045	Lee Foster (206) 568-1156
Resilient Flooring:	William Willey Co., Inc. PO Box 80356 Woodinville, WA 98075	William Willey (206) 673-4567
Fire Sprinkler:	Fire Sprinkler Co., Inc. 10005 E. Montgomery Bellevue, WA 98034	Larry Garbe (509) 928-3498 Harold Harris (206) 454-2068
Glazing & Storefront:	Sparkling Glass Company 1120 W. Lewis Seattle, WA 98006	Simon Shoe (206) 456-9807
Finish Hardware:	Plaza Hardware Co. 1315 Plaza Street Seattle, WA 98010	Richard Simms (203) 823-6078
HVAC & Plumbing:	Smith & Sons Co., Inc. 11078 Pacific Highway Bellevue, WA 98044	Ron Smith (206) 763-8900

EXHIBIT 2.11 *(Continued)*
LIST OF SUBCONTRACTORS

Thermal Insulation:	Insulation Service Co. 9944 · 152nd Avenue NE Redmond, WA 98045	Bob Burton (206) 885-5145
Millwork:	Coastcraft Mill Work PO Box 1888 Tacoma, WA 98401	Larry Jacobs (206) 839-9578
Painting & Vinyl:	Smith & Son Painting Contractors 465 Park Avenue NW Renton, WA 98056	John Smith (206) 229-3597
Reinforcing Steel:	Strong Steel Corporation PO Box 668 Kirkland, WA 98045	Terry Strong (206) 827-5887
Roof Hatch:	Foster-Bray Co., Inc. PO Box 5432 Seattle, WA 98005	Ed Bray (206) 323-8787
Roof Structure:	Kirkland Structures, Inc. 10909 - 154th Avenue SE Kirkland, WA 98034	Kay Jones (206) 823-5698
Roof Trusses:	Roof Trusses, Inc. 3163 "C" Street SW Auburn, WA 98002	Randy Jones (206) 823-1050
Built-Up Roofing & Rigid Insulation:	Rogers Roofing & Insulation PO Box 1554 Kirkland, WA 98033	Roger Gates (506) 525-3045 (506) 821-6934**
Site Utilities:	Jones & Smith Construction 11156 E. Imperial Avenue Seattle, WA 98168	Betty Jones (206) 823-2387
Sitework:	L. W. Kidd Co., Inc. PO Box 345 Seattle, WA 98045	Alan Mason (509) 265-8954
Structural & Misc. Steel:	Big Time Welders 6820 - 178th SW Redmond, WA 98052	Pat Meek (206) 885-9622
Stucco & Drywall:	ABC Drywall 10607 E. Wesson Drive Seattle, WA 99035	Gary Black (509) 934-1732
Toilet Accessories:	Shiny Brite Accessories, Inc. PO Box 1234 Seattle, WA 98114	Cliff Bray (206) 546-8756
Prefinished Wallboard	William Willey Co., Inc. PO Box 80365 Bellevue, WA 98004	Karin Stromberg (206) 454-9008

tenant improvements can become a profit center for the manager and enhance client relationships.

Some managers have the capability of providing full contracting services and charges for these services just as an independent contractor would. This involves a contractor's license and bonding requirements in most states. Something as simple as arranging for painting a suite or cleaning drapes requires no special licenses and is often part of the management services.

Regardless of the degree of involvement, the manager should be aware of building limitations, local building codes, costs for construction items, and time involved. Enthusiasm and optimism can lead the parties to believe that construction can be performed faster and less expensively than is realistic, and the reality can cause hard feelings, expensive delays, and even lawsuits. Any time the building owner is completing work for the tenant there should be a written agreement as to what is being furnished and when it will be completed. Commercial leases generally have a section that spells out the owner's responsibilities and clearly states that all other work is the responsibility of the tenant (see Exhibit 2.12).

§ 2.26   CONSULTING SERVICES

The property manager should not overlook the opportunity to provide consulting service. This is an opportunity to add profit to the company for little additional expense. One benefit of a consulting service is that it may lead to management accounts.

Consulting services can be marketed directly and indirectly. Direct marketing includes potential client contact and advertising. The firm must first determine the primary and secondary geographic areas it plans to service. For instance, a Seattle firm's primary market may be the Northwest and Alaska, and its secondary market the rest of the western United States or even the rest of the country. Next, the property manager identifies potential clients in the market (e.g., pension fund advisors, small developers, institutions, government agencies, and lenders). The person responsible for property management or leasing in each organization is identified. A letter is sent to the prospective client detailing specific consulting services that would meet the needs of the client. A letter to a developer might address the firm's ability to assist in organizing a property management department. A letter to a lender with properties in a depressed area might focus on the firm's expertise in managing and leasing problem properties. The information packet should include a brochure and a brief description of the firm. This is followed by a phone call and a request for a meeting.

Indirect marketing is one of the most effective ways to promote one's consulting services. Serving on committees and holding office in local

EXHIBIT 2.12

Description of Landlord's and Tenant's Work

Landlord agrees that it will, at its sole cost and expense, commence the construction of the demised premises and pursue the completion (with the exception of delays or conditions beyond the Landlord's control) in accordance with Landlord's or Landlord architect's designs and plans, which construction shall include the items generally described in Landlord's work below:

Tenant agrees to prepare, or cause to be prepared, and to submit the Landlord's architect two sets of fully dimensioned one-quarter (¼") scale drawings showing the layout of the demised premises including store front, trade fixture plans and any other matters which would affect the construction design of the demised premises, within thirty (30) days after the date that this lease is fully executed. Said plans shall be in conformity with the hereinafter set forth description of "Tenant's Work."

LANDLORD'S WORK for which Landlord is obligated to initially construct and pay:

1. Exterior building walls, roof, all structural items, including store front, per Landlord's design and specifications.

2. A flat concrete floor slab to receive Tenant's finish floor. **Tenant to pay the cost for utility lines and undergrounding for Tenant's needs within the demised premises.**

3. One toilet room including plumbing with Landlord's standard toilet room fixtures to include standard toilet, lavatory, water heater above toilet room for lavatory only, and mirror, all in a location selected by Landlord and per Landlord's design and specifications. Wall and floor covering to meet Health Department codes.

4. Landlord's standard type finished 2' x 4' x ⅝" grid ceiling at a height of 8 feet or higher to cover the demised premises.

5. Demising partitions or walls, including common walls to major tenants, will consist of wood or metal studs (at Landlord's selection), sheet rock, taped and sanded, or unfinished concrete and/or block on rear walls to receive Tenant's finish, where shown on Landlord's drawings.

6. Installation of air conditioning and heating system per Landlord's plans and specifications, adequate to condition, in accordance with the **A.S.R.A.E.** guideline for the geographical location, a standard retail store having electrical fixtures and equipment consuming no more than two and one-half (2.5) watts per square foot of leased area. If Tenant's requirements are in excess thereof, Tenant shall pay the increased cost.

7. Electrical. All electrical work not expressly provided for below shall be a part of Tenant's work.

    (a) An electrical panel at the rear of the space as applicable:

0 - 1200 s.f.	100 amp	Single phase
1200 - 2250 s.f.	100 amp	3 phase 4 wire
2250 - 2800 s.f.	125 amp	3 phase 4 wire
2800 - 3375 s.f.	150 amp	3 phase 4 wire
3375 - 4500 s.f.	200 amp	3 phase 4 wire

    (b) Convenience outlets (fed from the Tenant's panel) located approximately 15 feet on center on the side demising partitions.

    (c) Four tube recessed 2' x 4' fluorescent light fixtures per Landlord's plans and specifications. Light fixtures shall be provided at a ratio of not greater than one (1) per eighty (80) square feet of floor area of the demised premises.

    (d) Conduit and "J" box for the Tenant's sign.

    (e) "J" box, conduit, wiring and fixture for incandescent light and exhaust fan in the toilet room.

8. Landlord will provide a means of supplying telephone service to the Tenant's space.

9. Landlord will install sprinklers in the demised premises at the rate of one (1) head per 125 square feet without any interior partitions. Any additional sprinklers and/or changes required as a result of Tenant improvements, by local fire codes other than the Landlord's standard layout will be at the cost of the Tenant, and must be made by Landlord's contractor.

10. Standard aluminum and glass store front, 8 feet or higher (at Landlord's option), with a single-acting entrance door to include mail slot, not to exceed a maximum of 3'0" in width.

TENANT WORK:

1. Tenant shall provide, administer and pay for any and all work done to the demised premises other than that provided under LANDLORD'S WORK hereinabove. Tenant shall procure and pay for any and all plans, drawings, permits, etc., necessary to do said work in a legal and workmanlike manner. Upon completion of Tenant's work, Tenant shall provide Landlord a copy of the certificate of occupancy issued by the appropriate governmental agency.

2. Should the Tenant request, in writing, and the Landlord agree, in writing, to have Landlord's contractor perform any of the Tenant's work, it is agreed that the Tenant shall pay for all costs of said work in accordance with Landlord contractor's requirements. In

    addition, Tenant shall make arrangements for said work on or before _____ . If said arrangements are not made by said date, then Landlord or Landlord's contractor shall have no obligation to provide for said work.

Landlord's Initials   _____

Tenant's Initials   _____

chapters of IREM or BOMA as well as teaching and writing are the best indirect ways to market consulting services.

There are countless opportunities to teach. The major real estate organizations are usually looking for speakers for their local miniseminars. A property manager can develop a topic from his or her experience or participate in a panel. Community colleges, too, often look for guest speakers and instructors to teach a property management course. IREM has developed three community college courses—Introduction to Property Management (201), Apartment Management (202), and Commercial Property Management (203). IREM provides the instructors with a course outline, lecture outline, exams, and textbook. If the local community college doesn't offer any of these courses, someone in the management firm might want to contact the school to discuss the possibility of doing so. Serving on the national faculty of one of the real estate organizations provides an excellent teaching experience.

Writing is another good way to indirectly market consulting services. Local business magazines and daily newspapers are often interested in receiving general interest articles on real estate. After conducting a market survey of, for example, suburban office buildings, a property management firm can develop a feature article from the data. Another possibility is to turn a unique experience into an article for a national magazine. The article "The Property Manager as Consultant," in the *Journal of Property Management*, July/August 1986, is an excellent resource for developing consulting services.

Consulting fees are based on an hourly rate, a monthly retainer, or an agreed-upon amount. For example, a property manager in California was hired at a fixed fee to analyze the management and leasing operations of a failing community mall in the Northwest. Another manager was paid an hourly rate by a shopping center developer to review plans for a proposed office building. A property management firm was paid a monthly retainer for six months to develop the management and leasing plan and to supervise the on-site staff of an office building until the developer established its property management department.

When negotiating a consulting assignment, the property manager and client must agree on the type and frequency of reports. Reports will vary from a short, written and oral presentation when the assignment is completed, to monthly written reports, to an extensive management plan. Preparing and presenting the reports can be time consuming, and the manager must factor in that time when establishing a fee. The consulting agreement must explicitly address the service that will be provided, including the type and frequency of reports (see Exhibit 2.13). The American Society of Real Estate Counselors award the designation Counselor of Real Estate (CRE).

EXHIBIT 2.13

Sample Consulting Agreement

THIS CONSULTING AGREEMENT (hereinafter referred to as the "Agreement") is made and entered into this _____ day of _____, 19____, by and between _____, a _____ corporation (hereinafter referred to as "Consultant") and _____ (hereinafter referred to as "Owner"):

WHEREAS, Owner is the ground lessee or fee owner of certain real property situated in _____ (city, state), which real property is more fully described in the legal description hereof attached hereto and made a part hereof as Exhibit "A"; and

WHEREAS, Owner has purchased or developed certain improvements on and to said real property for the purpose of conducting thereon and therein a Shopping Center known as _____; and

WHEREAS, said real property and improvements are referred to herein as the "Property"; and

WHEREAS, Owner has or will employ an individual to act as its on-site manager of the Property (hereinafter referred to as "Manager") for the leasing of space in the Property, the collection of rents, day-to-day management of the Property, and the management and control of the association formed or to be formed among Owner and tenants of space in the Property (hereinafter referred to as the "Merchants' Association", and

WHEREAS, the Owner desires to employ Consultant as an independent contractor and consultant to provide Owner with advisory, consultative, and supervisory services concerning management of the Property as hereinafter set forth;

NOW, THEREFORE, in consideration of the mutual terms and conditions set forth herein and for $_____ and other good and valuable consideration, the receipt and sufficiency of which is hereby acknowledged, the parties hereto hereby agree as follows:

1. *ENGAGEMENT OF CONSULTANT; TERM*

(a) The Owner hereby employs and engages Consultant, and Consultant hereby accepts such employment and engagement, as an independent contractor to provide the consulting services described below. It is understood and agreed that Consultant is not an employee of Owner and is not, except to the extent set forth herein, Owner's agent for any purpose.

(b) *Term.* The term of the Agreement shall be for _____ and shall commence on _____, and terminate at 12:00 midnight on _____.

(c) *Cancellation.* Either party may cancel this Agreement upon not less than sixty (60) days prior written notice to the other.

2. *CONSULTING SERVICES*

(a) *Services.* Consultant shall provide Owner with advisory, consultative and supervisory services, including without limitation, supervision of the on-site Manager employed by Owner (hereinafter "the Services") and assistance in the development and implementation of the procedures and operational standards which are reasonably required for the management of the Property as a

EXHIBIT 2.13 *(Continued)*

shopping center and the establishment and operation of a Merchants' Association (hereinafter "Management Procedures").

The Services to be performed by Consultant in accomplishing the foregoing shall consist of the services set out in the Schedule of Services attached hereto and made a part hereof as Exhibit "B". The Management Procedures shall be established and the Services shall be performed as deemed reasonably necessary and appropriate for the efficient and successful management and operation of a shopping center of a size and type similar to that constructed on the Property.

(b) *Scope.* For the purposes hereof, the Services to be performed by Consultant shall include meetings by authorized employees of Consultant with Owner and/or Manager to be conducted at reasonable times upon reasonable notice taking place during the initial term on an average of _____ times each calendar month and consisting of up to _____ per month of actual meeting time; provided that Consultant shall participate in additional meetings and devote additional hours in the case of emergencies. Consultant shall have no obligation to undertake any unreasonable action or activity in order to accomplish its obligations hereunder. Consultant shall be under no obligation to maintain any employee or agent on the Property.

3. *FEE.*

For its services hereunder, Owner shall pay to Consultant a consulting fee in the amount and manner set forth on Exhibit "C", attached hereto, on or before the last day of each month during the term hereof. In addition to the consulting fee to be paid Consultant, the Owner agrees to pay in advance, or upon demand, as Consultant may determine, all of Consultant's actual expenses in performing its obligations hereunder.

For the purposes hereof, the term "actual expenses" shall include transportation expenses and airline tickets to and from _____ for all the meetings with the on-site Manager, and from Seattle to _____ for emergencies or other special trips, meals, lodging, and similar expenses and costs incurred in performing services on behalf of Owner.

4. *LAW.*

This Agreement shall be interpreted and enforced pursuant to the laws of the State of _____.

5. *WAIVER.*

It is understood and agreed that Consultant makes no representations or warranties with respect to the effectiveness of any of the Management Procedures or the profitability of the Property. Owner specifically assumes all risk of the use of any or all of the Management Procedures. Further, Owner hereby waives and releases and indemnifies Consultant, its agents, and employees from any and all claims, costs, losses, expenses, injuries, or damages suffered, incurred, or claimed by any person, entity, partnership, or joint venture and arising by reasons of the Agreement or the Management Procedures except if caused as a result of the negligence, breach, or misconduct of Consultant or any agent, employee, or associate of Consultant in performance or non-performance of Consultant's duties under this Agreement.

EXHIBIT 2.13 *(Continued)*

6. *COMPETITION.*

Nothing herein contained shall in any way prohibit Consultant from engaging in the management of, or entering into any other consulting agreements with respect to, other properties or ventures of any type or kind whatsoever even though the same may be in direct or indirect competition with the business conducted by Owner on the Property.

7. *ATTORNEYS' FEES.*

In the event either party shall commence any action to enforce its rights hereunder, then the prevailing party in such action shall recover against the other, reasonable attorneys' fees in addition to any costs incurred in the defense or prosecution of such action.

8. *NO ASSIGNMENT.*

This Agreement and the rights, benefits, and obligations hereunder shall not be assignable by any party hereto.

EXHIBIT B

Schedule of Services

Advisory, consultative, and supervisory services to be provided by Consultant:

1. Assist on-site Manager with training and direction for day-to-day shopping center management.
2. Assist in preparing annual operating budget and periodic review of budget.
3. Assist in setting up a maintenance management program, which includes bidding services and recommending vendors for selection.
4. Periodically supervise vendors and janitorial/maintenance operation.
5. Prepare monthly gross sales reports and analysis. Tenants' sales reports shall be obtained by the mall Manager and provided to Consultant.
6. Conduct tenant-mix analysis and make leasing recommendations.
7. Make recommendations to Owner for project improvements, both in physical modifications and in management/operation procedures.
8. Review Merchants' Association budget with income/expenditure plans.
9. Assist on-sit Manager in operation of Merchants' Association and development of an advertising and promotion plan.
10. Attend a monthly Merchants' Association meeting.
11. Prepare monthly deferred conditions. Lease summaries will be prepared by the mall Manager and provided to Consultant.
12. Provide Consultant's standard shopping center (mall) lease and management agreement. Said contracts will be reviewed by ＿＿＿＿＿ (attorney) before they are used.
13. Provide and instruct the mall Manager in the use of Consultant's management forms.
14. Provide training to mall personnel at the Bellevue and Anchorage offices of Consultant.

Source: R. F. Muhlebach & A. A. Alexander, "The Property Manager as Consultant" 51 *J. Prop. Mgmt.* (July/August 1986). Copyright © 1986 by the Institute of Real Estate Management. Reprinted by permission.

§ 2.27   DEVELOPING A COMPANY EDUCATION PROGRAM

Commercial property management is a dynamic profession. Each element in the effective management of a property is constantly changing. These changes in accounting, leasing, merchandising, insurance, maintenance, administration, and legal matters are precipitated by a number of factors, including industry innovation, government and tax regulations, economic conditions, technological advances, legal rulings, and shifts in society's values.

No individual can be an expert in every field. Property managers can master some of these elements and have a working knowledge of the others. The administrative and clerical staff must be proficient at their particular responsibilities and have a general familiarity with the other areas.

A company education program is an effective way to maintain a high level of professionalism for the entire staff. It can inform the staff about other aspects of property management and create a flow of shared information throughout the company. The education program can include membership in professional organizations, subscriptions to relevant publications, classes at local educational institutions and real estate organizations, and participation in in-house seminars.

The core of an effective education program is the in-house seminar. Staff members may meet annually for a one- or two-day presentation on chosen topics of interest. Depending upon the size of the company, the group will be divided into sections to cover a variety of subjects according to job responsibility, or presentations may be given to the entire group followed by small group discussions.

An effective in-house seminar must be carefully prepared. A committee with a representative from each department is formed and solicits topic suggestions from staff members. In collaboration with the director of property management, speakers are contacted and a program formulated.

Suggested topics for staff seminars include:

1. *Insurance.* Reporting claims, review of property coverage, review of employee benefits. Guest speaker: company's insurance agent.

2. *Legal Issues.* Eviction procedures, effects of bankruptcy laws on the landlord/tenant relationship, explanation of lease clauses. Guest speaker: company's legal counsel.

3. *Maintenance.* Roofing and parking lot inspections, landscaping, heating, ventilation and air-conditioning. Guest speaker: contractors or consultants. Film and slides are available from

the Asphalt Institute, Asphalt Institute Building, College Park, MD 20740.

4. *Accounting.* New tax laws. Guest speaker: company's accounting firm.

5. *Asset Management.* Review needs of the asset manager. Guest speaker: a local asset manager.

6. *Advertising and Public Relations.* Guest speaker: ad agency representative.

7. *Leasing.* Review state of the art in commercial leases, marketing techniques. Guest speaker: attorney discussing lease provisions.

Another portion of an in-house seminar is a presentation given by one or several staff members. For example, the company's controller can review the procedures for approving and paying bills and explain what causes bills to be held. Other talks could include: a property manager reviewing procedures for handling emergencies; a leasing agent reviewing market conditions; or the director of property management reviewing monthly management reports and annual management plans.

Depending on the seminar's structure, department sessions may run concurrently during the day, with a summary meeting for the entire group to conclude the session.

Another useful in-house educational program is the year-end review. This may be either an all-company or a single department meeting at which employees are given an opportunity to assess the year just passed, to give feedback on current operating practices, and to offer suggestions for improvement in the future. Staff members can also recognize company and personal accomplishments. An excellent format combining an informal and formal agenda is a two-hour session beginning at noon with lunch provided.

The property management company that does not have an ongoing education program will slowly lose its competitive edge. Providing a varied program of educational opportunities in a property management company benefits both the individual staff member and the company as a whole.

§ 2.28 CONVERTING TO ANOTHER SOFTWARE PROGRAM

Nearly every commercial property management firm is computerized. Most firms entered the computer age in the early 1980s. Many firms, not finding acceptable commercial property management software programs in the late 1970s and early 1980s hired a programmer and developed their own in-house software programs. By the mid-1980s, several excellent commercial property management software programs were available. Many commercial property management firms have been operating on their original software and hardware that dates back 12 to 15 years. Their software programs may be adequate, but not state of the art, and their hardware does not support new computer programs, nor does it have the capacity, the speed, or the flexibility of new hardware.

Institutional owners are placing greater financial reporting demands on commercial property management firms. Property management firms have new competition, the developer's property management company. In order to meet the needs and demands of institutional owners and sophisticated private investors and remain competitive, commercial property management firms must evaluate their present software programs and hardware. If their computer program is no longer state of the art, they should explore the possibility of converting to another software program.

Most commercial property management firms have not converted to a new software program or analyzed, evaluated, and compared available programs. The following is a step-by-step process to guide the property manager in such an analysis:

1. Appoint a committee to analyze the needs of the company. The committee should have a representative from each department of the firm who uses computers in his or her accounting or word processing position. Suggested members are the director of property management or the owner of the firm, the treasurer or controller, a property manager, an administrative assistant or secretary, and the office manager.

2. Choice of which software program to purchase should be software-driven, not hardware-driven.

3. Select the software program that meets the needs of the commercial property manager's clients and not the one that is the favorite program of the accounting department. If the commercial property management firm's primary clients are institutions, poll the asset managers for the software programs they prefer. Ask them what they like and do not like about some of the reports from their property management firms. Inquire if they have any special needs or anticipate special needs in the future. Remember, the primary objective of the financial reports is to meet the needs of the firm's clients.

4. The Institute of Real Estate Management (IREM) has developed minimum standards for property management software

programs in its publication "Minimum Standards for Property Management Accounting Software." This report should be reviewed by the committee.

5. Each committee member should review articles comparing and rating software programs. The *Journal of Property Management*, published by IREM, is an excellent resource on computers for the property management industry. Each issue of the *Journal* has a column on computers.

6. Compare your client's needs and your firm's needs to the features of each software program.

7. Meet with other property managers and discuss what they like and don't like about their software and hardware.

8. Select three to five software vendors that appear to meet your client's needs and your needs.

9. Contact the vendor's sales representative and arrange a meeting in your office. A meeting in the commercial property management firm's office will allow the vendor's representative to review your software and hardware and find out your likes and dislikes. This meeting should include a thorough discussion of the commercial property management firm's objectives in converting to another software program and acquiring new equipment.

10. Review the software vendor's financial condition. You want to be certain that the firm will be available to service the equipment and troubleshoot problems on a long-term basis.

11. Ask the vendor's representative for references from commercial property management firms that have been using the system/program for at least two years. When one property manager on the East Coast inquired of one of the vendor's references, she found out that the firm had replaced the system because it didn't perform as the company had been led to believe. Ask the references what they like and don't like about the system and what the software can and cannot do.

12. Review the strengths and flexibility of the report writer. This feature allows the user the ability to create custom reports.

13. Determine if the software operates on an industry-standard operating system as opposed to a proprietary operating system that is limited to one manufacturer.

14. Narrow the selection down to two or three software vendors.

15. Enter accounting data from one of your firm's properties into the equipment you are evaluating. Either visit the vendor's office, borrow equipment from the vendor, or use a terminal at the office of a property management firm that uses this particular system. Set up a lease, perform a billing including a Consumer Price

Index (CPI) adjustment, tenant reimbursement of pass-through operating expenses, and a minimum rent step-up adjustment.

16. Choose word processing software according to word processing needs, compatibility with other staff members and colleagues, availability of support, and user-friendly qualities.

17. As a committee, meet to discuss, analyze, and debate the strengths and weaknesses of each program.

18. Select the software programs that best meet the needs of present clients, future clients, and the office staff.

19. Evaluate alternative hardware vendors.

20. Negotiate the right to obtain the source code for the software program.

21. Negotiate the price of the software and hardware. Software vendors will negotiate their price only if you start the negotiations.

22. Develop a plan to convert from your existing software program to the new program. Training for everyone on the new system is essential and should be built into the contract.

    Timing for converting to the new equipment depends on the workload during the year. Most commercial property management firms are thoroughly involved in budgets and annual management plans from mid-September to mid-December, followed by year-end adjustments and percentage rent calculations after the first of the year. A good time to initiate the conversion is from March to early summer.

    The goal is to have each property running on the new system before the new year's budgets are completed. Depending upon the number of properties the firm manages, it may be necessary to place only two properties per week or per month on the new system. Always continue to run the old system in tandem with the new system to ensure that accounting and/or word processing functions can continue until the conversion is complete and everyone is satisfied with the new equipment.

23. Publicize your new computer system to your clients and prospective clients.

The complete new hardware system and software package(s) can cost between $20,000 and $200,000 for most commercial property management firms. The investment is not only monetary but must be measured in terms of time necessary to convert to a new system. Selecting the wrong system affects both the direct costs, as stated above, and the indirect cost of not being able to meet client's and prospective client's needs.

§ 2.29 RECEIVERSHIP

One of the outcomes of the depressed real estate market is the opportunity for the property manager to be appointed as a receiver for a distressed property. Each jurisdiction has its own concept of what receivers are and what duties they perform. For example, the Illinois Court of Appeals has defined a receiver as one who acts as a custodian of assets which are the subject of litigation, where title of such assets remains with a party litigant. The California Court of Appeals has defined a receiver as a ministerial officer, agent, creator, hand, or arm of, and a temporary occupant and caretaker of the property for, the court and he represents the court appointing him, functioning as the medium through which the court acts.

The court order appointing the receiver is the best source for determining the obligations and authority of the receiver. As an officer of the court, the receiver has only those duties which are expressly delineated in the order.

When a lender has a loan that is in default and there is concern with how the property is being managed or how the property's income is allocated and accounted for, a lender will petition the court for a court-appointed receiver. The lender will select a receiver and submit an "Order to Appoint Receiver" to the court. The property owner may contest the request for receiver. In most states the receiver is an individual and not a corporation.

In some states, individuals must first be approved by the state's Superior Court before they can be appointed a receiver. In these situations, the individual fills out an application, shows evidence of competence and knowledge of real estate, and submits the application to the court for approval.

Once approved, a lender could request that the individual be appointed receiver. A lender selects a receiver based on the individual's expertise in a particular property type and/or property management and leasing skills. The selection process for a receiver is often no different than the evaluation of a property management company. When the receiver is a property manager, it is often the director of property management who is appointed the receiver, and he or she appoints the company as the property management firm to manage and lease the property. Basically, the lender is appointing a property manager to be a receiver because the lender wants that property management firm to manage and lease the property. Often the receiver is not a property manager, but rather an attorney or an accountant who hires a property management firm to manage the property.

The receiver's scope of authority is specifically stated in the court order appointing the receiver. The intent of the order is to empower the receiver to act on the court's behalf to manage the asset. The court order should provide the receiver with the authority to manage, operate, and lease the property within specific guidelines. The court order should not be so broad that it requires the receiver to do things he or she is not capable of. The court order should allow the receiver to sue for debt, (for example, back rent), initiate litigation due to tenant's lease default, lease the property, collect rents and other income, maintain and preserve the property, pay authorized costs and expenses including real estate taxes and insurance, obtain insurance coverage, and employ legal counsel. The receiver will usually be required to post a surety bond in an amount usually no less than $100,000.

The court order will state what the receiver's and/or property management fees will be. In some states, the lender will appoint a receiver, pay the receiver an hourly or fixed monthly fee, and the receiver will hire a property management firm that will charge a management fee. Other lenders will appoint a property manager as the receiver and agree to a typical property management fee for a distressed property. When establishing a property management fee, the property manager must realize that the property is distressed and will usually require more management, administrative, and leasing time than that of a typical property. The fee should be based on the time and expertise required to manage the property. The management fee will usually be on the high end of the typical management fee range for that property type.

Frequently, the property will be in disarray and the property owner will not fully cooperate with the receiver. It is not uncommon for the property management firm to receive an initial set-up fee. For instance, the minimum monthly fee may be doubled for the first two or three months. The receivership order should allow for additional appropriate fees (for example, leasing, construction supervision, tax appeals, sale of the property). The leasing commission should depend upon the difficulty of the leasing assignment. The following questions should be considered:

- Is an incentive commission offered to the brokerage community to encourage their participation in the leasing of the property, for example, full commission to outside broker and half commission to property management firm?
- Will the property management firm's duties include remodeling supervision or tenant improvement coordination? If so, will the fee be a percentage of the construction cost (for example, 5 percent) or based on an hourly fee?
- If the property manager appeals the taxes, will the fee be based on a percentage of the tax savings or an hourly fee?
- If the management fee is a fixed amount or a percent of the collected income, will the court order allow the fee to be paid automatically

each month, or will the property management firm be required to receive court approval for payment?

If there are fees that are based on an hourly service, the property manager must justify and document the activities and the hours spent on these activities. The property management firm's standard accounting reports should be attached to the court order as an exhibit. Banks and savings and loans are concerned that the receiver's fees are not excessive. When the lender requests that a property manager be the appointed receiver, it is likely that the lender will retain the property management firm if it acquires the title to the property. In this situation, a management agreement would be negotiated with the lender when the receivership expires.

It is imperative that the property manager operate the property with strict impartiality. Even though the receiver was selected by the lender, the receiver must treat all parties equally and show no favoritism. All reports should be sent to the court, the property owner, and the lender. Most property management firms' standard monthly management and accounting reports will be adequate for the court, the property owner, and the lender. A comprehensive property management monthly report is described in § 11.2(b). It is important that the lender and property owner agree on the monthly accounting reports. As stated above, the accounting reports should be an exhibit to the court order. If additional accounting reports are required, the property management firm should be allowed to charge an additional fee.

Immediately after the receiver is appointed, the property manager should visit each tenant. The tenants are likely to know that the property's loan has been in default or that the property is distressed. Some of the tenants may have had disputes with the property owner, maintenance may have been neglected, and no doubt there are several vacancies. The property manager should instill confidence in the tenants that the property will be professionally managed. Each tenant should be provided with a letter from the bank's or property manager's attorney, possibly with a copy of the court order, as evidence that all rent payments should be made to the property management firm.

The receiver will select and direct an attorney to represent the property and the receiver. An attorney may be needed to initiate litigation, communicate with an uncooperative owner, and to communicate with and petition the court for specific approval. The attorney should copy the lender's and property owner's attorney on most of his or her correspondence. The cost of the attorney is an expense of the property, not the property management firm or the receiver.

The property management firm's accounting department should immediately summarize the property's leases and ascertain if the tenants are being billed properly for base rent and pass-through charges. The property owner may not have been aggressive in collecting the rents and some tenants may have significant arrearages. Other tenants may be withholding their rent claiming the developer/property owner hasn't fulfilled all lease obligations or promises. The property manager needs to address the problems immediately.

One of the first responsibilities of the receiver is to develop a month-to-month operating budget. The property will have limited funds. Sufficient funds may not be available from the monthly rents and tenant charges during the months that real estate taxes and insurance premiums are due. Delinquent taxes may need to be paid to prevent a sheriff's sale of the property.

The receiver should request all the records, leases, and construction documents held by the property owner. If the owner is not cooperating, the receiver's attorney will first contact the property owner's attorney and if the property owner refuses to cooperate the attorney can petition the court for the owner's cooperation.

If the property has a cash deficit, the property owner will be reluctant to contribute funds because he/she may lose the property to the lender. The lender may be reluctant to contribute funds because the lender may not acquire title to the property. Since the operating expenses are typically paid before the mortgage payment, there usually are sufficient funds to operate the property. However, there may not be excessive funds to pay for tenant improvements or major maintenance expenses.

The receiver should not enter into any agreement (for example, maintenance agreement and leases) when the terms of the agreement extend beyond the receivership period without obtaining approval of the court. Most maintenance agreements can be negotiated with a 30-day cancellation provision. If a long-term maintenance agreement is prudent (for example, a five-year elevator maintenance agreement with a substantial discount), the receiver should first obtain the consent of the property owner and lender and then approval of the court. The court order may allow the receiver to enter into a lease based on pre-agreed terms. For instance, a retail lease may be no longer than five years, at a rate no less than $15 per square foot per year, with no more than one month free rent for each year of the lease, with a standard percentage rate, with tenant improvement allowance not to exceed $5 per square foot and provided that the tenant's use is compatible with the property's tenant mix. It is advisable for the receiver to discuss each lease deal with the property owner and lender and then obtain court approval. The receiver should be certain that sufficient funds are available for tenant improvement and commission before entering into a lease.

One potential problem is that the court order doesn't provide the receiver with adequate authority or sufficient direction to operate the property. These problems can be alleviated with a properly drafted court order. The receiver/property manager should review the court order before it is submitted to the court.

If a property manager is interested in serving as a receiver, he or she should contact and market its services to lenders and attorneys who work for lenders or have been appointed as a receiver and need to hire a property management firm. Receivership became a new opportunity for property management firms in the late 1980s and early 1990s. Receivership can replace management business lost to developer and other property owners who have taken their property to manage in-house.

§ 2.30 CONCLUSION

Most property management companies are small, and it is easy to become so engrossed in managing properties that managing the company is overlooked. However, a small company requires the same attention to its administration and development that larger firms enjoy.

Three

Budgeting: Income and Expense Components

---

§ 3.1 THE PURPOSE OF A BUDGET

The effective budget is a financial road map of the property. The purpose of a budget is to provide financial guidance to the property manager and the property owner. A good budget will not prevent problems from happening, but it will allow the manager to anticipate and properly respond to financial changes.

For example, if the property will not have sufficient funds to pay the first real estate tax installment, this will be obvious when the budget is developed. The property owner then has sufficient time to plan for the cash shortfall. Conversely, if the property will generate a positive cash flow by midyear, the property owner can plan how these funds will be used.

Without a budget these two situations would go unnoticed until either the property ran out of funds or the owner realized more cash was available than anticipated. In either case, the owner is likely to be surprised. The property manager is responsible for minimizing or eliminating surprises for the property owner.

§ 3.2 TYPES OF BUDGETS

All but the most simple commercial properties have subbudgets that make up the entire budget. In a complex situation, a property can have several of the following subbudgets:

Expense

1. Capital expenditure budget
2. Owner's expenses
3. Common area—parking lot
4. Common area—mall
5. Escalation expenses—office building
6. Merchants' association/marketing fund
7. Property taxes
8. Insurance
9. Utility reimbursement
10. Reimbursement for repairs
11. Debt Service

Income

1. Base rent
2. Percentage rent
3. Reimbursement of tenant charges
4. Merchants' association/marketing fund
5. Miscellaneous income

1. *Capital Expenditure Budget.* The capital portion of the budget includes those items not generally expensed in one year and that are amortized over more than one year. These will include major repairs, tenant improvements, and leasing commissions.

2. *Owner's Expenses.* These expenses are paid by the owner and not reimbursed by tenants. They generally include merchants' association or marketing fund dues, legal expenses, business licenses, office expenses, and possibly property management fees.

3. *Common Area—Parking Lot.* In an enclosed mall, all tenants commonly share the parking lot expenses, and only those tenants on the mall share the mall expenses. Parking lot expenses are exterior items of maintenance, including but not limited to parking lot sweeping, landscaping, security and utilities for the parking lot, and the property management fee if the lease allows.

4. *Common Area—Mall.*   These expenses are generally shared by tenants whose stores open onto the mall. Major tenants are not always required to share these expenses, which include but are not limited to janitorial services, air-conditioning, maintenance, utilities, security, and interior landscaping.

5. *Escalation Expenses—Office Building.* Office tenants will share in the expenses of operating the building. These escalation charges include janitorial service, building repairs, insurance, property taxes, pest control, utilities, and, in some situations, property management fees.

6. *Merchants' Association/Marketing Fund.*   The owner's contribution to either the merchants' association or marketing fund is generally budgeted in this category. If the landlord collects the merchants' dues and pays the bills, it is generally not a part of the overall property budget but is handled separately.

7. *Property Taxes and Insurance.*   Most owners want a careful evaluation of the amount of taxes and insurance being paid and the percentage of these expenses that are being recaptured from the tenants. In the typical commercial lease, tenants will reimburse the landlord for their pro rata share of these expenses.

8. *Utility Reimbursement.*   The owner may pay for the utilities in bulk—known as a master meter—or have a central plant and recover the costs from the tenants on a pro rata basis.

9. *Reimbursements for Repairs.*   Large properties often have an on-site maintenance staff to provide repairs for a fee for tenants, who are responsible for the cost of the work.

§ 3.3   BUDGET DEVELOPMENT AND EVALUATION

One important factor in evaluating a property manager's performance is his or her ability to develop accurate income and expense projections. Although the budgeting process is not difficult, it can be time-consuming, and it requires a thorough knowledge of budget development and evaluation.

The budget must be consistent with the property owner's goals and objectives. This means that the manager must meet with the owner to discuss both short- and long-term goals. Was the property purchased for long-term appreciation? If so, the owner will want to invest in preventive maintenance and capital improvements. Does the owner have cash flow problems? Does the owner live off the property's income and need all the cash for personal use? In both these situations, the owner would be reluctant to spend any more money than was necessary to maintain the current status of the property.

The property manager should bring to the owner's attention all of the major maintenance and capital improvements and justify the need for this work. The property manager reviews the necessity of the work and recommends which items should be completed in the budget period and which can be deferred. It is an exercise in futility to develop an operating budget and then discover that the budget is not consistent with the owner's goals and objectives for the property.

(a) BUDGET TEAM

Developing an accurate budget requires the input of several members of the property management company along with outside consultants. The property manager is primarily responsible for developing the budget and should use the knowledge and experience of maintenance personnel, contractors, the accounting department, the leasing agent, the property's insurance agent, consultants, and the manager's supervisor.

The maintenance supervisor is often most familiar with the maintenance and mechanical operations of the property, yet this person's input is sometimes overlooked when the budget is developed. The maintenance supervisor should meet with the maintenance personnel to review the property's condition and then submit a brief status report to the manager.

Smaller commercial properties seldom have on-site maintenance personnel. They generally contract all maintenance, whereas most large properties contract only specific maintenance. The property manager should meet with all contractors to review their area of maintenance and solicit their opinion on future maintenance needs. For example, the HVAC service contractor may make recommendations for repairs beyond the preventive maintenance contract or recommend upgrading the filters. (See Chapter 9 for more information on maintenance agreements.)

Consultants may be added to the budget team for specific expertise, such as parking lot maintenance or roofing. Consultants are hired to analyze, make recommendations, develop specifications, and estimate costs for specific work.

The leasing agent should provide the leasing projections. The property manager needs to know the occupancy level in order to estimate janitorial and utilities costs in an office building. The manager also needs to know which spaces will be leased, the required amount of tenant improvements, and the amount of space that will be leased and renewed to project commission expense.

The property manager and the insurance agent should meet with the owner to discuss the existing insurance program and the cost of alternative insurance coverage.

The accounting department is an integral part of the budget team. The bookkeeper will provide historical expenses and actual expenses for the current period combined with the property manager's estimate of the expenses for the balance of the current budget period to arrive at the estimated expenses for the current year or budget period. Besides calculating the tenant's charges and reimbursements, the bookkeeper may be asked to determine specific expenses such as real estate taxes.

(b) BUDGET SCHEDULE

A budget is developed over a two- to four-month period. Each commercial property has multiple income components and up to four operating budgets. Every source of income in each income component and every line item expense in each operating budget must be analyzed to prepare an accurate net operating income (NOI) projection.

Multiply the time required to develop one property's income and expense projections by the number of properties managed and it is obvious that cooperation among the staff and close internal budgeting control are critical. Losing control of the budgeting process will result in inaccurate projections, missed deadlines, loss of confidence in the property manager, frustration in the office, and the possibility of losing management accounts.

The budgeting process must be planned, communicated to everyone involved in the budgets, and monitored. As a first step in developing the plan, the controller reviews the management agreements to determine when each budget is due to the owner and then prepares a proposed timeline for each budget. The timeline is developed in reverse chronological order, starting with the date the budget is due to the property owner, and includes the following steps: mail budget to owner, complete final review and corrections, submit for review by property manager's supervisor, type and edit written narrative, obtain income and expense data from the property manager, obtain historical and current data from the accounting department.

The timeline should be distributed to all staff members, and progress should be monitored. One staff person, such as an administrative assistant, can act as coordinator to keep the process flowing smoothly. Delays should be identified and corrected immediately. Staff members also should be recognized for meeting each deadline. Teamwork is essential.

Exhibit 3.1 is a sample budget timeline. This form is just one of many ways to organize the budgeting process. Each company must develop a timeline that suits its operations. Following is an explanation of the terms on the timeline:

Numbers to the project administrator—The property manager provides the income and expense projections to the project administrator (bookkeeper) who enters the numbers in the computer.

EXHIBIT 3.1

1993 Budget Timeline

No.	Project Name	PA/PM	Expense Numbers to PA	Income Numbers to PA	Numbers to PM	To Typist	PM/Super Review	Corrections	Mail to Owner
8186	Anch Bus Pk	Debbie/Charlene	7-15	8-17	8-3	9-10	9-10	9-11	9-12
8187	Anch Dist I	Thom/Charlene	7-15	8-7	8-3	9-10	9-10	9-11	9-12
8213	Anch Dist II	Jane/Charlene	7-15	8-17	8-3	9-10	9-10	9-11	9-12
3083	A5A	Thom/Jo	8-3	9-2	9-8	9-14	9-15	9-16	9-17
3065	Belgate	Billie/Jessica	9-18	10-20	10-24	10-30	10-31	11-3	11-4
3016	College Pl	Jane/Jessica	8-21	9-22	9-25	10-1	10-2	10-3	10-6
3026	Copper City	Marla/Rick	10-2	11-3	11-6	11-12	11-13	11-14	11-17
3075	Cottonwood	Billie/Marsha	8-14	9-15	9-18	10-6	10-7	10-8	10-9
3091	Crossroads	Rick	2-2	3-2	3-8	3-14	3-15	3-18	3-22
3007	Ellensburg	Marla/Jessica	10-2	11-3	11-7	11-11	11-12	11-13	11-14
1101	Fifth & I	Billie/J D.	9-30	10-30	11-6	11-11	11-16	11-19	11-20
3056	Forest Park	Thom/Rick	7-1	7-31	8-7	8-14	8-18	8-21	8-28
3044	Frontier	Debbie/J.D.	9-15	10-15	10-22	11-3	11-4	11-5	11-6
3001	JAFCO	Melody/Bob	9-4	10-6	10-10	10-15	10-16	10-17	10-20
2089	Kennewick	Billie/Bob	8-4	9-4	9-17	9-24	9-25	9-28	9-30
3067	Mill Creek	Melody/Rick	9-18	10-20	10-23	10-29	10-3	10-31	11-3
4015	Mountain Sq.	Rick	9-3	3-2	3-8	3-14	3-15	3-18	3-22
3012	Northway	Jane/Terry	8-7	9-8	10-5	10-19	10-20	10-22	10-23
3079	Oak Tree	Marla/Bob	9-11	10-13	10-17	10-23	10-24	10-27	10-28
1290	Overlake E.	Billie/Rick	8-3	9-3	9-10	9-14	9-16	9-23	9-25
3064	Regional	Melody/Terry	9-1	10-1	10-8	10-19	10-21	10-22	10-26
3011	Silverada	Billie/Bob	8-21	9-22	9-25	10-1	10-2	10-3	10-6
PR607	Spanaway	Marla/Rick	8-7	9-7	9-14	9-21	9-25	9-28	9-29
2020	Sunset Vil	Marla/Bob	10-9	11-9	11-14	11-17	11-18	11-19	11-22
3077	TRF Annex	Marla/Jessica	9-25	10-27	10-3	11-4	11-5	11-6	11-7
2095	TRF Office	Marla/Jessica	8-28	9-29	10-5	10-9	10-12	10-13	10-14
3063	Twin Lakes	Jane/Jessica	10-9	11-10	11-13	11-20	11-21	11-24	11-25
3033	Wash Plaza	Melody/Bob	8-14	9-15	9-28	10-6	10-8	10-29	10-30
3040N	Westgate N	Thom/Diana	9-21	10-21	10-24	10-30	10-31	11-3	11-4
3040S	Westgate S	Melody/Diana	9-4	10-7	10-10	10-16	10-17	10-20	10-21
30C0	Westwood	Marla/Rick	10-16	11-17	11-19	11-21	11-24	11-25	11-26
3028	Woodinville	Debbie/Rick	9-4	10-6	10-9	10-15	10-16	10-17	10-20

PA - Project Administrator   PM - Property Manager   PM/Super - Property Manager Supervisor

Numbers to the property manager—The project administrator provides the property manager with a spread sheet showing the income and expense projections on a monthly basis.

Typist—The budget, along with the annual management plan narrative, is given to the typist for first-draft typing.

Property manager and supervisor review—The property manager's supervisor reviews the first draft of the management plan and budget. The management plan is proofread for errors.

Corrections—The typist makes corrections.

Mail to owner—Before mailing to the owner, the property manager makes a final review of the management plan.

§ 3.4   DEVELOPING THE OPERATING EXPENSE BUDGET

Each item in the operating expense budget needs to be analyzed on a month-by-month basis to arrive at the total expenses for each month. A budget input form is used for each operating budget. Exhibit 3.2 is an example of a shopping center common area maintenance budget. By listing each expense for each maintenance item on a monthly basis, the manager develops a month-by-month operating expense. Combining all the operating budgets, landlord's and common area maintenance (CAM), along with the expenses for taxes, insurance, and any other expenses provides a month-by-month operating expense budget. When the monthly operating expenses are subtracted from the monthly income components, the result is a month-by-month net operating income (NOI) projection.

With this budget format, any month with a negative NOI or negative cash flow after debt service and capital expenses can be identified in advance and the timing of some expenses, especially major nonrecurring expenses, can be shifted to a period with positive cash flow. Identifying months with negative cash flow allows the property owner to plan for cash shortages. Conversely, positive cash flow projections are monitored for cash management planning.

The property manager must consider seven elements before arriving at expense numbers.

(a)   INSPECTIONS

It is impossible to develop an accurate and meaningful budget without an inspection. The property manager reviews prior inspection forms, and notes future maintenance items and capital improvement items on these forms. The manager then inspects the property. If major maintenance or capital improvement is needed, such as roof repair or replacement, a consultant is hired to analyze the problem.

EXHIBIT 3.2

Budget Input Form

PROJECT NO: _____ PROJECT NAME: _____ PERIOD: _____ PREPARED BY: _____ PAGE _____ OF _____

DATE: _____

GEN. LEDGER ACCT. NO.	DESCRIPTION	JAN.	FEB.	MARCH	APRIL	MAY	JUNE	JULY	AUG.	SEPT.	OCT.	NOV.	DEC.	TOTAL YEAR	% Gross Sched @ 100%	$/SQ FT
	PAGE TOTAL															
	CARRY FORWARD															
	TOTAL															

INPUT DATE: _____ REVISION DATE: _____ APPROVED BY: _____ DATE: _____

Carry Forward — If the income or expense items are too numerous for one page, the total of these items on the other page(s) is included on this line.

% Gross Schedule — The percentage this income or expense total is to the entire budget.

$/sq. ft. — The income or cost per square foot of the total building. For example, janitorial services may be $ .95 per square foot

(b) HISTORICAL DATA

One method of developing an operating budget is to add an inflation factor to the current year's budget. However, this method doesn't take into consideration nonrecurring expenses, capital improvement, the market's impact on the property, and major cost adjustments for specific expenses such as substantial increases in electrical rates or real estate taxes. This budget approach is not usually accurate.

Former President Carter popularized the zero-based budget that required analyzing each expense without consideration for past and current expenditures. The budget method that will be outlined in this chapter is similar to a zero-based budget. However, historical expenses and current expenditures will provide a frame of reference when developing the operating budget.

Historical and current expense data can assist in developing the operating budget in the following ways:

- Comparing the proposed budget to prior budgets on a per-item basis will ensure that an expense category is not missing from the proposed budget.
- Through use of historical data trends may be identified. For example, an older medical building was undergoing continued plumbing repairs. This trend suggested that a major plumbing problem was about to occur.
- Expenditures over several years can be used for reference to validate bids. If the janitorial costs have been around 80 cents per square foot per year, and the janitor's new bid is in the high 90-cent range, the present janitorial contractor may be overly confident about winning the contract award. In this case additional bids are necessary.
- Historical data can indicate that either the maintenance specifications are wrong or a contractor misinterpreted the bids. For instance, if full-service landscaping service has been costing $1,000 a month and some bids are coming in at $600 to $800 a month, the property manager should check the bid specifications against the contractor's specifications for missing items such as pruning or weed control.

(c) PUBLICATIONS

Publications distributed by real estate associations are another source for comparing operating expenses. The Institute of Real Estate Management (IREM) publishes *Office Buildings Income and Expense Analysis* (Exhibits 3.3 and 3.4) as well as Income and Expense Analysis Shopping

EXHIBIT 3.3

Operating Expenses for Suburban Office Buildings
Selected Metropolitan Areas

METROPOLITAN ANALYSIS BY RENTAL RANGE   SUBURBAN

SUBURBAN OFFICE BUILDINGS				RENTAL RANGE DALLAS, TX				$0.01 - $9.99			
CHART OF ACCOUNTS	\$/GROSS AREA OF ENTIRE BLG.			\$/GROSS RENTABLE OFFC. AREA				\$/NET RENTABLE OFFC. AREA			
	BLGS SQ. FT. (10000)	MED.	RANGE LOW / HIGH	BLGS SQ. FT. (10000)	MED.	RANGE LOW / HIGH		BLGS SQ. FT. (10000)	MED.	RANGE LOW / HIGH	
INCOME											
OFFICES	35	589	7.62	6.55 8.81	14	181	7.53	6.90 9.08	32	513 8.45	6.96 9.02
GROSS POSSBLE INCOME	35	589	7.51	6.47 8.82	14	181	7.33	6.67 8.31	32	513 8.50	7.22 9.09
VACANCY/DELIN.RENTS	35	589	2.23	.16 2.83	14	181	1.97	.02 2.83	32	513 2.40	.45 3.07
TOTAL COLLECTIONS	35	589	5.44	4.43 6.56	14	181	6.43	5.07 7.10	32	513 6.20	5.18 7.16
EXPENSES											
SUBTOTAL UTILITIES	35	589	1.22	1.00 1.43	14	181	1.42	1.11 1.54	31	513 1.37	1.10 1.56
JAN.PAYROLL/CONTRACT	34	583	.35	.25 .46	13	175	.37	.33 .57	31	507 .38	.28 .45
SUBTOT JAN/MAINT/RPR	35	589	.93	.75 1.15	14	181	1.05	.72 1.20	32	513 .99	.84 1.26
MANAGEMENT FEE	35	589	.29	.21 .36	14	181	.30	.26 .34	32	513 .30	.21 .38
SUBTOTAL ADMIN/PAYRL	35	589	.86	.60 1.07	14	181	.87	.44 1.11	32	513 .98	.66 1.13
INSURANCE	33	501	.11	.09 .13	14	181	.12	.10 .14	30	435 .11	.08 .13
SUBTOTAL INSUR/SRVCS	35	589	.47	.36 .54	14	181	.52	.36 .66	32	513 .52	.41 .59
NET OPERATING COSTS	35	589	3.64	2.97 3.99	14	181	3.80	3.39 4.26	32	513 3.86	3.47 4.26
REAL ESTATE TAXES	35	589	.90	.72 1.03	14	181	.87	.73 .92	32	513 .95	.84 1.04
TOTAL OPERATNG COSTS	35	589	4.53	4.09 4.98	14	181	5.00	4.26 5.29	32	513 4.91	4.47 5.29

SUBURBAN OFFICE BUILDINGS				RENTAL RANGE DALLAS, TX				$10.00 - $12.99			
CHART OF ACCOUNTS	\$/GROSS AREA OF ENTIRE BLG.			\$/GROSS RENTABLE OFFC. AREA				\$/NET RENTABLE OFFC. AREA			
	BLGS SQ. FT. (10000)	MED.	RANGE LOW / HIGH	BLGS SQ. FT. (10000)	MED.	RANGE LOW / HIGH		BLGS SQ. FT. (10000)	MED.	RANGE LOW / HIGH	
INCOME											
OFFICES	31	548	11.13	10.21 11.70	12	231	12.00	11.57 12.50	25	471 11.51	10.70 12.00
GROSS POSSBLE INCOME	31	548	11.58	10.55 12.19	12	231	12.46	11.71 12.82	25	471 11.95	11.48 12.27
VACANCY/DELIN.RENTS	31	548	2.95	.46 3.60	12	231	1.84	.46 2.38	25	471 3.29	1.13 4.13
TOTAL COLLECTIONS	31	548	8.53	7.19 10.18	12	231	10.76	9.15 11.57	25	471 9.02	7.43 10.52
EXPENSES											
SUBTOTAL UTILITIES	31	548	1.34	1.11 1.62	12	231	1.51	1.34 1.63	25	471 1.48	1.19 1.64
JAN.PAYROLL/CONTRACT	31	548	.47	.36 .54	12	231	.47	.44 .52	25	471 .49	.37 .57
SUBTOT JAN/MAINT/RPR	31	548	1.19	.94 1.33	12	231	1.31	1.12 1.38	25	471 1.19	1.02 1.38
MANAGEMENT FEE	31	548	.30	.26 .40	12	231	.36	.27 .42	25	471 .34	.27 .43
SUBTOTAL ADMIN/PAYRL	31	548	.88	.73 1.07	12	231	.81	.76 1.02	25	471 .95	.80 1.22
INSURANCE	31	548	.09	.07 .13	12	231	.10	.06 .12	25	471 .11	.08 .16
SUBTOTAL INSUR/SRVCS	31	548	.43	.42 .48	12	231	.46	.42 .48	25	471 .47	.44 .56
NET OPERATING COSTS	31	548	3.86	3.49 4.21	12	231	3.80	3.71 4.36	25	471 4.01	3.71 4.94
REAL ESTATE TAXES	31	548	.98	.89 1.14	12	231	1.06	.95 1.18	25	471 1.12	.98 1.25
TOTAL OPERATNG COSTS	31	548	5.03	4.40 5.36	12	231	5.03	4.69 5.41	25	471 5.25	4.50 6.00

SUBURBAN OFFICE BUILDINGS				RENTAL RANGE DALLAS, TX				$13.00 - $15.99			
CHART OF ACCOUNTS	\$/GROSS AREA OF ENTIRE BLG.			\$/GROSS RENTABLE OFFC. AREA				\$/NET RENTABLE OFFC. AREA			
	BLGS SQ. FT. (10000)	MED.	RANGE LOW / HIGH	BLGS SQ. FT. (10000)	MED.	RANGE LOW / HIGH		BLGS SQ. FT. (10000)	MED.	RANGE LOW / HIGH	
INCOME											
OFFICES	22	641	12.98	12.70 13.52	11	346	13.85	13.44 13.93	18	385 14.34	13.67 15.05
GROSS POSSBLE INCOME	22	641	13.55	12.92 15.40	11	346	14.33	13.56 15.09	18	385 15.06	14.31 16.22
VACANCY/DELIN.RENTS	22	641	3.19	1.42 5.57	11	346	5.07	1.14 6.00	18	385 3.40	1.53 5.91
TOTAL COLLECTIONS	22	641	10.01	8.20 12.23	11	346	9.67	7.04 12.47	18	385 12.26	9.42 14.55
EXPENSES											
SUBTOTAL UTILITIES	22	641	1.31	1.16 1.40	11	346	1.45	1.22 1.46	18	385 1.42	1.22 1.57
JAN.PAYROLL/CONTRACT	22	641	.48	.39 .53	11	346	.46	.32 .56	18	385 .52	.42 .60
SUBTOT JAN/MAINT/RPR	22	641	1.14	.93 1.37	11	346	1.15	.94 1.41	18	385 1.18	1.08 1.48
MANAGEMENT FEE	19	563	.32	.23 .55	9	320	.34	.24 .49	15	316 .39	.27 .56
SUBTOTAL ADMIN/PAYRL	21	640	.91	.68 1.05	10	345	1.08	.71 1.11	17	384 .97	.67 1.22
INSURANCE	22	641	.11	.08 .14	11	346	.13	.10 .15	18	385 .13	.09 .16
SUBTOTAL INSUR/SRVCS	22	641	.54	.36 .67	11	346	.57	.36 .61	18	385 .60	.41 .70
NET OPERATING COSTS	22	641	3.97	3.49 4.18	11	346	4.19	3.29 4.34	18	385 4.29	3.77 4.41
REAL ESTATE TAXES	22	641	1.31	1.11 1.43	11	346	1.40	1.06 1.45	18	385 1.42	1.22 1.70
TOTAL OPERATNG COSTS	22	641	5.33	4.80 5.61	11	346	5.33	4.74 5.95	18	385 5.63	5.19 6.15

FOOTNOTE: SQUARE FOOTAGE FIGURES (SQ.FT.) ARE REPORTED IN MULTIPLES OF TEN THOUSAND. SEE GUIDELINES SECTION FOR EXPLANATION OF REPORTS AND INTERPRETATION OF DATA. COPYRIGHT 1989, IREM.

Income/Expense Analysis: Office Buildings, Downtown & Suburban (1989)

Source: Reprinted with permission from the Institute of Real Estate Management.

EXHIBIT 3.4

Income/Expense Analysis: Shopping Centers
Open and Enclosed 1991

SELECTED METROPOLITAN AREAS   **OPEN**

OPEN SHOPPING CENTERS																
						METROPOLITAN DENVER, CO										

CHART OF ACCTS	$/TOTAL POTENTIAL GLA				$/TOTAL AVG. ACTUAL OCCUP.				$/BALANCE TOTAL POTENTIAL GLA			$/BALANCE AVG. ACTUAL OCCUPANCY		
	CENTERS	SQ. FT. (10000)	MED.	RANGE LOW / HIGH	CENTERS	SQ. FT. (10000)	MED.	RANGE LOW / HIGH	CENTERS	SQ. FT. (10000)	-$- MED	CENTERS	SQ. FT. (10000)	-$- MED
EXPNS-OPEN/CA														
MAINT & REPAIR														
PRKG LOT/SDWLK	5	58	.03	.01 .03	5	52	.04	.02 .04	5	35	.07	5	30	.07
SWEEPING	6	71	.10	.04 .13	6	63	.13	.04 .14	6	40	.17	6	34	.19
ROOF REPAIR	3	31	.04	.00 .04	3	27	.04	.01 .04	3	22	.05	3	18	.06
PLUMBING	4	50	.01	.00 .01	4	45	.01	.00 .01	4	33	.01	4	28	.01
ELECTRICAL	6	71	.03	.00 .03	6	63	.03	.01 .03	6	40	.04	6	34	.05
PAINT/DECORATE	5	66	.02	.02 .11	5	61	.02	.02 .11	5	35	.05	5	31	.07
OTHER	4	48	.05	.03 .05	4	43	.05	.03 .05	4	30	.09	4	25	.10
SUBTOTAL M & R	6	71	.29	.10 .30	6	63	.30	.21 .31	6	40	.51	6	34	.56
SERVICES														
OUTDR LANDSCAPE	6	71	.04	.02 .16	6	63	.05	.02 .17	6	40	.11	6	34	.14
SNOW REMOVAL	6	71	.10	.03 .12	6	63	.13	.03 .18	6	40	.15	6	34	.18
SECURITY	4	50	.35	.02 .35	4	45	.37	.02 .37	4	33	.37	4	28	.73
TRASH REMOVAL	5	58	.06	.01 .11	5	52	.07	.01 .12	5	35	.11	5	30	.23
CLEANING	4	53	.08	.01 .08	4	50	.08	.02 .08	4	30	.15	4	27	.16
OTHER	4	48	.00	.00 .00	4	43	.00	.00 .00	4	30	.01	4	25	.01
SUBTOTAL SRVCS	6	71	.59	.19 .64	6	63	.67	.23 .76	6	40	.61	6	34	1.18
UTILITIES														
ELECTRICITY	4	56	.06	.05 .06	4	51	.07	.05 .07	4	30	.12	4	26	.14
HVAC FUEL-ELEC	1	5	.14	.14 .14	1	2	.28	.28 .28	1	5	.14	1	2	.28
-OIL														
-GAS	1	8	.02	.02 .02	1	7	.03	.03 .03	1	3	.07	1	2	.10
-STEAM														
-OTHER														
WATER & SEWER	6	71	.07	.01 .11	6	63	.12	.02 .12	6	40	.15	6	34	.17
COMB ELEC	1	10	.23	.23 .23	1	10	.24	.24 .24	1	5	.44	1	5	.47
OTHER	2	22	.08	.01 .08	2	21	.08	.01 .08	2	10	.15	2	9	.17
SUBTOTAL UTILS	6	71	.16	.09 .21	6	63	.17	.11 .41	6	40	.27	6	34	.40
OTHER														
ADMIN FEE														
OTHER CA EXPNS	1	5	.02	.02 .02	1	2	.03	.03 .03	1	5	.02	1	2	.03
TAXES														
R/E TAX	6	71	1.04	.78 1.73	6	63	1.55	1.08 1.82	6	40	2.40	6	34	3.08
-ANCHOR OWNED	2	35	.48	.21 .48	2	33	.52	.22 .52	2	22	.66	2	20	.72
-ANCHOR G/L														
-ANCHOR B/L	2	18	.48	.37 .48	2	17	.56	.38 .56	2	8	1.51	2	7	2.02
-OUTPARCEL G/L														
-OUTPARCEL B/L	2	22	.49	.09 .49	2	21	.55	.09 .55	2	10	1.17	2	9	1.60
-BALANCE	6	71	.78	.53 1.26	6	63	1.35	.60 1.55	6	40	1.27	6	34	1.72
OTHER TAX/FEES	2	29	.00	.00 .00	2	28	.00	.00 .00	2	16	.01	2	15	.01
INSURANCE	6	71	.16	.12 .16	6	63	.18	.15 .19	6	40	.29	6	34	.32
-LIABILITY	3	37	.08	.02 .08	3	33	.08	.02 .08	3	20	.11	3	17	.12
-PROPERTY	3	31	.08	.03 .08	3	28	.08	.04 .08	3	13	.15	3	11	.16
-OTHER	3	37	.01	.00 .01	3	33	.01	.00 .01	3	20	.02	3	17	.03
SUBTOTL INS/TAX	6	71	1.15	.90 1.89	6	63	1.80	1.17 2.00	6	40	2.75	6	34	3.73
OTHER EXPENSES														
ADMIN PAYROLL	1	12	.01	.01 .01	1	11	.01	.01 .01	1	5	.02	1	4	.03
MANAGEMENT FEE	5	66	.40	.37 .51	5	61	.42	.39 .54	5	35	.71	5	31	.76
MERCH/MKTG	1	19	.08	.08 .08	1	18	.08	.08 .08	1	11	.14	1	10	.15
PROF SRVCS	3	31	.07	.06 .07	3	28	.07	.06 .07	3	13	.13	3	11	.18
MARKETING	1	7	.01	.01 .01	1	7	.02	.02 .02	1	3	.05	1	2	.06
OTHER MAINT	2	13	.19	.19 .19	2	10	.39	.22 .39	2	8	.59	2	4	.79
OTHER HVAC	4	45	.03	.01 .03	4	39	.03	.01 .03	4	23	.03	4	18	.05
FOOD COURT														
OTHER	1	8	.01	.01 .01	1	7	.01	.01 .01	1	3	.02	1	2	.03
TOTAL EXPENSES	6	71	3.02	2.04 3.02	6	63	3.31	3.14 3.71	6	40	5.76	6	34	6.20

E/I RATIO (TAE/TAI) .31	MGT FEE CAM REIMBURSABLE (% YES) 50%

FOOTNOTE: SQUARE FOOTAGE FIGURES (SQ.FT.) ARE REPORTED IN MULTIPLES OF TEN THOUSAND. SEE GUIDELINES SECTION FOR EXPLANATION OF REPORTS AND INTERPRETATION OF DATA. COPYRIGHT 1991, IREM.

Source: Reprinted with permission from the Institute of Real Estate Management.

Centers (Open and Enclosed). The Building Owners and Managers Association (BOMA) publishes the *Experience Exchange Report* (Exhibit 3.5). These two annual publications analyze office building operating expenses for every major metropolitan area and several secondary cities in the United States. Analyses are classified by size and age of buildings. The International Council of Shopping Centers (ICSC) routinely publishes the *Shopping Center Operating Cost Analysis Report* (Exhibit 3.6). This report provides operating expenses for strip centers and enclosed malls within different regions. Samples of reports found in these three association publications are shown in Exhibits 3.3 to 3.6.

All of these publications are used to compare expenses. A major variance in an expense category in one of the publications indicates the expense should be further analyzed. For instance, if real estate taxes in any of these publications average 75 cents per square foot per year for the city in which the property is located and the current projected tax expense is $1.10, this variance should be further analyzed and possibly a tax consultant called in to compare the assessed valuation with comparable building valuation. If there is no apparent justification for the variance, the taxes should be appealed.

(d) COMPARING EXPENSES WITH BUILDINGS IN THE AREA

Information is shared freely in the property management profession. Active membership in IREM, ICSC, and BOMA provides an opportunity to meet other property managers and to share experiences. It is common for property managers to seek information from each other. This professional network is invaluable when developing a budget for a building when historical expenses are not available or for a building under construction or proposal.

(e) CURRENT YEAR'S EXPENSES

A budget is usually developed some time between the middle to the end of the current budget period and is finalized a month or two before the current budget period ends. Some of the most helpful information for developing a budget can be obtained from the current budget period's actual and estimated expenses. The actual expenditures and estimates of the expenses for the remaining budget period are the best guidelines for preparing a budget.

The property manager takes the current year's expenses to date and estimates the expenses for the remaining budget period. Actual and projected expenses are combined to obtain accurate estimates for the current year's budget. The property manager then reviews the budget explanation information (See the discussion of budget explanation information in § 3.5.) and determines if the reasoning for the remaining expenses is still

EXHIBIT 3.5

1989 BOMA Experience Exchange Report

CITY ANALYSES 1988   **U.S. PRIVATE SECTOR**

Washington, DC
DOWNTOWN 50,000-100,000 SQ. FT.

		TOTAL BUILDING RENTABLE AREA				TOTAL OFFICE RENTABLE AREA			
7 BLDS		561,014 SQ. FT.				550,357 SQ. FT.			
	#	DOLLARS/SQ. FT.		MID RANGE		DOLLARS/SQ. FT.		MID RANGE	
INCOME	BLDS	AVG	MEDIAN	LOW	HIGH	AVG	MEDIAN	LOW	HIGH
OFFICE AREA	6					21.01	22.04	15.27	26.88
RETAIL AREA	3	33.47	25.79						
OTHER AREA	2	8.56	9.79						
TOTAL RENT	6	21.21	23.01	15.27	26.27				
MISCELLANEOUS	4	.28	.34	.15	.41				
TOTAL INCOME	6	21.39	23.21	15.27	26.56				
EXPENSE									
CLEANING	7	1.12	1.14	1.02	1.19	1.14	1.17	1.04	1.23
REPAIR/MAINT	7	1.59	1.61	1.37	1.97	1.62	1.70	1.39	2.01
UTILITIES	7	2.30	2.02	1.91	2.52	2.34	2.12	1.96	2.56
RDS/GRNDS/SEC	7	.41	.51	.18	.55	.42	.54	.19	.55
ADMINISTRATIVE	7	.81	.80	.51	1.02	.82	.80	.52	1.07
TOTAL OPER EXP	7	6.25	6.46	5.68	6.74	6.37	6.80	5.79	6.91
FIXED EXPENSES	7	3.23	3.45	3.12	3.52	3.29	3.55	3.14	3.62
TOTAL OPER + FIX	7	9.48	9.87	8.58	10.35	9.67	10.40	8.78	10.61
LEASING EXP	6	2.34	.54	.37	5.54				
TOTAL PAYROLL	7	.96	.76	.70	1.23				
TOTAL CONTRACT	7	2.26	2.13	1.41	3.08				

OCCUPANCY INFO.		BLDS
AVG SQFT/OFFICE TENANT	4479	7
AVG SQFT/RETAIL TENANT	1526	3
AVG SQFT/OFFICE WORKER	272	6
AVG % OFFICE OCCUPANCY	92.0	7
AVG % RETAIL OCCUPANCY	84.3	3
AVG $ RATE YR-END RENT	25.74	7
RENTABLE/GROSS SQFT	90	5

DETAIL*	AVERAGE	BLDS	DETAIL*	AVERAGE	BLDS	DETAIL*	AVERAGE	BLDS	DETAIL*	AVERAGE	BLDS	DETAIL*	AVERAGE	BLDS
CLEANING TOTAL	1.12	7	UTILITIES TOTAL	2.30	7	SECURITY TOTAL	43	5	FIXED EXP TOTAL	3.40	6	TOTAL PAYROLL	96	7
PAYROLL	53	2	ELECTRICAL	1.79	7	SEC PAYROLL			REAL ESTATE TAX	3.08	6	CLEANING	53	2
CONTRACT	1.04	6	GAS	08	6	SEC CONTRACTS	37	5	BUILDING INS	17	6	REPAIR/MAINT	75	7
SUP/MAT/MISC.	02	6	FUEL OIL	43	3	SEC OTHER			PERS PROP TAX	00	6	RDS/GROUNDS		
TRASH REMOVAL	07	6	PURCH STEAM			**ADMIN TOTAL**	.81	6	OTHER TAX	14	6	SECURITY		
REPR/MAINT TOTAL	1.59	7	PURCH CH WTR			PAYROLL			LEASING EXPENSES	2.71	5	TOTAL CONTRACTS	2.26	7
PAYROLL	75	7	COAL			MGMT FEES	80	5	ADV/PROMOTION	24	3	CLEANING	1.04	6
ELEVATOR	17	7	WATER/SEWER	30	6	PROF FEES	13	3	COMMISSIONS	56	3	REPAIR/MAINT	49	7
HVAC	18	7	**RDS/GNDS/SEC**	.39	6	GEN OFC EXP	05	5	PROF FEES			RDS/GROUNDS	05	4
ELECTRICAL	05	6	TOTAL			OTHER ADM EXP	04	5	TENANT ALTS	1.78	4	SECURITY	37	5
STRUCT/ROOF	09	4	RDS/GNDS TOTAL	06	4				BUY-OUTS			ADMINISTRATIVE	88	5
PLUMBING	07	5	RDS/GNDS PAYRL						OTHER LEASING	1.39	3			
FIRE/LIFE SFTY	01	2	RDS/GNDS CONTR	05	4									
OTHER MAINT/SUP	35	7	RDS/GNDS OTHER	02	3									

*TOTAL BUILDING RENTABLE AREA-AVERAGE DOLLARS/SQ. FT.   ©1989 BOMA Experience Exchange Report

DOWNTOWN 100,000-300,000 SQ. FT.

		TOTAL BUILDING RENTABLE AREA				TOTAL OFFICE RENTABLE AREA			
46 BLDS		8,694,819 SQ. FT.				8,033,078 SQ. FT.			
	#	DOLLARS/SQ. FT.		MID RANGE		DOLLARS/SQ. FT.		MID RANGE	
INCOME	BLDS	AVG	MEDIAN	LOW	HIGH	AVG	MEDIAN	LOW	HIGH
OFFICE AREA	42					22.72	21.81	18.20	26.89
RETAIL AREA	36	20.69	22.29	15.36	30.94				
OTHER AREA	15	6.56	9.40	5.22	10.82				
TOTAL RENT	45	22.62	22.11	18.60	26.04				
MISCELLANEOUS	44	.45	.17	.03	.40				
TOTAL INCOME	45	23.06	22.35	18.88	26.44				
EXPENSE									
CLEANING	46	.99	1.02	.92	1.08	1.06	1.08	.97	1.16
REPAIR/MAINT	46	1.25	1.23	1.00	1.45	1.34	1.31	1.06	1.55
UTILITIES	43	1.67	1.69	1.50	1.88	1.75	1.75	1.60	1.96
RDS/GRNDS/SEC	46	.27	.25	.11	.35	.29	.26	.11	.38
ADMINISTRATIVE	45	1.04	1.09	.90	1.24	1.12	1.22	.91	1.35
TOTAL OPER EXP	42	5.18	5.33	4.60	5.81	5.61	5.82	5.04	6.19
FIXED EXPENSES	46	3.49	3.62	3.07	4.07	3.78	3.91	3.47	4.35
TOTAL OPER + FIX	42	8.65	8.91	7.89	9.75	9.37	9.56	8.72	10.43
LEASING EXP	44	.81	.27	.11	.64				
TOTAL PAYROLL	42	.75	.71	.59	.90				
TOTAL CONTRACT	42	2.47	2.62	2.15	2.91				

OCCUPANCY INFO.		BLDS
AVG SQFT/OFFICE TENANT	6798	46
AVG SQFT/RETAIL TENANT	3045	39
AVG SQFT/OFFICE WORKER	328	22
AVG % OFFICE OCCUPANCY	94.1	46
AVG % RETAIL OCCUPANCY	91.4	39
AVG $ RATE YR-END RENT	25.52	36
RENTABLE/GROSS SQFT	95	40

DETAIL*	AVERAGE	BLDS	DETAIL*	AVERAGE	BLDS	DETAIL*	AVERAGE	BLDS	DETAIL*	AVERAGE	BLDS	DETAIL*	AVERAGE	BLDS
CLEANING TOTAL	1.00	42	UTILITIES TOTAL	1.69	39	SECURITY TOTAL	19	40	FIXED EXP TOTAL	3.58	42	TOTAL PAYROLL	75	42
PAYROLL	13	10	ELECTRICAL	1.53	39	SEC PAYROLL	14	7	REAL ESTATE TAX	3.19	42	CLEANING	13	10
CONTRACT	92	41	GAS	04	15	SEC CONTRACTS	16	40	BUILDING INS	15	41	REPAIR/MAINT	63	41
SUP/MAT/MISC.	02	42	FUEL OIL	05	24	SEC OTHER	18	11	PERS PROP TAX	00	22	RDS/GROUNDS		
TRASH REMOVAL	06	42	PURCH STEAM			**ADMIN TOTAL**	1.06	42	OTHER TAX	26	37	SECURITY	14	7
REPR/MAINT TOTAL	1.24	42	PURCH CH WTR			PAYROLL	12	26	LEASING EXPENSES	85	40	TOTAL CONTRACTS	2.47	42
PAYROLL	63	41	COAL			MGMT FEES	80	41	ADV/PROMOTION	04	35	CLEANING	92	41
ELEVATOR	14	42	WATER/SEWER	11	39	PROF FEES	15	38	COMMISSIONS	38	36	REPAIR/MAINT	46	42
HVAC	15	42	**RDS/GNDS/SEC**	.26	42	GEN OFC EXP	02	42	PROF FEES	03	8	RDS/GROUNDS	05	35
ELECTRICAL	03	38	TOTAL			OTHER ADM EXP	04	36	TENANT ALTS	17	32	SECURITY	16	40
STRUCT/ROOF	15	31	RDS/GNDS TOTAL	05	35				BUY-OUTS			ADMINISTRATIVE	92	42
PLUMBING	02	37	RDS/GNDS PAYRL						OTHER LEASING	37	13			
FIRE/LIFE SFTY	01	19	RDS/GNDS CONTR	05	35									
OTHER MAINT/SUP	16	42	RDS/GNDS OTHER	01	19									

*TOTAL BUILDING RENTABLE AREA-AVERAGE DOLLARS/SQ. FT.   ©1989 BOMA Experience Exchange Report

Source: Reprinted with permission of Building Owners and Managers Association (BOMA) International, Washington, DC.

EXHIBIT 3.6

Shopping Center Operating Analysis Report, 1989

Item	N	Mean	Median	Q1	Q3
Maintenance & Repair	46	0.621	0.441	0.270	0.713
Exterior	26	0.690	0.286	0.102	0.489
Parking Lot	26	0.253	0.150	0.094	0.211
Janitorial	19	0.168	0.108	0.063	0.196
Repairs	13	0.113	0.065	0.036	0.188
Landscaping	17	0.146	0.097	0.047	0.207
Miscellaneous	12	0.165	0.094	0.057	0.191
Building/Structural/Systems	22	0.070	0.059	0.021	0.091
Exterior Electricity	15	0.035	0.027	0.011	0.046
Insurance	24	0.073	0.054	0.036	0.096
Fire	12	0.048	0.037	0.024	0.081
Liability	13	0.042	0.025	0.015	0.067
General & Administrative & Marketing	43	0.414	0.293	0.198	0.465
Leasing & Management Fee	30	0.260	0.230	0.166	0.302
Leasing Fee	20	0.120	0.108	0.070	0.146
Management Fee	28	0.219	0.204	0.149	0.257
Professional Fees	19	0.069	0.047	0.020	0.096
Legal Fees	15	0.031	0.020	0.014	0.048
Marketing	11	0.036	0.024	0.016	0.038
Miscellaneous Aggregations:					
Interior & Exterior (M&R)	28	0.339	0.286	0.138	0.428
Interior & BSS (M&R)	23	0.094	0.082	0.024	0.140
Exterior & BSS (M&R)	30	0.374	0.327	0.146	0.533
Water & Sewer (Utilities)	11	1.205	0.084	0.018	0.167
Payroll & G&A&M	31	0.259	0.223	0.167	0.293
M&R & Security	47	0.640	0.465	0.276	0.722
G&A&M & Security	43	0.417	0.293	0.196	0.500

Source: International Council of Shopping Centers

valid or if the situation has changed and new assumptions will require revised estimates.

(f) COMPETITION'S IMPACT ON THE BUDGET

Outside influences may impact a building's operating and capital budgets. This in turn affects the marketing and leasing of the building. New developments and upgrading of existing competition always require careful analysis of a building's marketing features. The property manager drives through the area in which the competition is located looking for new and upgraded buildings. These buildings should be toured, compared, and assessed for their impact on the subject building. A site that is vacant when the budget is developed can become a competing building ready for occupancy during the budget period. Low-rise office buildings, industrial properties, and shopping centers can be constructed in less than a year.

It is important to consider such additional competition from new developments and upgraded buildings in formulating a building's leasing and occupancy projections. The city or county building department will usually provide information on plans for new developments. The property manager analyzes the impact of these plans on his or her building and considers whether additional improvements to the building must be included in either the operating or the capital budget.

(g) MARKET CONDITIONS

Market conditions will affect the operating and capital budgets and the income projections. In a soft leasing market, capital improvements and/or upgrading maintenance is often necessary to maintain or improve the building's market position. A market survey, which is part of the management plan, needs to be conducted in the early stages of the budget process. (See Chapter 7 for more information on market surveys.) The market survey will provide the data necessary to project leasing activity and occupancy, which in turn are needed to project all of the income components. This information is helpful when determining whether to upgrade the common areas and the exterior of the building.

§ 3.5 BUDGET FORMAT

All property owners require accurate budget forecasting. Owners need to plan for those months that have a deficit and those months that have excessive cash. A detailed month-to-month budget will provide a monthly net operating income (NOI) forecast. When the property's debt service and capital expenses are included in the budgeting process, a monthly cash flow projection can be developed

Each income component, base rent, percentage rent, and recovery of operating expenses from the tenants is budgeted separately. Each operating budget, owner's nonreimbursable expenses, common area maintenance, escalation expense, and other expenses are also budgeted separately. The budget input form (Exhibit 3.2) can be used for each income component and each operating budget. A similar format is found in most property management software programs. When each income component and each operating expense is budgeted and totaled and the expenses are subtracted from the income, a NOI forecast is produced.

The budgeting process is straightforward but time-consuming. Creating the proper procedures, budget format, and forms will assist in developing an accurate and timely income and expense analysis.

(o) BUDGET EXPLANATION FORM

The property owner's approved budget forms the basis upon which the property is managed. A commercial property manager manages either a portfolio of several small- to medium-sized properties or serves as an on-site manager for a large project. In both of these situations, the property manager will have a large number of monthly line items to budget.

It is easy to overlook budget items planned that occur several months after the budget is developed. A budget explanation form (Exhibit 3.7) allows the property manager to explain each budgeted expense item. The property manager is able to plan, bid, and administer the budgeted nonrecurring expense items by periodically referring to the form throughout the year. The nonrecurring maintenance items can easily be tracked throughout the year by placing them on a calendar or entering them into a computerized deferred conditions or a maintenance report. This form can be included in the property's annual management plan.

§ 3.6 CHART OF ACCOUNTS

Until the 1980s, property management firms developed and used their own chart of accounts for segregating and identifying income components and operating expenses. When institutions became the major owners of medium- to large-sized commercial properties, property management firms found, to their dismay, that many of their clients would no longer accept their standard chart of accounts and financial reports. Institutional owners, who contract with large numbers of property management firms, cannot operate efficiently and develop

EXHIBIT 3.7

Budget Explanation Form

GENERAL LEDGER ACCT NO	DESCRIPTION	EXPLANATION

PROJECT NO _____ PROJECT NAME _____ PERIOD _____ PREPARED BY _____ DATE: _____

PAGE ____ OF ____

INPUT DATE: _____ REVISION DATE _____ APPROVED BY: _____ DATE: _____

their internal reports if every property management firm reporting to them uses a different chart of accounts and reporting format. Property management firms must be able to accommodate the financial reporting requirements of each client and potential client. However, there are some clients, primarily private investors, developers, and some institutional owners, who will accept the property management firm's standard chart of accounts and financial reports.

Provided in Exhibit 3.8 is a commercial property management firm's chart of accounts listed numerically. In Exhibit 3.9 the same chart of accounts is listed alphabetically. These forms need to be modified for use with residential properties.

Commercial properties have several operating budgets. All properties will have a landlord's operating budget for expenses that are not reimbursed by the tenants. These expenses include legal fees, partnership audit, utilities cost for vacancies, the cost to clean vacancies in shopping centers and industrial properties, and the landlord's share of the merchants' association or marketing fund dues for shopping centers.

Office buildings will have a second operating budget for the building's operating expenses, sometimes referred to as escalation costs or charges billed to the tenants. Multitenant industrial properties may have a common area operating or escalation budget that is charged to the tenants.

Shopping centers can have multiple operating budgets. A non-enclosed or open shopping center, also referred to as a strip center, will have a common area maintenance (CAM) budget. If the shopping center is an enclosed mall, a second common area maintenance budget for the enclosed mall is developed. The reason for two CAM budgets is that tenants who are not on the mall, such as a bank or a fast food restaurant located on a pad or outlot, or a strip building out in the parking lot with shops, will not be charged for the cost to maintain the enclosed mall common areas.

In addition, major tenants, primarily department stores, often negotiate to pay only common area maintenance for the parking lot and not for the mall areas. The major tenant contends that it does not need the draw of the mall, and its customers have access to the store from the parking lot. Landlords disagree with this position. During lease negotiations, department stores are usually in a stronger negotiating position and often negotiate to pay no enclosed mall common area maintenance charge or just a nominal amount.

The shopping center may have a merchants' association or marketing fund that will also need an operating budget. These costs are covered by the dues paid by the merchants and landlord. This budget is developed by the shopping center's marketing director. If the shopping center doesn't have a marketing director, the property manager will develop this budget.

EXHIBIT 3.8

Chart of Accounts—Numerical List

Administrative—71000

71100	Advertising
71101	Merchants assoc. contributions
71105	Entertainment & promotion
71110	Contributions
74105	Automobile lease expense
74108	Parking/ferry tolls
74110	Automobile repairs & maintenance
74810	Management fees
74875	Management fees—cash
75510	Insurance expense
76100	Air freight
76105	Bank charges
76110	Dues and subscriptions
76115	Office equipment rental
76120	Office supplies
76125	Postage
76130	Repairs and maintenance
76135	Telephone expenses
76140	Miscellaneous expense
77100	Accounting fees
77105	Consulting fees
77110	Legal fees
77115	Architect fees
77120	Leasing commissions
78100	Business tax
78105	Licenses
78110	Permits
78115	Personal property tax
78120	Real estate tax
78125	Sales tax on capital additions
79100	Air fare
79105	Car rental
79110	Lodging
79115	Meals
80100	Salaries
80105	Payroll taxes
80110	Profit sharing expenses
80115	Insurance—life
80120	Insurance—medical/dental
80130	Gasoline
80135	Management training

Utilities—81000

81100	Electricity
81200	Gas

Utilities (cont.)

81300	Oil
81400	Water
81500	Sewer
81900	Other utilities

Building supplies—83000

83100	Licenses & permits
83150	Alarm
83200	Music
83300	Signs
83350	Supplies
83400	Tools/equipment/uniforms
83450	Rentals
83500	Trash removal

Repairs, maintenance & contract service—84000

84110	Salaries
84120	Payroll taxes
84130	Employee benefits
85100	Building repairs/ maintenance
85200	Flooring
85300	Ceilings
85400	Landscaping
85410	Window maintenance
85500	Roof
85600	Elevator/escalator
85700	Plumbing/sprinklers
85800	Parking lot
85900	Security
86000	Janitorial
86100	Painting
86200	Sweeping/snow removal
86300	Electrical
86400	HVAC
86500	Insurance damage
86600	Reserve account

Tenant costs—89000

89100	Tenant repairs
89200	Tenant improvements
89220	Landlord improvements
90000	Rent expenses
96000	Federal income tax expense

EXHIBIT 3.9

Chart of Accounts—Alphabetical List

Administrative—71000

Accounting fees	77100
Advertising	71100
Air fare	79100
Air freight	76100
Architect fees	77115
Automobile lease expense	74105
Automobile repairs & maintenance	74110
Bank charges	76105
Business tax	67100
Car rental	79105
Consulting fees	77105
Contributions	71110
Dues & subscriptions	76110
Entertainment & promotion	71105
Gasoline	80130
Insurance—life	80115
Insurance—medical/dental	80120
Insurance expense	75510
Leasing commissions	77120
Legal fees	77110
Licenses	78105
Lodging	79110
Management fees	74810
Management fees—cash	74875
Management training	80135
Meals	79115
Merchants assoc. contributions	71101
Miscellaneous expense	76140
Office equipment rental	76115
Office supplies	76120
Parking/ferry tolls	74108
Payroll taxes	80105
Permits	78110
Personal property tax	78115
Postage	76125
Profit sharing expenses	80110
Real estate tax	78120
Repairs & maintenance	76130
Salaries	80100
Sales tax on capital additions	78125
Telephone expenses	76135

Building supplies—83000

Alarm	83150
Licenses & permits	83100

Building supplies (cont.)

Music	83200
Rentals	83450
Signs	83300
Supplies	83350
Tools/equipment/uniforms	83400
Trash removal	83500

Repairs, maintenance & contract services—84000

Building repairs/ maintenance	85100
Ceilings	85300
Electrical	86300
Elevator/escalator	85600
Employee benefits	84130
Flooring	85200
HVAC	86400
Insurance damage	86500
Janitorial	86000
Landscaping	85400
Painting	86100
Parking lot	85800
Payroll taxes	84120
Plumbing/sprinklers	85700
Reserve account	86600
Roof	85500
Salaries	84110
Security	85900
Sweeping/snow removal	86200
Window maintenance	85410

Tenant costs—89000

Federal income tax expense	96000
Landlord improvements	89220
Rent expenses	90000
Tenant improvements	89200
Tenant repairs	89100

Utilities—81000

Electricity	81100
Gas	81200
Oil	81300
Other utilities	81900
Sewer	81500
Water	81400

Since almost all commercial properties have two or more operating budgets, the property management firm needs to develop a simple method of identifying which expenses are the landlord's nonreimbursable cost, or an escalation or common area maintenance expense. This can be accomplished by adding a prefix identifying the particular budget to the expense account number.

For instance, 1 is the landlord's nonreimbursable budget prefix; 2 is shopping center common area maintenance/parking lot budget; 3, shopping center common area maintenance/enclosed mall budget; 4, office building and industrial property escalation budget; 5, merchants' association/marketing fund budget and so on. The cost to wash the windows in a vacant shopping center space would be a landlord's nonreimbursable expense 1-84510, while the cost to wash the windows on the mall entrance would be a common area maintenance/mall expense, 3-85410.

§ 3.7   ANALYZING OPERATING EXPENSES

Each expense item is analyzed separately. When analyzing each expense, do not determine the annual cost and divide this number by twelve to arrive at a monthly expense. Since an expense is seldom a constant amount for every month, each expense has to be analyzed on a month-by-month basis. Even when a maintenance contract has a fixed monthly price for full service such as landscape maintenance, there is usually periodic maintenance that is not part of the contract, or a need may arise for emergency repairs that cannot be included in the base contract.

An analysis of several expense components follows. Once the manager understands the process and rationale behind each item, any expense item can be analyzed and budgeted.

(a)   AUDIT FEES

The landlord's expenses may include a partnership audit fee. Consult with the property owner for the cost of this service. Retail tenants' sales should be audited periodically to ensure that they are submitting accurate sales figures and paying the correct amount of percentage rent. After determining the number of tenants to audit, the property manager can obtain cost estimates from firms specializing in tenant audits.

(b)   COMMISSIONS

Commissions are estimated by first determining the amount of new space that will be leased and the amount of space that will be renewed. Next, the property manager reviews the leasing agreement to determine the commission schedule for new space, renewals, and pad tenants. These two variables are used to compute the commission expense.

(c) ELEVATORS

Most property managers know less about elevator maintenance than they do about HVAC maintenance, so they usually rely on a maintenance contractor. Bid specifications must be carefully prepared or, if they originate with the bidders, they must be carefully compared. Will the contract be a full maintenance contract? If a local small contractor with a lower bid than a national contractor is hired, the property manager must determine if the contractor has an adequate supply of parts and sufficient service people available for emergency and after-hours service. Should the property manager enter into a long-term maintenance agreement, usually five years, to receive a discount?

All of these issues must be considered when developing elevator maintenance costs. A light-load credit should be negotiated in the contract. This provides a discount for occupancy below a certain level and is usually a series of discounts based on different occupancy levels

(d) HVAC MAINTENANCE

This is another area in which property managers generally rely on the service contractor. When bidding the preventive maintenance, the contractor usually will provide the maintenance specifications, which can vary significantly from contractor to contractor. Each bid must be compared for frequency of maintenance, the items to be inspected and how often, and the type of filters provided by the contractor.

The property manager may hire a consultant to develop the preventive maintenance specifications. The manufacturer of the equipment may also provide such specifications. Some buildings hire building engineers to perform all HVAC maintenance. In Los Angeles, the building engineers' union has an education program for its members, and many buildings hire these engineers for an in-house maintenance program. If this is the case, the budget will reflect the number of engineers or chief engineers and their payroll costs.

The HVAC contractor can usually estimate accurately the cost of nonpreventive maintenance work and work not covered in the maintenance contract.

(e) INSURANCE

Insurance expense is based on the type of coverage and its cost, which depends on the type of building, the building's features, and its location.

The property owner will determine the type and limits of coverage for the building, and the insurance agent will provide the estimated cost of the coverage.

(f) JANITORIAL

Janitorial costs for office space may be determined by dividing the cost into two areas—common areas and occupied spaces. The cost to clean the common areas is not affected by occupancy unless a floor is totally vacant. Obtain a cost, either a dollar amount or a cost per square foot, for the common area. Then obtain a cost per square foot for occupied space. The common area cost for occupied floors is added to the cost to clean the tenants' spaces. To determine the cost to clean the tenants' spaces, multiply the cost per square foot per month to clean the occupied spaces times each month's projected occupancy.

Another approach is to obtain a price to clean the entire building based on 100% occupancy and allow a credit for each square foot of vacant space.

Shopping centers have only common areas to clean. The property manager determines the number of janitors needed each day and their schedule. The number of janitors will vary based on weekdays, nights, weekends, and peak selling seasons. The janitorial company will bid on these hours and the specifications for cleaning. If the janitorial service is in house, the property manager can calculate janitorial expense by determining the payroll cost of each janitor, the number of hours worked each week, and the cost of the supervisor.

(g) LANDSCAPING

There are three components to the landscape expense: the monthly maintenance contract fee or monthly in-house maintenance cost, periodic maintenance expenses, and the cost of replacing and upgrading planting materials. When developing the monthly maintenance cost, the property manager must carefully review the contractor's specifications. Some specifications will provide for full maintenance, including pruning, weed control, and spraying, while others will provide for the minimum monthly maintenance.

After calculating the monthly charge, the cost of the periodic maintenance, pruning, and weed control is determined if it is not included in the monthly maintenance service.

The third variable is plant replacement and upgrading. The property manager should inspect the property with a landscaper, checking for plants and trees that have been damaged or stolen. The manager reviews the landscaping needs and decides if upgrading is necessary to maintain the property's image or to be more competitive in the market. An estimate from a landscaper is submitted with the list of new planting materials.

(h) LEGAL FEES

Legal fees are usually the result of evictions, landlord-tenant disputes, or lease negotiations. Current cases are reviewed with an attorney to estimate what it would cost to resolve the disputes. The delinquencies are reviewed to determine which tenants will require legal action and, based on present legal costs, an estimate can be determined.

(i) MAINTENANCE PAYROLL

Maintenance employees' costs include salaries, payroll costs, and employee benefits. These are estimated by determining the specifications or job requirements, the number of maintenance personnel needed, the salaries for each person, the number of hours each staff person will work, cost of overtime, and the hours for replacement help for vacations and sick leave. The cost is usually constant each month except for additional personnel added for specific maintenance jobs, seasonal needs such as the Christmas period for shopping centers, possible bonuses or incentive pay, and periodic salary reviews.

(j) MANAGEMENT FEE

The management fee is relatively easy to estimate for properties with a high occupancy. Management fees are generally a percentage of income collected or a flat fee. In some cases, the management fee is a percentage versus a minimum fee, whichever is greater.

First review the management agreement, which will define how the management fee is calculated. If the fee is a percentage of income, it is either a percentage of the base rents and percentage rents collected or a percentage of all income collected. All income will include the base and percentage rent plus the income from tenant charges such as escalation or common area maintenance charges and reimbursement for taxes and increased expenses.

After estimating the income components, multiply these components by the management fee percentage. Apply this formula to each monthly income projection to arrive at a monthly management fee. If the building is in a lease-up stage, the process is the same but the accuracy of the estimated management fee is based on the accuracy of the lease-up projections. When the management fee is a minimum fee rather than a percentage, the minimum fee is budgeted for each month.

(k) MERCHANTS' ASSOCIATION/MARKETING FUND

If the shopping center has a merchants' association or marketing fund, the landlord is usually a major contributor. The tenant's lease generally stipulates both the landlord's and the tenant's obligation. Landlords usually pay between 25 and 33 percent of what the tenants contribute.

The property manager must first total the contributions from all the tenants and then multiply this amount by the percentage of the landlord's contribution. If the center opens with a low occupancy, the landlord may be willing to pay dues based on a 100 percent occupancy to provide the association or fund with operating capital.

If the center is new, the tenants and landlord may have a grand opening contribution. In this case, the method for calculating the landlord's obligation is the same. If the center is opening with a low occupancy, some landlords will contribute the tenant's grand opening dues and collect this amount from tenants that open within one year of the center's grand opening. However, it is difficult to collect grand opening dues from tenants who open a year later.

(l) PAINTING

Painting expense consists of contract painting and painting supplies. Before developing the numbers for the budget, the property manager inspects the property and identifies areas that will need painting and bids these jobs. On-site maintenance personnel will need painting supplies for small jobs and touch-ups.

(m) PARKING LOT MAINTENANCE

The parking lot must be thoroughly inspected for signs of cracking, raveling, or alligatoring. If major repairs are needed, a parking lot consultant should develop specifications for repair and their estimated cost. If only minor repairs are needed, a reliable asphalt or concrete contractor can provide a cost estimate for the budget. A month or two before the work begins, the job is bid by three or more contractors, including the contractor who provided the estimate for the budget.

The Institute of Real Estate Management publishes two excellent bulletins on parking lot maintenance: Bulletin 365, *Pavement Rehabilitation*, by Edward Cook; and Bulletin 381, *Effective Maintenance of Asphalt Paving*, by David J. Garber, CPM. The Asphalt Institute in College Park, Missouri, has produced an audio and visual tape series on asphalt maintenance. This series is excellent for an in-house seminar. Such instructional materials help the property manager identify problems and take corrective action. Accurate projections of parking lot maintenance costs are essential in developing this line item expense.

(n) REPAIRS AND MAINTENANCE

This category is often divided into several accounts, such as plumbing, electrical, and painting. If no major problem exists or is anticipated in these areas, historical expense data are usually a good reference in estimating the expenses for the next budget period. If inspection or service requests indicate major problems in any of these areas, a consultant or contractor should inspect the building to determine the problem, possible solutions, and the estimated cost for each solution.

(o) ROOFS

The process for budgeting roof maintenance is the same one used for budgeting parking lot maintenance. The International Council of Shopping Centers publishes an excellent bulletin on roof maintenance titled *The Worry-Free Roof*. The Institute of Real Estate Management publishes three bulletins on roof maintenance: Bulletin 354, *Roof Repair and Maintenance*, by Kai W. Adler; Bulletin 367, *Why Comprehensive Roof Inspection?* by H.Z. Lewis, P.E.; and Bulletin 374, *The Maintenance Roof*, by Heydon Lewis, P.E. These bulletins explain how to conduct a roof inspection, what to look for, and how to develop a roof maintenance program.

(p) SECURITY

The security needs of the building must be regularly assessed. Security can be a drive-by patrol, part-time to full-time on-site guards, and monitoring devices. Once the property manager has analyzed the building's security needs, the security program is bid. If on-site guards are part of the security program, the property manager must develop the hours per day the guards will be on site and provide the schedule to security companies bidding the assignment. Most security contracts are bid on an hourly rate. The rate for drive-by security patrols is usually based on the number of times the property is visited each night. (See Chapter 4).

(q) SNOW REMOVAL

Snow removal is one of the most difficult expenses to estimate because it is dependent primarily upon the weather. However, even with this uncontrollable factor the property manager can develop a prudent and economical strategy.

The first step is to develop a snow removal strategy as outlined in § 10.15. Next, the cost to remove the snow, push the snow to a different area of the parking lot, and clear the sidewalks can be calculated. Then the property manager must determine how often per month each of the above will be required during a normal year's snowfall.

(r) SUPPLIES

Paper supplies are either provided by the janitorial company and included in the janitorial costs or purchased by the property manager. The amount of paper products used by the tenants depends upon the occupancy of the building. The company that supplies the paper products can usually provide a fairly accurate estimate of the amount of paper products used if the property manager tells the supplier how many people work in the building. Another approach to estimating paper cost is to compare the estimated occupancy for the budget period with occupancy for the current year and adjust the cost of paper products accordingly.

The amount of paper products used in a mall's common area doesn't change significantly from one year to the next unless the mall expands or the occupancy level drops. If the amount of products consumed is approximately the same, the other variable is a change in the cost of the product caused by a price increase or by changing suppliers.

Other types of supplies such as hardware, tools, or uniforms are usually insignificant expenses that do not vary from year to year but need to be estimated and included in the budget.

(s) PARKING LOT SWEEPING

Parking lot sweeping is usually contracted. The property manager determines the frequency of sweeping, develops sweeping specifications, and accepts bids. In many areas, sweeping is dependent upon the weather. Sweeping is not needed when snow is on the ground, but a major spring cleanup is necessary to remove dirt and gravel that build up during the snow season. In other areas, sweeping is needed more frequently during the windy winter months than in the summer months.

(t) TAXES

Estimating real estate taxes is similar to estimating utility costs in that all of the information often is not available when the budget is prepared. The two factors required for estimating this expense are the assessed valuation and the millage rate. The safe method of estimating the assessed value for a new building is to combine the cost of construction and the land value and multiply this amount by the projected millage rate. It is highly unlikely that the first year's assessed value will exceed this estimate.

When a building is assessed while it is under construction, the assessed value represents the value of the land and the cost of the construction as of the date the building is assessed. In this situation, the property manager confirms with the assessor's office the date the building will be assessed and estimates the cost or value of the construction as of that date. Some municipalities assess all buildings on the same date—December 31, for example. Existing buildings have the benefit of the current year's valuation for reference.

The other factor is the millage rate. This rate is set by the city or county government. If the new millage rate hasn't been established, the property manager can review the changes in the millage rate over the past five years to establish trends along with proposed increases as reported in the local newspaper. Multiply the millage rate by the assessed valuation to determine the tax amount.

If the property was recently sold, the assessor may use the sale price as the market value and hence the assessed value. The property manager must constantly monitor the property's assessment to assure that it is fair and consistent with the assessment of comparable properties. Budgeting the real estate tax estimate provides an additional opportunity to review the current year's assessment. The fairness of the assessed value can also be reviewed when the assessment is received.

(u) TELEPHONE AND ANSWERING SERVICE

There are a few telephone charges that can be classified as either an escalation/common area expense or a landlord's expense. All elevators should have a telephone connected directly to a 24-hour answering service or a 24-hour guard station. The telephone and answering service expense is a building's escalation expense. If the building has an on-site management office, the answering service, which is needed for after-hours emergencies, is a building expense.

(v) TRASH REMOVAL

This expense is somewhat like a utility expense. Seldom does the property manager select the trash removal company. Either the municipality removes trash or a private contractor has an exclusive contract with the municipality to serve an area. Rates are determined by frequency of service and/or volume of trash removal and are established or approved by the municipality.

The volume of trash removed from the building is determined by the building's occupancy level and use. The property manager must determine the frequency of trash pickup and/or the size and number of trash receptacles. After determining this, the trash removal company can quote a monthly fee. Community and regional shopping centers may need to budget for additional trash removal during the Christmas season and other peak selling periods.

(w) UTILITIES

The two factors to consider when estimating utility expense are the billing rate and consumption. Keep in mind, however, that billing rates can change during a budget period and that consumption during lease-up time is difficult to predict.

When estimating the rate, the property manager should contact the utility company's representative for the property's area. The representative can provide the current billing rate and information concerning any rate increase during the budget period. This information cannot usually be obtained by just calling the utility company, so the property manager needs to develop a working relationship with the utility company's local representative. One way to build rapport is to request an energy audit of the building. Another opportunity is to work with the utility company when developing the building's emergency procedures.

If the projected rate increases cannot be obtained from the utility company, the property manager will project a rate increase by analyzing the rate increases during the past three to five years. Special note should also be given to recent rate adjustments and news stories about the local and national cost of energy as well as the financial condition of the utility company.

The other factor in estimating utility cost is the building's monthly consumption, which is based on the number and types of fixtures, the mechanical equipment, the occupancy rate, and the type of occupant.

Estimating utility costs for a shopping center differs from estimating an office building's costs. A shopping center's utility costs include common areas, vacancies, and utilities that are master-metered to all the tenants. The parking lot common area utilities include electricity for lighting and water for irrigation. To estimate parking lot lighting, calculate the hourly kilowatt usage and the number of hours the lights will be on each month. The type and number of fixtures will provide the amount of kilowatts consumed each hour. The property manager can estimate the hours the lights will be on each day. In the southern part of the United States, these hours will be fairly constant year round; in the northern states, parking lot lighting hours vary as much as four to five hours per night from summer to winter.

The formula for determining water consumption is not as simple as that for electricity consumption. The total expense for water can usually be obtained from the landscaper or the water company's representative. If the property is more than a year old, both the electricity and the water usage amounts are available for the prior twelve-month period. In this case, the property manager need only apply the projected billing rate to the prior year's usage.

The utilities for an enclosed mall are the lighting, water for irrigation, and the gas/electricity for the HVAC units. The manufacturer or installer of the HVAC equipment can estimate the kilowatts of electricity or BTUs of gas that will be consumed in an hour and the number of hours the equipment will operate during each month. This information, along with the billing rate, will provide the utility cost for the

HVAC equipment. Again, if the shopping center has been in operation for more than a year, the historical utility consumption is available.

If a utility—water, for example—is master-metered, the property manager can provide the utility company with a list of the types of businesses in the center, and the utility company will estimate the average consumption for each business.

In an office building, the utility consumption includes interior common area lighting, parking lot or garage lighting, lighting for occupied spaces, gas or electricity to operate the mechanical systems, and water consumption. The common area lighting and mechanical systems usage is estimated the same way as the shopping center common area utilities and HVAC units are estimated. The occupied space consumption is based on the average usage per 1,000 or 10,000 square feet with adjustment for tenants with overstandard usage.

Another way to estimate usage for new buildings is to request the utility consumption from other property managers who manage similar buildings. Estimating utility consumption on existing buildings with a history of usage is fairly simple; estimating consumption for a new building or a building in lease-up is difficult. The utility's cost will vary each month based on consumption, and the monthly variance can be significant.

(x) VACANCY EXPENSE

Vacant spaces incur expenses. Vacancies in shopping centers and industrial properties have more direct expenses than vacancies in office buildings. Because of the separate utility metering and the street frontage of shopping center and industrial space, these spaces have a utility cost. Most municipalities assess a minimum meter charge whether or not the utility is used. In cold-weather regions, the space must be heated during the winter to prevent water freezing in the pipes. Since these are street front spaces, the exterior of the windows must be washed monthly or quarterly, and the inside windows washed semiannually.

It is important to the leasing effort that all vacancies be placed in condition to "show" as soon as possible because a dirty and unattractive space is difficult to lease. Accumulations of business cards, junk mail, cobwebs, and expired bugs must be removed regularly or they will create a very negative image for the prospective tenant. The interior of all vacant spaces must be cleaned periodically. Some spaces may need walls or ceiling repaired and painted and windows and floor coverings cleaned.

(y) WINDOW WASHING

In an office building, the property manager must determine how often interior and exterior windows should be washed and whether the ground floor windows need to be cleaned more frequently. Once the specifications have been developed, bids are requested from contractors. Industrial and shopping center tenants are responsible for cleaning their windows. For a mall, the property manager budgets the window washing in the common areas.

(z) EXPENSE EXPLANATION

Budgets are developed a few months before they go into effect. Each property has at least two operating budgets: the common area maintenance or escalation budget and the landlord's non-reimbursable budget. Each budget has multiple expense categories. Multiply the amount of data for each budget by the number of properties managed by a property manager and it becomes obvious why it is almost impossible to remember all the budgeted items, why they were included, how each expense was determined, and when each expense is to be incurred.

The budget explanation form (Exhibit 3.7) can be used to list each expense, how it was determined, and how the budget amount will be used. For example, under the landscaping category for a mall, a monthly $500 maintenance expense is budgeted, but lilies are added at Easter at a cost of $300, poinsettias are added in December at a cost of $400, and new plants are added in January for $750. The budget explanation form provides a quick and accurate explanation for each expense item and is a reminder of why an amount was budgeted.

§ 3.8   CAPITAL BUDGET

A capital expenditure is one that is expected to yield benefits in future accounting periods. Capital expenditures are recorded as assets and amortized over the periods believed to be benefited.

Capital improvements are usually nonrecurring expenses. Most capital improvements to a property are major expenses. Examples include carpeting over a concrete mall floor, replacing a roof, remodeling a lobby, installing extensive energy conservation or life safety equipment, and making tenant improvements.

The same principles used in developing an operating budget are applied to developing a capital budget. All budgets start with a property inspection. Many capital improvements, such as the ones listed above, require an expert's opinion and recommendation since few property managers have an in-depth knowledge of construction and engineering. When a consultant is needed, monies should be budgeted for the consultant's time.

Capital improvements to marketing features of the building, such as lobbies, restrooms, elevators, and lighting in a building's exterior and center court areas, have a direct impact on the leasing. Maintaining a building's competitive position is essential to maintaining its occupancy level and rental rates. The property manager, whether serving as the leasing agent or not, must continually analyze market conditions and be aware of the building's position in the market. One way to keep apprised of the building's position in the market is to compare its features with the competition's. The office building market survey form in Chapter 7 (Exhibit 7.2) provides a checklist of features for comparison.

After inspecting the building and determining its position in the market, the manager compiles a list of suggested capital improvements and develops estimates to present to the owner. The property manager must prepare thoroughly for this meeting to be able to explain why the expenditures are needed. The owner will often take the manager's recommendation under advisement and consider the expenditure in relation to the goals of the property and the owner's ability to fund the cost of the improvements. When the owner approves any of the recommended capital improvements, the property manager will have specifications for the work prepared and bid the job.

Property owners and their accountants do not always agree on whether an expense is a capital expense or an operating expense. One owner may take an aggressive position on how an expense should be treated, while another may take an opposite view. The property manager needs to understand how the owner treats these expenses.

§ 3.9   DEVELOPING INCOME PROJECTIONS

Each income component must be analyzed and projected on a monthly basis along with the operating expenses to develop a month-by-month net operating income and cash flow. The first step in developing the income projection is to review the tenants' lease summaries, which state the obligation to pay rent, percentage rent, and tenant charges. Exhibit 3.10 is a sample tenant roster that summarizes the terms of each lease in the Washington Plaza shopping center. The CAC column is for common area charges. "Yes" indicates that the tenant pays those charges.

(a)   BASE RENT

The base rent is the easiest income component to project. The lease summaries are reviewed to determine the monthly rent during the budget period. Careful attention is given to any fixed step-ups in the rent. If a lease expires during the budget period, the property manager ascertains whether the tenant will renew and estimates the renewal rate. If the tenant is not renewing, or the landlord refuses to renew, the property manager must estimate how long the space will remain vacant and during which months. Since it is wise to initiate renewals at least six

EXHIBIT 3.10

Tenant Roster

Bldg. Washington Plaza

Date 5-1-93

TENANT	SUITE #	TYPE OF STORE	SQ FT	RENT			SECURITY DEPOSIT	TERM YEARS	LEASE DATE	COMMENCE-MENT	TERMINA-TION DATE	% RENT	SPECIAL NOTES	C A C
				YEAR	$/SF	MONTH								
J & B Supermarket	A-1	Supermarket	40,000	201,000	5.03	Step-up	-	30	1984	4-1-85	3-31-15	2	Option	Yes
Ice Cream Store	A-2	Ice cream	1,200	15,600	13.00	1,300	1,300	7	1985	4-15-85	4-14-92	6	-	Yes
Karen's Beauty Supply	A-3	Beauty products	1,000	12,480	12.48	1,040	1,000	5	1985	6-1-85	5-30-90	6	-	Yes
Tony's Pizza	A-4	Restaurant	2,400	26,400	11.00	2,200	2,200	10	1985	7-15-85	7-14-95	5	Option	Yes
Cats and Dogs	A-5	Pet store	1,800	23,400	13.00	1,950	1,950	5	1985	6-1-85	5-30-90	6	-	Yes
Discount Shoes	A-6	Shoe store	2,400	22,800	9.50	1,900	1,000	7	1985	4-1-85	3-31-92	4	-	Yes
Hair Cuts	A-7	Barber shop	500	7,500	15.00	625	625	5	1985	4-1-85	3-31-90	8	-	Yes
Saver's Drugs	B-1	Drug store	20,000	120,000	5.00	10,000	10,000	20	1985	4-1-85	3-31-05	2	Option	Yes
Vacant	B-2	-	1,200	-	-	-	-	-	-	-	-	-	-	
Family Video	B-3	Video rental	2,400	31,200	13.00	2,600	2,600	5	1985	10-1-85	9-31-95	5	-	Yes
White's Cleaners	B-4	Cleaner	1,200	17,400	14.50	1,450	1,450	7	1986	2-1-86	1-31-93	7	-	Yes
Elegant Fabric	B-5	Fabric store	3,000	33,000	11.00	2,750	2,750	6	1985	11-1-85	10-31-91	6	-	Yes
Western Bank	B-6	Bank	1,800	27,000	15.00	2,250	-	10	1988	4-15-89	4-14-99	-	-	Yes
Vacant	B-7	-	1,100	-	-	-	-	-	-	-	-	-	-	
Burgers and Burgers	P-1	Fast food	3,540	30,000	Gro/rent	2,500	5,000	20	1987	2-1-88	1-31-08	3	Option	Yes

188

months before the lease expires, only tenants whose leases expire later in the budget period will need to be contacted.

Another determination in projecting base rents is the tenant's rent payment history. Financially weak tenants may move out before their lease expires, may make only partial payment, or may stop paying rent altogether. If any tenants fall in this category, the property manager needs to decide what course of action to take. Usually the tenant is evicted, and legal action is taken to recover the lost income. If the market conditions and the area's economy warrant, a retail tenant may be offered rent relief. In either case, the property manager must consider the financial impact of such adverse situations on the base rent income projections.

Each tenant's monthly rent for the budget period is recorded on a budget input form (Exhibit 3.11). After calculating the income that will be received each month from each space, the property manager totals each monthly income column. If the management company is computerized, it can print a monthly rent projection.

Note in Exhibit 3.11 that the supermarket rent stepped up in July. The form lists vacancies and the month in which a new tenant commences paying rent. Note that one space was projected to remain vacant until June and another until September. Adding each tenant's rent by month provides the monthly base rent income projection.

A similar analysis is prepared for percentage rent, escalation or CAM income, reimbursement of taxes and insurance, and any other income components. Adding all the income component budgets together provides a month-by-month income projection.

(b) LEASE-UP AND VACANCY PROJECTIONS

Vacant space will not remain vacant forever. The property manager must estimate when the space will be leased, at what rate, and when the rent will commence. The leasing agent is consulted for this projection. If the property manager is the leasing agent, a market survey must be conducted to determine the property's market rental rate and to project the amount of space that will be leased in the building and when.

Each vacant space is analyzed for its desirability, the rental rate it can command, and its probable lease date. For example, a shopping center has four vacancies: two 1,400-square-foot spaces, an 1,800-square-foot space, and a 5,500-square-foot space. The property manager projects that one 1,400-square-foot space will be leased in March with the tenant opening April 15 with one and one-half months' free rent. Rent payments begin June 1. The 1,800-square-foot space is projected to be leased in July with tenant occupancy in September and rent to commence October 1. There is little demand for the odd-shaped space of 5,500 square feet, which is projected to be leased in November with three months' free rent, which extends beyond the budget period. No base rent is projected for this space

EXHIBIT 3.11
Budget Input Form
Income

Project No.: 3032   Project Name: Washington Plaza   Period: 1994   Prepared by: RFM   Date: 11-5-93

Base Rent Income Projection

GEN. LEDGER ACCT.NO.	DESCRIPTION	JAN.	FEB.	MARCH	APRIL	MAY	JUNE	JULY	AUG.	SEPT.	OCT.	NOV.	DEC.	TOTAL YEAR	% Gross Sched @100%	$/SQ. FT.
	J & B Supermarket	16,500	16,500	16,500	16,500	16,500	16,500	17,000	17,000	17,000	17,000	17,000	17,800	201,000		
	Ice Cream Store	1,300	1,300	1,300	1,300	1,300	1,300	1,300	1,300	1,300	1,300	1,300	1,300	15,600		
	Karen's Beauty Sup	1,040	1,040	1,040	1,040	1,040	1,040	1,040	1,040	1,040	1,040	1,040	1,040	12,480		
	Tony's Pizza	2,200	2,200	2,200	2,200	2,200	2,200	2,200	2,200	2,200	2,200	2,200	2,200	26,400		
	Cats and Dogs	1,950	1,950	1,950	1,950	1,950	1,950	1,950	1,950	1,950	1,950	1,950	1,950	23,400		
	Discount Shoes	1,900	1,900	1,900	1,900	1,900	1,900	1,900	1,900	1,900	1,900	1,900	1,900	22,800		
	Hair Cuts	625	625	625	625	625	625	625	625	625	625	625	625	7,500		
	Saver's Drugs	10,000	10,000	10,000	10,000	10,000	10,000	10,000	10,000	10,000	10,000	10,000	10,000	120,000		
	Vacant	-	-	-	-	-	1,400	1,400	1,400	1,400	1,400	1,400	1,400	9,800		
	Family Video	2,600	2,600	2,600	2,600	2,600	2,600	2,600	2,600	2,600	2,600	2,600	2,600	31,200		
	White's Cleaners	1,450	1,450	1,450	1,450	1,450	1,450	1,450	1,450	1,450	1,450	1,450	1,450	17,400		
	Elegant Fabric	2,750	2,750	2,750	2,750	2,750	2,750	2,750	2,750	2,750	2,750	2,750	2,750	33,000		
	Western Bank	2,250	2,250	2,250	2,250	2,250	2,250	2,250	2,250	2,250	2,250	2,250	2,250	27,000		
	Vacant	-	-	-	-	-	-	-	-	1,375	1,375	1,375	1,375	5,500		
	Burgers & Burgers	2,500	2,500	2,500	2,500	2,500	2,500	2,500	2,500	2,500	2,500	2,500	2,500	30,000		
	PAGE TOTAL	47,065	47,065	47,065	47,065	47,065	48,465	48,965	48,965	50,340	50,340	50,340	50,340	583,080		
	CARRY FORWARD															
	TOTAL	47,065	47,065	47,065	47,065	47,065	48,465	48,965	48,965	50,340	50,340	50,340	50,340	583,080		

INPUT DATE: _____   REVISION DATE: _____   APPROVED BY   AAA   DATE: 11-5-93 during this budget period. The second 1,400-square-foot space is expected to remain vacant during the entire budget period.

The lease-up of a new office building is projected in a similar way, except that the manager looks at square footage instead of spaces leased. For instance, a 95,000-square-foot office building opens with 30,000 square feet occupied. With 7,500 square feet per month projected to be leased during the first six months and 5,000 square feet per month projected leased over the next three months, the building's occupancy is expected to stabilize at 90,000 square feet. Just as in the shopping center example, after projecting the amount of space that will be leased each month, the property manager tries to anticipate how long it will take to build out the tenant's space, when the tenants will move in, how much free rent will be offered, and when they will commence paying base rent.

Vacancy and lease-up projections are the most complex income projections. They are more likely to be accurate if the manager takes time to study the market, know the building and its competition, evaluate the leasing effort, and understand the owner's ability to make a deal.

(c) PERCENTAGE RENTS

Percentage rent is a significant income component in many shopping centers. Office buildings and multitenant industrial buildings can have percentage rental income from retail or service tenants such as restaurants and health clubs.

Percentage rent is also a difficult income component to project because the property manager has limited influence over the tenant's sales volume. A quick but imprecise way to project percentage rent is to increase every tenant's sales by a given percent over the prior year and compare that estimate with the tenant's breakpoint (the natural breakpoint is determined by dividing the tenant's annual rent by the percentage rate). The amount of sales in excess of the breakpoint is multiplied by the percentage rate to arrive at the percentage rent owed.

A more accurate method is to analyze each tenant separately to estimate its sales for the budget period. The first step in this process is to compare each tenant's breakpoint with its sales for the most recent twelve-month period. Tenants whose sales either exceed or are within 20 percent of their breakpoint are then analyzed. The remainder of the tenants have little if any chance of their sales exceeding their breakpoint and paying percentage rent.

Several criteria are used to estimate the sales of those tenants who are likely to pay percentage rent, including:

- Sales projections. This is the best source, but some managers and store owners will not share this information.
- Sales trends. If the tenant's sales have increased between 6% and 8% during each of the past five years, a similar increase is probable.

- New competition. A local hamburger restaurant is experiencing 10% increases every year; but if a new McDonald's comes into the area, the local restaurant's sales will undoubtedly drop.
- Tenant mix. If a shopping center is adding another major tenant, the center will have additional traffic, and the other tenants' sales can be expected to increase. Conversely, if a major tenant vacates the center, the other tenants' sales probably will decline.
- Product demand. The property manager must be aware of fads in the marketplace. Hula hoops and drive-in carhops on roller skates were popular in the 1950s, and in the early 1980s tanning salons and take-and-bake pizza operations were popular. However, novelties wane over the years, and many businesses that were once the rage lose their popularity and close.
- Managerial change. An exceptionally good store manager may be promoted to regional manager and replaced with an inexperienced and less capable person. Or, the reverse can happen: a store with poor sales growth may replace its management with an aggressive person, and sales will increase dramatically.
- Merchandise or design changes within the store. Has the store remodeled or added new lines of merchandise? Has merchandise of lesser quality replaced quality items? These moves will affect sales.

The above information can be used to estimate the tenant's sales for the budget period. If sales exceed the breakpoint, this amount is multiplied by the tenant's percentage rate.

Before the estimated amount of percentage rent can be included in the income projection, the property manager must check the tenant's lease for rights to recapture certain charges from percentage rent. In the 1950s and 1960s many national tenants, especially major tenants, negotiated the right to recapture some or all of their tenant charges—common area maintenance, taxes, and insurance, for example—from their percentage rent. This right has seldom been granted a tenant since the 1970s.

An example of a tenant's percentage rent estimate follows:

Last year's sales	$650,000
Projected sales increase	+ 52,000
Projected per annum sales	$702,000
Tenant's breakpoint	− 600,000
Sales in excess of breakeven point	102,000
Percentage rate 6%	× .06
Percentage rent	$ 6,120
Recapture from percentage rent	-0-
Percent rent projected	$ 6,120

This analysis is applied to each tenant whose sales are likely to exceed its breakpoint or breakeven point.

After estimating the percentage rent, the manager must project which months the tenant will pay it. Remember, percentage rent is paid when sales are reported, usually a month after they take place.

Most shop tenants pay their percentage rent monthly. Some national tenants pay on a quarterly basis, and major tenants usually pay annually. Most tenants will pay their percentage rent in December and January for November and December sales. Some tenants, such as a candy store where sales peak in February, April, June, November, and December, may pay percentage rent several months of the year, whereas a restaurant's sales and percentage rent can be constant each month. The tenants' monthly sales will indicate the months they are likely to pay percentage rent.

The last factor to consider in this income component is percentage rent refunds. Even though most tenants report sales figures monthly and pay percentage rent on a monthly basis, their sales are annualized. If a tenant's sales exceed the breakpoint one month, with payment of percentage rent the following month, but sales are below the breakpoint on an annualized basis, the percentage rent paid is then refunded.

A tenant's breakeven point is determined by dividing the percentage rate into the annual rental rate for the annual breakeven point and dividing this number by 12 to determine the monthly breakeven point.

The rent paid in excess of the base or minimum rent is known as percentage rent or overage rent (rent in excess or over the minimum rent).

(d) CONSUMER PRICE INDEX (CPI)

The consumer price index (CPI) is a monthly measure of changes in the prices of goods and services consumed by urban families and individuals. Compiled by the Bureau of Labor Statistics, the index is based on about 125,000 monthly quotations of prices, rents, and property tax rates collected from about 65,000 sources. The items range from food to automobiles and from rents to haircuts. The relative importance given to individual items in the index is based on periodic surveys of consumer expenditures. Current prices are expressed as a percentage of average prices during 1982–1984, but the 1967 base year figures are still being published. The monthly index is prepared for the nation as a whole, for each of 17 large metropolitan areas, for individual items, and for commodity and service groupings. All data are published in the U.S. Department of Labor's *Monthly Labor Review*.

Many leases have rent adjustments based on the increases in the CPI. The tenant's rent can be adjusted over any period of time, such as annually or every three years. The increase can be based on the percentage increase in the CPI or a fraction of that increase.

Most commercial leases use the CPI for metropolitan areas. All items are indexed for the nearest geographical area published for the population area of the property. The CPI adjustment is determined by comparing the current month's index for the selected city with the same index in the preceding year. Below is an example of an adjustment in the San Francisco area CPI:

January 1993 CPI	145.1
January 1992 CPI	140.3
Index adjustment	+4.8

To calculate the percentage adjustment in the CPI, divide 4.8 (the index adjustment) by 140.3 (the preceding year's index) for an increase of 3.4%.

If a tenant's rent was $1,000 per month, with an annual increase based on the January CPI increase, the increase in base rent would be $34 ($1,000 × 3.4%). The tenant's adjusted monthly rent would become $1,034.

If the increase was based on two thirds of the increase in the CPI, the increase would be 2.27% (3.4% × 0.66%). The increase in monthly rent would be $22.68.

(e)   COMMON AREA MAINTENANCE (CAM) INCOME

The property manager determines what percent of the CAM budget will be collected. Each tenant's lease summary states the tenant's share of the CAM budget. The percentages for all tenants are totaled for each month. The CAM budget is divided by twelve, and each month the percent of space that will pay reimbursements is multiplied into one month's CAM budget. If a tenant is not required to pay a pro rata share of a particular expense, such as security, the landlord will not be reimbursed for that portion of the expense. These figures can be calculated in minutes if the accounting system is computerized. Chapter 4 on shopping centers explains in detail the exceptions to a tenant paying the full pro rata share of CAM charges. The common area calculations form in Exhibit 3.12 is designed for easy calculation of each tenant's pro rata share of all tenant charges. The form indicates how each calculation was derived. Note that the denominator for the CAM is larger than the denominator for taxes and insurance by 3,540 square feet. Burgers and Burgers (P-1) is a pad tenant that pays its pro rata share of CAM but has a separate tax parcel and maintains its own insurance coverage. HVAC (heating, ventilating, and air-conditioning) is a charge from the landlord for the cost to contract the HVAC maintenance. The two major tenants—the supermarket and the drugstore—and the pad tenant maintain their own HVAC units.

After the percentages are established, tenant charges can be calculated in dollar amounts as shown In Exhibit 3.12. This type of form is
used when quoting estimated charges to prospective tenants.

(f) ESCALATION INCOME

Escalation income is billed to the office building tenants in one of three
methods: base year, stop clause, or triple net charge. First, develop the
building's operating expenses. Then review each tenant's lease summary
to determine the method of billing and which expense items are treated
as escalatable operating expenses. Calculate each tenant's pro rata share
of the operating expenses. If the tenant pays a base year escalation, establish the expenses for the base year and subtract them from the projected
operating expenses for the budget period. Multiply the increase in operating expenses above the base year by the percentage of space occupied by
the tenant to determine the tenants' share of the escalation budget.

When the operating expense stop clause is used, the dollar per
square foot of the stop is subtracted from the dollar per square foot of
operating expenses for the budget period. The tenant's square footage
is multiplied by the increase in operating expenses per square foot
above the stop expense. The resulting number is the amount of escalation income the tenant will pay.

Triple net leases are common in single-tenant industrial properties,
but some office buildings also use this method of escalation charge. The
tenant's percentage of occupancy of the building is multiplied times
the building's operating expenses.

When reviewing the lease summary, the property manager checks for
caps on the escalation charges. For instance, a tenant may pay its full pro
rata share of the escalation charge but not exceeding $1 per square foot
during each of the first three years of the lease.

A source of escalation income that is easy to overlook is space that will
be leased during the budget period. The lease up projection is reviewed,
and tenants who will occupy space that was recently vacant and commence paying escalation charges in the budget period are included in the
escalation income projections. Escalation income, like all other income
components, is estimated on a month-by-month basis.

(g) TAXES AND INSURANCE

Real estate taxes and building insurance are not included in the shopping center common area maintenance budget and usually are billed
separately in industrial properties. Although most office buildings include these expenses in their escalation budget, some office buildings
separate one or both of these expenses from the escalation budget. In
each of the above situations, except where these expenses are included

EXHIBIT 3.12
Tenant Common Area Calculations

Bldg: Washington Plaza

Tenant	Suite #	CAM			CAM Mall			Taxes			Insurance			Merchant Assoc.			Misc.	
		T.T. Sq.Ft.	Denom.	%	T.T. Sq.Ft.	Denom.	%	T.T. Sq.Ft.	Denom.	%	T.T. Sq.Ft.	Denom.	%	T.T. Sq.Ft.	$/SF	$	H.V.A.C.	Misc.
J & B Supermarket	A-1	40,000	83,540	47.9	-	-	-	40,000	80,000	50.	40,000	80,000	50.	40,000	.15	5000	-	
Ice Cream Store	A-2	1,200	"	1.4	-	-	-	1,200	"	1.5	1,200	"	1.5	1,200	.50	600	180	
Karen's Beauty Supply	A-3	1,000	"	1.2	-	-	-	1,000	"	1.3	1,000	"	1.3	1,000	.50	500	180	
Tony's Pizza	A-4	2,400	"	2.8	-	-	-	2,400	"	3.0	2,400	"	3.0	2,400	.50	1200	360	
Cats and Dogs	A-5	1,800	"	2.2	-	-	-	1,800	"	2.3	1,800	"	2.3	1,800	.50	900	240	
Discount Shoes	A-6	2,400	"	2.9	-	-	-	2,400	"	3.0	2,400	"	3.0	2,400	.50	1200	360	
Hair Cuts	A-7	500	"	0.6	-	-	-	500	"	0.6	500	"	0.6	500	.50	250	100	
Saver's Drugs	B-1	20,000	"	24.0	-	-	-	20,000	"	25.	20,000	"	25.	20,000	.25	5000	-	
Vacant	B-2	1,200	"	1.4	-	-	-	1,200	"	1.5	1,200	"	1.5	1,200	.50	600	180	
Family Video	B-3	2,400	"	2.8	-	-	-	2,400	"	3.0	2,400	"	3.0	2,400	.50	1200	360	
White's Cleaners	B-4	1,200	"	1.4	-	-	-	1,200	"	1.5	1,200	"	1.5	1,200	.50	600	180	
Elegant Fabric	B-5	3,000	"	3.6	-	-	-	3,000	"	3.8	3,000	"	3.8	3,000	.50	1500	400	
Western Bank	B-6	1,800	"	2.2	-	-	-	1,800	"	2.3	1,800	"	2.3	1,800	.50	900	240	
Vacant	B-7	1,100	"	1.3	-	-	-	1,100	"	1.4	1,100	"	1.4	1,100	.50	550	180	
Burgers and Burgers	P-1	3,540	"	4.2	-	-	-	-	-	-	-	-	-	3,540	.50	1770	-	
TOTAL		83,540						80,000			80,000			83,540				

in the escalation budget, the tenants must be billed separately for real estate taxes and insurance expenses.

Most commercial leases require the tenants to pay their full pro rata share of these costs. In the 1950s and 1960s, tenants often paid these expenses above a base year. Both of these methods of charging tenants are explained in the escalation billing section.

Most leases allow a special tax assessment, known as a Local Improvement District (LID) or bonded indebtedness, which is a charge for street improvements such as traffic lights and sidewalks, to be included in the real estate tax billings.

§ 3.10 BASE-YEAR TAX MODEL

The theory behind using the base-year approach to determining a tenant's pro rata share of expenses is that the minimum or base rent incorporates the operating expenses for the first year of the lease and any increases in operating expenses are paid by the tenant.

Although very few base-year leases are being negotiated in shopping center leases today, many older shopping center leases, along with office building and industrial property leases, exist that have these clauses. To be accurate, it is necessary to trace the base-year expense back to the original calculation. This figure should be included in the formula. Then calculate the current expense taking into account the proper base-year information.

The tenant's lease will state which year is the base year. This is usually the year the tenant moves into the building. If a tenant is in a strong negotiating position, the base year may be the year *after* the tenant takes occupancy of the leased premises. The base-year method for determining a tenant's share of an expense can be used for real estate taxes, insurance, office building escalation (operating expenses), or a shopping center's common area maintenance charges. (See Exhibit 3.13.)

(a) BASE-YEAR MODEL—OFFICE BUILDING

The base-year model for allocating operating expenses is used as an on-going record of the cost of operating the building and each tenant's specific agreement relative to those costs. The lease is the source document of the base year. Once the base year has been established, the actual costs for that year are recorded. When the current year's costs are known, the base-year costs are subtracted and the individual tenant's percentage is applied to that figure. If there are exceptions to the costs, they are generally noted after the percentage allocation so everyone is aware of them.

EXHIBIT 3.13

Base-Year Tax Model Form

Base-Year Tax Model
Parcel 860-31-7266

19X2–X3—29089.00
19X3–X4—30544.00
19X4–X5—32071.00
Current Year—48383.00

	Base Year[a]	Tenant Share[b]	Base-Year Tax[c]	Current Tax Year[d]	Net Due[e]
Pizza	X2–X3	12.38	3601.22	5989.82	2388.60
Jeweler	X3–X4	1.55	473.43	749.94	276.51
Clothing	X2–X3	7.59	2207.86	3672.27	1464.41
Clothing	None	4.95	-0-	2394.96	2394.96
Restaurant	X2–X3	4.95	1439.91	2394.96	955.05
Pool supplies	X2–X3	3.25	945.39	1572.45	627.06
Video	X2–X3	8.66	2519.11	4189.97	1670.86
Shoes	X2–X3	4.02	1169.38	1945.00	775.62
Clothing	None	8.87	-0-	1872.42	1872.42
Photo	X3–X4	3.53	1078.20	1707.92	629.72
Restaurant	X3–X4	3.53	1078.20	1707.92	629.72
Computer	X2–X3	3.53	1026.84	1707.92	681.08
Beauty salon	X2–X3	3.02	878.49	1461.17	582.68
Cleaners	X2–X3	6.03	1754.07	2917.49	1163.42
Yogurt	X2–X3	4.33	1259.55	2094.98	835.43
Title company	X2–X3	2.72	791.22	1316.02	524.80
Realty	X2–X3	2.04	593.42	987.01	393.59
Insurance	None	1.53	-0-	740.26	740.26
Shoe	X2–X3	1.53	445.06	740.26	295.20
Pet	X2–X3	3.06	890.12	1480.60	590.40
Travel	X2–X3	3.25	945.39	1572.45	627.06
Fast food	X2–X3	3.25	945.39	1572.45	627.06
Dentist	X2–X3	7.43	2161.31	3594.86	1433.55

[a]Tenant agrees to pay increases in taxes above the base year.
[b]The tenant's percentage of the total expense. This percentage is usually determined by calculating the percentage of the building that the tenant occupies.
[c]The pro rata share of the tax bill attributed to the tenant's premises in the base year.
[d]Same as above except ends in the current year.
[e]This amount is the difference between the current year tax and the base-year tax.

The tenant's insurance clause must be reviewed carefully to determine if the tenant pays a pro rata share of all of the landlord's insurance coverage. Some leases, especially with major tenants, will exclude certain coverage or place a limit on the amount of liability insurance they will reimburse the landlord.

(b) TENANT EXTRA SERVICES

Office building leases allow for a charge if the tenants request extra services. These services can consist of overstandard janitorial services, maintenance that is the responsibility of the tenant, and other miscellaneous jobs. This income component is projected by reviewing the tenant's extra service charges in the current year and determining if any new tenants will have a similar need.

(c) UTILITY INCOME

In the 1960s and early 1970s, several types of developments, particularly enclosed malls, billed electricity to tenants for a profit. The developer would contract with the utility company to purchase electricity that was metered on one master meter. The developer then paid the cost to run lines to submeters for each tenant. Tenants were billed the same rate they would be charged if they purchased the power directly from the utility company. The developer earned a profit by purchasing the electricity at a bulk rate (similar to a wholesale rate) and charging the tenants a retail price. Developers justified their profit by stating that it was a return on their investment of installing at their cost the utility lines and submeters. When managing a property with this situation, the manager must monitor the billing rate to ensure the tenants are being billed based on the correct rate.

(d) OVERSTANDARD UTILITIES

Some office building tenants consume more utilities than is normal for their space size, and most leases allow the landlord to bill the tenants for their overstandard usage. This extra usage is usually the result of special equipment, an excess of equipment consuming an inordinate amount of electricity, or after-hours use of lighting and HVAC service. The property manager must monitor the tenant's use of utilities. When a tenant has additional utility requirements, a consultant may be called in to determine the amount in excess of standard usage. The income received is credited to the building's escalation expenses because the expense will be charged to the escalation expenses. A simpler method is to separately meter the tenant's premises.

(e) OVERSTANDARD HVAC

Overstandard HVAC is a need of tenants who must keep their offices open beyond the building's hours of operation and tenants who need supplementary cooling. The property manager determines an hourly cost for HVAC, which includes the cost of electricity, the wear on the equipment, and the cost of the building engineer's time if he or she is required to be on site while the equipment is operating. The income generated is credited to the building's escalation expenses because this is where the expense is charged.

(f) TENANT IMPROVEMENT PROFIT

When tenant improvement work is performed by the building owner or property management company, a profit is added to the cost of the work. The profit is the typical profit a general contractor would earn and is either credited to the building owner or the property management company or is shared.

The property manager estimates the amount of tenant improvement work based on the amount of space that is projected to be leased and renewed, the type of tenant build-outs that new tenants are likely to need, and the improvements, if any, that will be required to renew leases. Tenant improvement fee is usually a percentage of the construction cost. Office tenants and most industrial tenants in multitenant buildings will require that tenant improvement be performed by the landlord. Shopping center tenants almost always perform their own tenant work.

(g) INTEREST INCOME

Interest income is a component that can easily be overlooked. Income received from each property should be deposited in an interest-bearing account. The property manager determines the average balance each month and multiplies this number by the interest rate paid on that account.

§ 3.11   RESERVES FOR REPLACEMENT

In any large income-producing property, major components will have to be replaced or major repairs will be needed at some point. It is prudent to estimate these needs, quantify them, and set aside sufficient cash to cover them.

Many owners choose not to set aside cash reserves. They prefer to use available monies as they are earned and worry about major repairs or replacements when they are needed. This is not an irresponsible approach, since the owner is counting on either increased cash flow, the likelihood of refinancing, or the probability of secondary financing or a line of credit.

Even if the final decision is not to reserve for replacement, the prudent manager will still estimate the reserves that may be needed and share this information with the property owner. It is not uncommon for a manager to evaluate the cash flow and arbitrarily set aside a percentage for reserves. Such a figure is more likely to be what the manager believes the property could afford rather than what the property may really need.

Taking a slightly different approach, the manager may set a reserve based on cents per square foot per year. A common reserve figure in a shopping center may be five cents per square foot per year. Obviously, a large reserve is not built up in this short time frame.

(a) NEEDS ESTIMATE

The most effective method of determining reserves that will be needed is to consider each major building component.

First, review which major components must be analyzed. In a strip shopping center, these components include the roof, the parking lot, and the exterior painting. Tenants are generally responsible for the air-conditioning unit.

The holding period of the property must be taken into consideration. No owner is going to worry about what work will have to be done after the property is sold. For easy calculations, our example will be a 100,000-square-foot strip shopping center. The owners will hold the center for ten years. The evaluation of each component is as follows:

- *Roof.* An evaluation of the roof indicates that it is generally in good condition, but one large section of 25,000 square feet will have to be replaced within five years. The estimated cost for this repair in five years is $30,000. To reserve for this cost, the $30,000 is divided by the five years available to accumulate the monies, for an annual reserve in the amount of $6,000. Dividing the cost by the square footage of the center—100,000 square feet—provides a reserve of six cents per foot per year.
- *Exterior Painting.* A physical inspection indicates that the center will need a complete paint job at the end of the eighth year. The estimated cost will be $80,000. Again, $80,000 divided by the years to accumulate the reserve indicates $10,000 per year will be needed. On a square footage basis the reserve is ten cents per square foot per year.
- *Major Parking Lot Repairs.* The parking lot is sound, but after three years it will need patching, resealing, and restriping. The cost

is estimated to be $30,000. The annual reserve is $10,000, and the per square foot reserve per year is ten cents.

(b) COLLECTION OF RESERVES

To establish a reserve fund, the center manager would set aside twenty cents per square foot for the next three years and ten cents per square foot for the following three years. These funds would likely be held in an interest-bearing account during this time. The manager would calculate the interest to be earned and reduce the amount set aside by the interest earned so that the interest and the actual reserves would provide the needed cash. Another approach would be to allow the interest to accumulate as a cushion if the original cost estimate were too low.

If the reserves for common area items are to be paid by the tenants, the method of calculation would be the same. However, the leases must permit charging a reserve for replacement to the tenants. Most major or anchor tenants will not pay into a reserve. They will pay their pro rata share when it is due rather than have the landlord hold their funds.

If the leases do allow for the collection of reserves, those monies should be placed in a trust or escrow account earning interest and held in the tenants' behalf until major work is done. If the center is sold, the trust account should be transferred to the new owners to be held on behalf of the tenants. If a tenant has paid into reserves but vacates before the monies are spent, the tenant does not receive a refund of the reserves paid.

§ 3.12   REVIEWING AND REVISING THE BUDGET

About sixty days before the budget period begins, the budget is completed and approved by the property owner based on the best information available at the time. Ideally, the budget will be accurate for the entire year with no revisions necessary.

It is possible, however, that changes will occur that will require revision. A major tenant may move out. An unusually heavy snowfall may result in being significantly over budget. A long-term, difficult vacancy may be filled unexpectedly. A major replacement of a building component may substantially reduce operating expenses. In all cases, the budget should be revised, for the change is likely to be significant. When such a change occurs, the new assumptions are incorporated into the budget, the budget is dated, and the owner is given a new cash flow projection.

Even if no major changes have taken place, the budget should be carefully evaluated periodically. Some owners of income property zero out all budgets at midyear. The actual income and expenses become the budget for that period, and all accounts are in balance, or "zeroed" out. This is intended to prevent the manager from borrowing from one account to support another. Any excess funds are automatically withdrawn

It is more common, however, for the manager to prepare an analysis of income and expenses at midyear, evaluate what the current position means for the balance of the year, and report that position along with recommended changes to the owner. Such a midyear adjustment allows the manager and owner to plan the balance of the year so that the desired goals will be reached, given the existing circumstances.

Should income be running ahead of budget, and it appears that such will be the case at year-end, the decision may be made to proceed with some capital expenditures that were shelved due to lack of funds. Conversely, if funds appear to be running behind schedule, some discretionary expenditures may be eliminated from the budget for the balance of the year.

A "deep pocket" owner may not be too concerned that the budget is under expectations for the year, whereas a "cash flow" owner may be keenly aware of every dollar. It is important for the property manager to understand the owner's position and be sure that the owner is informed of anything that might have an impact on that position.

Because of the very real possibilities of large swings in the cash flow of commercial properties, it is critical that the actual figures be compared with the budget on a monthly basis and that those comparisons be analyzed for significant differences. Most owners will accept a variance between 5 and 10 percent in any one line item without too much concern. Quite often the manager is not even asked to comment on variances more or less than 10 percent. However, the current monthly variance may be indicative of a larger problem coming up. The manager must be sensitive to this possibility and inform the owner even if the current variance is within the agreed-upon range.

When the monthly operating statements are forwarded to the owners, the statements should contain a narrative report that evaluates the numbers for the owner. Numbers by themselves do not always give a complete picture.

§ 3.13 CONCLUSION

Budgeting is not a difficult process, but it can be time-consuming. Once the property manager understands how to determine each income and expense component, an accurate NOI or cash flow projection can be developed. This is needed to maintain financial control over the property. All property owners require accurate budgets.*

---

* *Preparing a Budget for a Small Shopping Center,* Alan A. Alexander, CSM, International Council of Shopping Centers, 1988.

Four

Shopping Center Management

§ 4.1 INTRODUCTION

While shopping centers as we know them are only about 50 years old, the concept is as old as society itself. In the past, farmers came to town on the weekend and traded, bought and sold at a common market. The market was located in the center of town to be accessible to the greatest number of people. The farmers grouped together because collectively they could offer more and attract more people—the basic concept of the shopping center.

While many aspects of the management and leasing of shopping centers are quite similar to office buildings, industrial parks, and even apartment buildings, there are significant differences. The major difference is the interdependence between the tenants and the shopping center for their success. The involvement of management in selecting the right tenant for the center and then maximizing that tenant's sales potential and, therefore, the center's potential through high sales and percentage rents provides a unique approach to real estate leasing and management.

In a poll conducted by the Institute of Real Estate Management (IREM), members were asked to rank the management difficulty of various properties. Shopping centers were ranked as the most difficult to manage. Reasons cited were complexity of the tenant mix, the element of percentage rents, and involvement with tenants in promoting and advertising the shopping center. Despite its complexity and difficulty in operation, however, the shopping center also provides tremendous satisfaction when the results are positive.

204

Management has little involvement with office or industrial tenants beyond collecting the rent, establishing an emergency procedures program, making sure the tenant is not doing anything detrimental to the facilities or other tenants and developing a tenant retention program. In the shopping center, the landlord's challenge is to select tenants whose merchandise and marketing program complement the demographics of the trade area and the other tenants in the center.

Once the tenant mix has been established, steps must be taken to assure that the tenant generates high sales. High sales usually bring increased customer traffic, helping all of the tenants in the center. Furthermore, the tenant's success produces increasingly higher rents, both minimum and percentage, over a longer period of time.

The astute shopping center manager will be knowledgeable in many areas, including leasing, operations, security, business law, contract law, real estate law, human relations, accounting, finance, marketing, community relations, demographics, and maintenance.

While there are many sources for this information, one stands out—the International Council of Shopping Centers (ICSC), the trade association for the shopping center industry. The ICSC has been in existence for more than thirty years and was founded on the premise that sharing ideas makes all members more knowledgeable in the field.

ICSC conducts excellent training in all aspects of shopping centers. Its School of Professional Development offers intensive classes in almost every facet of the business, from marketing to management to development. The ICSC also offers management, marketing and maintenance institutes, seminars on construction, legal issues, accounting, leasing, and other topics. ICSC is responsible for testing and certifying shopping center managers and marketing directors. Managers are recognized with the Certified Shopping Center Manager (CSM) designation. Marketing directors receive the Certified Marketing Director (CMD) designation, formerly Accredited Shopping Center Promotions Director (ASPD).

For several hundred years, downtown was the center of social and retail activity until the end of World War II, when the exodus to the suburbs began. Sears, with its freestanding buildings, was the first major retailer to move to the suburbs to be closer to the customer. As more and more shoppers showed preference for the suburbs, small centers were built there to accommodate their needs. Developers and the retail industry followed the market, and shopping centers proliferated throughout the United States.

§ 4.2 SHOPPING CENTER CLASSIFICATIONS

Shopping center classifications have traditionally been based on the size of the shopping center and the type of major tenant that anchors it. The size of the shopping center is determined by the amount of gross leasable area (GLA)—the area occupied by the tenants. All other areas in the shopping center are referred to as common areas.

(a) BY SIZE AND MAJOR TENANT

The following are the major classifications of shopping centers as defined by GLA and major tenant:

- *Neighborhood Center.* The neighborhood center ranges in size from 50,000 to 150,000 square feet of gross leasable area and is usually anchored by a supermarket. Some neighborhood centers may have a drugstore or home improvement store as additional major tenants. The small shops are generally service tenants such as laundromats, cleaners, videotape rentals, and food services such as restaurants and specialty food stores. The neighborhood center usually has one to three pads for use by restaurants or banks. A pad is a parcel of land within the shopping center that is either leased or sold to a tenant. The merchants of the neighborhood center offer primarily convenience goods and services.
- *Community Center.* The community center ranges in size from 150,000 to 400,000 square feet of GLA. The community center is anchored by one or a combination of the following: supermarket, drugstore, home improvement center, variety store, and junior department store. The small shops are a combination of convenience and service stores, restaurants, and general merchandise and fashion stores.
- *Regional Center.* The regional center ranges in size from 400,000 to 1,000,000 square feet of GLA. It is anchored by at least one full-line department store and is tenanted predominantly by fashion, gift, and general merchandise stores, and restaurants. The regional shopping center was originally developed as an open-air mall, but most regional malls developed since the early 1970s are enclosed malls. Most open-air malls have been converted to enclosed malls.
- *Super-regional Center.* The super-regional center is in excess of 1 million square feet of GLA. The superregional center is anchored by four or more full-line department stores with more than 100 small shops like those in a regional mall.
- *Specialty, Theme Center, or Festival Center.* The specialty or theme center is either a conversion of an existing nonretail facility or a center developed around an architectural theme such as an Old World or nautical theme. The festival or specialty center is generally tourist oriented. Ghiradelli Square in San Francisco is a specialty center that was converted from an old chocolate factory. Trolley

Square in Salt Lake City is an old trolley barn converted to a specialty center. The specialty center usually doesn't have a major tenant; however, a restaurant or various food services frequently serve as the center's main draw. The center is tenanted by specialty and boutique stores such as a music box store or a leather goods shop. Such stores require a tremendous amount of traffic to survive, as their merchandise appeals to a limited number of people and most of the items are not necessities. Specialty or theme centers typically range in size from 50,000 to 300,000 square feet of GLA.

- *Outlet, Off-Price, and Discount Center.* Outlet, off-price, and discount centers are generally classified as one type of center, but each category is slightly different. The outlet merchant is the manufacturer who is also selling merchandise in retail stores, but at a bargain price. The off-price merchant is selling branded merchandise such as Nike and Jordache at less than traditional retail prices. The discount merchant sells merchandise at less than traditional retail prices, but it is not necessarily branded merchandise.

  The size of these centers ranges from neighborhood centers to community centers. They are anchored by a junior department store with merchandise falling in one of the above categories. The anchored store ranges in size from 30,000 to 100,000 square feet. The rest of the center is tenanted by merchants who also sell discounted or off-price merchandise, and food service tenants.

  These centers are usually located well away from traditional shopping centers to avoid conflicts with the suppliers of traditional retailers and to keep the rental factor lower as demanded by these tenants with low margins. A lower rental rate is also achieved by the developer by limiting the amenities in the center.

- *Power Center.* The power center is a relatively new type of shopping center. The anchors or major tenants are heavy promotional and price promotional merchants. These major tenants, ranging in size from 15,000 to 100,000 square feet of GLA, have a following of small shop tenants who market to the same customer and prefer to locate in the same centers. They include high volume stereo stores, home improvement centers, discount women and mens apparel, import stores, and warehouse clubs. These centers range in size from 50,000 to 500,000 square feet of GLA. The most recent change in this category is the "Box Farm" or center made up entirely of very large (20,000 sq. feet to 100,000 sq. feet) stores, all of which are mass merchandisers, highly promotional, and very high volume producers. Parking ratios are higher in this category than those of more traditional centers. These merchants are known as category killers, because they attempt to dominate their product line in their trade area.

- *Unanchored Centers.* The unanchored center is the newest concept in the industry. Centers of up to 150,000 square feet of GLA are being built without traditional anchors such as a supermarket or drugstore. The size of the center, its location, and the mix of merchandise is intended to provide the attraction and the traffic. It is too early to gauge the success of this concept.

(b) BY MARKET SERVED

Another consideration in classifying shopping centers is how the center operates in the marketplace. A center that has the square footage and anchor tenants of a community mall may function as a regional mall. For instance, until the late 1980s, Anchorage had no regional center. Three centers in that city were anchored by, respectively, a junior department store, a supermarket, and a super drugstore, with 50 to 100 small shops. Although the centers met the size and major tenant criteria of community malls, they functioned as regional malls. The small-shop tenant mix in these community centers is similar to the regional center's. These centers also are managed, leased, and marketed like regional malls.

A center that meets the size criteria of a neighborhood center but is located in a rural area may have a tenant mix similar to a community center and serve the area as a community center.

It is more important that the property manager understand how the shopping center functions in the community than it is to classify a shopping center by its size. The tenant mix must meet the needs of the shopping center's trade area. Once this has been determined, the manager can develop and implement an effective leasing program.

§ 4.3 DOWNTOWN REDEVELOPMENT

The late 1970s and early 1980s saw a move to revitalize downtown areas to create a shopping district similar to shopping centers. Municipal governments and redevelopment agencies assist in assembling land, provide low-cost loans, help in abating or deferring real estate taxes, provide infrastructure at no cost to the project, and even help with ongoing maintenance costs. Downtown revitalization has had mixed results throughout the country. Like shopping centers, downtown areas, even when revitalized, must have market support and the conveniences that shoppers demand.

§ 4.4 PARKING REQUIREMENTS

A shopping center's size is determined primarily by the amount of gross leasable area the developer can build on a parcel of land. The developer will usually build the maximum amount of GLA allowable. The amount of buildable GLA is restricted by the parking ratio (the number of parking stalls per GLA) and the amount of landscaping that is required by the municipality. The more GLA that can be built on a site, the greater the potential income that property can produce.

Parking restrictions for shopping centers are determined by the municipality. The city, county, or borough will have a parking code stating the minimum number of parking stalls per 1,000 square feet of GLA for a shopping center. A parking ratio of six per thousand (6/1,000) means that six parking stalls are required for each 1,000 square feet of GLA.

Other parking restrictions may be found in the tenant's lease. Seldom would a small tenant's lease address parking requirements; however, the major tenant's lease may require either a minimum number of parking stalls for the entire shopping center or a specific parking ratio of stalls per GLA. A major tenant wants to be sure that adequate and convenient parking exists for its customers.

Parking requirements also may be found in the reciprocal easement agreement (REA), the covenants, conditions and restrictions (CC&R), or common area agreements. These agreements place various restrictions on the use of the property. (See § 4.7.)

Most of the parking ratios for shopping centers were created several years ago and are outdated. This is evident by the fact that very few neighborhood centers have days when the entire parking lot is full; even most regional and superregional malls have very few days during the year when all stalls are occupied.

The International Council of Shopping Centers, under the auspices of the Urban Land Institute (ULI), funded a study on parking requirements for shopping centers. In 1982 the ULI published its findings in *Parking Requirements for Shopping Centers: Summary Recommendations and Research Study Report*. This 136-page report concluded that adequate parking for a typical shopping center would require:

- Four spaces per 1,000 square feet of GLA for centers having a GLA of 25,000 to 400,000 square feet
- Four to five spaces in a lineal progression with an average of 4.5 spaces per 1,000 square feet of GLA for centers having 400,000 to 600,000 square feet
- Five spaces per 1,000 square feet of GLA for centers having GLA of over 600,000 square feet

Additional parking was recommended for shopping centers with office space, cinemas, or food services exceeding a predetermined percentage of the shopping center's GLA. The significance of this report is that the parking requirements of many municipalities exceed the recommendations in the ULI report.

§ 4.5   CREATING ADDITIONAL INCOME AND GLA ON EXISTING CENTERS

An opportunity may exist to create additional income by building additional GLA if a shopping center's parking ratio exceeds ULI recommendations. Additional GLA can be created by adding onto an existing building, constructing another building, or creating a pad for a restaurant or bank in the parking lot. Creating and leasing additional GLA will generate additional income, thus increasing the income of the shopping center and its value. For instance, if a pad were created by changing the parking requirements, and the pad were ground leased to a national fast-food restaurant for $40,000 per year, the additional income generated from this pad would be just under $40,000 per year after subtracting expenses associated with the increased income such as increased management fees. The net operating income would be increased by approximately $40,000; if the center was valued at a cap rate of 10 percent, the value of the center would increase approximately $400,000.

If the municipal code's parking requirements are higher than those in ULI's report, property managers should consider obtaining a variance or working with the building department for possible changes to the municipal code. It may be easier to obtain a variance for one shopping center than to request the municipality to change its code for all present and future shopping centers.

Before action is taken to add GLA to the shopping center, the property manager must review the tenant's leases, the REA, CC&Rs, and common area agreements for parking restrictions. If any of these documents have a parking restriction, the property manager must obtain an agreement with the signators of these documents amending the parking requirements before changing the center's parking ratio.

Another possible restriction would be a tenant's lease or any of the above mentioned documents that may provide a tenant, usually the major tenant, with the right to approve the redesign of a shopping center. The addition of a pad or additional buildings would probably be considered as redesigning the shopping center.

The property manager should be well prepared when pursuing a change in the parking code or a variance with the municipality, amending the tenant's lease or the REA, CC&Rs, and common area agreements. In addition to using the ULI report, the property manager may need to hire a consultant to conduct a parking survey of the shopping center. A survey of the percentage of vacant parking stalls at different times on different days could provide invaluable information. The property manager may also want to obtain aerial photos of the parking lot taken at different times of the day.

In addition to obtaining a variance in the parking ratio for the shopping center, the property manager may ask the municipality for a change in the number of compact parking stalls that can be provided in the shopping center. The ULI *Parking Requirements for Shopping Centers* has estimated that in the 1990s, most automobiles in use will be compact cars. Creating compact parking stalls out of regular-sized ones will yield more total parking stalls, in many cases as much as a 20 percent increase, and provide more efficient use of the parking area, thus allowing for more buildable GLA.

The property manager should evaluate the shopping center's parking requirements, and if the number of parking stalls exceeds the recommendations in the ULI report, the manager should consider reducing the ratio of parking stalls per GLA. This reduction will provide additional building opportunities and generate further income for the shopping center, thus enhancing the value of the center.

§ 4.6   OPERATING AGREEMENTS

There are agreements that place restrictions on the landlord's and tenants' use of shopping centers and assign rights and obligations to the landlord and the major tenants. These restrictions, rights, and obligations are usually found in the shopping center's reciprocal easement agreement, common area agreement, or covenants, conditions, and restrictions.

(a)   RECIPROCAL EASEMENT AGREEMENT

The REA is an agreement between the landlord and the major tenants that describes the property, defines the common area, and establishes the rights and obligations of the major tenants and the landlord. This agreement will usually appoint the landlord as the manager of the common area, establish the maintenance standards for the common area, and provide the major tenants with the right to remove the landlord as the manager of all or a portion of the common area if the maintenance does not meet the agreement's standards. The major tenants are given rights to approve changes or additions to the common area.

These rights may even include the major tenant's approval of the landlord's plans for remodeling the property. When major tenants own their building and the adjacent parking areas, this agreement provides crossover rights to use each other's common area. Occasionally the lender is a party to these agreements. REAs are most often found in regional and community shopping centers.

(b)   RECIPROCAL EASEMENT AGREEMENT (REA) AND
COMMON AREA AGREEMENT SUMMARY

Because buildings in a shopping center may be under different ownership, it requires an agreement between the parties as to how the shopping center will be operated. Another document often found in shopping centers is the common area agreement. This is an agreement between the property owner and the major tenant as to how the property will be operated. These documents are lengthy, and a summary of points related to the daily operation of the property will save time for the property manager as well as maintenance, accounting, and leasing personnel. Periodic review of this summary will keep the property manager aware of the restrictions in the agreement, thus minimizing the possibility of an inadvertent violation of the agreement. (See Exhibit 4.1.)

(c) COMMON AREA AGREEMENT

The common area agreement is a document between the landlord and the major tenant(s) describing the common areas and buildable area and establishing the rights and obligations of each party within these areas. A common area manager is appointed, usually the landlord. Each party's pro rata share of the expenses of the common area is established. The agreement provides the major tenants with approval rights to changes to the common area. These agreements, which are most often found in neighborhood or community centers, include the following provisions:

- Recitals
- Maintenance standards
- Lighting
- Taxes
- Maintenance director
- Reimbursement of maintenance director
- Billing for expenses
- Effect of sale by owner
- Default in payment of expenses
- Lien for expenses or taxes
- Right to maintain parcel separately
- Responsibility if no maintenance director
- Sale and leaseback of the major tenant's parcel
- General provisions
- Sale and sale-leaseback purchaser

(d) COVENANTS, CONDITIONS, AND RESTRICTIONS

CC&Rs are restrictions on the use of the property. They convey the rights and obligations to the owners of the property.

These various operating agreements can easily be violated. For example, the REA may restrict kiosks, the use of common areas for selling,

EXHIBIT 4.1

Reciprocal Easement Agreement and Common Area Agreement Summary Form

	MERCHANT	PARCEL	PERCENTAGE
PARTIES:	Supermarkets	2	34.30%
	The Drug Store	4	17.98%
	Fast Food	5	2.32%
	Fast Food	6	2.32%
	Auto Parts	7	4.74%
	Developer	1,3,8	37.86%

SECTION I - DEVELOPMENT

NO BUILDING IN EXCESS OF STATED FOOTAGE WITHOUT APPROVAL OF 90% OF THE PARTIES TO THE REA - MUST ANSWER WITHIN 30 DAYS OR APPROVED BY DEFAULT.

NO SIGNAGE TO BE INSTALLED OTHER THAN THOSE PRE-APPROVED IN REA WITHOUT APPROVAL OF 90% OF THE PARTIES TO THE REA.

NO FENCES OR OTHER IMPEDIMENTS TO TRAFFIC TO BE INSTALLED THAT MIGHT IMPAIR FREE ACCESS BETWEEN THE PARCELS.

ALL BUILDINGS IN SHOPPING CENTER MUST BE FIRE SPRINKLERED.

SECTION II - COMMON AREA MAINTENANCE

A. EMPLOYEE PARKING TO BE DETERMINED BY COMMON AREA OPERATOR AND ALL PARTIES AGREE TO USE BEST EFFORTS TO REQUIRE ALL EMPLOYEES TO PARK IN DESIGNATED AREA.

B. ALL PARTIES AGREE TO PAY ALL REAL ESTATE TAXES PRIOR TO DELINQUENCY.

C. DEVELOPER SHALL BE NAMED "MANAGER" OF COMMON AREA. EACH MAJOR TENANT MAY ELECT TO MAINTAIN OWN PARCEL OR BY VOTE OF 50% OF TOTAL SQUARE FOOTAGE MAY TAKE OVER AS COMMON AREA MANAGER.

D. MANAGER MUST PROVIDE LIABILITY INSURANCE OF $2,000,000 COMBINED LIMITS, PROVIDE FOR 10 DAYS ADVANCE NOTICE OF CANCELLATION AND NAME ALL PARTIES AS ADDITIONAL INSURED.

E. MANAGER TO MAINTAIN COMMON AREA IN GOOD CONDITION. ANY EXPENDITURE ABOVE $10,000 MUST BE PRE-APPROVED BY THE PARTIES.

F. MANAGER TO SUBMIT ANNUAL BUDGET TO THE PARTIES PRIOR TO JANUARY 1ST OF EACH YEAR AND EACH PARTY AGREES TO PAY PRO RATA SHARE MONTHLY WITH A FULL ACCOUNTING AND ADJUSTMENT WITHIN 90 DAYS OF THE END OF EACH CALENDER YEAR.

G. PARTIES HAVE THE RIGHT TO AUDIT RECORDS AND OBTAIN COPIES OF ALL INVOICES AND BACK UP DOCUMENTS.

SECTION III UPKEEP AND MAINTENANCE

A. EACH OWNER AGREES TO KEEP ALL BUILDINGS IN GOOD CONDITION TO ASSURE FIRST CLASS APPEARANCE.

B. ARCHITECTURAL CHARACTER OF REPLACED OR REMODELED BUILDINGS AS WELL AS NEW CONSTRUCTION MUST CONFORM WITH ARCHITECTURAL CHARACTER OF EXISTING BUILDINGS.

EXHIBIT 4.1 *(Continued)*

SECTION IV — INDEMNITY

A. ALL PARTIES AGREE TO INDEMNIFY THE OTHER PARTIES AGAINST LOSS FROM THEIR OWN NEGLIGENCE.

SECTION V — RESTRICTIONS ON USE

A. NO PORTIONS OF PARCELS 1, 3, 5, 6, 7 OR 8 CAN BE USED FOR A DRUG STORE OR SUPERMARKET. NO PORTION OF CENTER CAN BE USED FOR A SKATING RINK, THEATER OR BOWLING ALLEY. NO PORTION OF PARCELS 3 OR 8 CAN BE USED FOR SIT DOWN FOOD, MEDICAL OR DENTAL OFFICE OR LIQUOR STORE.

SECTION VI — GENERAL PROVISIONS

A. ALL EASEMENTS, RESTRICTIONS AND COVENANTS RUN WITH THE LAND.

B. DOCUMENT IS VALID FOR 99 YEARS EXPIRING DECEMBER 10, 2083.

C. DOCUMENT MAY NOT BE MODIFIED UNLESS 100% OF PARTIES AGREE IN WRITING.

D. BREACH OF DOCUMENT SHALL NOT PERMIT TERMINATION.

E. DOCUMENT DOES NOT CONSTITUTE A PARTNERSHIP BETWEEN THE PARTIES.

or the leasing of the common area to a temporary tenant. Adding a pad tenant to the common area may violate the common area agreement. The courts have found that ignorance is no excuse for violating a tenant's rights.

Violations of these agreements, whether intentional or not, can be costly to the landlord and possibly the property management company. The property manager should meet with the owner of the shopping center to determine if the property has any of these agreements. If it does, the property manager should request a copy of the agreement and determine the landlord's rights and obligations as they effect the operation, development, and leasing of the property. If the owner is not familiar with the agreements, the owner's attorney should review them and summarize the rights and obligations of the parties that are signators to the agreement.

§ 4.7   THE CUSTOMER SURVEY

One of the critical elements of any shopping center's success is serving its trade area properly. The market survey, in contrast to the customer survey, provides most of the necessary information on demographics, competition, traffic, ingress, and egress, but it does not evaluate customer response to a particular shopping center. If the center does well in sales and occupancy, it can be assumed that the center is serving the area well. Even in this situation, however, it is possible that the center might do even better if it were more responsive to consumers' needs. The customer survey provides a way to determine shoppers' perceptions of the center and to invite suggestions for improvement.

Before a customer survey is conducted, specific goals must be developed. Is the purpose to evaluate maintenance and cleanliness of the center? Is it to define tenant mix and determine just what the public thinks is missing? Is it to measure the impact of outside events, such as teenage cruising, major street work, or the opening of a competing center, on the success of the center? Once goals are defined, the survey must be carefully drafted to assure that the responses will provide the necessary information.

Surveys can take various forms. The most expensive and extensive survey is an interview in the customer's home. Less expensive is a customer interview conducted on site or focus groups. Visiting civic clubs and neighborhood groups for discussions can be very productive and provide opportunity for a dialogue rather than just filling in blanks on a form.

Professional marketing organizations have the background and experience to design the survey, formulate the correct questions, recommend the methods of polling, and determine the proper number of customers to contact to validate the survey. A comprehensive customer survey for a regional shopping center with known problems can easily cost in excess of $40,000 and take months to develop and evaluate.

At the other end of the spectrum, an owner or manager of a small center can use a simple customer survey to determine what the customer wants and to evaluate maintenance and management. A simple questionnaire like the one in Exhibit 4.2 can be prepared and, when filled out and deposited in one of the center's stores, becomes an entry blank for a prize drawing. A small ad in the local paper or placards in each store promote the program and keep the cost low.

A neighborhood shopping center may conduct a survey in conjunction with one or more major tenants. For example, if the tenant is a supermarket, the survey asks questions about the center and the supermarket. The survey forms are placed in the customer's shopping bag at the supermarket and a free loaf of bread is presented if the form is returned within 10 days. The cost of the bread and copying the forms is minimal, and is shared by the supermarket and the center.

Questionnaires provide focus and can be handed out by all merchants or mailed to the trade area or zip code residents. The decision about which form to use will be influenced by the degree of the problem to be resolved, the owner's resources, outside or out-of-pocket costs, and the time frame in which the information is desired.

Another method of evaluation is to attend civic group meetings to obtain impressions of the center. A contribution to the group's favorite charity or local civic program may help gain entrance, the expenditure justified by gaining worthwhile information. The group can be approached with a questionnaire to be filled out and then discussed, or those in attendance can be questioned. In any case, questionnaires should be brief or customers may become annoyed and not complete them.

A license plate survey can be very effective in determining where customers are coming from. One method is to note license numbers for every fourth car in the lot using random times and days. Be careful to avoid employee automobiles. After collecting 500 to 800 license numbers, submit them to the state motor vehicle department which will, generally for a fee, provide addresses. The addresses are then plotted on a map of the area, giving a good approximation of the center's trade area. Independent companies also survey license plates for a center and compile useful data.

Most store owners or store managers spend upwards of 70 hours in their stores and talk with hundreds of customers. Hence a survey of merchants can yield valuable information about center maintenance, customer preferences, effective advertising media, lighting, security problems, and even problems with other tenants (see Exhibit 4.3). Care must be exercised in evaluating merchant responses, for they can be self-serving.

EXHIBIT 4.2

Customer Survey

1. What is the primary purpose of your visit to this shopping center today?
    - (1) Specific purchase
    - (2) Work in store
    - (3) Specific store/restaurant
    - (4) General shopping
    - (5) Special shopping center or store event
    - (6) Other purpose (specify) _____
2. What is your next destination?
    - (1) Other shopping area
    - (2) Work
    - (3) Home
    - (4) Other
3. Which of the following categories best describes the length of your shopping visit?
    - (1) Less than 1 hour
    - (2) 1 to less than 2 hours
    - (3) 2 to less than 3 hours
    - (4) 3 hours or more
4. How did you get to this shopping center today?
    - (1) Taxi
    - (2) Walk
    - (3) Tour bus
    - (4) City bus
    - (5) Car
    - (6) Bicycle
    - (7) Other
5. Did you come to this shopping center today from home, work, another shopping area, or some other place?
    - (1) Work
    - (2) Other shopping area
    - (3) Home
    - (4) Other
6. Which of these categories best describes the total amount you spent at the center today, including expenditures for food?
    - (1) Nothing
    - (2) Less than $10
    - (3) $10–$24.99
    - (4) $25–$49.99
    - (5) $50–$99.99
    - (6) $100–$199.99
    - (7) $200–$399.99
    - (8) $400–$599.99
    - (9) $600 or more

EXHIBIT 4.2 *(Continued)*

7. Which of the following stores did you visit today?
   - (1) Restaurant
   - (2) General merchandise
   - (3) Shoe store
   - (4) Yogurt shop
   - (5) Print shop
   - (6) Fabric store
   - (7) Dentist office
   - (8) Electronic equipment
   - (9) Cleaners
   - (10) Pizza parlor
   - (11) Bicycle shop
   - (12) Telephone equipment
   - (13) Fish & seafood market
   - (14) Video store
   - (15) Optometrist
   - (16) Beauty supply
   - (17) Apparel shop
   - (18) Post office
   - (19) Gift & card shop
   - (20) Computer store

8. What is the primary reason for your being in downtown Happytown today?
   - (1) Employed in office or store in the center
   - (2) Work in downtown
   - (3) Conducting business downtown
   - (4) Shopping
   - (5) Live downtown
   - (6) Other (specify): _____
   - (7) Visiting (tourist)
   - (8) Visiting (conventioneer/conference attendee/out of town business traveler)

9. How often would you say you visit the following shopping centers or areas for shopping/dining?

	Frequently Once/week or More	Occasionally Once/Month or More	Seldom Less Than Once Month	First Time/ Once	Never
(1) Happytown Plaza	5	4	3	2	1
(2) Happytown Mall	5	4	3	2	1
(3) City Center	5	4	3	2	1
(4) Riverfront Commons	5	4	3	2	1
(5) Downtown stores	5	4	3	2	1

10. Where do you work?
    Cross streets _____ and _____.

11. Which stores did you make purchases in:
    - (1) Restaurant
    - (2) General merchandise
    - (3) Shoe store
    - (4) Yogurt shop
    - (5) Print shop
    - (6) Fabric store
    - (7) Dentist office
    - (8) Electronic equipment
    - (9) Cleaners
    - (10) Pizza parlor
    - (11) Bicycle shop
    - (12) Telephone equipment
    - (13) Fish & seafood market
    - (14) Video store
    - (15) Optometrist
    - (16) Beauty supply
    - (17) Apparel shop
    - (18) Post office
    - (19) Gift & card shop
    - (20) Computer store

EXHIBIT 4.2 *(Continued)*

12. Which of these publications do you read regularly?
    (1) *Happytown Weekly*   (3) *Morning News*
    (2) *Great Area Gazette*   (4) *Happytown Shopper*

13. When you go to the shopping center, why do you choose it over some other shopping centers?
    (1) No reason
    (2) Close to home or work/convenience
    (3) Like stores/restaurants generally
    (4) Like specific center store or restaurant. Specify: _____
    (5) Other reason. Specify: _____

14. Which of these radio stations do you listen to regularly?
    (1) WZRR-AM (800)
    (2) WPON-FM (91)
    (3) WKKY-FM (99.9)
    (4) WERT-AM (610)
    (5) WYZZ-FM (103.1)

15. Why don't you visit this shopping center more often for shopping/dining?
    (1) Don't have enough time
    (2) Prefer other centers
    (3) Too confusing to find my way around the center
    (4) No reason
    (5) Too far to drive/walk
    (6) Not open weekday evenings
    (7) Cannot find merchandise I'm looking for
    (8) Too tourist oriented
    (9) Don't shop anywhere often
    (10) Other centers closer
    (11) Too expensive
    (12) Not open Sundays
    (13) Don't like stores
    (14) Parking too difficult

16. If the center had a multiscreen movie theatre, would you patronize it?
    (0) Don't know/No response   (2) Probably no   (4) Definitely yes
    (1) Definitely no   (3) Probably yes

17. Which of these television programs do you watch on a regular basis?
    (1) 5:30 P.M. News,   WAJY Channel 12   (ABC)
    (2) 6:00 P.M. News,   WERT Channel 30   (NBC)
    (3) 6:00 P.M. News,   WKYT Channel 21   (CBS)
    (4) 11:00 P.M. News,   WQZV Channel 17   (ABC)
    (5) 11:00 P.M. News,   WERE Channel 35   (NBC)
    (6) 11:00 P.M. News,   WSTS Channel 10   (CBS)
    (7) CBS Morning News,   WUYU Channel 19   (CBS)
    (8) Good Morning America, WNCR Channel 37   (ABC)
    (9) Today Show,   WPPT Channel 6   (NBC)

18. What additional stores, services, or eating places would you like to see added to the center? _____

EXHIBIT 4.2 *(Continued)*

19. What other improvements or changes would you like to see at the center or in the stores? _____

_____

20. How many children under age 18 live in your household?

    1   2   3   4   5   6 or more   7 no children

21. Which of the following categories best describes the number of years of education you have completed?

    (1) Up to 11 years   (4) 4 years college
    (2) Completed high school   (5) Graduate school
    (3) 1–3 years of college   (6) Refused/No answer

22. What is the zip code of your home?

    _____   _____   _____   _____

23. Which of these categories best describes your age?

    (1) 12–16   (2) 17–21   (3) 22–29   (4) 30–44   (5) 45–54
    (6) 55–64   (7) 65–Plus   (8) Refused/No answer

24. Which of these categories best describes the total annual income of everyone in your household?

    (1) Less than $10,000   (5) $35,000–$49,999
    (2) $10,000–$14,999   (6) $50,000–$74,999
    (3) $15,000–$24,999   (7) $75,000 or more
    (4) $25,000–$34,999   (8) Refused/No answer

25. Describe your occupation

_____

_____

26. Gender

    1   Male   2   Female

27. Race

    1   Caucasian   2   African-   3   Hispanic-   4   Asian   5   Other
                        American   American

EXHIBIT 4.3

Shopping Center Merchant Survey

(To be completed by on-site store manager or store owner, if applicable)

Note: Some aspects of this questionnaire may not apply to your specific store.

Store/Management Profile

1. What store within the Happytown trade area do you consider to be your primary competition?

   _____

2. What are your store's peak hours at Happytown? _____
   Which of these categories best reflects your store's total advertising budget during 1986?
   ____ Don't know   ____ $1,000 to $5,000   ____ $10,000 or more
   ____ Less than $1,000   ____ $5,000 to $10,000

3. Does your firm conduct regularly scheduled selling training programs for managers?
   ____ No ____ Yes—How often? _____

4. How many people are employed in your store?
   Full time _____
   Part time _____

5. Please list which credit cards your store accepts. _____

   _____

6. How long have you (manager/owner) been employed with your company?
   ____ Less than one year   ____ Five years to less than ten yrs
   ____ One year to less than two yrs   ____ Ten years or more
   ____ Two years to less than five yrs

7. Does your firm conduct regularly scheduled selling training programs for employees?
   ____ No ____ Yes—How often? _____

8. Check those which best describe your store's advertising program.
   ____ National advertising   ____ Local advertising
   ____ Regularly scheduled   ____ Regularly scheduled
   ____ Sporadic   ____ Sporadic

9. Please list all of your stores' locations in the Happytown market and rank them in order of sales volume.

                                                                    Rank

   _____   _____

   ____ _____
   ____ _____
   ____ _____
   ____ _____

10. Does your store maintain a mailing list of active customers?
    ____ Yes ____ No

11. Are you provided with a store plan for merchandising/display?
    ____ No ____ Yes

12. If yes, how often? _____
    Do you have flexibility to make changes? ____ No ____ Yes

EXHIBIT 4.3 *(Continued)*

13. What is your (manager/owner) highest level of completed education?
    ____ Some high school   ____ Master's degree
    ____ Graduated high school   ____ Doctor's degree
    ____ Some college   ____ Associate or business degree
    ____ Bachelor's degree
14. Please describe your merchandise return policy? _____
    _____
    _____

15. Does your store use professional visual merchandising display services?
    ____ No   ____ Yes—In House ____   Outside Resources ____
16. Do you offer merchandise layaways?   ____ Yes   ____ No
17. What are the best aspects of the Happytown Center?
    _____
    _____
    _____

18. What are the worst aspects of the Happytown Center?
    _____
    _____
    _____

19. What additional services should be offered to customers/merchants by the Happytown Center?
    _____
    _____
    _____

20. What suggestions for center improvements do you have?
    _____
    _____
    _____

21. What additional stores, services and eating places are needed at this center?
    _____
    _____
    _____

22. Please rate the following aspects of the Happytown Center.

	No Opinion N/A	Excellent	Above Average	Average	Below Average	Poor
Center Management						
Common area maintenance	6 ___	5 ___	4 ___	3 ___	2 ___	1 ___
Security	6 ___	5 ___	4 ___	3 ___	2 ___	1 ___
Heating, ventilating, air-conditioning	6 ___	5 ___	4 ___	3 ___	2 ___	1 ___
Communications with center management	6 ___	5 ___	4 ___	3 ___	2 ___	1 ___
Management responsiveness to store problems	6 ___	5 ___	4 ___	3 ___	2 ___	1 ___

EXHIBIT 4.3 (Continued)

Management responsiveness to mall problems	6 ___	5 ___	4 ___	3 ___	2 ___	1

Center Marketing

Quality of execution and

effectiveness of: Events	6 ___	5 ___	4 ___	3 ___	2 ___	1 ___
Decor	6 ___	5 ___	4 ___	3 ___	2 ___	1 ___
PR/community relations	6 ___	5 ___	4 ___	3 ___	2 ___	1 ___
Advertising campaign	6 ___	5 ___	4 ___	3 ___	2 ___	1 ___

Advertising media

placement	6 ___	5 ___	4 ___	3 ___	2 ___	1 ___

Other merchant
participation in:

Center events	6 ___	5 ___	4 ___	3 ___	2 ___	1 ___

Center group

Advertising	6 ___	5 ___	4 ___	3 ___	2 ___	1 ___

Competiveness with

other centers	6 ___	5 ___	4 ___	3 ___	2 ___	1 ___

Communications with

marketing staff	6 ___	5 ___	4 ___	3 ___	2 ___	1 ___

Marketing staff

responsiveness	6 ___	5 ___	4 ___	3 ___	2 ___	1 ___

Center Qualities

Length of center hours	6 ___	5 ___	4 ___	3 ___	2 ___	1 ___
Uniformity of store hours	6 ___	5 ___	4 ___	3 ___	2 ___	1 ___
Traffic in center	6 ___	5 ___	4 ___	3 ___	2 ___	1 ___

Traffic in your area of

the center	6 ___	5 ___	4 ___	3 ___	2 ___	1 ___
Tenant mix	6 ___	5 ___	4 ___	3 ___	2 ___	1 ___

23. If you advertise, in which media?

Publications	Radio	Television
___ *Courier Journal*	___ WHAM-FM	___ WTZZ (12)
___ *Happytown Times*	___ WAFC-AM	___ WTTY (1)
___ *Business Journal*	___ WCCR-FM	___ WQQM (42)
___ *Happytown Magazine*	___ WPOI-AM	___ WSAS (54)
___ *Happytown Sun*	___ WTRE-FM	___ Billboards
___ Other _____	___ WTUI-AM	___ Other ___
		___ Other ___
		___ Other ___

24. Please estimate the percentage of sales volume this demographic group
contributes to your store sales:

By age group

Persons under 22 years	_____	%
Persons 22 to 44 years	_____	%
Persons 45 plus years	_____	%
Total	100%	

EXHIBIT 4.3 *(Continued)*

25. Please estimate the percentage of sales volume this demographic group contributes to your store's sales:
    By racial group
    Caucasian   _____%
    African-American   _____%
    Hispanic-American _____%
    Asian   _____%
    Other races   _____%
    Total   100%

26. Please estimate the percentage of sales volume this demographic group contributes to your store's sales:
    By gender
    Male   _____%
    Female   _____%
    Total   100%

27. Please estimate the percentage of sales volume this demographic group contributes to your store's sales:
    By household income group:
    Income earners under $20,000   _____%
    Income earners $20,000 to $50,000   _____%
    Income earners $50,000 plus   _____%

28. In which of the following merchandising/advertising programs can your store participate?

	Can/Could		Already Do/Could	
Group Ads in				
Newspaper tabloids	____ Yes	____ No	____ Yes	____ No
Newspaper sections	____ Yes	____ No	____ Yes	____ No
Magazine sections	____ Yes	____ No	____ Yes	____ No
Coupons	____ Yes	____ No	____ Yes	____ No
Direct mail catalogs	____ Yes	____ No	____ Yes	____ No
Direct mail flyers	____ Yes	____ No	____ Yes	____ No
Radio advertisements	____ Yes	____ No	____ Yes	____ No
Television advertisements	____ Yes	____ No	____ Yes	____ No
Group Merchandising Events				
Sales events	____ Yes	____ No	____ Yes	____ No
Fashion shows	____ Yes	____ No	____ Yes	____ No
Contests	____ Yes	____ No	____ Yes	____ No

Generally, the center's owners pay for these surveys because merchants' association funds are usually limited and because the owner will use the information for management and leasing considerations in addition to the merchandising interests of the tenants. If the survey is to be used for leasing, it should include a disclaimer on the accuracy of the information and how it was obtained.

A potential customer survey for a center yet to be built may be conducted, but such a survey is more likely to be used if there is a problem in an existing center, a rehab is contemplated, or a major tenant is leaving and additional input is needed about what the customers want or need.

The customer survey (Exhibit 4.2) is meant to evaluate many aspects of the center. Questions 1, 2, 4, 5, 7, and 8 explore what brings customers to the center. Questions 12, 14, and 18 evaluate advertising media for the center's customers. Questions 7, 11, 13, 17, and 19 will help management evaluate the current tenant mix and determine the nature and thrust of future leasing efforts. Questions 22, 24, 25, 26, 27, and 28 seek to identify the customer of the center so that amenities and tenant mix can be matched to customer preferences.

§ 4.8 TENANT MIX

The concept of tenant mix is not limited to shopping centers but is more critical to the success of a shopping center than it is to office buildings, medical buildings or industrial parks. Tenant mix must be consistent with the trade area as well as within the center itself.

No one formula exists for correct tenant mix, but there are helpful guidelines to determine the most likely mix for a given shopping center. The best tenant mix for a specific shopping center will provide the broadest range of goods and services consistent with the shopping patterns of the people in the trade area. If customers in the trade area are affluent, the shops are more likely to cater to higher income tastes. If, on the other hand, the trade area is made up of families at the lower end of the income spectrum, the successful shops are more likely to carry lower cost merchandise. It does not make sense to put K-Mart in Beverly Hills or Saks Fifth Avenue in a blue-collar neighborhood.

Sources such as *Sales and Marketing Management's Annual Survey of Buying Power* detail how people spend their money in every major metropolitan area of the country. By evaluating that information, a tenant mix can be developed. If, for example, a study of supermarket sales shows higher than average figures, an opportunity may exist for another supermarket. Studying the average sales per square foot of existing supermarkets can indicate whether a new store in this category will be successful. (See Exhibit 4.4.)

EXHIBIT 4.4

Sales Comparisons by Store Categories

| | SEPTEMBER | | OCTOBER | | NOVEMBER | |
	1991	1992	1991	1992	1991	1992
Women's Wear	269140	338903	253822	319805	293432	402006
% Change		+25.9		+26.0		+37.1
Mens Wear	61490	70593	74652	76626	124956	122154
% Change		+14.8		+2.6		−2.3
Restaurants	136443	159741	148354	157131	150101	166404
% Change		+17.0		+5.9		+10.8
Food To Go	52034	36352	58819	53912	136455	143761
% Change		−30.2		−8.4		+5.3
Shoes	219946	255303	165640	208488	187532	233014
% Change		+16.0		+25.8		+24.2
Jewelry	79002	70074	57612	95680	92192	158609
% Change		−11.3		+66.0		+72.0
Gifts	39611	37456	34355	36165	51119	66319
% Change		−5.5		+5.2		+29.7
General Merchandise	213735	230953	204704	241872	282749	378021
% Change		+8.0		+18.1		+33.6
Center Total	1071401	1199375	997958	1189679	1318536	1670288
% Change		+11.9		+19.2		+26.7

Multiplying the number of people in the trade area by the average purchases per person to arrive at the potential sales in the area. We can then estimate the sales of the existing market. Sales tax figures can also be used to determine if the area has excess potential that would suggest support for a new supermarket.

Studying how people in the trade area spend their money reveals percentages of sales in various uses such as women's wear, men's wear, shoes, and restaurants (see Exhibit 4.4). These percentages are then modified based on the competition and type of center involved. Every category of merchandise can be evaluated in the same way. The sales potentials indicated by this type of study are meant to be a guideline and not an absolute figure. Analyzing the area's growth rates, traffic patterns, and quality of existing competition provides additional indicators for probable success.

A supermarket and drugstore serve as anchor tenants in a neighborhood center. They provide the traffic to support the smaller merchants. Both should be either high end or low end rather than appealing to different market segments.

The actual placement of specific tenants within a given center is not a science. The property manager's experience and general know-how play an important part in determining tenant mix. The goal, however, is to mix goods and services to encourage impulse shopping while the customer is looking for something specific. Beauty and barber shops do not usually need a high traffic location as they are a destination-type tenant. A jewelry store will usually want to be in a high traffic location so customers can see something they like and buy on impulse.

A pet store or hair salon is not a good neighbor for a restaurant because unpleasant odors may flow into the restaurant. A record store is not a good idea next to a bookstore since bookstore patrons could be disturbed by loud music from the adjoining premises. Placing an auto parts store between two dress shops will not benefit any of the retailers involved.

The center's management must also take great care not to put in tenants that would cause customers discomfort or would take away from the overall shopping experience. (See § 4.20 for a discussion of potential problem tenants.)

§ 4.9 PERCENTAGE RENT ADMINISTRATION

Rent paid above the minimum rent is referred to as percentage rent or overage rent—rent over the minimum rent. The theory is that merchants in a shopping center should be able to generate more sales than they would if they were freestanding without the drawing power of the additional merchants. The payment of percentage rent by a tenant is meant to recognize the increased sales realized by combining the merchants in the shopping center environment. The landlord should benefit if the retail environment results in the tenant's achieving higher sales.

Percentage rent is administrated on three levels: (1) accounting for any percentage rent due, (2) measuring the success of each tenant and of the center as a whole, and (3) collecting the monies due.

The percentage rental rate for any given tenant is based on the profit margin of that type of business. A supermarket has a very low profit margin and the lowest percentage rental rate in the industry at 1 to 1½ percent of sales. Most retail soft goods, shoe stores, restaurants, and specialty stores are in the midrange of profit margins and pay from 5 to 7 percent of gross sales. Service tenants such as beauty and barber shops have a higher profit margin and will pay 7 to 10 percent of sales (see Exhibit 4.5). These figures are all negotiable but should be kept within reasonable ranges to be fair to both landlord and tenant. Percentage rental rates are applied to gross sales, less sales tax and any negotiated exclusions.

Typically, the tenant will pay minimum rent on the first of each month and any percentage rent due above the minimum as called for in

EXHIBIT 4.5

Percentage Rent Record

Tenant	Footage	Percent	Notes
Friendly Market	42,000	1.5	Reports & pays 45 days end calendar year
Kathy's Kards	2,000	7.0	Reports 20 days, pays end calendar quarter
Today's Styles	1,500	5.0	Reports 10 days, pays end month
White Cleaners	1,600	6.0	Reports 20 days, pays end lease year 6/30
Advance TV	2,000	0	No requirement
Vacant	700		
Kings Hardware	5,000	3.0	Reports 10 days, pays end of month
Pizza Plus	3,200	6.0	Reports 10 days, pays end of month
Fast Sell Realty	1,500	0	No requirement
Goodies Ice Cream	1,700	5.0	
Fancy Fabrics	3,400	4.5	
Slim & Trim Salon	3,200	7.0	
Family Shoes	2,600	3.0	
Speedy's Bikes	1,600	5.5	
Discount Drugs	22,000	3.0	
Dine 'n Dash	3,600	6.0	
Home Town Bank	2,400	0	
Totals:	100,000		

the lease. The point at which a tenant is obligated to pay percentage rent is known as the *breakpoint,* which can either be a natural breakpoint or a negotiated breakpoint referred to as an artificial breakpoint.

The natural breakpoint is determined by dividing the minimum rent by the percentage rental rate. Example: $12,000 minimum annual rent ÷ 6 percent percentage rental rate = $200,000 annual breakpoint. If the tenant's sales are less than $200,000—$175,000, for example—percentage rent is not owed ($175,000 annual sales × 6 percent = $10,500 total percentage rent vs. $12,000 minimum annual rent = no balance due). If, however, the tenant's sales were $240,000 for the year, the annual percentage rent would be $2,400 ($240,000 annual sales × 6 percent = $14,400 total percentage rent − $12,000 minimum rent paid = $2,400 percentage rent due).

Tenants in a shopping center pay either a minimum rent or a percentage of their sales, whichever is greater. The percentage rent for a tenant whose rent is $12,000 a year with a 5 percent rate and sales of $300,000 is $3,000 ($300,000 × 5 percent = $15,000 − $12,000 = $3,000 percentage rent). If the same tenant's sales were $200,000, there would be no percentage rent ($200,000 × 5 percent = $10,000 − $12,000 = no percentage rent).

Major tenants will report sales and pay the percentage rent owed annually. Smaller shop tenants should report their sales and pay the percentage rent owed monthly. After the year ends, the tenant's sales are adjusted based on the tenant's annual sales, which even out the seasonal highs and lows of the year. Even though a tenant may pay percentage rent in April and December, the annual sales may be below the breakpoint. In this case, the percentage rent paid would be refunded.

(a) NEGOTIATING PERCENTAGE RENT RATES

Percentage rent calculations can vary. The breakpoint can be negotiated up or down; one percentage rate can be used to determine the breakpoint and another for sales above the breakpoint; there can be a declining rate; or the tenant may have the right to deduct taxes, insurance, and common area costs from percentage rents.

Negotiating the Breakpoint Downward

The tenant may demand a higher level of interior improvements to the store than the landlord is willing to provide and is unwilling to pay a higher rent to offset the cost of these improvements. The landlord may propose that the breakpoint be lowered to offset the landlord's additional investment. In the above example, the natural breakpoint of $200,000 could be negotiated to a $150,000 breakpoint. If the tenant generated $50,000 in sales above the breakpoint at a 6 percent rate, $3,000 in additional percentage rent would be paid to the landlord.

Negotiating the Breakpoint Upward

A tenant may be forced to pay market rent for a space that is in poor condition. As an inducement, the landlord might agree to move the natural breakpoint up to allow the tenant to recapture the additional cost to improve the premises. For example, a natural breakpoint of $200,000 negotiated to a $230,000 breakpoint is $30,000 above the natural breakpoint times a 6 percent rate provides the tenant with $1,800 a year to offset the additional improvements.

Higher Percentage Rate to Breakpoint and Lower Percentage Rate Thereafter

Sometimes the landlord and the tenant cannot agree on the percentage rental rate. The tenant might want 5 percent and the landlord 6 percent. A compromise, aside from the obvious rate of 5.5 percent, is 6 percent to the breakpoint and 5 percent thereafter ($12,000 minimum rent ÷ 6 percentage rate = $200,000 natural breakpoint; $12,000 minimum rent ÷ 5 percentage rate = $240,000 natural breakpoint).

Calculate the breakpoint by dividing 6 percent into the annual rent and multiplying the sales in excess of the breakpoint by 5 percent. The result is the amount of percentage rent. To determine the total rent, add the minimum rent to the percentage rent. (For example, sales are $500,000. $12,000 minimum rent ÷ 6 percent = $200,000 breakpoint. $300,000 is subject to percentage rent at 5 percent: $300,000 × 5 percent rate = $15,000 percentage or overage rent + $12,000 minimum rent = $27,000 total rent.)

Declining Rate

A high-volume tenant might be willing to pay percentage rent, but not at the same rate for all sales. A declining rate may be the answer. For example, a 30,000-square-foot supermarket generates $18 million in annual sales—very high volume by industry standards. The tenant may feel the percentage rent paid based on a constant rate is too high under the circumstances. A compromise might be 1 percent for the first $12 million ($12,000,000 × 1 percent = $120,000); 0.75 percent for the next $3 million ($3,000,000 × 0.75 percent = $22,500); and 0.50 percent thereafter ($3,000,000 × 0.50 percent = $15,000). Total rent is $157,500.

Deductions from Percentage Rent

While it is rare today to allow a tenant to deduct expense items from percentage rent due—known as recapture—some major tenants demand, and get, the right to do so. In the following example, the tenant is allowed to deduct (recapture) its share of the taxes and insurance from any percentage rent owing.

Total sales		$5,000,000
1.5 percent gross		75,000
Less minimum rent		50,000
Percentage rent due		$ 25,000
Less taxes paid	$18,000	
Less insurance paid	9,000	
	$27,000	
Actual percentage rent owed		-0-

§ 4.10   PERCENTAGE RENT THEORY

Some retail tenants object to paying percentage rent versus a minimum rent. Many of these tenants do not understand the rationale for percentage rent and the concept of the shopping center. When these concepts are explained to tenants, most will no longer resent paying percentage rent.

A logical reason for the landlord to receive percentage rent, sometimes referred to as overage rent—rent over the minimum rent—is that the landlord has created a unique retailing environment. This distinctive environment can be the result of a combination of the shopping center's tenant mix, major tenants, location, or design of the shopping center. The tenant that locates in the shopping center has the opportunity for additional business because of this unique retail environment. If the tenant is more profitable in this environment, the landlord, as creator of the shopping center, should benefit by receiving additional rent. The additional rent is based on a percentage of the tenant's sales above a predetermined amount (known as the tenant's breakpoint). If the location in the shopping center doesn't benefit the tenant's sales, no percentage rent is owed.

The letter of explanation in Exhibit 4.6 advises the tenant on how to fill out the percentage rent report. The example given in the letter helps the tenant compare its sales with the figures in the letter and complete the report satisfactorily.

§ 4.11 SALES REPORTS

The tenant's sales reports are collected and analyzed for several reasons. First, the sales report determines if the tenant owes percentage rent. The sales report also provides indications whether the tenant is successful, a potential rent collection problem, or an impending failure. A tenant's performance is included in evaluating whether or not to renew the tenant's lease.

When all the tenant's sales reports are combined, the property manager can analyze the performance of categories of businesses and the entire center. This analysis will point out weak areas in the shopping center's tenant mix and is also used when developing the shopping center's leasing plan.

(a) SALES REPORTS—MONTHLY

If the lease requires that a tenant reports sales for percentage rent purposes and/or evaluation of the tenant's sales, it is helpful to provide the tenant with a blank form (Exhibit 4.7). The form will assure that the reports are submitted in consistent form and will also help the tenant to understand how percentage rent is calculated.

The tenant is provided sufficient forms at the beginning of the year to complete a full year's reports. For example, if the tenant reports monthly, a supply of 14 or 15 blank forms is sufficient. A letter accompanying the forms (Exhibit 4.6) explains how percentage rents are calculated.

EXHIBIT 4.6

Percentage Rent Letter

Mr. Thomas Black
Blacks Gifts
838 Main Street
Happyville, Maine 02713

Dear Mr. Black:

Welcome to Happyville Center. Many merchants find it helpful to receive a brief explanation of the percentage rent clause and the reporting that goes with it. A supply of forms is enclosed.

Sales reports are due 20 days after the end of each month, and must be signed by the business owner or designated accounting personnel.

Gross Sales include all sales from or because of the business. Sales taxes are deducted as are any items that may have been excluded in the lease agreement. The remaining balance is subject to percentage rent. Multiply the balance times your percentage rent rate and from that figure deduct your montly minimum rent. If there is a balace, that amount should be forwarded with the report. If the minimum rent exceeds the calculated percentage figure, no additional monies are due. Example:

	MONEY DUE	NO MONEY DUE
Sales:	$27,315.00	$21,315.00
Less taxes	(1,366.00)	(1,066.00)
Exclusions	-0-	-0-
Adjusted gross	$25,949.00	$20,249.00
% rent rate 6%	1,556.94	1,214.94
Minimum rent	1,400.00	1,400.00
net due:	$ 156.94	-0-

The annual sales report will be used to reconcile monthly reports for a final accounting. Please make all checks payable to Happyville Center and mail to Alexander Consultants at the below address.

Please call if you have any questions.

Very truly yours,

HAPPYVILLE CENTER

Alan A. Alexander
Manager

AAA:nmt

EXHIBIT 4.7

Monthly Sales Report Form

Date: _____

Merchant: _____   Center: _____

Month: _____

Gross receipts as defined in lease agreement		$_____
Less: Sales tax	$_____	
Other exclusions	_____	
Sub total	_____	$_____
Sales for rental calculation		_____
Percentage rental		_____
Less monthly minimum	_____	
Sub total		$_____
Amount due		$_____

I hereby certify that the above is true and correct.

By: _____

Due by the 10th of following month.

Make all checks payable to:
Plaza Shopping Center

_____

_____

The form should indicate the merchant's name and the name of the center. The month is the month being reported. Gross sales include all income earned from activities at the premises as defined in the individual lease agreement. Sales taxes are always excluded, and some leases have other exclusions such as sales to employees, wholesale items, and so on. The balance of the sales are then subject to the percentage rent calculation.

The percentage rate is the rate stated in the lease agreement. The sales for rent calculation is multiplied by the percentage rate. The minimum rent is then deducted from that amount. If there is a balance due, the tenant should forward that balance to the landlord with the sales report. If there is no balance due, the tenant sends in the report only.

The form should be signed so that the manager can refer to that person if there is a question. It is important to indicate the due date on the form; tenants can easily forget to return the form if no deadline is shown. Also, it is important to include to whom and where to send the form.

When the reports are received in the owner's or manager's office, they should be checked for accuracy and whether any unpaid rent is due. Once the form has been evaluated for percentage rent due, it generally becomes part of a sales analysis report.

(b) COLLECTING SALES REPORTS

Collecting sales reports is more difficult than collecting rent. The property owner wants to know how each tenant and the center is performing. An accurate analysis cannot be provided unless most if not all tenants report their sales on time.

The typical retail lease provision (Exhibit 4.8) will require shop tenants to report their sales between the 20th and the 30th of the month following the sales period. Even national tenants will report sales monthly. Major tenants usually negotiate the right to report sales annually. If the property manager has a rapport with the manager of the major store, verbal reporting may be provided monthly. This is not recommended since there would then be no records to refer to.

Independent merchants often are either late or ignore reporting their sales. They do this for one of several reasons. They don't understand their reporting requirements, their bookkeeping procedures are inadequate, they don't want to pay percentage rent, or they just don't want to be bothered.

Collecting sales reports starts by explaining to the tenant the requirements of the sales reporting provision in the tenant's lease. Someone, usually an administrative person, in the property management office or the on-site mall management office is assigned to collect the sales reports. If the tenant refuses to report its sales, the property manager

EXHIBIT 4.8

Sales Reporting Lease Clause

(a) *Tenant's Obligation.* In addition to the Minimum Rent to be paid by Tenant pursuant to Section 4.1.(a) above, Tenant shall pay to Landlord, at the time and in the manner herein specified, additional percentage rent in an amount equal to _____ percent (_____%) (hereinafter referred to as the "Percentage Rent") of the Tenant's gross sales made in, upon and/or from the Premises, less Minimum Rent paid by Tenant, all as more fully set forth below.

(b) *Monthly Statements.* Within thirty (30) days after the end of each calendar month of the Lease Term, commencing with the 30th day of the month following the month in which the Fixed Minimum Rent Commencement Date commences hereunder, and ending with the 30th day of the month next succeeding the last month of the Lease Term, Tenant shall furnish to Landlord a written statement certified by Tenant to be correct, showing the total gross sales made in, upon and/or from the Premises during the preceding calendar month, and shall accompany each such statement with a payment to Landlord equal to said hereinabove stated percentage of the total monthly gross sales made in, upon, or from the Premises during said calendar month, less the Minimum Rent for each such calendar month, if previously paid. Anything herein to the contrary notwithstanding, in the event the Tenant shall fail or refuse to submit the above monthly statement within said thirty (30) day period, then it shall be deemed that the gross sales for that month are double that necessary for the payment of the Percentage Rent, which Percentage Rent shall be immediately due and payable; provided, that there shall be an actual adjustment for actual gross sales made on an annual basis as set forth herein.

(c) *Annual Statement.* Within thirty (30) days after the end of each calendar year of the Lease Term, Tenant shall furnish to Landlord a written statement, certified by Tenant to be correct, showing the total gross sales made in, upon, or from the Premises during each month of the preceding calendar year, at which time an adjustment shall be made between Landlord and Tenant to the end that the total Percentage Rent paid to Landlord for such calendar year shall be a sum equal to said hereinabove stated percentage of the total gross sales made in, upon, and/or from the Premises during each calendar year of the Term hereof, less the Minimum Rent pursuant to Section 4.1.(a) for such calendar year, if previously paid, so that the Percentage Rent, although payable monthly, shall be computed and adjusted on an annual basis. Any overpayment of Percentage Rent by Tenant shall be credited towards the next Minimum Rent payments due. Tenant shall attach its check to such annual report, which check shall be in an amount equal to any underpayment revealed by such annual report.

(d) *Definition.* The term "gross sales," as used herein, means the selling price of all goods, merchandise and services sold in, upon and/or any part of the Premises by Tenant or any other person, firm or corporation, and shall include, but not be limited to, sales or charges for cash or credit regardless of collections, sales by vending devices, including coin telephone, rent income, mail or telephone orders received or filled at the Premises, all deposits not refunded to purchasers, orders taken although filled elsewhere, fees, commissions,

EXHIBIT 4.8 *(Continued)*

catalog sales, and sales by any sublessee, concessionaire, licensee or otherwise. Excluded from gross sales shall be returns and refunds to customers and the amount of any sales tax or other excise tax imposed upon said sale and charges (but only if such sales tax, excise tax or similar tax is billed to the purchaser as a separate item). Each sale upon installment or credit shall be treated as a sale for the full price in the month during which such sale is made, regardless of the time when Tenant receives payment from its customer.

(e) *Records.* The Tenant shall keep full, complete and proper books, records and accounts in accord with generally accepted accounting principles of its daily gross sales, both for cash and on credit, of each separate department, subtenant, and concessionaire at any time operated in the Premises. The Landlord and its agents and employees shall have the right at any and all reasonable times, during the regular business hours, to examine and inspect all of the books and records of the Tenant, including any sales tax reports pertaining to the business of the Tenant conducted in, upon, and/or from the Premises, for the purpose of investigating and verifying the accuracy of any statement of gross sales. Tenant shall keep all said records for five (5) years. All records shall be maintained by Tenant on the Premises. The Landlord may once in any calendar year cause an audit of the business of Tenant to be made by an accountant of Landlord's selection, and if the statement of gross sales previously made to Landlord shall be found to be inaccurate, then and in that event, there shall be an adjustment and the Tenant shall pay to the Landlord on demand such sums as may be necessary to settle in full the accurate amount of said Percentage Rent that should have been paid to Landlord for the period or periods covered by such inaccurate statement or statements. If said audit shall disclose an inaccuracy of greater than a two percent (2%) error with respect to the amount of gross sales reported by Tenant for the period of said report, then the Tenant shall immediately pay to Landlord the cost of such audit; otherwise, the cost of such audit shall be paid by Landlord. If such audit shall disclose any willful or substantial inaccuracies, this Lease may thereupon be canceled and terminated, at the option of Landlord.

becomes involved. The first step in collecting delinquent sales reports is a phone call to the tenant. If the property has an on-site manager, a personal visit to the tenant is more effective. If the phone call and visit produce no results, and the store is part of a chain, its district manager should be called. A letter can be sent to the tenant following the conversation (Exhibit 4.9). Continual nonreporting of sales figures may indicate that the tenant's sales are above the breakpoint and he owes percentage rent. This tenant should be considered for a sales audit. The sample lease provision states a penalty of double the base rent if a tenant fails to report its sales on time. The tenant's handbook should contain an explanation of the sales reporting procedure (§ 4.13). The penalty for late sales reporting, as stated in the lease, should be enforced. If the current lease doesn't provide a penalty, it should be included in the lease at renewal time. The ultimate step, one which is seldom taken, is to place the tenant in default of its lease and seek legal action.

§ 4.12   SALES ANALYSIS—COMMUNITY OR REGIONAL SHOPPING CENTER

Sales analysis in a larger shopping center is a significant management tool that can be provided to the tenants on a monthly basis. This summary enables merchants to evaluate their performance compared to other merchants in the center and to the center as a whole. The sales reports are gathered and placed in predetermined categories such as women's wear, men's wear, gifts, shoes, food, and so on.

Each merchant is assigned a letter known only to management, and its sales are then compared on a sales-per-square-foot basis and percentage of change. The numbers are compared to the same month in the previous year and to sales in the area for a comparison in the marketplace. It is not unusual to use these figures to evaluate an area in a center, a merchandise category, or specific sizes of stores. Quite often, sales figures will reveal certain areas of the center are stronger than others which is helpful in locating specific tenants or uses.

The sales per square foot can also be compared to those in *Dollars and Cents of Shopping Centers* to see how the merchants compare to the same categories of merchandise on a national basis.

It is best to compile this information and return it to the merchants each month to give immediate feedback.

(a)   SALES COMPARISONS BY STORES

Each category of merchandise is analyzed to see how each merchant is performing compared to others in the category. The sales are reduced

EXHIBIT 4.9

Missing Sales Report Form

DATE:

TO:

In Reply Refer To:

RE: **MISSING SALES REPORTS**

We are still missing sales reports for the following months for your store. Your lease requires that sales be reported on a monthly basis. Please submit the missing reports to our office within five days of receipt of this notice.

_____	$_____
_____	$_____
_____	$_____
_____	$_____
_____	$_____
_____	$_____
_____	$_____
_____	$_____
_____	$_____
_____	$_____
_____	$_____
_____	$_____
_____	$_____

Sincerely,

to sales per square foot and listed by a predetermined code to make sure that no merchants sales can be directly identified. The sales are then compared for the same period in the previous year and stated as a percentage of increase or decrease. The entire category is compared in the same way so the merchant and the management can determine how well the specific merchant is doing in relation to the other merchants in that category (Exhibit 4.10).

This information is used in discussions with the merchant about improving sales and for letting them know how well they are doing. The information is also used in analyzing tenant mix.

§ 4.13 SALES ANALYSIS—SMALL SHOPPING CENTER

In a small shopping center or office setting with few retail tenants, it is not practical to analyze sales by merchandise categories. Instead, the retailer's sales figures are compared in three ways: (1) to the individual retailer's figures from the previous year, (2) to all merchants in the center, and (3) to sales per square foot. By comparing the individual tenant's sales to the same period the year before, progress or decline is evident. Comparing percentages of increase for all merchants and the center shows the bigger sales picture.

The report is also used to determine both individual sales per square foot and the entire center's sales per square foot. A third comparison can then be made with the sales figures in *Dollars and Cents of Shopping Centers* to see if sales figures meet national averages. Comparing a tenant's sales per square foot to those of a merchant in a different category is usually not valid since different merchants produce substantially different sales results even when both are quite successful. Tenants that do not have percentage rent clauses are not included in this report.

The tenants are listed according to their place on the tenant roster. Sales are entered for the current period and added to the previous period for year-to-date figures. Most reports round the sales off to the nearest dollar. The sales breakpoint is the dollar amount of sales the tenant must exceed before percentage rent is paid to the landlord. The breakpoint is calculated by dividing the minimum rent by the percentage rate, or if the breakpoint is artificial, it is entered in the appropriate column in the percentage portions of the report. The reason the column is headed "percentage rent potential" is that a tenant could owe percentage rent one month, but by year-end the annual sales could be less then the required amount of sales for percentage rent (Exhibit 4.11).

The sales increase (or decrease) can also be compared to sales reports for the city or county to see if the center is holding its market share over a period of time.

EXHIBIT 4.10

Sales Comparisons by Stores

	SEPTEMBER Sq. Ft.	%	OCTOBER Sq. Ft.	%	NOVEMBER Sq. Ft.	%	DECEMBER Sq. Ft.	%	JANUARY Sq. Ft.	%	FEBRUARY Sq. Ft.	%
WOMEN'S WEAR												
A	4.33	- 12.3	4.37	.04	4.96	+ 9.2	13.37	+ 2.7	4.20	+ 21.8	3.27	- 10.2
B	6.18	+ 61.6	4.25	+ 28.9	5.80	+ 26.2	13.61	+ 71.2	3.33	+ 68.9	3.77	+ 78.9
C	5.83	- 0 -	6.51	+ 31.6	7.77	- 47.7	23.70	+ 35.4	4.61	+ 57.8	5.51	+ 78.9
D	11.28	+108.2	7.56	+ 47.7	8.22	+ 36.2	15.51	+ 41.2	4.69	+ 61.9	4.67	+ 67.9
E	6.56	- 29.5	4.40	- 13.2	6.07	- 26.3	14.35	+ 42.2	4.39	+ 42.6	4.56	+ 51.0
F	5.00	- 6.6	4.80	- 12.8	5.50	- 19.2	11.76	- 19.1	3.22	- 14.4	4.76	- 3.3
G	4.56	+155.8	4.62	+ 32.0	5.44	+ 27.5	11.41	+ 26.8	3.91	+ 58.0	3.68	+ 45.6
H	11.63	+ 76.6	11.26	+ 85.6	12.48	+ 69.8	22.17	+ 66.0	6.37	+ 23.5	7.20	+ 4.3
I	4.78	- 7.1	3.66	+ 44.1	3.50	+ 9.9	6.86	- .5	1.65	- 40.2	2.67	+ 16.0
J	6.92	+ 18.5	6.68	+ 31.6	8.47	+ 32.1	11.68	+ 38.5	5.77	+ 65.2	7.74	+ 38.4
K	5.60	- 6.7	4.59	- 3.2	5.48	+ 23.6	15.28	+ 41.3	4.37	+ 16.9	5.41	+ 57.1
L	6.20	- 0 -	4.77	- 0 -	7.64	- 0 -	11.98	- 0 -	5.83	- 0 -	5.06	- 0 -
M	5.06	+129.3	5.53	+ 65.2	5.90	+ 57.8	13.10	+ 44.7	6.46	+ 83.7	5.00	+ 28.9
N	5.61	- 9.0	5.29	+ 25.3	5.65	+ 52.7	9.97	+ 22.8	2.63	+ 66.9	3.98	+111.2
O	4.57	+ 18.9	3.82	- 0 -	5.08	+213.0	11.09	+ 54.9	3.46	+ 62.3	3.52	+133.8
P	3.50	+ 8.8	3.28	+ 90.8	3.79	- 34.3	8.77	+ 6.9	3.19	+ 21.0	2.65	+ 11.7
Q	6.49	+ 8.8	5.53	+ 35.9	6.27	+ 25.8	15.00	- 20.4	3.87	+ 23.1	4.46	- 2.3
R	4.00	- 0 -	4.28	+ 15.5	5.39	- 0 -	9.16	- 0 -	2.97	- 0 -	3.62	+ 31.7
Category Average	5.62	+ 25.9	4.95	+ 26.0	5.64	+ 37.0	13.19	+ 31.2	4.07	+ 37.8	4.24	+33.6
MEN'S WEAR												
A	4.79	- 12.6	4.39	+ 15.4	5.36	+ 10.7	11.68	- 8.1	3.39	+ .7	3.55	- 11.0
B	4.40	- 0 -	4.59	- 0 -	7.17	- 0 -	12.45	- 0 -	4.48	- 0 -	7.17	- 0 -
C	7.43	+ 38.0	5.47	+ 2.6	9.16	+ 26.2	17.81	+ 27.2	3.55	- 9.9	9.27	+ 85.5
D	4.13	- 0 -	4.16	- 0 -	4.59	- 0 -	12.78	- 0 -	4.43	- 0 -	3.11	- 0 -
E	- 0 -	- 0 -	- 0 -	- 0 -	2.72	- 0 -	10.03	- 0 -	3.67	- 0 -	3.57	- 0 -
F	4.34	+ 2.3	3.25	+ 4.9	7.17	- 17.0	14.14	+ 17.0	1.80	+ 19.8	3.70	+ 46.8
G	16.20	- 0 -	8.48	- 0 -	11.21	- 0 -	31.85	- 0 -	8.92	- 0 -	8.90	- 0 -
H	4.32	- 0 -	4.23	- 5.1	6.11	- 46.2	10.62	- 13.8	3.02	- 21.5	2.79	- 19.3
I	3.86	+, 45.7	4.62	- 1.7	5.81	+ 1.9	14.60	- 7.3	3.93	- 28.6	3.99	+ 21.5
Category Average	5.42	+ 14.8	4.58	+ 2.6	5.88	+ 2.3	14.00	+ 6.0	4.08	+ 6.7	4.49	+ 32.0
RESTAURANTS												
A	10.01	- 12.3	8.53	- 13.2	10.12	- 7.2	17.22	+ 5.0	7.56	- 7.5	7.17	- 19.1
B	8.84	+ 62.5	8.75	+ 19.0	9.38	+ 25.7	11.16	+ 20.5	8.73	+ 16.5	8.79	+ 28.2
C	8.90	- .18	9.01	- .01	9.18	+ 3.6	11.01	+ 9.9	8.77	+ 5.7	8.32	+ 5.9
Category Average	8.99	+ 17.0	8.84	+ 5.9	9.36	- 10.8	11.72	+ 11.4	8.63	+ 8.8	8.41	+ 11.9

EXHIBIT 4.11

Sales Analysis Form

CENTER Neighborhood Center

MONTH: _____

MERCHANT	AREA	MONTHLY SALES COMPARISON					YEAR-TO-DATE COMPARISON					BREAK-POINT	OVERAGE POTENTIAL EVALUATION				
		MONTH	MONTH	% CHANGE	SQ. FT.	SQ. FT.	CURRENT YEAR	PREVIOUS YEAR	% CHANGE	SQ. FT.	SQ. FT.		CURRENT MONTH		% CHANGE	YEAR-TO-DATE	% CHANGE
Supermkt	A-1	885,000	835,500	5.9	41.07	19.89	3,640,111	3,258,111	8.4	84.29	77.58	816,667	1,025	282	363	4,102	0	-
Malls Cards	A-2	34,380	29,101	18.14	17.19	14.55	120,380	101,31%	18.85	60.17	50.68	27.783	396	79	500	351	0	-
Styles	A-3	7,315	6,812	7.38	4.88	4.54	28,500	27,150	4.90	19.80	18.10	17,000	0	0	0	0	0	0
Cleaners	A-4	10,150	9,230	9.97	6.34	5.77	40,510	38,003	6.59	25.12	23.75	19,529	0	0	0	0	0	0
TV & Stereo	A-5	44,144	38,887	13.51	22.07	19.44	175,112	161,201	8.75	87.36	80.60	41,675	99	0	-	344	0	-
Hardware	A-7	37,500	34,111	9.93	7.50	6.82	149,012	137,800	7.41	29.30	27.56	96,350						
Pizza	A-8	61,500	57,111	7.68	19.22	17.84	245,500	228,211	8.53	76.22	70.49	52,000	475	256	185	1,875	1,016	18%
99 Flavors	A-10	18,312	1,66	10.77	10.60	70.151	69,135	1.47	41.28	40.67	26.917	29,040						
Fabric	A-11	38,900	33,612	15.73	11.44	9.89	135,000	114,350	13.33	39.71	35.04	55,260						
Salon	A-12	19,151	17,999	6.40	5.98	5.62	76,011	72,003	5.57	23.75	21.18	40,000						
Shoes	A-13	41,512	33,667	23.38	14.97	12.95	158,333	135,898	16.51	69.90	62.27	37,917	216	0	-	4,090	0	-
Bikes	A-14	18,858	19,312	(2.35)	11.79	12.07	74,312	75,889	(2.08)	46.45	47.43	28,000						
Drug	A-15	285,011	245,811	15.95	12.96	11.17	1,100,101	895,994	22.8%	59.00	50.73	244,433	1,217	46	252	6,621	46	1.376
Dime	P-1	101,560	97,013	4.69	26.95	26.95	400,850	385,856	3.43	111.34	107.11	108,000	322	0	-	-	-	-
Remaining merchants report yearly.																		

(a) SALES COMPARISONS BY CATEGORIES

Each category of merchandise is analyzed, using total dollar sales, against the same period for the previous year and converting that into a percentage of increase or decrease. All categories are then totaled and this provides a figure for the shopping center as a whole. These figures can then be used to compare the centers market share to that of the city or county to see if the center is gaining or losing sales in the market place.

The sales for the entire center are useful in measuring the individual merchant but some categories are typically higher volume than others so a direct comparison with all categories may result in a meaningless comparison (Exhibit 4.10).

§ 4.14   COMPARATIVE SALES ANALYSIS— INDIVIDUAL TENANT

This report gives information to the tenant about how it is doing in comparison with other merchants in the same category and in the center as a whole. Obviously, in the compilation of sales data, great care must be taken to ensure there are sufficient merchants in a category so that individual tenant sales are not revealed. The report covers both the current month being analyzed as well as the year-to-date figures.

The report is most effective if hand-delivered to the store manager. The property manager can use the report as a public relations tool to congratulate the merchant for a job well done or to discuss low sales as compared to other stores that are producing at a higher level. Further, the report provides valuable information for individual merchants in comparing the center's sales with those of the community to see how the center is doing with the market share (Exhibit 4.12).

§ 4.15   ACCOUNTING

Generally, the accounting department needs a lease or a billing to trigger a receivable. In the case of percentage rent, the accountant first has to collect sales reports from the tenants. A master list of all tenants should be prepared indicating whether sales reports are required and, if so, when they are due and at what point will percentage rent be due (see Exhibit 4.13).

It is helpful to provide sales report forms to less sophisticated tenants. The due dates of sales reports for all tenants should be recorded in a tickler file and, if not received as agreed, the tenant should be notified. A close follow-up on sales reports can improve cash flow substantially.

EXHIBIT 4.12

Comparative Sales Analysis Form

Center:_____

Store Name:_____ Sales Category:_____

		Cumulative
Month_____, 19_____		_____Months, 19____
1. Your sales per sq. ft.	_____	_____
2. Number of stores reporting in category.	_____	_____
3. Category average per sq. ft.	_____	_____
4. Highest sales per sq. ft.	_____	_____
5. Your ranking in category.	_____	_____
6. Your increase (decrease) vs. prior year. (%)	_____	_____
7. Category average increase (decrease).	_____	_____
8. Highest increase.	_____	_____
9. Total Center's increase (decrease) excluding	_____	_____

_____
Center Manager.

Once the reports are received they should be checked by the accounting personnel for mathematical accuracy and any percentage rents due. If monies are due, the tenant should immediately be billed and the amount entered on the tenant ledger card or on the computer so that the billing is not lost in the system. The bookkeeper would then pass the report on to the property manager for sales evaluation and possible tenant audit.

(a) AUDITING TENANT'S SALES

The typical lease with a retailer and some service tenants calls for minimum rent versus a percentage of sales, whichever is greater. Tenants

EXHIBIT 4.13

Percentage Rent Formula—Neighborhood Center

			Date:	
Tenant Name	Percentage	Reports	When Due	Break Point
Friendly Market	1.5	Annual	Feb/NY	14700000
Kathy's Kards	6	Qtrly	Qtr + 20	316667
Today's Styles	7.5	Monthly	Mth + 10	16250
White Cleaners	7	Monthly	Mth + 10	18571
Advance TV	4	Monthly	Mth + 10	39583
Vacant				
Kings Hardware	4	Annual	Feb/NY	1093750
Pizza Plus	5	Monthly	Mth + 10	49333
Fast Sell Realty	0			
Goodies Ice Cream	5	Monthly	Mth + 10	26916
Fancy Fabrics	5	Monthly	Mth + 10	52417
Slim & Trim Salon	7	Monthly	Mth + 10	35809
Family Dis Shoes	6	Qtrly	Qtr + 20	108333
Speedy's Bikes	5	Monthly	Mth + 10	27333
Discount Drugs	See Below	Annual	Mar/NY	2640000
Dine N Dash	5	Monthly	Mth + 10	96000
Home Town Bank	0			

Discount Drugs

3% up to 2,640000
2% for the next 1500000
1% everything above 4,140000

who have a percentage rent provision in their lease should be considered for a sales audit.

The property manager analyzes which tenant should be audited based on several factors. The first factor is whether or not the tenant is paying percentage or overage rent. Percentage or overage rent occurs when a tenant's sales exceed its breakpoint to pay percentage rent. The natural breakpoint is calculated by dividing the tenant's minimum rent by the percentage rate. Every tenant paying percentage rent is a candidate for an audit. Tenants may not be calculating their sales correctly or they may be understating sales to avoid paying additional rent. It can also be helpful to compare tenant's sales to those in the *Dollars and Cents of Shopping Centers* (Exhibit 4.14).

Another situation when a sales audit may be performed is when tenants' sales are within 20 percent of their breakpoint. These tenants may also be understating their sales to avoid paying percentage rent. Most tenant whose sales are less than 80 percent of their breakpoint are not likely to be submitting incorrect sales reports.

There are many shopping centers where no tenants are candidates for an audit. This can occur when all the tenants' sales are low or when the minimum rent is so high that the tenants' breakpoints are high and it is not likely any of them will reach their breakpoint during the initial term of their lease.

The property manager reviews the tenants who are likely candidates for an audit and selects which tenants to audit based on:

1. Who is likely to be understating sales
2. Whose business appears to be increasing but sales figures show very little growth from prior years
3. Which tenants would tell other tenants that they were audited. The property manager wants all the tenants to know that the landlord conducts regular sales audits. This may deter any tenants who might be thinking of understating their sales figures.
4. When each tenant was last audited
5. Which tenants were found owing percentage rent during their last audit.

Some landlords will automatically audit 10 percent of their tenants each year. This program is not recommended, for many tenants' sales will never come close to their breakpoint.

Prior to selecting tenants for an audit, the property manager should have designated an auditor who could be either a national or a local accounting firm that specializes in conducting tenant audits.

After the tenants to be audited have been carefully selected, a letter is sent to them stating that they have been selected for an audit (Exhibit 4.15). Once the tenants receive their letter, the property manager needs to schedule the audit and a premeeting with the tenant to explain the purpose of the audit and emphasize that it is a routine procedure and does not indicate that the landlord believes the tenant is submitting incorrect sales reports. The auditor will provide the property manager with a checklist of items to provide for the audit.

After the audit is completed, the property manager and the auditor should meet with the tenant and review the results. If the tenant owes percentage rent, the lease should state when it is due.

(b) EVALUATING EXISTING TENANTS

Each tenant's sales should be compared with national averages and with similar uses within the center. For example, a neighborhood center has a national chain 45,000-square-foot supermarket. It produces $9,360,000 in

EXHIBIT 4.14

Comparative Measure of Tenant Sales

U.S. Neighborhood Shopping Centers
Hobby/Special Interest, Gifts/Specialty

Tenant Classification	No. in Sample	GLA in Sq. Ft. Median Lower Decile	Upper Decile	Sales per Sq. Ft. Median Top 10 Percent	Top 2 Percent	Rate of Percentage Rent Median Lower Decile	Upper Decile
Cameras	18	1.630		217.67		5.00	
M04		920	2.900	268.96	281.22	2.00	6.00
National Chain	5	1.600					
Local Chain	2						
Independent	11	1.766					
		920	2.900				
Toys	13	1.900		82.10		6.00	
M05		150	5.250	107.07	151.59		
National Chain	0						
Local Chain	5	3.260					
Independent	8	1.750		82.10		6.00	
Bike Shop	16	1.350		103.93		5.00	
M06		970	3.312	139.98	159.54	4.00	6.00
National Chain	0						
Local Chain	3						
Independent	13	1.350		103.93		5.00	
		900	3.312				
Arts and Crafts	28	1.200		69.11		6.00	
M07		900	10.400	104.76	138.83	5.00	8.00
National Chain	3						
Local Chain	4						
Independent	21	1.200		60.29		6.00	
Coin Shop	5	1.032					
M08							
National Chain	0						
Local Chain	2						
Independent	3						
Outfitters	9	1.378		127.06			
M09							
National Chain	0						
Local Chain	4						
Independent	5	1.400					
Imports	7	2.800					
N01							
National Chain	0						
Local Chain	1						
Independent	6	2.800					
Cards and Gifts	84	2.310		73.87		6.00	
N03		1.200	3.600	133.44	170.00	5.00	8.00
National Chain	9	3.000		80.46		6.00	
Local Chain	17	2.310		63.67		6.00	
		1.352	3.000	109.38	120.77	5.00	7.00
Independent	58	2.200		75.26		6.00	
		1.200	3.515	132.03	170.00	5.00	8.00

Source: Urban Land Institute, *Dollars and Cents of Shopping Centers*, 192–193 (1987).

Total Rent per Sq. Ft.		Common Area Charges per Sq. Ft.		Property Taxes and Insurance per Sq. Ft.		Total Charges per Sq. Ft.		Total Charges as Percent of Sales	
Median		Median		Median		Median		Median	
Top 10 Percent	Top 2 Percent	Top 10 Percent	Top 2 Percent	Top 10 Percent	Top 2 Percent	Top 10 Percent	Top 2 Percent	Lower Decile	Upper Decile
9.24		.41		.54		10.03		5.57	
14.49	16.26	.88	1.88	1.01	1.25	15.74	17.08	3.18	13.80
9.75		.41		.77		11.31			
9.03		.37		.32		9.33			
9.84	10.50	.63	.74			10.56	13.53		
8.83		.63		.63		10.53		15.79	
14.00	20.07	2.08	2.73	1.06	1.15	16.96	22.54	6.29	31.31
5.93						6.86			
9.60		.73		.63		10.92		18.67	
8.06		.80		. 63		10.79		8.64	
11.96	12.70	1.74	1.61	1.06	1.06	13.99	14.64	4.65	19.98
8.06		.72		.63		10 79		8.55	
11.28	11.96	1.46			1.74	1.309	13.99		
9.00		.60		.61		10.00		12.29	
12.21	14.40	1.32	1.81	1.18	1.32	14.16	16.01	6.80	41.06
8.76		.57		.61		9.68		12.29	
11.00	12.00	1.08	1.18	.96	1.16	12.23	12.59	5.16	41.06
8.25						8.55			
12.00		6?		.24		12.24		7.75	
12.00				.24		13.84			
9.16		1.04		.51		10.41			
9.16		1.04		.51		10.41			
8.75		.62		.65		9.88		13.29	
12.49	18.67	1.46	1.73	1.28	2.17	14.55	20.51	6.73	27.61
7.25		.80		.95		10.08		12.97	
9.18		.81		.80		11.04		13.29	
11.00	12.49	1.73	1 73	1.16	1.93	14.52	14.55	5.91	31.10
8.70		.53		.61		9.63		14.68	
12.00	15.00	1.03	1.73	1.22	1.92	13.73	16.36	6.99	27.61

EXHIBIT 4.15

Tenant Audit Letter

March 5, 19____

Mr. George_____
George's Barber Shop
_____

Dear Mr. _____

George's Barber Shop at Sunny Hills Shopping Center has been selected for a sales audit for the period January 1, 1988 through December 31, 1990. This examination is being done in accordance with your lease to determine the accuracy of the sales figures reported to us. This letter will serve as the formal notice required in your lease agreement.

Selection of tenants for audit is based on several factors including lease expiration date, sales performance relative to breakpoint, nature of business, and date of last audit. In addition, many of the tenants are selected at random.

In connection with the examination, our independent auditors, Thompson Associates, will require that the following be available for inspection:

1. Sales journal/Cash receipts journal
2. General ledger
3. Profit and loss statements
4. Bank statements
5. Sales tax returns
6. Federal income tax returns
7. Any records necessary to substantiate deductions from reportable sales
8. All of the above for any subtenant, licensee, or concessionaire

Thompson Associates will also require the following daily documentation for the test months March and September 1988, April and October 1989, June and November 1990:

1. Daily cash register tapes and sealed continuous tapes, and/or original sales slips (both tapes and sales slips are required if used to record sales.
2. Daily/weekly sales reports.

A representative from Thompson Associates will be contacting you to arrange a mutually convenient time and location to perform the examination. With your cooperation you will find that the time required to perform the audit is normally only a few hours and you will experience only a minimal disruption of your daily operations.

Your cooperation in this matter is certainly appreciated. If you have any questions, please contact Thompson Associates, 345-0096.

Sincerely,

XYZ Management Company

sales, which is $280 per square foot. *Dollars and Cents of Shopping Centers* (1993) indicates that a supermarket will average $346.79 per square foot. A comparison shows that the store is average for a national chain and above average for supermarkets in general.

In larger centers, a form like the one in Exhibit 4.10 would be used to evaluate a specific tenant. Comparing the tenant with the category reveals whether the tenant is doing well, poorly, or average. The manager must also consider store size, specific type of merchandise, time of year, and any store changes that have taken place.

Once the sales figures are gathered, the property manager should schedule a meeting with each tenant to open up a dialogue. The tenant in the supermarket example above should not be a future rent collection problem: It is generating very good sales, is number two in its category, and is well above average in its percentage of increases. Congratulations are in order during the meeting.

(c) EVALUATING PROSPECTIVE TENANTS

Sales comparison figures can also be used to evaluate prospective tenants. For example, in a negotiation with two prospective men's wear stores, assume that Prospect 1 is negotiating for lower rent and that Prospect 2 seems willing to accept your terms. Prospect 1 has another shop averaging $350 per square foot in sales and feels she will do at least that volume in your center. Prospect 2 believes he will average sales of $120 per square foot but will pay your asking rent of $12 per square foot per year. Men's wear stores generally pay about 5 percent of sales. Prospect 1 would pay a total rent of $17.50 per square foot based on her sales, if the rent would be 5 percent of gross sales, a very comfortable rent-to-sales ratio. Prospect 2 would produce only rent of $6 per square foot based on projected sales, but the minimum rent is $12 and the ratio of rent to sales is 10 percent. All things being equal, Prospect 1 would make the better long-term tenant. Note: Rent to sales ratio is determined by dividing the tenant's sales into its rent. When a tenant's rent-to-sales ratio exceeds 12 to 15 percent, the tenant is probably not generating a profit and is a candidate for failure.

(d) EVALUATING THE CENTER'S SALES

Sales figures can be used not only to evaluate each tenant but to evaluate the center as a whole and to measure the success of various merchandise categories within the center (see Exhibit 4.3). Each category is totaled, averages set, and each tenant in the category compared with the whole. Comparisons can be made on sales per square foot as well as sales increases or decreases.

Great care must be taken not to reveal individual tenant's sales figures to others in this process. If there are three or fewer merchants in a category, revealing the total sales would automatically provide each tenant with the sales of the others. For that reason, it is very difficult to calculate category breakdowns in neighborhood centers. Sales analyses in such centers are limited to confidential individual tenant analysis and an overall center analysis. If the center is in a state where sales taxes are collected, those figures can be used to measure the market share of an individual center on an ongoing basis.

Here are several indicators why a tenant's sales should be audited.

- Tenant's sales have steadily increased in a specific pattern but have leveled off just below the breakpoint for percentage rent.
- The tenant paid percentage rent last year but is now reporting sales just below the breakpoint.
- The store is always busy, but the sales volume does not seem to match the activity.

The property manager should pay close attention to sales when the center has been remodeled, expanded, or has added a major tenant and the given tenant's sales do not increase. Even if nothing seems to be amiss, auditing a tenant who is close to the breakpoint may reveal enough additional sales to require paying percentage rents. Auditing the most vocal tenant in the center can produce excellent results because as other tenants find out about the audit they often take more care in reporting their sales.

Physical observation of a store can turn up questionable activities. One drugstore operator was observed diverting cash sales to a cigar box in a drawer below the cash register. It was also noted that some of the store's employees were stealing from the cigar box.

A useful technique in auditing tenants' sales is to send a letter to all tenants in the center announcing a routine audit of a percentage of all tenants' sales on a regular basis. This starts tenants thinking about the accuracy of their sales reports. In states with sales taxes, the property manager may ask for a copy of the tenant's state sales tax reports and compare them with the sales reports made to the center. If the tenant cannot explain any discrepancies, it is prudent to conduct an audit.

In deciding who should audit tenants, several factors should be considered. The property manager's accounting staff provides the greatest flexibility and is the least expensive. However, unless they are knowledgeable in retail accounting important items might be overlooked such as missing cash register tapes, missing invoices, imbalance between inventory and sales. In addition, the tenants might not take the staff accountant as seriously as they would an outside auditor.

The use of a large national CPA firm specializing in tenant audits has advantages if the tenant has many locations and the books are centrally located. Using a nationally recognized company also indicates the serious nature of the audit because these companies have the expertise to find clever manipulations or obscure errors. If a national company is used, however, it will often schedule the audit for its convenience rather than the shopping center's.

A local CPA firm generally knows more about the area's business climate, is more flexible in schedule, and can return for another look if the situation warrants.

Unless there is reason to believe there may be many auditing problems in a center, it is suggested that not more than 10 percent of the tenants should be audited in any given year because of the expense of conducting audits. Even though a tenant may be suspected of not accurately reporting sales, there are times when an audit is not indicated. If the tenant's actual sales are not likely to produce percentage rent, and the lease is expiring shortly, there is no point in spending money on an audit. The same holds true if the tenant is underreporting but sales are not likely to exceed the breakpoint. Also, as a practical matter, if the tenant and landlord are having ongoing problems concerning other matters, an audit can easily aggravate an already difficult situation.

The auditor should send a completed written report outlining any problems, the scope of the problem, and recommendations for prevention. As quickly as possible, the property manager should meet with the tenant, review the report, and make appropriate requests for any monies due and procedural changes to prevent future discrepancies.

If the discrepancies are large enough, or deliberate in nature, the manager may need to consider a possible lease default, checking with legal counsel before proceeding. Whatever the outcome of an audit, it is personal business between tenant and management and not a topic to discuss with other tenants or outsiders.

§ 4.16   THE MERCHANTS' ASSOCIATION

No matter how small the shopping center, it can always benefit from a good merchants' association. Although they do have problems, and many property owners would just as soon not have the merchants organized for any reason, an effective association is worth any small problems it may cause.

The purpose of a merchants' association is to advertise and promote the center and to foster good business practices, thereby encouraging the public to shop at the center. It is not the purpose of the association to operate the common areas, oversee leasing efforts, supervise on-site employees, or set rents and center hours. It is critical for the long-range success of the association that these purposes be kept clearly in mind and that the property manager maintain sufficient control to see that the association does not deviate from its intended purpose.

When properly run, the merchants' association benefits all parties. The merchants gain the benefits of joint advertising and reach a larger audience for less individual investment, particularly when the landlord contributes toward their advertising efforts. The merchants' association also provides a forum to discuss good business practices and share common concerns.

The property owner gains by having this forum to help guide the center in an effective merchandising program. The property owner will see direct benefits in terms of high center sales, which produce additional percentage rents.

Even the community gains when a center has an organized promotional effort. The public becomes aware of merchandising events, sales, and community interest programs. Large centers put on shows and events with broad public appeal, often at little or no cost to the customer.

There are three approaches to advertising and promoting shopping centers: traditional merchants' association, marketing fund, and owner-sponsored program.

(a) TRADITIONAL MERCHANTS' ASSOCIATION

For many years, the traditional merchants' association was the choice of almost all shopping center owners. This association is set up by the center's owners or developers as a nonprofit corporation. Nonprofit status gives the association effective buying power because they do not pay taxes and, as a corporation, the association's liability is limited.

There are three approaches to membership. The most effective is mandatory membership in the association as a lease requirement. The second approach, and a weaker one, is a lease provision that requires a tenant to join the association if 80 percent of the merchants belong. The last and least effective is voluntary membership. In all cases, tenants who are members of the merchants' association are required to pay minimum dues set by the landlord and often are required to participate in a minimum number of advertising campaigns each year.

The association is governed by bylaws prepared by the property owners and administered by a board of directors elected by the merchants. The property owner or property manager always has a permanent seat on the board of directors and has veto rights over programs in the common areas that are deemed undesirable for the center.

Major tenants often refuse to join a merchants' association, causing a split between large and small tenants. This is one reason for setting the participation level at 80 percent rather than 100 percent. The major tenant is generally one of the largest advertisers in the center and does not want to be controlled by the smaller tenants.

The most effective merchants' associations allow one vote for each merchant rather than weighted votes for store size. Some centers allow for one vote per 1,000 square feet of leased space, which may seem equitable but can cause serious problems if five smaller tenants in favor of a program are voted down by a 14,000-square-foot tenant acting alone. Although the property manager can veto any activity in the common area because the landlord controls that space, the veto should be used only when absolutely necessary. Tenants will feel that they have no real say if they are continually overruled.

The association generally meets monthly to plan programs for the future and discuss items of mutual interest. In smaller centers, merchants may be reluctant to participate. Many are small business owners who already spend long hours at their stores. The property manager needs to encourage participation and show consistent support for the association without appearing to control it. For this reason, the manager would be ill advised to act as an officer of the association or to take on many of the administrative tasks.

In very large shopping centers, the merchants' association is administered by a full-time professional marketing director. The International Council of Shopping Centers (ICSC) has a program for training and certifying marketing directors. The professional designation is Certified Marketing Director (CMD), which recognizes a high level of experience and training in that field.

The bylaws of the association should give the landlord the right and obligation to hire, fire, and oversee the marketing director. The cost is generally part of the property owner's contribution to the association, if the property owner makes a contribution. The marketing director is not a member of the board but carries out most of the business of the association and serves as its executive director.

Because of limited funds available, promotions and advertising in smaller centers are handled in various ways. The center can hire a part-time marketing director who is paid an hourly or monthly fee, or it can retain the services of a public relations or marketing company.

The least effective approach, often used in neighborhood centers, is for the merchants to run the association. Although better than no effort at all, this arrangement does not work very well. Merchants lack experience in shopping center advertising and promotion and are already too busy to devote much time to further activities. However, when merchants are in charge, the property manager generally types and mails minutes, meeting notices, annual calendars, and other administrative materials so that the merchants can concentrate on advertising and promotion.

(b) MARKETING FUND

A more recent innovation in handling shopping center advertising and promotions is the marketing fund. In the late 1970s, a number of regional and super-regional malls set up an advertising or marketing fund in lieu of a merchants' association. This method has been fairly effective in large centers; in smaller centers it is not as workable since merchants may resent paying into a fund with little or no say in its disposition.

If the center has a marketing fund, the lease will require each merchant to contribute. The landlord then administers the fund in the best interests of the center. Although there is no association and no monthly merchant meetings, an advisory committee of merchants will provide guidance and ideas for the fund's administrator. Merchants can also meet quarterly to review past promotions and suggest future events.

(c) OWNER-SPONSORED PROGRAM

The center's owner has the largest single investment in the center and must be concerned with its long-term success even if the merchants are not enthusiastic about advertising and promotions. The third approach is for the landlord to advertise and promote independently with no support or involvement from the merchants. In a problem property, where the merchants seem unwilling to cooperate in advertising and promotion, this may be the only alternative. In this case the landlord independently sets up a program, implements it, and pays the costs.

One effective advertising program is a weekly ad that uses a standard format but features different merchants or events each week. This keeps the center's name in front of the public and attracts prospective tenants. The landlord in this case arranges for centerwide sales, civic programs, or paid promotions throughout the year. (See Exhibit 4.16.)

(d) DUES STRUCTURES

Dues vary widely but will generally range from 35¢ per square foot per year to as high as $2 per square foot per year in specialty centers. Neighborhood center dues usually range from 35¢ to 50¢ per square foot per year. Regional mall dues will vary from 50¢ to $1.50 per square foot per year.

The amount of dues is generally spelled out in the lease. Dues for major tenants are usually negotiated at a lower rate per square foot than for smaller tenants. It is not unusual for major tenants to have a permanent seat on the board of directors of the Merchants' Association.

There should be an automatic mechanism for increasing dues over the term of the lease to keep up with inflation. This can be an agreed-upon annual increase—3 or 5 percent—or an increase tied to the consumer

EXHIBIT 4.16

Landlord Sponsored Ad

price index (CPI). The main idea is to protect the purchasing power of the association. The dues are paid either quarterly or monthly. In neighborhood centers they are administered by the association and in larger centers by the marketing director or owner. If a problem arises, it is the landlord's responsibility to collect the dues because they are a provision in the lease agreement.

(e) GRAND OPENING DUES

New or revitalized centers usually plan a grand opening or reopening. It is not unusual to require each merchant to contribute to the grand opening. Dues vary widely, but 25¢ to $1 per square foot is most common. This is generally paid at the time the lease is signed.

The grand opening is usually arranged by the property owners because the merchants are not organized at that point to handle it themselves. Tenants who open up to one year after the grand opening are also assessed grand opening dues. Quite often the landlord will contribute the share allocated to vacancies. This amount is reimbursed when the space is leased.

(f) OWNER'S CONTRIBUTION

It is difficult to have an effective merchants' association or marketing fund without a contribution by the property owner, usually between 25 and 33 percent of what the association collects from the merchants. The contribution can be cash or "in kind," such as providing the services of a marketing director. Cash contributions should be timed to coincide with dues collection from tenants so that the association has a steady and predictable cash flow.

(g) USE OF FUNDS

Regional and superregional shopping centers have annual budgets that allow for television advertising, shuttle buses, ads in tourist publications, national celebrity visits, full-scale theme productions, extensive community involvement activities, direct mail brochures and Christmas decorations. Smaller centers cannot generate the income for such a broad approach and must use their funds carefully.

In both cases, the funds are generally allocated over the year on the basis of the center's sales distribution (see Exhibit 4.17). The largest expenditures are saved for November and December, when most centers will do 20 to 25 percent of the year's business. Most centers will allocate the least amount of funds for February because it is the lowest month in terms of sales. Those tenants who do well on Valentine's Day will be the exception. It becomes very important to prepare an annual budget and

EXHIBIT 4.17

Month	Department Stores	Jewelry Stores	Men's and Boys' Wear	Women's Apparel and Accessory Stores	Gift Shops
Jan.	7.4	6.2	6.7	6.5	4.2
Feb.	7.4	6.6	6.0	6.2	4.9
Mar.	7.9	6.7	6.8	7.5	5.5
Apr.	7.9	6.2	7.1	7.9	5.8
May	8.3	7.3	7.7	8.0	6.8
June	8.1	6.6	7.9	7.2	6.6
July	8.3	6.1	7.0	7.5	5.7
Aug.	8.5	6.5	8.5	8.7	6.5
Sept.	8.1	6.5	7.6	8.3	6.1
Oct.	8.8	7.5	8.7	9.1	8.0
Nov.	8.8	9.4	10.0	9.3	13.2
Dec.	10.5	24.4	16.0	13.8	26.7
Total	100	100	100	100	100

Source: Shopping Center World

program to be sure the association is not out of funds in December when it needs them most (see Exhibit 4.18).

Small centers generally have direct-mail programs, coupon advertising, shared newspaper ads, Boy Scout or 4H activities, art shows, car shows, sidewalk sales, community promotions such as a used book collection for a library, and local celebrities. The National Research Bureau publishes a monthly report of effective shopping center advertising and promotion.

(h) STARTING A MERCHANTS' ASSOCIATION

The property manager should take the lead in starting the merchants' association. The first step is to review tenant leases and determine which tenants are required to join. Next, select a date and a place to hold the first meeting. This can be a landlord-sponsored breakfast, lunch, or dinner meeting. Prior to the meeting, the property manager should call or visit each merchant to explain the purpose of the association and to invite the merchant personally to the first meeting. If the tenant's lease requires membership and dues, the property manager simply reminds the tenant of this obligation. If the lease is silent on the issue, the property manager must persuade the tenant to join on a voluntary basis.

EXHIBIT 4.18

Simplified Small Center Annual Budget Merchants' Association

			Percent of Budget
Dues Income 58,000 feet × .35		$20,300.00	
Owners Contribution 30%		6,100.00	
Total Income		$26,400.00	100
January	January Sidewalk Sale & Clearance Ad & Banners	2,100.00	8
February	Valentines Day—Coloring Contest	2,300.00	9
March	No activity	-0-	-0-
April	Spring Mailer	500.00	3
May	Mother Day—Coloring Contest & Newspaper Ad	2,400.00	9
June	Summer Boat Show & Vacation Contest	2,200.00	8
July	Anniversary Promotion	3,000.00	11
August	Back to School Ad—Posters & Banners	3,200.00	12
September	Art Show—No cost to Association	-0-	-0-
October	October Clearance Direct Mailer and Window Signs	2,200.00	8
November & December	Christmas Decorations Christmas Kick Off Ad	8,500.00	32
Totals		$26,400.00	100

The property manager prepares an agenda for the meeting that includes the following:

- The purpose of the merchants' association
- An income projection
- Statement on the landlord's role as major dues payer with the right to veto activities in the common area
- Suggested activities
- Suggested committees
- Nomination of officers.

The manager then chairs the first meeting, making sure to limit discussion to the subjects on the agenda. If issues not included on the agenda are raised, the property manager must be able to deal with them; unresolved items can destroy a merchants' association before it even gets off the ground.

(i) POTENTIAL PROBLEMS

The following are some typical problems that can beset a merchants' association meeting:

- *The meeting becomes a gripe session.* The main fear landlords have of merchants' associations is that meetings will turn into gripe sessions. Tenants will complain that the common area maintenance charges are too high, or the parking lot sweeper is doing a poor job, or the landlord should be spending time leasing the vacancies and not in a merchants' meeting. The property manager should not allow these unrelated issues to be discussed at a merchants' association meeting.

    The manager can prevent this by clarifying the purpose of the merchants' association and stating at the outset that questions or discussions that are not related to advertising or promotion will not be allowed. The property manager should indicate willingness to meet with merchants at any other time either at the property manager's office or at the merchants' store to discuss issues related to the merchant or the shopping center. If a tenant insists on discussing an unrelated item, the property manager should firmly but politely inform the tenant that the matter will be discussed at a later date and continue with the meeting. The property manager can state that he or she will not bring up landlord's concerns, such as, delinquent rent or other lease violations and the tenant's shouldn't bring up their problems with the landlord during these meetings.

- *"Why should I pay dues when the major tenants don't?"* Some major tenants refuse to belong to the merchants' association, and seldom is the landlord in a strong enough position during lease negotiations to include mandatory membership in the major's lease. The property manager should inform the small shop merchant that the landlord was unable to persuade the major to join the association and remind the tenant that the major tenant spends millions of dollars on advertising and is the main traffic draw to the center. The property manager also should let the tenant know that he or she will continue to encourage the major tenant to join on a voluntary basis. As a compromise, the property manager may be able to solicit the major tenant's participation by contributing to specific events such as Christmas decorations or turkeys for a giveaway the week before Thanksgiving.

- *"Why should I be involved when my neighbor never attends a meeting?"* A simple and direct reply from the property manager is, "Why should a few tenants who either do not care or do not have the time to participate cause the rest of us to lose the benefits of working together and the benefits of the merchants' association?"
- *"We're tired of doing all the work."* As with all organizations, a few members do most of the work. The property manager needs to encourage participation from a sufficient number of merchants so that there is a regular change of officers and committee chairpersons. Two or three active committees will relieve the board of much work and provide a training place for future board members. If the workload is too heavy for a few merchants, the small center's association could hire either an advertising agency or a person to work part time as the marketing director.
- *"The dues are too high."* Inform tenants that they will receive a return in advertising and promotional benefits far greater than their individual dues. By combining the tenants' dues and the contribution of the landlord, the association can purchase more advertising and promotional activities than the tenants could afford individually. In addition, advertising rates for the association are usually lower than the tenant could purchase individually.
- *"A few merchants run the association."* This statement is usually overcome by inviting the tenant to join or chair a committee or by having the tenant nominated to the board of directors.

(j) COMMUNICATING WITH MERCHANTS

It is important that the property manager and the shopping center marketing director communicate regularly with the merchants to keep them informed on upcoming events. A monthly newsletter, usually only a few pages in length, informs the merchants about new retailers in the center, new store managers, the shopping center sales comparisons by category, the leading store in each category, upcoming events, copy deadlines, and miscellaneous information about the shopping center and merchants. These newsletters usually have catchy names such as "Mall Talk" or "S'mall Talk," and merchants are encouraged to submit information about their stores and their employees.

Larger shopping centers develop marketing calendars listing the advertising and promotional events through the year. The calendar gives the dates of each event, a brief description of each, deadlines for ad copy, and a projected budget for each event.

The merchants' association handbook includes a directory with phone numbers of all the stores and the name of their managers; shopping center hours; employee parking information; meeting dates of the merchants' association or marketing fund; and information on the community booth, community room, information booth, and the center's gift certificate program. The handbook also includes a marketing plan that outlines the association's or fund's objectives, strategy, and tactics. The marketing plan exemplifies the shopping center's primary, secondary, and tertiary trade areas and describes the demographics and psychographics of each. It explains the marketing budget and analyzes income and expenses in a monthly breakdown. The handbook is an excellent addition to the leasing package because it shows the prospective tenant the aggressive advertising and promotional program of the center. Smaller shopping centers can scale down the handbook to suit their particular needs.

An advertising session informs the merchants of media publishing dates and media contacts at the newspaper and radio station. It may list all upcoming events and the association's plans for supporting the events with print or electronic media advertising.

§ 4.17 LANDLORD-TENANT RELATIONS

Landlord-tenant relations are more critical in the shopping center than most other types of properties. In a shopping center the property manager must be concerned with the best tenant mix and within that mix must find the best operator for each category of merchant. The property manager then must make every effort to create an environment where the tenant can maximize their sales.

The landlord's approach to leasing, management, and maintenance will have a direct impact on the tenant. Tenants often overstate that impact and use it as an excuse for their nonperformance of the lease. Hence, a relationship with tenants should be established very early. It is of the utmost importance that tenants clearly understand their obligations and charges, the landlord's obligations, the purpose of each tenant's expense, and which items are the landlord's expenses. The lease documents, especially the construction exhibits, should spell out who is responsible for what.

One area that can cause tenant relations problems is the condition of the space when it is turned over to the tenant. Several arrangements are possible in the construction of the premises: the tenant provides all improvements in a pad location; the tenant takes the existing premises "as is"; the landlord completes the space except for floor covering and interior partitions; the landlord provides a turn-key store that has all improvements except trade fixtures and interior decor. The more precise the lease and construction exhibits, the less likely there will be disputes in the future.

Tenants are almost always responsible for maintaining the premises, which generally includes exterior doors, glass, and utility lines serving the premises even if they are outside the tenant's premises. Pad tenants will most likely handle their own roof repairs. In-line tenants will pay for their share of roof repairs, but the landlord is responsible for the work. In some leases the landlord repairs the roof at his or her own expense.

Once the lease is signed, the leasing agent should introduce the tenant to the property manager. This person should be prepared to explain the tenant's next steps and provide guidance where necessary, advising the tenant of critical construction and grand opening information. To protect tenants from unpleasant surprises, as part of the introductory program they should receive a statement showing their rents and tenant charges (i.e., common area maintenance, taxes, insurance, and merchants' association or marketing fund dues), and information on payment procedures. This information can be included in a welcoming booklet or tenant information kit. This information can be mailed, but delivering it in person gives the manager and the tenant an opportunity to get acquainted and begin their relationship. Tenants also appreciate a small gift and congratulations from the landlord when their store is opened. Just before the tenant opens for business, the manager should conduct a walk-through of the premises. This shows the tenant that the owner or manager cares, and it allows them to agree on any work to be completed. Obviously, at that point it is in everybody's best interest to have any necessary work done as quickly as possible.

Each retail tenant should be visited at least once a month. The purpose of the visit is to establish communication, so the manager must refrain from using this time to complain about late rents, poor sales, or parking violations. The visit should be short; if the tenant is busy with a customer, a nod and a wave will suffice.

A common complaint from tenants is that they only see the property manager when something is wrong. When it is necessary for the manager to bring an infraction or default to the tenant's attention, the tenant should be given the benefit of the doubt, at least for the first time. Tenants may not have understood the situation, or perhaps circumstances were beyond their control.

A provision in the lease prohibiting certain actions should not be stated as the reason for a rule. Rather, tenants should be informed of the business reasons underlying the lease provisions. For example, if the lease does not allow tenants to park in front of their store, referring to the employee parking clause is generally not productive. It is more beneficial to tell tenants that the reason for employee parking requirements is to allow two to four customers per hour the convenience of close-in parking.

Tenants often ask property managers for favors above and beyond the landlord lease requirements. There is no reason not to be understanding and sympathetic. Rather than responding with a flat no or chastising the tenant for asking more than the lease agreement calls for, the manager should reply sympathetically: "I'm sorry but I cannot do what you ask." If the manager decides to grant the request because it is an important tenant or a fair request, the tone should be sincere and gracious. Legitimate tenant requests should be acted on promptly. When complaints are ignored, tenants build up resentment that the landlord does not care or that they are not important. The property manager should either deny the request in a timely fashion or perform the work promptly.

All tenant billings should have sufficient detail to assure tenants that their billing is in accordance with the lease. Tenants should be given courteous, complete, and accurate answers to specific questions. Many local small shop tenants, in particular, sign leases with little real understanding of what they are signing. A complex common area billing is routine to the sophisticated manager, and it is easy to become impatient with tenants who appear to be questioning not only the billing itself, but the property manager's honesty and integrity. Patience and an understanding of the tenant's position will serve the property manager in this situation better than impatience.

When disputes arise between tenants, especially if they are related to lease requirements, the property manager should step in to mediate the dispute if it is related to the shopping center. Feuding tenants have a way of polarizing the other tenants, and part of that feud often winds up being antimanagement.

Finally, the manager should avoid communicating by sending "Dear Tenant" letters. Tenants like to think they are respected as successful business people as well they should be. If group letters must be sent, address them to "All Merchants" or, even better, to individual operators.

The tenant is the landlord's customer and should be treated as such. Every effort should be made to maintain an open businesslike communication with all tenants all of the time. Even when a tenant is being difficult, it is in the manager's best long-term interest to stay cool and rational and move any disagreements in a positive direction.

§ 4.18   TENANT REPAIRS

Most shopping center leases require tenants to maintain their premises at their own expense. It is not advisable to perform repairs that the tenants are responsible for and bill them back to the tenant. When this is done, the property manager often winds up defending costs or procedures. There are exceptions, however. Quite often it is desirable to have one contractor or owner's employee maintain the roof air conditioners to be sure that they are properly maintained and to prevent excess traffic on the roof. If possible, the landlord should control the maintenance work but have the contractor bill the tenants directly.

If the landlord provides the services through his or her staff, a profit is allowable, but the total cost of the service should be competitive in the marketplace, and the tenant is entitled to know the basis of the billings. Quite often the problems mentioned above far exceed the potential profits.

If general repairs are provided to the tenants for a fee, it is suggested that all work be performed on the basis of a written request by the tenant. The billing should be detailed and reflect the original request. If work is required over and above the original request, it should be discussed with the tenant before proceeding and the tenant should authorize in writing the additional work.

§ 4.19   MONITORING STORES' OPENING AND CLOSING HOURS

A major component in creating synergism in a shopping center is all or a majority of the merchants and service tenants maintaining uniform business hours. Shoppers expect all the retail tenants to be open during the hours of the shopping center. The tenant's lease will state what hours the tenant will remain open. Some service tenants, such as a bank, dentist, or insurance agent, will not be required to be open evenings and weekends.

The landlord should control the shopping center's hours and should never allow the merchants' association to determine them. It is best to avoid allowing a tenant's hours to be those of similar businesses in the area, and it is not always practical for most tenants to maintain the same hours of the major tenants. Most supermarkets are open from early morning to late in the evening, and some are open 24 hours a day.

If the shopping center has an on-site manager, maintenance personnel, or security staff, a form can be used to check each store's opening and closing hours (Exhibit 4.19). When a tenant violates its lease requirement, the property manager should discuss with the store's manager the purpose of uniform hours and the negative impact of opening late or closing early has on the store and the entire shopping center. If the tenant continues to violate the prescribed hours, the store's district manager or owner should be contacted. Some leases call for a fine if a tenant violates the opening or closing hours (Exhibit 4.20).

§ 4.20   FINANCIALLY TROUBLED RETAIL TENANTS

When merchants experience problems, the shopping center experiences problems. Merchant failures can give a shopping center a negative image among both existing and potential tenants, as well as customers. When tenant failures occur in conjunction with a soft leasing market, shopping centers are in serious trouble. Faced with the potential deterioration of a

EXHIBIT 4.19

Irregularity in Store Opening and Closing Hours Form

TO: OPERATIONS MANAGER   BLDG. _____

FROM: SECURITY   DATE: _____

STORES	OPENED	CLOSED	STORES	OPENED	CLOSED

EXHIBIT 4.20

Monitoring Opening and Closing Hours Lease Clause

5.3 **Operation of Business.** Tenant shall conduct its business on the Premises during the entire Lease Term hereof with diligence and efficiency so as to produce all of the gross sales which may be produced by such manner of operation, unless prevented from doing so by causes beyond Tenant's control. Tenant shall keep in stock on the Premises a full and ample line of merchandise for the purpose of operating its business and shall maintain an adequate sales force. Subject to the provisions of this Lease, Tenant shall continuously during the entire Lease Term hereof conduct and carry on Tenant's business in the Premises and shall keep the Premises open for business and cause Tenant's business to be conducted therein during the hours of 10:00 a.m. through 9:00 p.m. Mondays through Fridays; 10:00 a.m. through 6:00 p.m. Saturdays; and 12:00 p.m. through 5:00 p.m. Sundays unless Landlord notifies Tenant in writing of a change in such hours of operation; provided, however, that these provisions shall not apply if the Premises should be closed and the business of Tenant temporarily discontinued thereon on account of strikes, lockouts or similar causes beyond the reasonable control of Tenant.

---

shopping center, a property manager needs to search for practical short-term solutions that will enable the shopping center to endure this difficult economic period. Solutions to this problem can be both monetary and nonmonetary assistance to the financially troubled tenant.

The most obvious symptom of potential failure is late rent payment, but earlier indications may be obtained by monitoring a tenant's sales. (See § 4.12.) If the tenant's sales are appreciably below national averages, the tenant is probably operating the business at a loss. The tenant's sales should also be compared with prior periods to determine sales trends. If the sales are consistently declining, the tenant either now or in the near future will experience financial difficulties.

Other symptoms of potential tenant failure are reductions in inventory, store hours, staffing, advertising, and a lower merchandise turnover. When tenants have financial problems, they may be unable to purchase new inventory. Low inventory or old inventory that is not selling will continue the downward sales spiral. Tenants may respond to financial difficulties by attempting to reduce operating expenses. A reduction in store hours, staffing, and advertising generate immediate cost savings but result in the continuing sales decline.

A more effective means of monitoring a tenants' operations is to develop a good rapport with tenants so that they will inform the manager of potential problems.

The property manager must analyze the impact of various factors on the shopping center before deciding whether to offer monetary relief to a tenant. The most important consideration is the condition of the leasing market. Are there existing vacancies and, if so, how long will it take to lease them? If any tenants fail, how long will it take to re-lease their space? In estimating the time it will take to re-lease a space, the space in question should be analyzed in terms of its desirability; the adjacent tenants; visibility from common areas and fronting streets; and its size, configuration, and location. The property manager must also know the local retail leasing market.

Once the vacancy period for the space has been estimated, the property manager must consider what effect a vacancy might have on the tenant mix of the shopping center. Will the shopping center's ability to draw customers be significantly weakened if a tenant moves out? What effect would one tenant failure, or several tenant failures, have on the leasing program? In a soft leasing market it is difficult to find replacement tenants, and that difficulty is compounded when potential tenants notice vacancies and tenant failures in a center. A further consideration: Is the center developing a reputation among the merchants in the community as a place where a retailer is doomed?

Another consideration is the cost of replacing a tenant, which includes: loss of rent, rental concessions in the form of free rent or tenant allowances, remodeling costs, leasing commissions, possible legal fees, and possible lower percentage rents from other tenants resulting from reduced sales of merchants affected by the vacancy. Still another consideration is the financial position of the shopping center. At least partial rent payment may be essential for the normal operations of the shopping center.

If the property manager determines that the cost to replace the troubled tenant is too high, or if the tenant deserves assistance because of prior contributions to the shopping center, a temporary rent relief program should be considered.

(a) RENT RELIEF

Rent relief is designed to help a tenant overcome financial difficulty. Commonly used rent relief programs are: deferred rent, percentage rent only, waived rent, and use of security deposit.

- *Deferred Rent.* The merchant's current rent and an agreed-upon amount of future rent are reduced, and repayment is deferred to a later date. For example, a tenant's rent might be reduced from $1,000 per month to $400 per month for six months, then increased by $600 per month for six months later in the lease term. Delinquent rent can also be deferred to a later date. Many property managers prefer not to charge interest on the deferred rent because it hinders the tenant's recovery.

- *Percentage Rent Only.* The tenant's minimum base rent is eliminated for a specific period, and monthly rental payments are based on a percentage of the tenant's sales. The percentage used can be either a rate already established in the lease or a renegotiated rate, which generally is higher.
- *Waived Rent.* Past, present, or future rent is waived entirely. All or a portion of each month's rent for a period of time may be waived.
- *Use of Security Deposit.* All or a portion of the security deposit may be applied either to rent owed or future rent. Little is sacrificed with this method because the security deposit would be applied to delinquent rent or future rents if the tenant vacated before the lease expired. A condition of a rent relief program may be that the tenant spends a percentage of the waived or deferred rent on additional advertising or inventory.

When rent relief is granted to a tenant, the property manager is always concerned that the tenant will inform all the other tenants of the landlord's assistance and the other tenants will seek a similar program. Generally, most tenants are not going to tell their neighboring merchants that their sales are so poor that the landlord is granting them rent relief for their survival. Nevertheless, if the tenant does talk, and the property manager receives other requests for assistance, the other tenants should be informed that each tenant's situation is analyzed individually. The property manager and the landlord are the sole arbiters in granting a tenant's request.

When offering a rental concession to an existing tenant, a property manager can reopen lease negotiations. The lease may have one or more clauses detrimental to the shopping center, and the offer of rent relief can be contingent upon the tenant's agreeing to modify or eliminate these clauses.

(b) LEASE PROVISIONS IN RENTAL CONCESSIONS

Lease provisions that might be revised or eliminated include:

- *Options.* Either eliminate the option or tie the rental rate in the option period to the adjustment in the consumer price index or other predetermined increase.
- *Restrictions.* Eliminate the provision allowing tenants to approve remodeling or expansion plans of the center.
- *Exclusive.* The tenant's lease may prohibit similar uses within the shopping center. Such restrictions should be eliminated.

- *Use.* It may be desirable to place more restrictions on the tenant's use.
- *Assignment/Subletting.* Assignment or subletting should be subject to the landlord's prior written approval.
- *Merchants' Association.* Membership in the merchants' association or contribution to the marketing fund should be mandatory.
- *Signage.* Conformance to the shopping center's sign criteria should be required.
- *Store Hours.* The tenant should be required to maintain the same business hours as the rest of the shopping center.
- *Cancellation Clause.* The landlord may obtain the right to cancel the lease if the tenant's sales do not meet or exceed an agreed-upon minimum amount.

An amendment to the lease is required to formalize any modifications. If a portion of the deferred rental payment is due after the lease expires, the tenant should sign a promissory note for this amount.

Offering a tenant rent relief may be a distasteful solution to some owners or property managers, but sometimes it is the only way to save a shopping center's most valuable asset—its tenants.

(c)   NONMONETARY ASSISTANCE

Nonmonetary programs can be an alternative to monetary relief or used in conjunction with the rent relief program. The first consideration is, how can the property manager help the tenant reduce operating expenses without affecting sales? Reducing the tenant's square footage will reduce base rent, pro rata tenant charges, utility costs, and possibly the size of the tenant's staff. If the tenant's sales do not depend on walk-by traffic, the tenant could be relocated to a less desirable area of the center where the rent is lower. This solution is practical only if the tenant's fixturization costs are nominal. A hair salon could not afford to relocate because of the expense of the plumbing for its fixtures, but a florist could easily relocate.

It may be beneficial to expand the tenant's use provision. If the tenant is the only restaurant in the center, the tenant's use provision could be broadened to include other food-related items. The property manager must be certain, however, that this will not have a negative effect on the tenant mix of the shopping center or on the sales of other tenants.

If the tenant's problem stems primarily from mismanagement, a new operator may be able to turn the business around. Thus, permitting a lease assignment may be a simple solution.

Many small merchants do not have strong backgrounds in retailing and do not have the opportunity to seek professional retailing instruction.

Consequently, the merchant's employees do not usually receive the necessary sales training. The property manager should consider asking the shopping center owner to hire a retail consultant to provide seminars and individual consultations for tenants and their employees. These programs should not only be motivational training sessions, but also provide insight into the development of a merchandising plan, markdown policies, in-store signage, displays, budgeting, selling techniques, and other important retailing concepts and principles. The tenants benefit by acquiring valuable retailing techniques, and their employees receive professional sales training.

Most owners and managers who have provided this service to their tenants consider the expense an investment in the financial strength of the center. Through strong sales they can expect higher percentage rent and fewer tenant failures.

(d) LEASE TERMINATION

When the probability of a tenant's recovering from financial problems is slim, even though the landlord has assisted with either rent relief or nonmonetary assistance or a combination of the two, it may be best to seek a termination of the lease. Terminating the lease enables the property manager to regain possession of the premises and place the space back on the market. The lease can be terminated by eviction or mutual consent.

A mutual lease termination may be offered to the tenant for financial consideration. The property manager should request a current financial statement from the tenant before agreeing to the lease cancellation. If the tenant is a corporation, and the lease has personal guarantees, a financial statement should be requested of the corporation and the guarantors. If both party's financial statements are weak, a mutual cancellation with either no cancellation payment or a nominal payment to the landlord would be most practical.

One school of thought says that it is fruitless to incur the cost of taking a tenant to court for back or future rent if the tenant has no assets. Another approach is to file a judgment and wait for the day when the tenant gains financial stability. If the tenant's financial statement is healthy, the property manager can either negotiate a lease buy-out on the part of the tenant or enforce the lease, including the payment of rent and other tenant charges, until the space is re-leased. This is an area in which it is impossible to establish a standard operating procedure. Each case must be analyzed individually and with flexibility.

Although rent relief is not advocated by all property managers, it offers a temporary solution to an immediate problem. In fact, in some cases rent relief may be the only solution. But if problems are spotted early enough, less drastic solutions may be employed effectively.

§ 4.21   POTENTIAL PROBLEM TENANTS

Customers will avoid a shopping center that they find distasteful. Shoppers can be offended by the type of merchandise or service provided, and the actions of one merchant in the shopping center can disrupt another merchant's business. Customers can also be frightened by the patrons of a particular store or loiterers in the mall or parking lot. The property manager should avoid leasing to tenants who might cause problems, or structure the tenant's lease to prevent the problems from occurring, or provide the landlord with the right to cancel the lease if the problem persists.

Several uses can create problems. The property manager should carefully evaluate whether or not these uses should be included in the center's tenant mix. If they are included, the manager should have the above-mentioned lease restrictions to alleviate potential problems. Following is a list of tenants that can cause problems for a shopping center along with suggested lease modifications to alleviate these problems.

(a)   VIDEO ARCADES

Few property managers take a middle ground regarding this use; they either hate video arcades or they find them to be an acceptable use in a shopping center. Astute managers recognize that this tenant will pay top dollar for a space, with the potential for percentage rent.

Video arcades present few problems when they are located in an enclosed mall and must close when the shopping center closes. The video arcade in an enclosed mall does not face onto the parking lot, and young people do not have the opportunity to hang out in front of the arcade or in the parking lot in front of the arcade. Also, most malls have security guards who handle loiterers. Video arcade problems usually arise in open centers, particularly neighborhood and community centers.

The biggest potential problems with video arcades are excessive noise and unruly teenagers. The lease should call for additional insulation, especially above the ceiling and extending to the roof, to minimize the transfer of noise from the video machines to adjacent tenants. One center in the Northwest was sued by a craft merchant adjacent to a video arcade who claimed that the video arcade noise prevented the store from holding craft classes and thus reduced its sales and profits. The noise problem can be alleviated by stating that the tenant is required to take the necessary action to prevent noise from carrying over to the neighboring tenant spaces. If the tenant refuses to correct this problem, the lease should allow the landlord the right to make the corrections and bill the tenant for the cost of the work.

The potential problem with unruly teenagers and preteens also can be addressed in the lease by stipulating that an adult attendant must be on site during store hours and that the store must close at a specific time. The lease can state that at the request of the landlord the tenant will hire a uniformed security guard at the tenant's expense. The ultimate control the landlord can have is the right to cancel the lease if the tenant is unable to correct the problem within a specific period of time.

(b) VIDEO STORES

The popularity of the VCR in the early 1980s has created a proliferation of video stores throughout the United States. Most of these video stores opened in neighborhood shopping centers and are not a source of problems, but some customers might be offended by the explicit promotional posters and photos on X-rated videotape boxes. To prevent this potential problem, the property manager can state in the lease that the X-rated tapes will be placed in the rear of the store and not be visible from the storefront.

(c) TAVERNS

Opinions are mixed on whether taverns, often referred to as a sports tavern, should be in a shopping center. Some of the major tenants' leases in neighborhood and community centers either restrict taverns from the shopping center or restrict their location within a specific distance from the major tenant's premises. The concern with the tavern in a shopping center is the possibility of rowdy behavior in the parking lot and the negative image that this will create for the shopping center. Another concern is the littering of beer bottles and other trash in the shopping center late at night and into the early morning. This can be a serious problem if the shopping center is not swept daily and the litter accumulates in the parking lot. If the property manager decides to enter into a lease with a tavern, the lease restrictions may require the tavern to have a uniformed security officer on site during specific hours at the request of the landlord.

A further concern with taverns is the possibility of the tavern converting to a topless bar. Although this is unlikely, if it did occur it would have a tremendous negative impact on the center and its image. To prevent this from happening, the lease should restrict the type of live entertainment allowed on the premises. The property manager may find it prudent to seek an alternative use for a large space rather than leasing to a tavern.

(d) RECORD SHOPS AND HEAD SHOPS

Record shops are an acceptable use in a shopping center and a positive addition to a shopping center's tenant mix. The concern with a record shop is that the merchant might sell drug paraphernalia usually found in a head shop. To prevent a record shop from selling such items, the use provision should be very specific on which items can be sold. It should not state that the tenant may sell records, tapes, and "other related items or accessories," thus leaving the related items or accessories up for debate.

(e) ADULT GIFT STORES

In the early 1980s, a number of adult gift stores opened throughout the United States. These stores sell a combination of lingerie, adult cards, and adult gifts and may generate unpleasant controversy in the community. If adult stores are allowed in a shopping center, the property manager may want to specify in the lease that the X-rated materials and adult gifts be displayed in the back of the store.

(f) AUTOMOBILE SERVICE

Another use that became very popular in the early 1980s is instant oil and lube service for automobiles. These uses are usually freestanding buildings where an automobile is lubed and the oil changed while the owner waits. The operators of most of these establishments are professional, and their buildings are attractive and well maintained. A concern might be the number of cars that are parked in the shopping center to be serviced for pickup later in the day. The lease may restrict the number of cars that the operator can place in the shopping center.

(g) SERVICE STATIONS

Service stations have always been an acceptable pad use for shopping centers. The concern with service stations is the number of cars that are parked in the lot and the cleanliness of the service station. These items should be addressed in the tenant's lease.

(h) OFFICES

More and more office users are finding shopping centers an attractive alternative to an office building. The shopping center provides the office user with good exposure, comparable or lower rental rates than office buildings, more amenities, and free and abundant parking. The concern of the property manager is the long-term parking requirement of office users. Some major tenant leases will restrict office uses within a specific distance of their premises. The lease for the office user should designate the areas where employees may park.

(i) HAIR SALONS

Hair salons are found in most shopping centers. The problem that can arise with this use is the odor from the permanent wave solution that can filter into the adjacent tenant's space. The lease should require the tenant to have proper ventilation and address the maintenance of the HVAC unit.

(j) PET STORES

Pet stores are another acceptable use in all shopping centers. The concern with this use is unpleasant odors. The tenant must keep the store's cages and grooming area clean and have proper ventilation.

Most tenants do not create a problem for the customers or adjacent tenants. When a problem does arise, it can ruin a shopping center's image and create havoc with the other tenants and take a long time to correct. The property manager can alleviate potential problems by anticipating these concerns and addressing them in the tenant's lease. The placement of a pet store, along with a hair salon, can create problems. These stores should not be located next to a food operator.

§ 4.22   MERCHANDISING VACANT SPACES

A shopping center's vacancies should be merchandised to alleviate their negative impact on the customers, the merchants, and potential tenants. Vacancies in a shopping center are unlighted and give the appearance of a blank wall instead of a prospering business with interesting displays and activities. Vacancies also create pocket areas of little or no traffic and cause tenants in nearby spaces to lose some of the benefits of the shopping center environment. This loss is multiplied with each additional vacant space.

These vacancies can be viewed as an opportunity to help existing tenants merchandise their stores and to create goodwill in the community. These goals can be accomplished at very little expense.

The property manager should consider offering the vacant space or spaces to merchants in the center to display their merchandise. The merchants can decorate the show windows and have their merchandise displayed in another area of the shopping center. This offer is contingent upon the tenant's moving out of the vacancy on short notice, keeping the premises clean, abiding by the landlord's sign criteria, and relieving the landlord of all responsibility for missing or stolen items. The merchant should enter into a license agreement covering these and other obligations. The merchant should be encouraged not to display expensive items that are likely targets for theft. The selection of tenants to display their merchandise in the vacancies is based on which tenants can best utilize the space, which tenants need the most assistance, and the location of the tenant's space in relationship to the vacancy. Tenants may be offered the space on a rotating basis or on a longer term use.

(a) COMMUNITY'S USE OF VACANT SPACE

An alternative to merchandising vacant spaces is to allow community groups the opportunity to use the vacancies. If the spaces are anticipated to be vacant for a short period, they can be offered to groups for a specific short-term purpose such as a haunted house the week before Halloween, a white elephant sale, a collection area for toys at Christmas, or a dropoff point for a food drive. Organizations may use the space for their membership drive or to register children for sporting activities, such as Little League sign-ups. Other organizations such as the Girl Scouts, Boy Scouts, and the 4-H clubs can use the vacancies to display their activities and promote their organizations.

If the center is in an economically depressed area or is a distressed center with vacancies anticipated for an extended period, these spaces may be offered to community organizations on a long-term basis. Space may be offered to the community college or the high school adult education program for a classroom or to the chamber of commerce for a temporary office. The property manager should have the right to relocate these organizations to another vacancy or to terminate the use with sufficient notice to enable the organization to either complete its function or find another location.

Another use is to convert a vacancy into a community room. Even if the shopping center already has a community room, a second community room may be considered if demand justifies its use. If the community room is a temporary use, the property manager should not allow organizations to reserve the room more than two months in advance. Community groups should also enter into a license agreement for the use of the vacancy.

(b) CHARGING FOR VACANT SPACE

The property manager must decide whether to charge for the use of the vacancy. When the space is offered to community groups it should be provided at no charge. If the community group will use the space on a long-term basis, the group should be responsible for the utility costs and the costs to maintain the heating, ventilating, and air-conditioning unit. When tenants use the space to display their merchandise, the space should be provided free of all charges.

How will prospective tenants know that the vacancies are available to lease when they are temporarily occupied? This concern can be alleviated by maintaining a For Lease sign in front of the shopping center and a small For Lease sign located on the premises where it doesn't detract from the window display. Most prospective tenants are able to distinguish a permanent user from a temporary user.

If the vacancies are spaces that have never been occupied, the property manager must weigh the cost to finish these spaces against the benefits mentioned above. The cost to finish vacancies in a regional mall can be considerable. Many regional malls lease their spaces in an almost completely unfinished condition. The space is turned over to the tenant with a dirt floor, no ceilings, demising walls, store fronts, sprinkler system, or heating, ventilating, and air-conditioning duct work. If the regional mall has a high percentage of vacancies, the manager should consider selecting spaces in key areas of the mall that will have a severe negative impact on the mall if they remain vacant. Allowing long-term temporary tenants the right to occupy vacant space may be necessary to create a flow of traffic to areas of the mall that have few merchants. The landlord must reserve the right to relocate the temporary tenant.

There are no industry standards for finishing out spaces in neighborhood centers. One extreme is to turn space over to the tenants in the condition described above. The other extreme is for the landlord to build out, or finish, the space except for the floor covering and wall treatment. In between these extremes are countless ways to finish the tenant premises. If the spaces are built out in a near complete state, the property manager has little to do to turn the space over to a temporary tenant. If the use is for a short term or the space is being used by an existing tenant, the property manager should paint the walls. The user can be required to build the display platform. If the use is for a longer term, the user may be required to paint the walls and provide flooring. When the property manager incurs the expense to finish the space, the improvements may enhance the marketability of the space, and the improvement costs may be recaptured by leasing the space sooner than projected.

§ 4.23   SEMINARS FOR TENANTS

The success of a shopping center is dependent upon the success of its tenants. A center's base rent is in part determined by the potential or actual sales volume of the tenants. A shopping center in which most tenants' sales volume greatly exceeds the national average can justify charging a higher base rent than a shopping center in which the tenants' sales are at or below the national average.

The higher the tenants' sales volume, the higher the rental rates that can be achieved on vacancies and during lease renewals. When a tenant exceeds the breakpoint for paying percentage rent, additional rent in the form of percentage rent or overage rent will be paid. And when tenants' sales are stronger, there is less likelihood of tenant failure. Costs associated with tenant failure are lost rent, commission expense, and marketing costs.

Tenant failures are a major concern of the property manager because they give the shopping center a reputation that businesses cannot be successful in that location. Statistics prove that the most likely tenant to fail

is the small, independent business, with the first year being the most critical period. According to Dunn & Bradstreet, more than half of the approximately 57,000 businesses that failed in 1985 had been operating for
less than six years. Twenty-nine percent of the failures occurred in the
business's first two years. During the next three years, 28 percent of these
businesses failed. Only 20 percent of the failures occurred after the business's tenth year.

The property manager can help tenants maximize their sales by sponsoring retailing seminars designed to improve their business and merchandising skills and improve their sales volume. Such programs are of
particular importance in distressed centers and in areas with a weak
economy.

The seminar program should be designed around the needs of the
shopping center tenants. Those who need the most assistance are the local "mom and pop" retailers who, unlike managers of regional and national chain stores, do not have the opportunity to attend professional
retailing seminars. They also do not have the retailing expertise of a
large, sophisticated chain.

The property manager can offer many seminars to tenants free of
charge. Through business contacts the property manager often can
tap into valuable community resources. For example, the local police
department can present information on shoplifting. The Small Business Administration (SBA) can provide speakers on specific topics
ranging from budgeting to market research, and lenders are generally
willing to present seminars on cash management and financing. The
display manager of a department store may be willing to teach a seminar on window displays. A professor from the local university might
speak on motivational sales training. The cost of these one- to two-
hour seminars is nominal.

Retail consultants can present classes on specific retailing subjects
and meet with the merchants on an individual basis. These consultant's
fees are usually paid by the landlord. Occasionally the merchants' association will share the expense, but usually the association's budget cannot
afford this expense. The merchants are never charged for the general
seminar or the individual sessions with the consultant. If the tenant requests additional individual consulting, it is at the tenant's expense.

Topics for group sessions might include: in-store promotions, visual
merchandise, personnel management, retail salesmanship, customer
policies, return policies, sales forecasting, inventory planning, open-
to-buy, and stock pricing.

Even though the retail program is free to the merchant, many merchants need to be convinced to attend. Often small retailers have limited time available, do not believe the program will be worthwhile or,
even worse, believe that they know all there is to know about their business. The seminar should be publicized to all merchants; a bulletin

with pertinent information will be a first step toward gaining their interest. The property manager should then meet with each merchant to discuss the program and the benefits of participating in it. The manager should outline the program, provide the credentials of the instructors, and explain how the program worked at other shopping centers. If the property manager is assisting a tenant with a rent deferment program, financial assistance should be contingent upon the tenant's participation in the program.

The seminars should be held either in the morning, before the stores open, or in the evening. Two hours per session is the maximum length. The seminars should be held on site in a vacancy, the community room, or the conference room of a major tenant. Light refreshments should be provided at each class.

Advisors to Business Management (ABM) in Long Beach, California, has developed a program of successful seminars for merchants. ABM will conduct three two-hour seminars and will meet individually with merchants for a two-hour session. Most chain stores do not participate in individual consulting sessions, but many send representatives to the seminars.

The property manager should attend the seminars and the individual consulting sessions to gain an understanding of retailing and its problems, to learn to distinguish a poor tenant from a good one, and to gain insight into an individual tenant's strengths and weaknesses.

A resource library on retailing can be developed at the property management company's office or at the shopping center's on-site management office. The Small Business Administration and many leading banks have publications, pamphlets, and books for the small business. Examples are Bank of America's series called *The Small Business Reporter* and the National Retail Merchant Association's outstanding publications on retailing. ICSC publishes *The Retail Challenge Tips for Shopping Center Retailers.* A quarterly newsletter that many shopping center owners provide to their tenants.

Subscribing to the leading retail trade journals is not only an excellent way to collect information for the library, but also a way for the property manager to stay abreast of current trends in retailing. Included among these publications are *Nation's Restaurant News*, and *Chain Store Age Executive*, published by Lebhar-Friedman, Inc.; *Shopping Centers Today*, published by International Council of Shopping Centers; *Shopping Center World*, published by Communication Channels, Inc.; *Fairchild's Book and Visuals*, Fairchild Publications; Newspaper Advertising Bureau, Inc., for newspaper advertising plan book; Merrill Lynch's *How to Read a Financial Report;* NCR Corporation, Customer and Support Education, for its education publications catalog. Retailing consulting firms such as Robert Morris Company in Cleveland provide operating statement analysis, and Retail Merchandising Services Automation in Riverside, California, provides merchandising information systems for retailers.

Retail seminars can be used as a marketing tool in the shopping center leasing program. These educational opportunities tell prospective tenants that the manager and the landlord are concerned about the success of the tenants and are willing to take the lead in offering unique programs for them. The landlord should view the retail seminar program as an investment that will pay great dividends by helping tenants become better retailers who have higher sales and pay greater percentage rent.

§ 4.24 COMMUNITY SERVICES

(a) COMMUNITY ROOM

A community room gives the shopping center a chance to provide a service to the community, to promote positive public relations, to generate additional traffic to the center, and in some situations to merchandise a vacancy. It is a large room, sometimes a converted vacant space, that is offered as a meeting place at no charge to community groups and for a small fee to businesses. Community rooms are usually found in community or regional centers. If they are designed within the mall, they are located in an area that would be difficult or impossible to lease, and away from the storefronts and traffic areas. They are furnished with folding chairs, long folding tables, and a wall writing board. The facility is promoted through news releases to the media, direct mail invitations to community groups, information provided to merchants, and brief statements regarding the facility in the shopping center's advertisements.

The property manager must develop guidelines for the use of the community room. The guidelines have two purposes: to allow maximum use by the greatest number of organizations, and to maintain control over all aspects of the room's use. The guidelines will limit the times a group can schedule the room to prevent some groups from monopolizing it. A group might be allowed to reserve the room at least seven days but no more than ninety days in advance; or the room may be used by a group for a maximum of five days within any month.

If the community room is located in a mall, the use may be limited to mall hours. If the room has direct access from the parking lot or if security guards or maintenance personnel are available, they can provide access to the mall beyond business hours. Groups should be required to clean the room after using it and should not be allowed to affix any materials such as handbills to the walls. Public address systems or materials disturbing to shoppers are not allowed, and the property manager always retains the right to reclaim the room for other uses.

When community rooms are located in a mall, the maintenance or security personnel are given the room's daily schedule and are responsible for unlocking and locking the room for each group. If the community room is located in a shopping center without on-site personnel, a key to the room may be left with one of the tenants. The groups can be instructed where to pick up and return the key and how to secure the room. The room should be cleaned daily by the shopping center janitorial staff or a maintenance contractor.

The property manager can promote the mall to the captive audience in the community room by posting in the room a list of the merchants, a separate listing of the restaurants, including those that deliver, photos and ads of past and current promotions, and a calendar of upcoming promotional and merchandising events.

Organizations using the community room may be required to sign a license agreement or a hold harmless agreement.

(b) COMMUNITY BOOTH

Since the early 1970s, there have been conflicting rulings by the courts on all levels as to the public's right to use the shopping center as a public forum. The property manager must check with legal counsel on the rights of the public and the obligations of the property owners in each state regarding the public's access and right to use public property for noncommercial uses.

Many shopping center owners addressed this issue by building a community booth in the shopping center's common area as a public forum facility for individuals or groups. These booths are usually located against a blank wall in an area with ample pedestrian traffic. Managers of small centers that do not have a permanent booth can designate locations on the sidewalk where individuals or organizations may set up a table to distribute information.

The property manager must develop guidelines and enforce them equally with all individuals and organizations. The guidelines will include how an individual or organization applies for consent to use the shopping center's community booth. The application process may require that the booth be reserved a minimum number of days prior to the use. The application may ask for the name, address, and telephone number of the organization or individual sponsoring the activity and the names of the individuals participating in the activity. The guidelines may prohibit the sale of merchandise or service and limit the activities to the community booth. Signs may be restricted to a specific size. Individuals and organizations are responsible for cleaning the area inside and outside the booth. Public address systems or voice amplifying devices should be prohibited.

The property manager must stay current with the changing laws regarding the public's right to use private property, particularly shopping centers, as a forum to disseminate information to the public. The International Council of Shopping Centers is the best source of information on this issue.

If the property manager has followed the appropriate guidelines, the community booth can provide a public service to the community without creating problems for the shopping center.

(c) NONPROFIT USE OF STRIP CENTERS

Strip centers do not receive nearly as many requests from individuals or organizations to use the property to disseminate information. Guidelines for this use are important (Exhibit 4.21). Strip center managers will designate an area along the sideway to accommodate such requests.

(d) INFORMATION BOOTH

The information booth is an area in a mall that can provide customers with general information regarding the mall and its merchants. The staff of the information booth also can provide operational support for the mall's management and marketing staff. Information booths are usually found in larger shopping centers that have a budget to support this service.

The information booth can provide a variety of services to the customer, including information on mall hours, store locations, and upcoming events. The information booth can also handle lost and found items, deal with lost children or parents, issue wheelchairs, and rent strollers. A listing of positions available in the stores can either be kept or posted at the booth. The community booth staff can receive emergency calls to the management office and answer questions regarding the mall. The staff of the information booth may also serve as radio dispatchers for the mall's security and maintenance personnel.

The information booth can be a convenient place to sell mall gift certificates, which are valid in any mall store. Certificates can be sold in dollar increments, such as ten-dollar increments, or for a specific amount. In either case, they should state that they are valid only at the mall.

There are several approaches to the gift certificate. One approach is to sell it like a money order or check. The certificate is signed by a mall representative, a purchase is made at a mall store, and the store fills in its name as the payee. Depending on the program, the payee either deposits the check in its account or is reimbursed by the management office. The money received from selling the gift certificates is deposited in a special account.

The information booth's staff should be trained to handle emergencies, ranging from helping a customer find his/her car to coping with a bomb threat. The booth should have a procedure manual that lists emergency phone numbers, details the dress code, discusses the above-mentioned duties, includes procedures for personal calls and visits, and explains how to deal with the public and with irate customers.

EXHIBIT 4.21

Guidelines for Nonprofit Use of Strip Centers

Although _____ is private property, and despite the fact that it invites the general public to the center for the purpose of shopping, it recognizes its social commitment in allowing non-profit civic, social, political and religious groups to use the center for non-shopping purposes. In order to treat all organizations fairly and with no discrimination whatsoever, any clubs or organizations desiring to conduct activities in the center may do so, simply by following these rules and regulations:

1. Reservations—All clubs, organizations or individuals desiring to use the shopping center must make arrangements in advance, in writing, and must have written confirmation from the management office. Information regarding these reservations may be obtained by calling (206) _____, or by visiting the _____ Management Corporation's offices at _____, Anytown, USA.

2. Advance notice—All requests for use of the center must be received at least thirty (30) days, but not more than one hundred eighty (180) days, before the date requested.

3. Duration—The shopping center may be used for a maximum of three (3) days during any thirty (30) day period, during the hours that _____ is open for business.

4. Location—All activities connected with the use of the center must be confined within the area designated for such use and not conducted in the stores, or on the sidewalks, or in the parking lot.

5. Signing—All signing must be located within the designated area.

6. Cleanliness—During usage, the designated area must be kept in a presentable state. Upon conclusion of the activity, users must clean the area and repair or replace any damaged items. If said area is not cleaned and repaired and all refuse removed after use, _____ reserves the right to retain part or all of the $25.00 security deposit to defray cleaning/repair costs.

7. Handbills—Distribution of information is allowed only within the designated area. No handbills or other items may be distributed in the stores, the parking lot, or on the sidewalks.

8. Noise control—No public address systems, loud music, or other disturbing activities will be allowed within the shopping center property.

9. Deposit—A deposit of $25.00 is required for use of the shopping center. The deposit must be received at least one (1) week prior to the requested dates. The deposit will be refunded within one (1) week after use of the center, provided that all requirements for cleanliness and repair have been met.

(e) COMMUNITY BOOTH RULES AND REGULATIONS

Many malls across the country have created a booth on the mall where individuals or organizations can disseminate information although some mall's management prohibits such use. The booth is counter height and has room for two or three individuals. In most malls, community booths are booked every weekend and, in some malls, they are booked throughout the year. The mall management must provide rules and regulations for the orderly and nondiscriminating use of the community booth. Exhibit 4.22 is an example of the rules and regulations guide printed by one mall.

§ 4.25 CLEAN-UP FOR HOLIDAY SEASON

The success of most retailers depends on good holiday sales. Most retailers will receive 24 to 35 percent of their annual sales during the five to six weeks between Thanksgiving and Christmas. The shopping center and the tenants should look their best for this important buying season. Many merchants are so involved with preparing the interior of the store and their merchandise for the holiday season that they overlook some basic maintenance and housekeeping items. The letter in Exhibit 4.23 reminds the tenants of these items and encourages them to report any maintenance items in the common areas that the property manager may have overlooked.

§ 4.26 SECURITY

A shopping center's success depends on its acceptance by the community, and the community will not accept a center in which it does not feel safe. The shopping center manager needs to constantly monitor the security needs of the shopping center. The first step in developing a security program is to conduct a security audit of the shopping center. The security audit will consist of surveying the neighborhood and researching actual or potential security issues at the shopping center.

The police precinct captain is a good place to start the audit. Find out the type and frequency of criminal activities in the neighborhood. Find out if these incidents are also likely problems within the shopping center and ask for recommendations from the captain as to the appropriate action to be taken. Find out how often the police patrol the area and the shopping center in particular and if needed, how this frequency may be increased.

Drive through the neighborhood. Where are the schools, parks, residential areas, large apartment complexes, other business districts in

EXHIBIT 4.22

Mall Community Booth Guide

Although Main Street Mall is private property and despite the fact that it invites the general public to the center for the purpose of shopping, it recognizes its social commitment in allowing civic, social, political, and religious groups use of the mall for nonshopping purposes. In order to treat all organizations fairly and with no discrimination whatsoever, any clubs or organizations desiring to conduct activities in the mall may do so, simply by following these rules and regulations:

1. Reservation—All clubs or organizations or individuals desiring to use the Community Booth must make arrangements in advance and have a confirmed, written reservation from the management office.This reservation confirmation must be displayed in the Community Booth prior to its use.

2. Advance notice—All requests for use of the Community Booth must be received at least thirty (30) days but not more than one hundred eighty (180) days before the date requested.

3. Duration—The Community Booth may be used for a maximum of two (2) days within any thirty (30) day period, during the hours that Main Street Mall is open for business.

4. Location—All activities connected with public use of the Community Booth must be confined within the Community Booth and not conducted in the Main Street Mall stores, other mall areas, or the parking lot.

5. Signing—All signing must be located within the designated Community Booth area only.

6. Cleanliness—Upon conclusion of the activity in the Community Booth, users must clean the area and repair or replace any damaged items.

7. Handbills—Distribution of information is allowed within the Community Booth. No handbills may be distributed in the Main Street Mall stores, other mall areas, or the parking lot.

8. No public address system—No public address system or disturbing activities will be allowed within Main Street Mall property.

9. Deposit—A deposit of $25.00 is required for temporary use of the Community Booth. The deposit must be received at least one (1) week before the requested dates. This deposit will be refunded within six (6) days of the termination of use, if all requirements have been met.

EXHIBIT 4.23

Holiday Season Clean-Up Letter

TO ALL MERCHANTS:

With the holiday season fast approaching, we would all like to see the shopping center presented as attractively as possible. I would like you to direct your attention to the following:

1. Clean all framework on store fronts and doors.
2. Clean the terrazzo, carpet, or tile on the entryways or foyers.
3. Clean and repair your identification signs.
4. Keep your merchandise and displays inside your lease line.

I would appreciate your bringing to our attention any items we might have overlooked on the mall.

We wish you a happy and prosperous holiday season.

Sincerely,

XYZ Management Company

---

relation to your shopping center? Are there any areas where gangs tend to hang out? Is the shopping center on the path kids or gangs tend to frequent after school hours?

A physical inspection of your shopping center should be conducted for possible problem areas. A major area of concern are areas that are poorly lit. Good lighting is one of the best deterrents to crime. Check for overgrown landscape areas where someone would be able to hide either for the purpose of breaking into a building or accosting customers and/or merchants. In one shopping center, a bank was broken into late at night under the cover of a very large flowering bush that obscured the visibility of that area. The bank manager had long protected the bush as being very attractive, but after the incident the bush was trimmed back so the police would be able to see the windows easily.

Electrical, utility, and/or storage rooms can be a source of danger if they are not properly secured. Many of these areas also have roof access, allowing criminals to get on the roof and cut down into stores at will and with little chance of being observed.

Visit with the merchants to find out what they may observe at odd hours within the property. Having the benefit of the eyes and ears of all of the merchants will increase the chances of determining the source of potential problems early and taking preventative steps.

Review employee parking areas. It is not unusual for shopping centers to require that employees park in back and/or out-of-the-way areas, which are easy targets for vandalism, auto theft, or assault. Lighting again, is one of the best tools for protection, but it may also be necessary to have a security patrol. It may be possible to have the police make additional patrols or have the center security do additional checks as well as be available to escort employees to their cars after dark.

Most people feel safer at a shopping center than they do on city streets, and the shopping center manager must maintain this feeling by monitoring the center's security needs.

(a) NEIGHBORHOOD CENTER SECURITY

Strip centers and neighborhood centers seldom have a security problem other than minor vandalism in the parking lot and graffiti on the back walls of the center. Security problems that do occur are usually a result of one or a combination of four factors:

1. The shopping center is located in a high-crime area, and the problems at the shopping center are a reflection of the problems in the neighborhood.
2. Youth are using the shopping center as a place to hang out.
3. A rash of burglaries occurs in a short period as the burglars move from one area of the community to another.
4. A tenant is attracting a clientele that is causing the problems.

When there are no security problems other than minor vandalism, the shopping center manager's security program will consist of asking the tenants and maintenance personnel to report suspicious people and loiterers. The property manager should develop a rapport with the police precinct captain and ask that officers drive through the shopping center periodically.

Graffiti should be removed or painted over immediately or it will encourage more vandalism. If graffiti is an ongoing problem, the manager should try to determine when it is occurring—for instance, after school or late in the evening. The shopping center manager should then ask the police to drive through the shopping center during those hours. If that does not solve the problem, a private security patrol may be needed during the period of the day or evening when the problem occurs until it stops. Several city police departments now have very effective graffiti details and can help in identifying offenders and obtaining restitution.

Another problem may be teens cruising the parking lot. One approach to this problem is to request that the police enforce the motor vehicle code with regard to noise, speed, and drinking while driving.

A deterrent to vandalism and other security problems is good lighting in the common areas. Problems occurring in the evenings or early morning hours indicate that the shopping center manager must give extra attention to the shopping center lighting. Visiting the center in the evening, walking throughout the parking lot, behind the shopping center, and on all sidewalks will help the manager find areas that need better illumination.

(b) COMMUNITY MALL SECURITY

Smaller malls and enclosed community malls usually do not need security guards on duty 24 hours a day. Their security needs are similar to those of the nonenclosed neighborhood center with the exception that the mall will attract more shoppers and is a convenient place for teens to gather. If either of these situations warrants on-site security guards, the shopping center manager can schedule them based on the traffic and activities in the mall. A security program may be needed for the hours the mall has most of its traffic and the hours school is out. For instance, a security guard may be scheduled from 2:00 P.M. to 10:30 P.M., Monday through Friday, and during the hours the mall is open on the weekends, plus one-half hour after the mall closes. When school is out for the summer and during holidays, the starting time may be adjusted to an earlier hour. After mall hours, the night janitorial staff can clean the common areas, and the maintenance personnel can start their shift when the night janitorial crew leaves. Combining the maintenance and janitorial personnel and the security guards in such a manner provides on-site personnel twenty-four hours a day.

The shopping center manager develops a security program by first analyzing the hours the guards will be needed for each day of the week. Then additional guards are scheduled for peak selling seasons and special events. The cost of the guard service can be easily determined by multiplying the number of hours by the hourly rate.

The security schedule in Exhibit 4.24 is for an enclosed community mall. Note that the schedule provides security during the peak traffic periods of the week and takes into account the additional security needs for special events, the peak selling season, and evenings, when the probability of vandalism is greater.

The community mall security guard schedule provides guards during the peak mall traffic times each day of the week. Additional guards are on duty on New Year's Eve and Halloween, the two days when there is most likely to be vandalism. Three promotions—sidewalk sales, moonlight sales, and community bazaars—will generate extra traffic in the mall, and additional security is scheduled to handle this traffic.

The extra security for the Christmas season starts the Friday after Thanksgiving. Traditionally, this is the busiest shopping day of the year, which means additional security is needed on the three-day Thanksgiving weekend. Many malls extend their hours the two weekends before

EXHIBIT 4.24

Security Guard Schedule and Budget

Monthly Security Guard Schedule

Monday–Friday	1 guard	4:30 P.M. to 10:30 P.M.	= 6 hr × 5 days	= 30 hr
Saturday	1 guard	10 A.M. to 10 P.M.	= 12 hr.	= 12 hr
Sunday	1 guard	noon to 7 P.M.	= 7 hr	= 7 hr
				49 hr/wk

49 hr/wk × 4.33 wk/mo = 212 hr/mo

Additional Security Guards

Halloween night	1 parking lot guard	3 P.M. to 6 A.M.	= 15 hr
	1 guard in mall	3 P.M. to 9 P.M.	= 6 hr
			21 hr
New Year's Eve	1 guard	10 P.M. to 6 A.M.	= 8 hr
January Sidewalk Sale	1 guard	noon to 6 P.M.	= 6 hr
July Moonlight Sale	1 guard	6 P.M. to midnight	= 6 hr
September			
Community Bazaar	1 guard	10 A.M. to 5 P.M.	= 7 hr
			27 hr

Christmas Season

Thanksgiving weekend

Friday	1 mall guard	10 A.M. to 9 P.M.	= 11 hr
	1 parking lot guard	10 A.M. to 9 P.M.	= 11 hr
Saturday	1 mall guard	10 A.M. to 6 P.M.	= 8 hr
	1 parking lot guard	10 A.M. to 6 P.M.	= 8 hr
Sunday	1 mall guard	11 A.M. to 6 P.M.	= 7 hr
	1 parking lot guard	11 A.M. to 6 P.M.	= 7 hr
			52 hr

Second week before Christmas

Monday–Friday	1 mall guard	noon to 10 P.M.	= 10 hr × 5 days =	50 hr
	1 parking lot guard	noon to 10 P.M.	= 10 hr × 5 days =	50 hr
Saturday	1 mall guard	10 A.M. to 6 P.M.	=	8 hr
	1 mall guard	noon to 7 P.M.	=	7 hr
	1 parking lot guard	10 A.M. to 7 P.M.	=	9 hr
Sunday	1 mall guard	noon to 6 P.M.	=	6 hr
	1 mall guard	1 P.M. to 6 P.M.	=	5 hr
	1 parking lot guard	noon to 7 P.M.	=	7 hr
				142 hr

Week before Christmas

Monday–Friday	1 mall guard	10 A.M. to 10 P.M.	= 12 hr × 5 days =	60 hr
	1 mall guard	5 P.M. to 10 P.M.	= 5 hr × 5 days =	25 hr
	1 parking lot guard	noon to 10 P.M.	= 10 hr × 5 days =	50 hr
Saturday	1 mall guard	10 A.M. to 6 P.M.	=	8 hr
	1 mall guard	noon to 7 P.M.	=	7 hr
	1 parking lot guard	9:30 A.M. to 6:30 P.M.	=	9 hr

EXHIBIT 4.24 (Continued)

Sunday	1 mall guard	noon to 6 P.M.	=	6 hr
	1 mall guard	1 P.M. to 6 P.M.	=	5 hr
				177 hr

Total Christmas Period   371 hr

Cost of the Security Guard Program

Monthly schedule	212 hr/mo	× $9.50/hr	= $2,014.00/month
Halloween night	21 hr	× 9.50/hr	= 200.00
New Year's Eve	8 hr	× 9.50/hr	= 76.00
Jan. Sidewalk Sale	6 hr	× 9.50/hr	= 57.00
July Moonlight Sale	6 hr	× 9.50/hr	= 57.00
Sept. Community Bazaar	7 hr	× 9.50/hr	= 66.50
Christmas season			
Thanksgiving	52 hr	× 9.50/hr	= 494.00
December	319 hr	× 9.50/hr	= 3,030.50

Security Costs by Month

January	$ 2,014.00 monthly
	76.00 New Year's Eve and Day
	57.00 Sidewalk sale
	2,147.00
February	2,014.00 monthly
March	2,014.00 monthly
April	2,014.00 monthly
May	2,014.00 monthly
June	2,014.00 monthly
July	2,014.00 monthly
	57.00 Sidewalk Sale
	2,071.00
August	2,014.00 monthly
September	2,014.00 monthly
	66.50 Community Bazaar
	2,080.50
October	2,014.00 monthly
November	2,014.00 monthly
	494.00 Thanksgiving weekend
	2,508.00
December	2,014.00 monthly
	3,030.50 Christmas
	5,044.50
Total	$27,892.00

Christmas Day, and the security schedule reflects the longer Saturday and Sunday mall hours. A security guard is placed in the parking lot to direct traffic the three-day weekend following Thanksgiving and the two weeks before Christmas.

(c) REGIONAL AND SUPER-REGIONAL MALLS

Regional and super-regional malls usually schedule guards 24 hours a day, or all the hours the mall is open. They also have the parking lots patrolled. If the mall has two common area maintenance budgets, a mall budget and a parking lot budget, then separate security guard budgets would be developed for each area.

Extra guards need to be scheduled for the grand opening of a community or regional mall to direct traffic in the parking lot and to patrol the mall. A security incident during a grand opening can be more devastating than at any other time, so a security schedule that is more than adequate should be developed for the grand opening. Remember, you never get a second chance to make a first impression.

(d) SECURITY GUARDS

A key decision in developing a security guard program for a shopping center is whether the mall should hire the guards as employees of the mall or contract with an outside security guard company. There are advantages to both.

In-House Staff

The first advantage to an in-house guard staff is that the property manager has greater control over the entire guard program, including selection and supervision of the guards. If the guards are employees of the mall, they know they will not be transferred to another property. This can build allegiance to their job and result in a lower turnover. The in-house guards also have a better opportunity to become familiar with the layout of the mall, the store managers, and employees. Finally, the cost per guard may be less since the profit margin of the security guard company is saved. Off-duty police officers are an excellent source of guards.

Security Guard Company

There are also distinct advantages to contracting with a security guard company. First, the company provides an expertise that the property manager may not have, and is more likely to be current on the laws of citizen's arrest, detaining a person, curfews, and other law-enforcement regulations. Hiring an outside company relieves the property manager of hiring, training, and terminating security personnel. The security company will have additional personnel to substitute for those who are ill or on vacation and can provide additional security guards during peak mall traffic periods and special events. Finally, if a guard is involved in an incident that ends in litigation, the security guard company's insurance carrier can defend the shopping center's property management company and the mall. Since the shopping center manager has required the security guard company to have insurance naming the mall and the property management company as named insured on the policy, the mall's insurance carrier is not brought into the picture, and the mall's insurance rates are not affected.

Armed or Unarmed Guards

Another security question to be decided is: Should a security guard be armed? Generally, no. Most security guards do not receive ongoing training with firearms, and few security guards are qualified to handle a situation that requires the display and possible use of a firearm.

Armed security guards in a mall can give shoppers the impression that the mall is a dangerous place. It would be more reassuring, if a situation arises that requires the use of firearms, to call in the local police, who are trained to handle emergency situations.

If the mall is in an area where guards must be armed, the shopping center manager should work with the local police department in the selection of a security guard company. Some cities offer a parapolice program. This program allows the city to assign uniformed off-duty officers to patrol the mall. The shopping center would reimburse the city for the cost of the police patrol. The advantage to the city is that it has more officers on patrol at no additional cost to the city. The advantage to the officers is that they have an opportunity to moonlight at the approval of the police department and usually at a pay comparable to their city salary. A parapolice program costs more than contracting with a security guard company, but the police officers are professionals.

Security Guard Uniforms

Whether to outfit the security guards in either a police-type uniform or a blazer outfit is another decision for the property manager. If there is a need for a show of force, then the security guards should be in police-type uniforms. However, if the security guard's main responsibility is to serve a public relations function, then blazer uniforms may be more appropriate. Regardless of the type of uniform, it must be clean and easily identifiable.

Training the Security Guards

The shopping center manager should develop an ongoing training program for the mall's security force. The security program is an integral part of the entire management program for the shopping center, and the security guards must believe that they are an important part of the management team. Each new guard must become familiar with the property and receive a security guard's procedure manual. Regular training sessions should be conducted. At these sessions, the shopping center manager should review the security procedures for upcoming events and discuss how to handle specific situations. The police should be encouraged to attend these sessions. Other guest speakers that should be invited to these sessions are: fire department representatives, the mall's attorney and insurance agent or carrier, and the property manager's supervisor. The security guards should be encouraged to take an active role in these sessions and to discuss their problems and offer suggestions.

The shopping center manager should review the equipment needed by the security force. Will a car or motorized cart be needed for parking lot patrol? Should all security guards be in radio communication with the management staff and one another? What types of flashlights, first aid kits, and other equipment will be needed?

Each guard should receive a manual from the shopping center manager that covers every possible situation the guard might encounter. The manual should also include each guard's schedule; what happens when a guard is not relieved; areas the guard should patrol; areas that require more frequent patrols, such as restrooms; how to report vandalism and theft of the mall's property; how to assist customers with lost items, locked cars, and so on; how to handle loiterers; the mall's policy regarding skateboards, skates, and animals; the guard's responsibilities if an incident occurs in a store; areas to patrol; the procedures and requirements for using the community room and community booth; whether employees should be escorted to their cars or to on-site banks; what to do in different emergencies; responsibilities during a power failure; what happens when the fire or sprinkler alarm sounds; the location of shutoff valves; how to handle irate customers. The guards should check for burned out lights in the evening and slippery spots, especially in the exterior common areas, in the winter.

At the end of each shift, the guard should give the property manager a written report detailing the situations the guard was confronted with, how the situation was handled, and which topics should be discussed at the guards' meetings.

The guards can be assigned the responsibility to list the hours each store opens and closes. A form Irregularity in Store Opening and Closing Hours is filled out by the security guard each morning and evening and given to the mall manager or operations manager. The mall manager meets with the manager of any store that is opening too late or closing earlier.

(e) DEVELOPING A RELATIONSHIP WITH THE POLICE DEPARTMENT

The property manager should develop a working relationship with the community's public service departments, requesting the police and fire department to appoint a liaison to the mall. The police should be requested to report all incidents at the shopping center to the property manager. The department can be invited to use the shopping center after hours to practice emergencies and training. Some police departments will loan the on-site property manager a walkie-talkie for direct and immediate reporting of the incident to the police. A few regional malls have been able to locate a sheriff's or police department's substation at the mall. As a result, the sheriff or police are always cruising the parking lot and are visible within the shopping center.

Budgetary concerns should never be a factor in developing a security program. A shopping center cannot afford inadequate security.

§ 4.27 SAFETY AWARENESS BROCHURE

An innovative approach to safety awareness has been instituted by Tysons Corner Center in McLean, Virginia. They distribute a brochure throughout the shopping center outlining shopper safety and crime in the center. The brochure was developed in response to customer concerns about crime in the center.

The brochure provides statistics on crimes, which include robbery, murder and aggravated assault, rape, other violence, and auto theft. The statistics are based on the number of incidents per so many visits to put them in a proper context. Tysons Corner Center estimates that it has an average population of 4,200 at any given time, making it the equivalent of many small cities.

In addition to these statistics, the brochure carries safety tips as well as information on how to reach security and how to report a crime.

§ 4.28 MERCHANT RETENTION

Over the last several years, the United States has experienced one of the most difficult economic times in recent memory. In past years, the merchants had little choice but to meet the demands of the shopping center owners. However, with the change in the economic conditions, landlords have come to realize that the merchant is the customer and/or client of the property and should be treated with respect and concern at all times.

There is little doubt that the loss of a good merchant in a shopping center can be expensive. It also has a negative impact on the other merchants as well as the buying public. An effective, strong merchant contributes to the success of the shopping center, not only with the rent, but the successful draw of traffic to one store brings new customers to the surrounding stores.

The responsibility for good landlord/merchant relations should be with the landlord and the manager of the shopping center. In the past, the misconception that the landlord and the merchant have opposing views and that their interests are much different has been prevalent. The merchant needs a successful, well-operated shopping center in which to do business and the landlord, on the other hand, needs effective, well-run stores to make the center a success.

The relationship with the merchant should start with the initial meetings and never stop. The landlord representatives—starting from the leasing agent, center manager, maintenance personnel, marketing staff and administrative personnel—must be made aware of the importance of the landlord/merchant relationship.

The leasing agent must be knowledgeable and helpful and not combative or condescending. A professional approach with honest and direct answers will go a long way in building a relationship and not just trying to get a lease signed. Once the lease is signed, the leasing agent should introduce the merchant to the center manager and/or the construction coordinator so there is no gap in the communication. A letter should be sent to the new merchant by the leasing agent with the signed lease indicating who the next contact will be along with a phone number.

The center manager and/or construction coordinator should then either call or meet with the new merchant, answer any questions, and provide the new merchant with information on what will happen from that point on. That meeting should be followed up with a letter outlining what was discussed. This is an excellent time to give the merchant a tenant kit that provides operating information on the property.

If the merchant has tenant improvements to put in, he or she will be grateful for information on obtaining building permits, where to obtain temporary power for construction, how to get the store sign approved, how to contact the marketing personnel, how to get mail started at the store, who to contact for security, who to call for telephone service, who to call for utility services, and how to handle trash pick up.

The tenant kit should include all information on warranties, especially for a new project. It should inform the merchant what warranty exists on the basic construction and on the air conditioner compressor. The merchant may not be aware of these warranties and incur unnecessary expenses as a result. The air conditioning systems are often quite complex and the tenant kit is a good way to tell the merchant how to operate the system and how it works. This is a good place to tell the merchant how the thermostat works and where the various controls are located and how they are used. The kit should include such things as the breakers, reset switches, servicing shut offs, filters, and roof access. The tenant kit is also used to tell the tenant where to pay the rent, where to pay merchants' association or marketing fund dues, who to call for emergency repairs both inside the store and in the common areas, where employees are to park their cars, how to call security if needed. Typically, the mall's security staff does not operate inside the merchants premises and that fact should be spelled out in the tenant kit as well. Emergency escape routes should be shown in the kit along with other emergency information such as how to call the police and/or fire department and where emergency equipment is located.

The tenant kit will also show a shopping center plot plan with items of interest clearly marked. Those items would include emergency shut offs for electrical power, gas meters, water meters, the location of roof ladders, the location of sprinkler systems risers and controls, fire hydrants, sump pumps, electrical rooms, elevator rooms, and who has keys to these areas for emergency access.

While some national chain merchants are quite familiar with construction management and problems, the typical smaller merchant has little experience in that area and can use some help. During the construction process, it is helpful if the manager and/or construction coordinator can stop by the new store and inquire as to how things are going. If the merchant is having a problem with city hall, a contractor, or the physical plant, it is a nice touch for the center personnel to see if they can help clear away the problem. On a purely selfish level, it is in the best interest of the shopping center to be sure that the merchant completes construction and opens as soon as possible.

Once the merchant has opened for business, it is a good idea to stop by the store, congratulate the merchant on opening, and see if there are any lingering problems. If there are items that are the responsibility of the landlord, it is good business to get them resolved as soon as possible so that both the property manager and the merchant can get on with business. Many landlords find it a good policy to send the merchant a small gift for the opening—a plant, a small teapot or coffee pot, or some other way to say "congratulations."

At this point, the landlord should send the merchant a letter indicating that the lease is now in effect and showing the starting and ending dates of the lease, the amount of rent and common area charges along with the proper back up, where to send the rent, and any other information that would be helpful to the merchant. It is also helpful to send a letter to all of the other occupants in the shopping center introducing them to the new merchant and suggesting that they stop by and get acquainted.

Once the merchant is operating it is good business to stop by and visit at least once a month. In a troubled property, more frequent visits are suggested. The purpose of these visits is to let the merchant know that you care and are involved, but also to allow the merchant to bring problems and situations to your attention. It is much better to hear about a minor problem in time to get it taken care of than to receive an emergency call in the middle of the night about a major disaster that could have been prevented. If the manager does stop by for a visit and the manager or owner is not in, it is important to leave a business card letting them know that you stopped by. If you do not see the manager or owner in your regular visits, a phone call to "touch bases" is a great idea and lets the manager or owner know that you care enough to go out of your way to communicate.

All merchant phone calls should be returned promptly. A suggestion where the manager has multiple properties in other area codes is to install a custom 800 phone number so the merchant can reach management without making a long distance call. The cost is nominal and sends a good message to the merchants. For a manager who is in the field much of the time, both a pager and a car phone are great ideas. Often there are problems that need immediate attention and a quick response can save hard feelings. The cost of these tools is modest compared to the potential benefits. Because most shopping centers have activity of some sort 24 hours a day, every day of the year, it is critical that there be an "after hours" contact for the merchants. This can be an answering service or one staff member each week, but an answering machine is not sufficient because of the potential problems that can happen in a shopping center.

(a) TENANT REQUESTS

There will always be tenant requests. These requests should be handled in a timely and courteous fashion. The shopping center manager is not there to "win" arguments, but rather to solve problems. Even if the merchant calls in with a request for a service that should be taken care of by the merchant, the center manager should point that out in a courteous informative manner. A good approach is to say "I'm sorry but . . ." and provide an explanation why the service cannot be provided by the center management. It is also a good idea to suggest a contractor or source for the solution to the problem. Quite often the merchant or the merchant's manager really does not understand the lease provisions and will not appreciate learning that he or she is responsible for solving the problem as well as the cost that will go with it. A little sympathy will take the sting out of hearing this "bad news."

It is also important that legitimate requests be taken care of promptly. A dirty sidewalk in front of a retail store or burned out lights in the parking lot can be a real source of irritation to a merchant, or worse, loss of business. If the solution takes four or five days, the merchant can easily assume that the management does not care.

If the problem is a safety hazard or impairs the merchant's activity, a follow-up phone call to see that everything is taken care of will be appreciated. Every effort should be made to resolve the problem at the earliest possible time so it does not escalate out of proportion. At times, involving the merchant in the solution can be an excellent strategy, especially if the problem is a difficult one and you are not sure of the solution. The shopping center manager does not need to have the answer to every problem. Rather, being willing to discuss the problem with the merchant may elicit valuable input and a new perspective.

The shopping center manager should have a complete understanding of the property's lease documents and the individual terms so there is a clear knowledge of the responsibilities of both the landlord and the merchant. A misunderstanding of the landlord's responsibilities may well leave the merchant thinking that the landlord is trying to avoid his or her legal obligations. If a job is to be delayed or take longer than originally estimated, the merchant will appreciate a call advising him of what is being done and why there is a delay. Again, an apology for the delay will make the merchant feel better, even if nothing is being accomplished at the moment. Maintenance personnel and outside contractors should be instructed on the importance of the landlord/merchant relationship and should be courteous and helpful at all times. Because they are not aware of the lease provisions, they should refer any specific requests to management, but should not try to discuss the lease or specific responsibilities. It is not unusual for a maintenance person or contractor to pass along inaccurate information to the merchant and cause problems that take a long time to overcome.

If major repairs are planned for the property, it is common courtesy to inform the merchants ahead of time. Major parking lot repairs are very disruptive and the merchant may be planning a big sale that could be disrupted by such work. Roof work often requires that large sections of the parking lot be roped off causing parking problems. The work can be quite noisy, causing problems within the store. These large projects must be done, but informing the merchants in advance will give them a chance to raise legitimate objections or to change their plans to avoid the problems. They may also have some suggestions that will help minimize the disruption of the work.

(b) POSITIVE COMMUNICATIONS

It is not unusual for a merchant to say "the only time I hear from the landlord/shopping center manager is when there is a problem." This should not be the case. There are many opportunities for good, positive communication between landlord/shopping center manager and merchant and the astute manager will take advantage of all of them.

When a merchant reports a particularly good sales month, a letter of congratulations is a good public relations tool. If the center manager sees a good ad in the newspaper, it is a great idea to cut it out and sent it to the merchant with a letter thanking them for their advertising effort. A good window display is another opportunity to compliment the merchant on a job well done. Quite often a merchant will call the management office to point out a problem in the common areas that might have been missed by the manager. Every effort should be made to thank the merchant for this extra effort. Recently, in a West Coast shopping center, a common area billing was sent with an error that cost the merchants additional money. One merchant saw the error and reported it to the manager. The error was immediately corrected by management and the letter that went to all of the merchants thanked the merchant who reported the problem which improved the managers relations with that merchant, but also made the merchant somewhat of a hero with the other merchants.

Many merchants are active in the community in service organizations, city boards, church activities, and so on. When their activities are known to management, a letter of congratulations is a good idea. Merchants' Association activities are difficult for most merchants who already have full schedules, so that activity is also an opportunity to recognize their efforts with a letter of congratulations or a breakfast or lunch to say "thanks."

(c) ADVERTISING AND MARKETING

Bringing in an outside speaker to the Merchants' Association meetings can be an excellent tool for improving landlord/merchant relations. Topics for outside speakers can be window displays, advertising for the small merchant, how to minimize shoplifting, store security, employee relations, merchandising, or complying with the latest governmental program. The merchants can often be an excellent source of topics if they are asked.

In difficult times, the astute landlord will consider an ad campaign for the center, completely paid for by the landlord or heavily subsidized by the landlord. Even if the landlord is paying for all of the advertising, some of the more involved merchants should be asked for their input, or it is possible that the merchants will feel that the money has been wasted.

The advertising program should be designed to benefit the largest number of merchants in the center and then every effort should be made to be sure they are aware of the campaign. If there are specific positive results, these results should be shared with everyone in the center. If there is a way of transferring these benefits to all, that should also be shared. In some centers, a welcoming ad is placed for each new merchant and paid for by the landlord. The ad is stylized for the specific shopping center with a logo and location, but the center part of the ad is for copy from that specific merchant. The cost of such a program is minimal, but it is well-received by both the new merchant and the existing merchants.

Many small merchants have little access to helpful information on merchandising, advertising, and the general state of retailing. There are many good sources of such information and it is a good idea for the landlord/manager to collect this information and pass it along to the merchants. The International Council of Shopping Centers publishes a booklet called "The Retail Challenge." The center manager may subscribe to this publication in sufficient quantities to provide one to each merchant and send it along on a quarterly basis. Another excellent publication by the International Council of Shopping Centers is "Merchandise Index" published quarterly. With the permission of ICSC, some of this information can be passed along to the merchants. Quite often the local papers, *The Wall Street Journal,* or other trade publications have articles of interest to the merchants and the manager can pass these along to the merchants.

Some shopping centers with more active merchants' associations will host an annual breakfast, lunch, or evening social for the purpose of handing out awards, recognition for specific accomplishments, and just general good will. This gives the manager an opportunity to meet with the merchants in a more relaxed atmosphere and get better acquainted. It also provides a positive setting that can benefit both the landlord and the merchant.

(d) COMMON AREA BILLINGS

Common area billings are the source of many problems between landlord and merchant. Often, the merchant does not fully understand just what is involved. The costs may seem high relative to what the merchant sees being done on a daily basis. It is important to see that billings are accurate, that the services are competitive, and that the merchants are given sufficient explanation to understand what they are paying for.

Some of the more sophisticated merchants go to great lengths to negotiate limits on common area costs and/or exclusions to the billings, only to find that they are ignored when the bills arrive. It is very likely that such an error is an oversight, but it creates an atmosphere of doubt and mistrust. It is worthwhile to build a model of each common area lease provision for each merchant and then to be sure that each billing adheres to that model. Once a merchant receives a few carefully crafted common area bills, he or she is likely to look at future bills in a more positive light. Sufficient detail should be given so that the merchant can readily determine what was spent, when it was spent, and how the merchant's share was determined. It is not suggested that copies of the individual bills be sent to the merchants, unless the lease requires that, but rather that there be sufficient detail so the merchant can have a full understanding of the charges.

If a merchant questions part of the billing, the manager should provide a courteous, patient answer. It is not sufficient to say "it is in the lease," but rather to spend a moment to explain what was done and why. If the costs are higher than anticipated, a little sympathy will go a long way in getting the merchant to accept the higher amounts. Even though the merchant signed a lease agreeing to pay "all" of the charges, it is often quite frustrating to receive a very large common area bill, especially if it comes at a time of lower sales. A patient, sympathetic approach will generally get the bill paid a lot sooner than threats. Quite often giving the merchant a little extra time to make the payment will resolve any dispute and eliminate the need to reduce the billing.

Finally, a timely billing is helpful to all concerned. It is not fair to either the landlord or the merchant to wait nine months to send out a common area billing. The landlord loses the cash flow and the merchant may well have closed his books on that time frame, issued bonuses, or distributed profits, only to find that there is a large outstanding bill.

(e) MERCHANTS WITH FINANCIAL PROBLEMS

The merchant who is having financial problems needs special attention. The manager should keep in mind that the merchant who cannot pay bills is probably already under stress. A supportive and understanding manager will be most effective. Working out either financial or nonfinancial relief for a merchant can be in the best interest of merchant and landlord alike. Giving full attention to the merchant's problems and making every attempt to work them out will be to the ultimate benefit of the landlord/manager. This is not to say that the landlord should concede every time a merchant asks for relief, but the landlord should give full consideration to the problem and approach the merchant in a businesslike, sympathetic fashion. Saving the existing merchant is usually preferable to having a vacancy and the costs and problems that accompany it.

§ 4.29   PERFORMING A TENANT VISUAL AUDIT

In addition to being fully versed in all aspects of property operations, the shopping center manager must have knowledge for the viability of the retail operations. The property manager needs to understand what elements are needed for a successful retail store in order to help merchants maximize their potential.

The typical retail property manager, while not a retailing expert, should have a basic understanding of stocking, merchandising, personnel needs, signage, merchandise turns, markdown policies, window display, store arrangement, and advertising. The manager need not visit the merchants on a regularly scheduled basis to advise on store operation but should evaluate each store and offer suggestions to the stores that need help or request rent relief and other forms of landlord assistance.

The Tenant Visual Audit in Exhibit 4.25 serves as a guide for the shopping center manager who wants to understand and identify the characteristics of successful stores. Armed with these guidelines and the merchants' monthly sales reports, the manager should be in a good position to provide help and make informed decisions. The property manager who can visit a retail shop or study sales reports and quickly recognize that the shop is in trouble is ahead in the game of shopping center management.

(a) VISUAL MERCHANDISING

Much merchandise is sold to the customer who is "just looking." For many merchandise categories, the customer must look at what is offered before deciding on a purchase. "Just looking" is smart shopping, and any effort that enables the customer to see more is likely to produce additional sales.

Windows should convey what the store carries. Complicated windows are likely to be distracting. Props are passé as are window displays that conceal the shop's interior

Some window signage is often desirable. Shop names are better shown on windows than on blade signs, but it is vital to establish a standard for such signage and to maintain some degree of uniformity in the shopping center.

The usual recommendation is to change windows and major display areas every two weeks. This is based on the premise that some 60 percent of the customers shop a center twice a month or more frequently. In support of this, the surveys at Fashion Island, Newport Beach, California, and at South Coast Plaza, Costa Mesa, California, are representative. These surveys asked the question: How often do you usually shop?

	FI (%)	SCP (%)
Once a week or more	28.0	22.9
Three times a month	16.0	19.9
Twice a month	16.3	21.0
Once a month	14.2	16.8
Less than once a month	21.6	16.5
This is my first visit	2.9	2.5

EXHIBIT 4.25

Tenant Visual Audit for a Retail Specialty Shop

To be successful, a retail specialty store must be as good as or better than other similar stores in its trading area. There are six essentials in achieving this goal. The store must have:

1. A specialized merchandise mix.
2. Adequate representation in higher ticket merchandise.
3. Operation at an adequate initial mark-on.
4. Complete price competitiveness on identifiably identical merchandise.
5. A specific program for recognizing and getting rid of slow selling merchandise.
6. Personal involvement of the shop managers and owners in the store's operation.

The following questions explore these issues:

1. *Does the shop have a specialized merchandise mix?* Most specialty shop owners can best compete in high-ticket, fine merchandise that allows them to do things better than anyone else. The specialty store can be truly outstanding only with a narrow mix of merchandise.

Demographics are unimportant as long as a shop operates in a reasonably sized heterogeneous community. The smart merchant does not tailor a shop to the local demographics but instead chooses a merchandise category in which the shop can be the very best in the trading area. The interested customers (and there are always enough of them for the best shop) will find and support the shop.

2. *Is there adequate representation in higher ticket merchandise?* Small independent specialty shops that do not offer high-ticket items are rarely successful. If the average sale is low, the shop may enjoy many transactions; but at the end of the month, after paying for merchandise and paying the high current cost of operation, little if any funds may remain for ownership.

Even an experienced merchant can be misled by the numerous low-ticket transactions in comparison with a fewer high-ticket dollar sales.

The following analysis, for two different gift shops, demonstrate the importance of including substantial amounts of high-ticket merchandise in the store's inventory:

	Price Range	% Sold Trans	$s	Cumulative % Sold Trans	$s
I	Under $4.99	40.1	5.4	40.1	5.4
	$5.00– 9.99	21.9	7.6	62.0	13.0
	10.00–24.99	23.9	18.5	85.9	31.5
	25.00–49.99	9.4	16.0	95.3	47.5
	Over 50.00	4.7	52.5	100.0	100.0

EXHIBIT 4.25 (*Continued*)

	Price Range	% Sold Trans	$s	Cumulative % Sold Trans	$s
II	Under $4.99	42.0	8.0	42.0	8.0
	$5.00– 9.99	22.7	9.7	64.7	17.7
	10.00–24.99	22.1	21.4	86.8	39.1
	25.00–49.99	9.2	19.4	96.0	58.5
	50.00–99.99	2.5	9.9	98.5	68.4
	Over 100.00	1.5	31.6	100.0	100.0

In Case I, over 50% of the dollar volume came from sales over $50 each, only 4.7% of the transactions; 68.5% of dollar sales came from sales over $25, only 14.1% of the transactions. Similarly in Case II, 13.2% of the transactions were over $25 and accounted for 60.9% of the dollar sales. Having a significant portion of an inventory in higher ticket merchandise is vital.

3. *Does the shop maintain an adequate initial mark-on?* The small independent operator who is tempted to operate at a closer mark-on, need only make a straightforward breakeven calculation to be sold at discounted prices. Discounting requires management expertise and financial muscle not generally available to the specialty shop.

4. *Is the shop completely price competitive on identifiably identical merchandise?* Specialty store retailers that stock the same merchandise carried by large-scale discount operations can seldom be competitive with such retailers. Even small communities have been seriously affected by discounting. In areas that have this competition, small, independent specialty operations are no longer competing successfully in the sales of housewares, toys, traffic appliances, major appliances, radios, television, and audio equipment—all identifiable, identical branded merchandise. Many small jewelry stores have discontinued brand-name watches, and more recently, record shops and video rental shops have felt the impact of large discount chains.

It is impractical for the independent single-store operator or small chain operator to attempt to match the selection or prices of discount operations that have huge buying power, continuous market presence, and strong financial support

5. *Does the shop systematically recognize and take action on slow-selling merchandise?* The number one killer of speciality stores is not poor management skills or undercapitalization. Rather, it is the failure to deal with accumulated slow-selling merchandise and the associated inability to bring in fresh merchandise each month.

This problem with a recommended solution, is presented in detail in section (b).

6. *Is ownership personally involved?* Specialty store owners who are not prepared to give their time and energy wholeheartedly to the enterprise are seldom successful. Personal involvement is essential to a profitable operation

Prepared by Robert Bearson of Advisors to Business Management, Long Beach, California.

(b) SLOW-SELLING MERCHANDISE

The most troublesome problem facing store managements is the need to quickly identify and deal with slow-selling merchandise. It is vital to establish limiting time standards on the basis of acceptable stockturn rates.

It is reasonable to state that markdowns are unavoidable. There are strong psychological barriers to expeditiously taking markdowns. Therefore, it is necessary to set and implement standards. The result of doing so will be significant profit increase.

The magnitude of the problem is considerable because markdowns are increasing each year. The proportion of inventory that must be reduced to be sold is increasing each year.

The following questions focus on important aspects of slow-selling merchandise:

- *Is merchandise marked down after a specific number of weeks?* The most practical and effective approach to a markdown program is to establish and implement standards based on number of weeks on sale.

The basic criterion in the following calculations is that an item is not selling acceptably if it has not been sold in 25 percent more time than the average.

$$\frac{\text{Maximum Weeks}}{\text{on Hand}} = 52 \times 1.25 \times 1 \, / \, \text{Stockturn, or}$$

$$433 \times 1.25 \times 1 \, / \, \text{Stockturn} \times 1 \, / \, \text{Median \% Month}$$

$$\text{Stockturn} = \text{Net Sales} \times 1 \, / \, \text{Average Inventory @ Retail}$$

Example:

The National Retail Merchants Association, Merchandising and Operating Results, 1989, for the year 1988, indicates for department 1000, Female Apparel, a median and top quartile stockturn of 3.1 percent and 3.7 percent: Using 3.1 times the median monthly percentage of annual sales of 8.05 suggests that any item that has not been sold in 22 weeks should be marked down:

$$52 \times 1.25 \, / \, 3.1 = 20.97$$

$$433 \times 1.25 \times 1 \, / \, 3.1 \times 1 \, / \, 8.05 = 21.69$$

If one-half of a group has not been sold in one-half the above number of weeks, 11 weeks, the group should be marked down.

If in the first four weeks of sale, 18 percent of the group has not been sold, the group should be marked down.

- *Are the markdowns adequate?* After the first markdown has been taken, follow-up markdowns should be taken progressively until the merchandise is sold. The markdown amount in season should be 25 percent to 33⅓ percent off, to 50 percent off, to progressive 20 percent further reductions. The markdown amount out of season is generally 33½ percent off, to 50 percent off, to progressive 20 percent further reductions.
- *Are follow-up markdowns taken?* The markdown frequency in season is at four-week intervals to allow the typical customer two visits. The markdown frequency out of season is two- or three-week intervals. The spring/summer season ends the last week in June. The fall/holiday season ends December 26.
- *Do price tickets indicate when merchandise was put on sale?* A simple way to date merchandise is to enter a three-digit code on the price ticket. Each week number begins on Sunday and is applicable to the days that follow. The number begins with the first week (01) in January and ends with the last week (52) in December. The two-digit number is preceded by the year (1 = 1991). Using this system, the week beginning Sunday, 19 May 1991, would be 121. Exhibit 4.26 illustrates the use of the three-digit code, followed by a form (Exhibit 4.27) setting markdown standards.

(c) PROFESSIONAL PERSONAL RETAIL SELLING

The typical retail specialty store can increase sales significantly by providing employees with a basic training program in professional retail selling.

In the past few decades, personal retail selling diminished markedly, primarily because of the heavy demand for merchandise and the rapid growth of supermarkets and discount stores. Through reduced staffing, large retailers have realized significant expense savings, but small specialty stores must still maintain minimum sales staffs. This gives the small shop the opportunity to gain a competitive edge by utilizing professional personal selling. Unquestionably, the customer with whom the salesperson establishes rapport remains in the shop longer, sees more, considers more, and buys more.

In addition, the salesperson with superior selling skills finds that the day passes more quickly and pleasantly. The satisfying feeling of having functioned as a professional rather than as an order-taking clerk minimizes fatigue and bolsters self-esteem.

EXHIBIT 4.26

Inventory Management—Week Numbering System 1992

	Jan	Feb	Mar	Apr	May	Jun	Jul	Aug	Sep	Oct	Nov	Dec	
1	201	205	210	214	218	223	227	231	236	240	245	249	1
2		206						232					2
3					219								3
4										241			4
5	202			215			228						5
6									237			250	6
7						224							7
8			211								246		8
9		207						233					9
10					220								10
11										242			11
12	203			216			229						12
13									238			251	13
14						225							14
15			212								247		15
16		208						234					16
17					221								17
18										243			18
19	204			217			230						19
20									239			252	20
21						226							21
22			213								248		22
23		209						235					23
24					222								24
25										244			25
26	205			218			231						26
27									240			301	27
28						227							28
29			214								249		29
30								236					30
31					223								31

EXHIBIT 4.27

Setting Standards—Inventory Management/Markdown Program

The National Retail Federation, Merchandising and Operating Results, indicates:

Year of report	_____
Year reported	_____
Department Number	_____
Department	_____
Stockturn, median	_____
Stockturn, top quartile	_____

The median monthly percentage of annual sales as found in the 199_____ Newspaper Advertising Planbook, in the RAB Instant Background, Radio Advertising Bureau, Spring/Fall 199 ___ is _____. It then follows that:

Any item that has been in the shop _____ weeks should have been marked down:

$$52 \times 1.25 \times 1 / \underline{\quad} \qquad = \underline{\quad}$$
$$433 \times 1.25 \times 1 / \underline{\quad} \times 1 / \underline{\quad} = \underline{\quad}$$

If one-half of a group has not been sold in _____ weeks, the group should be marked down. This is one-half of the above number of weeks.

If in the first four weeks, _____%

If in the first eight weeks, _____%

If in the first twelve weeks, _____ % of the group has not been sold, the group should be marked down:

$$4 / \underline{\quad} = \underline{\quad}$$
$$8 / \underline{\quad} = \underline{\quad}$$
$$12 / \underline{\quad} = \underline{\quad}$$

	Markdown Amount In Season Out		Markdown Frequency In Season Out	
1st	_____	_____	_____	_____
2nd	_____	_____	_____	_____
3rd	_____	_____	_____	_____
4th	_____	_____	_____	_____
nth	_____	_____	_____	_____

Season End: Spring / Summer   _____ _____

The shop, meanwhile loses none of its self-selection business and picks up additional sales—often a 25 percent increase or more.

The following guidelines describe proven selling techniques for a wide variety of retail operations. In using these guidelines, the individual shop manager must determine which procedures would be most effective for the needs, characteristics, and personality of that particular store. Although each shop differs in its merchandise, presentation, price lines, and salespeople, many of the guidelines are applicable to all professional retailers. The suggested techniques reflect these premises:

- Every customer should be greeted within half a minute of entering the shop.
- Every entering customer should be approached while in the shop.
- Sales personnel should be on the selling floor except when it is necessary to be behind the service desk.
- Sales personnel should always use professional approaches with customers.

(d) GUIDELINES—SALES PERSONNEL

The customer who enters a retail store to look at the merchandise is sometimes searching for a specific item. In most instances, however, the customer enters the shop "just looking" to see what is new and makes most buying decisions while in the store.

It is a disservice to show only low-ticket merchandise in the belief that the customer wants to spend as little as possible. Most customers are interested in unique merchandise and, in specialty stores, this is usually the more expensive items. For most busy customers, shopping is not primarily a recreation: It is a necessary chore. Thus there is a sense of accomplishment in finding and purchasing desirable merchandise.

In choosing purchases, customers tend to buy close to the time of use. Retailers must always respect the customer's intelligence, attempting to influence buying decisions.

The customer is attracted to merchandise that is on sale, will come into a shop to check out sales, and appreciates being told of sale merchandise. The customer may require information or help in locating merchandise but does not like to be pressured. In most instances, the customer "sells" herself or himself.

In sharp contrast to other forms of selling, the function of the *retail salesperson* is less to "sell" the customer and more to "show" the customer. To fulfill the objective of encouraging the customer to remain in the store as long as possible, it is valuable to involve the customer in conversation. This creates an opportunity to show the customer more, to respond to questions, and to counter objections.

The salesperson must recognize the difference between being aggressive and being assertive. Aggressive behavior inhibits customer rapport, whereas assertive behavior indicates competence, knowledge, and professionalism, thereby encouraging the customer's feeling of confidence.

(i) Sales Elements

For purposes of analysis, although all elements are not present in every transaction, a retail sales transaction can be divided into the following segments:

1. Preplanning
2. Greeting
3. Identification of Customer's Area of Interest
4. Approach
5. Merchandise Presentation
6. Countering Objections
7. Closing
8. Security
9. Showing Additional Merchandise
10. Giving a Reason to Return
11. Follow-Up.

Preplanning. Salespersons should master these preplanning techniques:

- Learn at least three selling facts about each prominently displayed item in the store, for example, "You will always be able to add pieces"; "The price will increase soon"; "It was designed by _____."
- Select an item suitable for demonstration.
- To keep customers in the store longer, select an "Item of the Day" to show each visitor.
- Get out from behind the service counter and mix with your customers so that you can approach them easily to learn their areas of interest.
- Know the store's policies regarding returns, refunds, layaways, guarantees, and other procedures so that you can fulfill customer requests.
- Have someone to contact in any area in which you are not completely knowledgeable, so that you can provide accurate customer information, even if it has to be through a follow-up telephone call.

Greeting. A salesperson, without delay, should greet each customer who enters the store. This assures customers that the salesperson is ready to be of help. It has the additional benefit of deterring shoplifters.

The greeting should be warm, friendly, and sincere. It is best to avoid saying, "May I help you?" or "Are you looking for something special?" which can give the customer the opportunity to send the salesperson away.

Simple yet effective greetings are:

- "Hi!"
- "Good afternoon."
- "Welcome."
- "Happy Mother's Day."
- "Happy Holidays."

Identification of Customer's Area of Interest. By observing the customer, it is often possible to establish an area of customer interest. Make a mental note of any item that the customer:

- Stops to look at.
- Discusses with a companion.
- Studies with great care.
- Touches or picks up.

Approach. After establishing the area of interest, the salesperson can approach the customer. Ideally, the salesperson should be between the customer and the shop door. Since customers often back away from the salesperson, the customer backs into the shop, rather than out of it. The following approaches are useful:

- *A Merchandise Approach:*
    "That is a must—solid brass and it will not tarnish."
    "Isn't that great? You will be amazed at how easily it can be cleaned."
    "Let me show you how it works."
    "Let me open the case for you."
- *A Personal Approach:*
    "What a great tan. Hawaii?"
    "Great looking bag. Where did you find it?"
    I love your haircut. Where do you have it done?"
- *The Customer with a Child:* Approach and talk to the child. The customer will listen to anything that a salesperson says to the child, will appreciate the attention, and will enjoy the few minutes

of undisturbed shopping time. Occupying the child allows the customer to look around more comfortably.

"Are you having fun shopping with Mommy?"

"I'll bet your name is Charlie [wonderful fun when the child is a girl]."

"Let me tell you about something that I saw just yesterday . . ."

- *Having Overheard the Customer Express a Need:*

"If you're looking for a fishing rod, let me show you one that I've had great luck with."

"We have an outfit that is just the thing for a cruise."

- *Soliciting Advice:*

"This has just come in. I am not sure that I like it. What do you think?"

"Do you like these buttons?"

- *Where Security Is Involved:*

"Let me open that case for you. Our insurance company requires that we remove only one item from the case at a time."

"Isn't it a shame that we have to lock our leather goods?"

- *Item of the Day:* If the customer has not indicated an interest, an approach should be made with the "Item of the Day" when the customer is on the way out of the shop, but well before exiting.

"Isn't this interesting. Notice how it reflects the light."

"They say that this is unbreakable. I wonder." (And drop it.)

Merchandise Presentation. It is valuable to involve all the senses as shown in the following suggestions:

- Get the customer to handle the merchandise. If a salesperson offers an item, the customer will usually accept it. Holding the product implies ownership, and so it is a particularly effective sales device.
- If there is a scent, call it to the customer's attention.
- Demonstrate the merchandise, whenever possible.
- Share negative aspects of the merchandise, as well as positive ones, with the customer. A most effective way of establishing credibility is by volunteering a negative or limiting comment.

"It requires dry cleaning."

"It is fragile and must be handled with care."

- If the customer is showing poor judgment, suggest alternatives, but show respect for the customer's taste.
- Touching the customer can be very productive (adjust a collar, straighten a sleeve, shake hands).
- Treating the merchandise with care, respect, even affection, has a positive effect with customers.

- *Fitting Room Techniques:* A customer in a fitting room with selected merchandise is unlikely to search for additional merchandise. This usually calls for getting dressed, coming out and looking again, going back into the fitting room, getting undressed. Therefore it is desirable:

    To notice what a customer takes into the fitting room; the size, the color, the category of interest, and then to bring additional items without the customer's requesting them. These should be offered while the customer is still trying on clothes in the fitting room.

    To encourage a customer to come out to check the look in the mirror outside the fitting room. This gives the salesperson the chance to make comments, offer accessory ideas, and suggest variations.

- Desirable to state:

    "Our insurance requires that we limit taking three items into the fitting room."

    "I will be back to check with you and bring you anything that you like."

    "Why don't you take those three?"

    "Let me hold these for you. I can check with you in a few minutes."

- *Shoe-Selling Techniques:* The typical shoe customer has usually made a selection before asking for a salesperson's assistance. The customer usually knows the required size and asks for it. While acknowledging this request:

    Seat the customer and measure the foot. No foot is exactly size 8½. It is highly probable that the customer's foot size falls between two sizes. Either might fit equally well.

    Seated with one shoe off, the customer is not going anywhere and is likely to be quite patient while the salesperson searches for the requested shoe.

    Bring out no fewer than four pairs of shoes from the stock area—the requested shoe, a couple of others that are similar in color and style, and another that "is the most comfortable shoe in the shop" or "has just come in and you must try it." This approach will mean returning many shoes to the stockroom, but it will also increase sales, especially multiple sales.

Countering Objections. It is valuable to encourage the customer to voice any objections about a product. The salesperson should have enough knowledge of the merchandise to counter objections factually and intelligently, thus making the customer feel comfortable about the purchase:

- "Yes, this plate is delicate. We recommend hand washing."
- "That will not be a problem as long as you do not allow it to remain for any length of time at extremely high temperatures."

Stress benefits over features: Instead of saying "The lead content is 7.8 percent," say "Listen to the crystal clear tone."

Most customers find it easier to decide between items than to decide whether to purchase a particular item. Consequently, it is wise to give customers a choice:

- "You will enjoy the clear more than the frosted."
- "The red is more you."

Closing. Many customers are indecisive and require help in making a decision. The following suggestions deal with this problem:

- Where the customer needs a little encouragement to implement a desire to make a purchase, these statements can be useful:
  "Would you like to use your bank card?"
  "Will that be cash or charge?"
  "Is it a gift? Let me wrap it for you."
  "We have a great gift wrap. You can just sign the card and hand it to him."
  "It really is you. Why don't you take it with you?"
- If the customer wants a price guarantee, the salesperson can state:
  "Now if you are concerned about the price, we are determined to be as low as or lower priced than any other shop. If you find this item at a lower price anytime within the next 30 days, just come back and let me know. I will make an adjustment."
- A customer who wants the approval of another family member will often respond positively to a comment like this one:
  "Why not take it home and let your husband see it? He will love it. If he doesn't, of course, we will accept a return."
- Hesitant customers may like the idea of placing a purchase on a layaway plan:
  "Would you like to put it on layaway?"

Security. All salespeople share responsibility for security. In many instances, store policies limit the number of items that can be taken out of a case or into a fitting room at one time. It is good to alert customers to such rules and limitations in advance rather than to deal with violations. This approach avoids having the customer feel that the salesperson is making an accusation.

"It is a nuisance but our insurance requires that we take only one item out of the case at a time."

"Having to chain things down is awkward. But our insurance requires that we do this. Sorry."

Showing Additional Merchandise. It is important to recognize that a customer almost always enters a shop voluntarily, in the hope of buying something that pleases. Showing additional merchandise caters to that desire. Use the following approach:

- Show merchandise that is complimentary to articles the customer has already chosen.
- Show other merchandise that might appeal to the customer's demonstrated taste.
- Find opportunities to show merchandise when the customer first comes in, while he or she is browsing in the store, and at the completion of a transaction.

   "Whoops! I nearly forgot—let me show you something that I think is really special."

   "I have to show you a widget that has just come in. It is expensive, but it is irresistible."

(ii)   Giving a Reason to Return

The departure of the customer from the store seldom get proper attention:

- The traditional parting is, "Thank you. Have a nice day." A more professional parting is to offer a specific reason for the customer to return:

   "Be sure to come back on Thursday of next week: Our season-end sale begins."

   "We are expecting a new shipment of English bone china. It is due next week. You must come back and see it."

   "Did you notice that our Sidewalk Sale begins on Thursday? It is going to be big—really big."

- By this time, the salesperson has seen a charge card, or has asked the customer for her name to add to the store's mailing list. The salesperson should address the customer by name.

   "What an interesting name. What is the origin? How is it pronounced?"

   "Thank you so much, Ms. _____."

(III) Follow-Up

It is extremely valuable to develop a selected list of personal customers who can be contacted by telephone or by note:

- Some salespeople maintain a detailed card file. In many instances, it is adequate to have a "little black book" with names, telephone numbers, addresses, items of interest.
- A follow-up phone call or note of thanks, particularly one that includes the suggestion to come in again is smart. A note or postcard is likely to be more productive than a phone call, which may be viewed as an intrusion. Also, phone calls often miss the party sought.

    Always write the note as soon as possible after the sales transaction, even if it is not to be mailed immediately. Writing the mailing date so that the stamp will cover the notation at the time of mailing serves as an adequate "tickler."
- Where deliveries are involved, it is worthwhile to phone and ask if the delivery was made properly, on time, and whether everything is satisfactory:

    "Just realized that your delivery was to be made today. Any problem?"

    "Do let me know if everything is handled satisfactorily I can be reached at (_____) _____."

(e) ADVERTISING/PROMOTION

(i) In-Store Sales Promotions

One of the most effective in-store promotions is to have something on sale at all times, and to advertise this with signage either just outside or just inside the door. Another way to attract customers and keep them in the store is to offer some sort of refreshment, such as coffee, herb tea, fresh popcorn, or fortune cookies.

Merchants can choose among many other in-store promotions: giveaways, trivia games, guessing contests, rebates on purchases or rentals, and free customer access to copies of industry magazines. All these devices add to the shop's ability to attract customers.

Package stuffers can be valuable promotions; a typical format describes the shop's unique offerings on one side and advertises the current merchandise, coupons, and sale items on the other side.

The following list provides information about some widely used promotions:

- *Trivia Promotion.* A trivia question is written on a small black-board. The first customer to correctly answer is rewarded with a free drink, popcorn, coffee, or sandwich. This game brings many people into the shop twice a day—first to discover that they do not know the correct answer, and later to learn the correct answer.
- *Free Drawing.* Customers enjoy anything free. A fish bowl to collect business cards and a twice-monthly, or monthly, drawing is a popular arrangement. Registration cards should be available for those who do not have business cards. The reward does not have to be large.
- *Guessing Contest.* The question can involve the number of beans in a jar or coins in a sack, or something as esoteric as the number of cassettes sold in one year. The closest guess wins a small prize.
- *Periodicals.* Having a newspaper/magazine rack with current copies of periodicals applicable to the entertainment world encourages young customers to develop a habit of coming to the shop. For older customers, a shop might experiment with the local newspaper, *The Wall Street Journal,* or the national edition of the *New York Times.*
- *Giveaways.* Balloons for children of all ages and various refreshments are proven drawing cards.

(ii) Preseason Sales

The policy of offering customers reduced prices, for brief periods at the beginning of a season, on selected merchandise, is a relatively recent development. It was introduced to the Southern California retail community by Nordstrom's department store and Jay Jacobs specialty shop. It is now included in the promotional programs of virtually all major retailers in that part of the country.

Merchants must ask: Under normal circumstances, how much must net sales increase to maintain the normal gross margin dollars with a preseason discount?

The mathematical relationship is:

$$\% \text{ Sales Change} = \% \text{ Initial Mark-on} \times (100 - \% \text{ Reduction})$$
$$\times 1 / (\% \text{ Initial Mark-on} - \% \text{ Reduction}) - 100$$

Making this calculation for a typical 25 percent preseason sale of merchandise on which the initial mark-on is 54 percent give the following calculation:

$$\$ \text{ Sales Change} = 54 \times (100 - 25) \times 1 / (54 - 25) - 100$$
$$= 54 \times 75 \times 1 / 29 - 100$$
$$= 39.66$$

If sales increase 39.7 percent over what they would have been at the normal initial mark-on, the dollar gross margin dollars are maintained. Beyond that, gross margin dollars increase. And, an increase of 39.7 percent is certainly modest.

The following shows, for various discounts—10 percent through 33.3 percent—the equivalent percentage increase of net sales required to maintain the same gross margin dollars:

Discount Percentage	Initial Mark-On Percentage				
	54	50	45	43	40
10.0	10.5	12.5	15.7	17.3	20.2
15.0	17.7	21.4	27.5	30.5	36.0
20.0	27.1	33.3	44.0	49.6	60.0
25.0	39.7	50.0	68.8	79.2	100.0
30.0	57.5	75.0	110.0	131.5	180.0
33.3	74.0	99.7	156.5	195.7	298.2

At the beginning of the season, customers tend to be hesitant to purchase. They are also well aware, however, that stock can become depleted. Therefore a 25 percent preseason reduction is likely to be very productive. Since it is highly probable that resources will participate in such promotions, it is not at all surprising that so many stores have picked up this technique.

One chain has some of their merchandise marked with a price ticket that has a removable stub to allow for easy change to the full initial retail price.

(f) LIBERAL CUSTOMER POLICIES

Many independent specialty store operators are driving customers from their stores and into the major retailers because of an unwillingness to offer liberal customer policies. This is unfortunate and unnecessary.

In addition to being a matter of fairness, it is smart, good business to be liberal—to eliminate negative signage, to give cash refunds, to trust customers.

Merchants consistently relate that they must deal with troublesome customers only a very few times each year. They really do not need to have every eventuality spelled out in a rigid policy. The typical customer is not trying to take advantage of merchants, and so smart retailers are liberal to a fault.

This does not mean that "the customer is always right." There are times when merchants must say, "no." But these times are rare. When there is any doubt, the retailer will do well to go along with the customer.

A merchant who decides to be very liberal should list each instance in which the exceptional was done, the out-of-pocket cost of that incident, and relate the total costs to the total business for a period. This procedure will quickly provide convincing evidence that it is smart to be liberal, if for no other reason than that it costs so little. The sheet used to keep score usually remains blank: The cost is that small.

There are other reasons for a liberal policy: The customer who is comfortable with a merchant will make more purchases. Being liberal contributes to a pleasant workplace in which sales staff and supervision can work with a minimum of controversy to create a positive environment for everyone—customers, sales personnel, supervisory personnel, and ownership.

Technical Assistance Research Programs (TARP), a consulting firm in Washington, DC, states that most customers won't complain to management if something goes wrong with a purchase. But TARP found that, "depending on the severity of the problem, an average customer will tell between nine and sixteen friends and acquaintances of his bad experience. Some 13% will tell more than twenty people. More than two out of three customers who've received poor service will never buy from the store again, and worse, management will never know why."

(g) EXPANDED SALES HOURS

Many women as well as men hold full-time jobs outside the home. As a result, Saturday, Sunday, and evening hours provide more time for shopping and hence more business than do the daytime hours.

To be successful, independent merchants must maintain store hours that fulfill the needs of customers. Although remaining open evenings and Sundays can be difficult for the small shop owner, closing the doors is costly and detrimental to the image perceived by customers. If necessary, additional part-time personnel should be hired to achieve competitive business hours.

Five

Office Building Management

§ 5.1 INTRODUCTION

The office market has become both sophisticated and competitive over the last several years, requiring a more experienced and responsive management approach. A high-rise office building is a complex entity with many interrelated systems and a large number of occupants and visitors with varying needs that must all be integrated by the skillful manager.

The fact that office buildings are vertical structures on relatively small parcels of land presents unique management responsibilities. The office building's landlord through the property manager has more maintenance responsibilities than the shopping center and multitenant industrial property owner. Emergency procedures are more involved because of the large number of people concentrated in a vertical tower. Parking and the movement of people in and out of the building often are a concern of management. The mechanical, and life safety, and energy conservation systems are highly technical.

Security in an office building centers around controlling access into and out of the building. Medical buildings present an even greater security challenge. After-hours emergency access to the building, transportation of nonambulatory patients, storage of large quantities of medications, and disposal of medical waste all mandate special consideration.

Because of the proximity of office buildings to each other, tenants can easily compare buildings. Brokers and tenants often use a comparison

319

chart to assess their position when they are negotiating the lease. A tenant often needs to locate in a specific area, but seldom in a specific building. For a given building to be competitive, management must know which buildings are direct competition and make sure that the building measures up in terms of rental rates, maintenance, management, curb appeal, and tenant relations. If all buildings in the area provide air conditioning, and yours does not, you are likely to be at a considerable disadvantage unless there is an offsetting benefit such as a much lower rent.

Basic property management is similar for all types of properties, but each property type has its unique features. This chapter will review the subtle and unique differences in managing office buildings. Although management techniques and problem solving are similar for all types of office buildings, it is helpful to indicate the categories used as industry standards: garden office buildings, one to two stories; low-rise office buildings, three to four stories; mid-rise office buildings, five to ten stories; and high-rise office buildings, eleven or more stories. These categories will be used in this chapter when discussing management differences in each type of building.

§ 5.2 MANAGEMENT STAFFING

The basic criterion in determining whether an office building will have an on-site property manager is whether the building's income can support that cost in addition to the management fee.

Garden and low-rise office buildings are usually managed from a central office away from the project. Two questions must be addressed when managing office buildings without an on-site property manager. The first is, how many office buildings can one person manage? Several variables must be considered before answering this question. One is the level of service offered by the property manager and the management company. Obviously, many more properties can be managed if only the minimal services of rent collection and responding to maintenance calls are provided rather than a proactive property management program designed to enhance value.

The other variables are the location of each property, the size of each building, the number of tenants in each building, unusual problems with any building, and the level of administrative support available to the property manager. A rule of thumb for the number of garden and low-rise office buildings in the 40,000- to 80,000-square-foot range, all within driving distance from the central property management office, is five to eight buildings for a high level of service and eight to twelve buildings for a medium level of service.

The second question is, How can immediate response be provided when the property manager is not available or the property is more than thirty minutes from the office? It is prudent to have an arrangement with one of the tenants in the building who can provide keys to utility rooms, respond to a maintenance emergency and, in essence, be the eyes and ears of the building. Occasionally, this tenant may open a vacant space for a prospective tenant. Caution must be exercised, however, that the duties assigned to this person do not require a real estate license.

Mid- and high-rise office buildings are usually staffed with on-site managers and administrative personnel. On-site managers should be considered for office buildings exceeding 100,000 square feet, but are not necessarily needed. When a building exceeds 150,000 square feet, it will most likely need an on-site manager. When the building exceeds 200,000 square feet, an administrative assistant is usually added to the on-site staff. The square footages discussed above are a guide and just one of several factors used to determine if a building needs and can support an on-site manager.

High-rise office buildings are usually staffed with an on-site manager, assistant manager, and secretary or administrative assistant. A tenant relations coordinator, tenant improvement construction supervisor, and a chief engineer may be added to the staff.

§ 5.3   SPACE MEASUREMENT

The industry standards for measuring space in office buildings have been established by BOMA. These standards were revised in August 1980 and can be found in BOMA's annual *Experience Exchange Report.*

Measuring space in office buildings is a critical step in the overall management, operations, and leasing process. Management wants to be accurate in space measurements and, at the same time, competitive. The more the same standards are used, the easier it is to make valid comparisons between buildings and to reduce possible disagreements in the future.

There are several different measurements to be considered:

1.   Gross Building Area. This includes all the area between exterior walls, less elevator shafts, pipe shafts, and stairwells. This figure in most cases would be the same as the rentable area of the building.

2.   Usable Area. "The usable area of an office shall be computed by measuring to the finished surface of the office side of corridor and other permanent walls, to the center of partitions that separate the office from adjoining usable areas, and to the inside finished surface of the dominant portion of the permanent outer building walls."[1]

3.   Rentable Area. "The rentable area of a floor shall be computed by measuring to the inside finished surface of the dominant portion of the permanent outer building walls, excluding any major vertical penetrations of the floor."[2]

In the past, a tenant that leased a full floor in a building also paid rent on what was the common area that exclusively served its premises, such as hallways, restrooms, and telephone closets. Using this same theory, owners added a "load factor" to the usable footage of tenants on multitenanted floors so that even a small space user would pay its share of those common facilities.

For example, a building may have 50,000 square feet of usable area and 7,500 square feet of common area. Instead of collecting rent on only 50,000 square feet, the owner would add a load factor of 15 percent (7,500 ÷ 50,000) to each occupancy. A tenant that leased 1,000 square feet usable would pay rent on 1,150 rentable square feet, which would include its share of the common areas.

In a garden-style open corridor building, the load factor can be as low as 5 to 6 percent of the usable space since there are no hallways to allocate. Another possibility is a building with a large atrium court; here the true load factor can approach 30 percent of the usable area. Industry experience indicates that it is very difficult to bill load factors in excess of 17 to 18 percent regardless of the actual amounts involved. An acceptable load factor is between 8% and 12%.

§ 5.4   TENANT IMPROVEMENT

Tenant improvement work is an ongoing process in most office buildings. It is critical that all work be completed in a timely fashion to meet the tenant's needs and at a competitive cost.

Space planning is an important part of the construction process. Many tenants have little idea of how much space they need to operate their business or how to plan their space layout for efficient use. On the other hand, even the most sophisticated tenant is not always aware of the latest techniques in space utilization. A good space planner can be a great help in discussing "what if" options for the leasing personnel. The final space plan makes for an easy transition to working drawings for the actual construction.

---

[1] Building Owners and Managers Association International, *Standard Method for Measuring Floor Area in Office Buildings* (1980).

[2] *Ibid.*

There are several factors to consider when interviewing and selecting a space planner. Foremost, the landlord needs to know how many millions of square feet the space planner has planned and whether he or she understands the leasing business. All references should be checked.

The space planner's first question should be, What is the landlord's tenant improvement budget? The landlord's space planner is hired to lay out the prospective tenant premises and not to provide design services to the tenant. A good space planner will work within the landlord's budget. If the tenant asks for a relight (a glass wall used to allow light to enter an area), the space planner will explain that a relight costs five times the cost of studs, drywall, and paint, and the additional cost will be a tenant expense.

A good space planner will be motivated to keep tenant improvement costs down. After the tenant has signed the lease, the space planner can offer design services to the tenant. At this point, any extras beyond what the landlord agreed to provide is a cost to the tenant. A professional space planner is a valuable member of the building's marketing and leasing team. Ideally, most managers would have an on-site construction coordinator ready to contract the build-out. For most buildings, however, this is not practical. In the absence of a building construction coordinator, there are two choices for the use of outside contractors.

For minor tenant improvements, use unit prices. The property manager generally knows what kind of work will be provided to tenants, and contractors can provide specific prices for these items in advance. A contractor may agree to charge $120 for a two-by-four-foot light fixture, partition walls at $26 per linear foot, floor tile at $1.06 per foot, and carpeting at $18 per square yard. From this listing, the property manager can calculate the cost of the improvements while negotiating the lease.

The alternative is to bid the work for each job. This will generally assure the best price, but quite often this approach can delay the completion of the job. When bidding the job, contractors need to have complete plans. Contractors should be screened and selected on the basis of experience with office buildings, reputation, financial stability, and reliability in finishing the work on time. For a realistic bid, the process must be completely open and honest. If contractors are used to establish each other's prices, they will soon lose interest in providing costly bids that will not be accepted.

All contracts should be written and include an outside finish date with a penalty if the date is not met. Payment should be on a progress basis, and a 10% retention should be held to cover contingencies and get past the lien dates. Labor and material lien releases should be obtained before the contractor is paid. All work should carry a warranty, which in most areas lasts one year.

If possible, the building's contractor should finish its work before the tenant is allowed to start its work. Otherwise the tenant's work could hold up the landlord's contractor, and then a dispute will arise over when the work was completed and when the rental period is to start.

Seldom will the property manager allow a tenant to perform or contract for construction in the building. The primary reason is to ensure the quality of the construction and the integrity of the building and its mechanical systems. An unqualified contractor, or one who isn't familiar with the building, can disturb the HVAC and electrical systems. On the other hand, exceptions need to be made for sophisticated tenants with special needs or wants.

It is the exception to allow the tenant to perform or contract for improvements. However, the tenant may negotiate this right, or it may become evident that the work will be expedited by allowing the tenant to contract the improvements. Major tenants may require the right to perform their own improvements. An owner of a small office building may allow the tenants to contract nonstructural improvements. Medical tenants may be allowed to contract for the installation of their expensive medical equipment. The property manager should place restrictions and requirements on the tenant and its contractor. The plans should be reviewed and approved by the property manager or building owner's representative. The contractor should be licensed, bonded, and required to have insurance, naming the building owner and property management company as additional insured or named insured.

Core drilling is not allowed during the building's regular hours. Parking, unloading, use of the building's elevator, and whether there is a need for union employees should be discussed with the contractor. A consent to alteration agreement is signed by the tenant before the work is commenced.

If the tenant is contracting for improvements, the landlord should be protected from liens. Each state has methods of protecting the building owner, and the property manager should apply these methods whenever tenants are contracting work on the premises.

§ 5.5   MOVE-INS AND MOVE-OUTS

Relocation is a major disruption for a business and a major frustration for its employees. If handled properly, the actual move in or out of the office building can be a smooth transition. If not, the disturbance can cause problems for everyone and sour the manager-tenant relationship. If the process is not controlled, parking will be tied up and the elevators commandeered by the movers. The building's rules and regulations should address move-ins and move-outs, giving the building manager control over the hours that the move can be accomplished and what facilities the tenant will use in the process. The tenant is required to request a specific time for moving. Based on other building activities, the manager will then prepare a convenient schedule for everyone involved.

If the building doesn't have a freight elevator, a specific elevator will be assigned and padding blankets installed. The common areas in the building may need special covering placed over the carpeting and tile flooring. Temporary storage of furniture in the common areas is prohibited. If the building doesn't have a loading dock, an area in the parking lot may need to be roped off for the moving trucks. The moving company is required to submit a certificate of insurance that includes the building's owner and the property management company as additional insured or named insured.

If the move occurs on a weekend or in the evening, the elevator company should be notified and requested to have a maintenance person on call in case the elevator breaks down. If a major tenant is moving, a member of the building staff should be available during the entire move. A move into an area of 30,000 square feet or more can take an entire weekend. Building personnel should be assigned shifts, and coffee and light refreshments should be provided.

§ 5.6   ESCALATION CHARGES

Typically, the cost to operate the building, including maintenance, management, utilities, taxes, and insurance, are billed to the tenants. There are several different methods of billing the tenants for their share of the building's operating expenses. The two most common escalation methods are the base year approach and the operating expense stop. Two other methods, the triple net and gross leases, are seldom used to pass on all or none of the costs of operation to the tenants. Each of these escalation or bill-back methods is discussed in Chapter 8, Lease Administration.

§ 5.7   BUILDING MAINTENANCE

The office building owner assumes more maintenance responsibilities than does the shopping center or industrial property owner. Typically, the building owner will provide janitorial service five nights a week. Electricity, plumbing, HVAC, general maintenance, and light bulb replacement are also the building owner's responsibility. The tenant is generally responsible for the care and maintenance of the carpeting and window covering.

In small buildings, the maintenance services are usually contracted because the building cannot support an on-site maintenance person. An alternative is for the property management company to establish a maintenance company with roving personnel. A second alternative is to have a maintenance person, possibly a retiree, work a few hours a day policing the parking lot and handling minor maintenance problems. A third approach is to have the janitorial company provide light maintenance services. One last approach is to contract the work by job assignment.

Mid- and high-rise office buildings have several on-site maintenance employees. A day porter is responsible for keeping the common areas clean during the building's normal operating hours and possibly handling minor maintenance. One or several building engineers will handle the majority of the building's maintenance. Elevator maintenance, fire sprinkler inspections, and major plumbing and electrical maintenance will be contracted. HVAC maintenance can be handled in several ways. The maintenance staff may be responsible for first echelon maintenance with the balance of the maintenance contracted, or the entire HVAC maintenance may be either contracted or handled by the on-site staff.

§ 5.8   SECURITY

Security has become a concern in recent years in all types of buildings, including office buildings. An office building can be an easy target for a thief, who can enter a suite under the guise of doing business with the tenant and observe opportunities to make a return visit for illegal activities. Employees often leave purses and garments with wallets, money, or other valuables unattended, making them easy pickings for an alert thief. With the complex and costly office equipment used in most business, offices are targets for the burglar who, once inside, generally has easy access to most areas through the drop-ceiling construction.

(a)   SECURITY PERSONNEL

Garden and low-rise buildings in the suburbs seldom need security guards on site. A private security company can be employed to drive by the property several times a night at random times. Janitors can be utilized to watch for problems. The exterior doors can be locked at a specified hour. Access after hours may be by a coded card that registers the individual in and out of the building. The employees in the building are instructed to report suspicious people in or near the building.

Mid- and high-rise buildings will have either a security guard in the lobby 24 hours a day, or starting around 5:00 P.M. until the building opens the next day and through the weekends and holidays. People entering or leaving the building after 5:00 P.M. and before 7:00 A.M. and on weekends and holidays must sign in and out at the lobby desk and indicate the tenant they are visiting. Employees show their building identification card. Additional security can be provided by having the security guard call the tenants to verify the appointment before allowing the visitor to go beyond the lobby. The elevator can be programmed so the visitor has access to only one floor. To minimize theft of business equipment, a tenant should have a pass to remove equipment from the building. Many buildings with 24-hour lobby guards will not have tenant directories. The guard provides directory service.

Additional information on security is provided in Chapter 10, Developing Emergency Procedures.

(b) KEY CONTROL

Key control is critical to the security of the office building. A master key system is a must, but precautions must be taken to be sure that these keys do not get into the wrong hands.

The key system of the building should be designed and recorded by a qualified locksmith. Generally, there is a grand master key for all locks in the building. From that grand master, submaster keys can be made for janitor closets, telephone rooms, meter rooms, and individual floors. Each tenant's suite key is coded and marked "do not duplicate." Master keys should be numbered and issued only to individuals who need them and have signed out for them. This list should be as limited as possible, keeping in mind the operating efficiency of the building.

When a tenant moves out, the lock cylinder should be changed to assure security for the next occupant. This is easily performed by keeping four or five cylinders that have been set up for the system and rotating them throughout the building. If a tenant fires an employee and wants the locks changed, it should be done by the building's locksmith at the tenant's cost. This is the only way to preserve the original lock system in the building.

When a master key is lost or stolen, the building should be rekeyed as soon as possible. In the meantime, a security guard may need to be stationed in the building. If a security officer or janitor lost the keys, that contractor should pay for the cost to rekey the building.

Rekeying a building can be expensive, but with expensive high-tech business machines in office buildings and drugs in medical buildings, it usually is the prudent choice when master keys are missing.

§ 5.9 TENANT RETENTION

In 1991, the Institute of Real Estate Management (IREM) Foundation retained Arthur Andersen Real Estate Services Group to survey property owners about their characteristics and needs and to explore significant issues with industry leaders. The ensuing IREM Foundation study titled

"Managing the Future: Real Estate in the 1990s," included responses to the two questions asked of property owners. The first question asked property owners to rate the importance of 36 property management tasks on a scale of one to five. Property owners gave retaining tenants a 4.59 rating, making it the most important property management task. Handling tenant relations was selected as the fourth most important task with a rating of 4.39. The second question property owners were asked was to list the trends affecting real estate. Vacancy was the number one trend affecting real estate. *Tenant retention* has been a buzzword in the real estate industry since the early 1990s. A commercial building's most valuable asset is its income stream—the amount paid by the building's tenants in rent. In the early and mid 1990s, hundreds of distressed buildings were selling for 20 to 35 percent of their replacement cost because most of these buildings had high vacancy. When a building's income stream suffers from low occupancy, its value is diminished.

After a tenant has moved into a building, it is easier and less expensive to keep the tenant than to replace the tenant. Consider the potential costs of losing a tenant: (1) With the real estate market as soft as it is today, a vacancy can easily cost anything from a few months to a year or more of rent. (2) There is typically a leasing commission for a new tenant and quite often, especially in a tough market, new tenant improvements are requested. These can cost tens of thousands of dollars, particularly in an office building. (3) There is also the intangible effect that the loss of a specific tenant may have on other tenants or prospective tenants. Quite often the loss of a tenant conveys the impression that something is wrong with the property and this may hamper leasing and releasing efforts.

Whether the leasing market for office space is strong or weak, leasing agents regularly attempt to lure tenants from other buildings. They consider every tenant in a building a prospect for the building or buildings they are leasing. The best and most effective offensive to counter such activities is an effective tenant retention program. When a building's tenants are neglected by the property owner and property manager and tenant's requests are treated as an annoyance, tenants soon become dissatisfied with the building's management and the real estate community becomes aware that the building is poorly managed. Before long, the building becomes the favorite raiding ground for leasing agents.

The property manager needs to develop and implement an effective tenant retention program. A tenant retention program for an office or medical building will have several components. Though the property manager is responsible for developing and implementing the tenant retention program, he or she will need the cooperation of the building's staff and contractors for the program to be successful. the components of the tenant retention plan include: (1) How the tenant is treated while he or she

is a prospect; (2) the manner in which the lease negotiations, space planning, and space buildout are handled; (3) the move-in process; (4) the
building operations including maintenance, security, and parking contracts; (5) accurate and timely tenant billings; and (6) tenant's occupancy
cost. Understanding what alienates tenants enables the property manager
to be proactive in retaining tenants. Three additional components to the
building's tenant retention program are: (1) improvements to the building, (2) enhancing the building's tenant mix, and (3) providing building
amenities for the tenants and their employees.

The property manager serves as an ombudsman on behalf of the building. Building employees' loyalty to an office or medical building is a
unique opportunity to enhance a building's tenant retention program.
Community programs may be developed with the building's tenants and
their employees.

(a) LEASE NEGOTIATIONS TO MOVE-IN

A building's tenant retention program starts with the tenant's first contact with the building's staff. The initial contact is usually when the tenant was first contacted to lease space in the building. This is a period of
"courting" the tenant. Once the "courting" period is over, the tenant or
leasing agent negotiates the business terms of the lease and either this
party or the tenant's attorney negotiates the lease provisions. These
negotiations may take a few hours over coffee or they can be protracted
negotiations taking weeks or even months. the tenant and his or her representative must be treated professionally during the lease negotiations,
regardless of the actions of the other party or the final outcome of the
negotiations. If the tenant perceives that the landlord or its representative was mean-spirited and/or disrespectful, the tenant will not trust the
landlord or its property manager.

The leasing agent, having obtained a signed lease, moves on to finding
other prospects and negotiating their leases and the tenant often has no
one to turn to at a time when the tenant need guidance and, at the very
least, a sympathetic ear. It is important that the leasing agent complete
all of the lease documents and inform the tenant of all of his or her responsibilities before introducing the tenant to the manager. It is not
enough for the leasing agent to complete his/her tasks and then leave it
up to the tenant to find the next contact. Rather, the leasing agent should
introduce the tenant to the manager face to face or by conference call (a
letter is impersonal and is not the best approach) so there is not a gap in
the communication between the tenant and the building's management.
The property manager should become the source for information and
support for the tenant as he or she prepares to finalize the space plan for
their premises and commence construction of the tenant improvements. The space planner must understand the limits of the landlord's

contribution towards the construction of the tenant's improvements and the tenant's budget. Providing a tenant with a space plan and interior designs that exceed everyone's budget usually ends up with a dissatisfied tenant and a frustrated landlord. After the space plan has been approved by the tenant and landlord, the tenant improvement contractor turns the drawings into reality.

The tenants may become frustrated if the landlord's contractor seems uncooperative or unavailable while the tenant's improvements are being constructed. A message from the manager can usually alleviate concerns and misunderstandings and get things back on track. A tenant who needs building or health permits may not be aware of how or where to obtain them. The manager can often provide that information and make things easier for the new tenants.

The property manager's helpfulness may be limited to explaining how the situation can be handled, but even that can be of great assistance to a tenant faced with a multitude of problems. Quite often, a sympathetic approach to the tenant's problems is enough in a difficult situation. After the premises are completed, the property manager schedules a walk-through with the tenant and the contractor. Construction items that are not completed to the tenant's or property managers' satisfaction are placed on a punchlist. If these items are not completed shortly after the tenant takes possession of the premises, they will become a source of aggravation for the tenant. The property manager must follow up with the contractor to ensure that all of the items on the punchlist are promptly completed.

Some tenants have limited or no experience in relocating their offices. The astute property manager will realize that the opening of a new commercial office is a traumatic time for the tenant, especially if this is the tenant's first location or relocation. The property manager should make an effort to facilitate matters as much as possible and to help (even when it is not the property manager's responsibility to do so). This effort can go a long way in creating a good landlord-tenant relationship for the future.

(b) POSITIVE COMMUNICATION

Returning all phone calls is the first step toward establishing and maintaining good tenant/landlord communications. The property manager and tenant often keep quite different hours. If the property manager cannot return the call immediately, the secretary can call the tenant back and let him/her know when the property manager will be available, or see if anything can be done in the interim. The property manager must be available 24 hours a day, seven days a week to cover emergencies. Since problems do not limit themselves to business hours, the lines of communication must be open at all times. This can be achieved with the help of maintenance personnel, an answering service, or even a tenant in the property. If major repairs are planned for the property, the tenants should be notified at least two weeks in advance. The property manager does not need to ask the tenant's permission to schedule repair work. However, advance notice, especially where a large repair job is concerned, can prevent major disruptions to the tenant's business. Breaking up a large repair into smaller jobs may also reduce any inconvenience to the tenant. If the tenant's position is not considered, it can put the tenant out of business or destroy an event that was already planned and cannot be changed. Letters of appreciation and commendation can go a long way toward improving landlord/tenant relations. The best method of communication is personal visits with the tenant. Most managers are not "on-site" managers and are not usually visible on the property. Therefore, it is advisable to visit the tenants on a regular basis. At least one visit per quarter is suggested when properties are running well. In troubled properties or new properties with the usual start-up problems, more frequent visits should be made. Quite often, a tenant will be aware of a problem but will be too busy to alert the property manager; this visit gives the manager the opportunity to convey the message and to discuss any other items of mutual interest. This also enables the property manager to head off any potential problem at its earliest stage of development. For instance, it is better to hear about a roof leak immediately than to be called after the roof has collapsed. If the tenant is not in, a card may be left to indicate that the visit was made. Some tenants have claimed that they have never met the property manager, but they have a dozen calling cards in the front desk.

Many buildings will provide a monthly or quarterly newsletter. These newsletters are usually given a clever and catchy name, such as the newsletter for a building on Broadway Street was titled "On Broadway," a phrase from a popular song. The newsletter is an excellent means to communicate with the tenants and their employees on a host of issues. The newsletter may be used to inform the tenant of businesses that have recently signed leases and when they will open, of the accomplishments of the building's recycling program, and of information regarding the building's emergency procedures. It may also acknowledge tenants and individual employees for their accomplishments, promote the activities of businesses in the building, and discuss activities in the community. Newsletters are inexpensive to publish and distribute and can be prepared by the building's management staff or a public relations firm.

(c) BUILDING OPERATIONS

Several of the daily building management activities can be part of the tenant retention program. Many property managers provide a letter of introduction as soon as the lease is signed and enclose a "Tenant Kit and Emergency Procedures" booklet. This does not have to be an expensive production; a tenant kit may be prepared on the property manager's computer or desktop publishing.

The tenant kit informs the tenant of building activities and rules and regulations that will impact its business. The tenant kit will provide information on tenant directory listings, signage, after-hours heating ventilation and air conditioning (HVAC), maintenance of the premises, alterations to the premises, where to pay the rent and many other issues. The tenant kit also has a section on emergency procedures. Since the major San Francisco earthquake in 1989 and the bombing of the World Trade Center in New York in 1993, tenants are more concerned than ever with being prepared for an emergency or disaster. Reviewing your emergency procedures booklet with the tenant, along with conducting practice evacuations for mid- and high-rise buildings, provides the tenant and the tenant's employees with confidence that the building's management has prepared for a natural disaster or a manmade emergency. (Chapter 11 discusses developing emergency procedures.)

There will always be tenant requests. These requests should be handled in a timely and courteous fashion. The property manager is not there to "win" arguments, but rather to solve problems. If the tenant calls in with a request for service that is not covered by the contract, the property manager should explain in a courteous, informative manner and, where possible, give the tenant guidance in getting the work done. Quite often, the tenant really does not fully understand the lease and will not appreciate learning that he or she is responsible for the problem. It is also important that requests are a responsibility of the property manager and that they be taken care of in a timely fashion. A flickering light in an office building or a dirty sidewalk in front of a ground floor retail store can be very aggravating to a tenant, especially when the problems are not taken care of promptly. If the problem has been lingering or is a safety hazard, a follow-up call to see that everything has been corrected is appreciated. Property managers do not have time to follow up on every problem, but tenants appreciate the care shown by a follow-up call. Every attempt should be made to resolve problems immediately so they do not escalate out of proportion. Involving the tenant in finding solutions is a useful strategy, especially if the problem is very difficult. The property manager does not need to give the impression that he or she has the answer to every problem. Rather, discussing the situation with the tenant may elicit valuable input and a new perspective to the problem at hand. If the property is in another city far from the property manager's office, an off-premises extension phone in the tenant's area will allow the tenant to call the manager without making a toll call. An 800 number covering the property manager's properties is useful. This convenience makes communications much easier for the tenants. The cost for either phone program is minimal, considering the benefit of increased communication with the tenants. It is not unusual for a property owner to share in the extra cost of such a telephone program.

The property manager should have a complete understanding of all of the lease terms and be aware of which responsibilities belong to the tenant and which belong to the landlord. A property manager's misunderstanding of the lease may cause the tenant to feel that the landlord is trying to avoid his responsibilities. If a job is to be delayed or take longer than originally expected, a phone call to the tenant should be made. This will establish a basis for trust in the landlord-tenant relationship; the tenant will feel confident that he or she will be alerted to any similar situations in the future. Maintenance personnel should be instructed on the importance of the landlord/tenant relationship and their role in that relationship. They should be advised to be friendly, courteous, and understanding of the tenants' problems. Contractors should be advised not to discuss building problems with individual tenants, but rather to take them to management. It is not unusual for a contractor to pass along inaccurate information to the tenant, thereby creating ill will between tenants and management.

All tenants and their employees need to feel secure in the building. Most buildings do not need on-site security guards. When the property manager assumes the management of an office building, one of his or her first tasks is to conduct a security audit of the building. The security audit would include becoming familiar with possible criminal activities, if any, in the area; reviewing the interior and exterior common areas for poorly lit areas and areas where criminals could hide; and how to secure the building and provide after-hours access for the tenants.

The parking area can easily become a problem for many tenants. It must be kept clean, with a good snow management program in the winter in the northern tier of the country. The tenant's visitors and customers should have a sufficient number of convenient, dedicated parking stalls. A well-managed parking area will be an asset to the building and the tenant retention program.

(d) OPERATING COST

A component of a tenant retention plan that is frequently overlooked is the tenant's occupancy costs. The tenant's occupancy costs include base rent and pass-through operating expenses. The property manager should endeavor to keep expenses as low as possible while maintaining the property in a first class manner.

Building operating expense billings to tenants are the source of many problems between landlord and tenant. Often, the tenant does not understand just what is involved and almost always the costs seem quite high relative to the work that the tenant sees being done. For this reason, it is important to make sure the billings are accurate, timely, and understandable. Tenants often go to great lengths to negotiate operating expense provisions. It is irritating to the tenant to find that these provisions have been missed or ignored in the billings. It is worthwhile to build a model of the lease provisions for the operating expense billing for each tenant to be sure that all exclusions and/or special provisions are being compiled with. Once the tenant receives a carefully prepared operating expense billing, he or she is likely to look at future bills in a more positive light. Sufficient detail should be given so the tenant can readily determine what was spent, when it was spent, and how the tenant's share was computed. It is not sufficient to send a billing simply showing the amount owed by the tenant, with no indication that the tenant is paying the amount stated under the terms of the lease. It is not suggested that copies of individual bills be provided to the tenants, but rather that they be given enough detail to fully understand what he or she is being asked to pay for. This will speed up the process and help keep the relationship in good stead. If a tenant questions a portion of the billing, a courteous, patient answer is in order. It is not sufficient to say "it is in the lease," but rather, spend a few minutes explaining what was done and why. Be sympathetic to the impact on the tenant, regardless of the necessity of the work or the cost involved.

(e) DE-INSTITUTIONALIZING THE BUILDING

Most employees spend more time in their work environment than any other place except their home. The property manager can develop a tenant-retention program that makes the office building a pleasant, enjoyable, and sometimes fun place to work. When the tenant's employees are happy with their workplace, the tenant is less likely to move out. Tenant appreciation luncheons or outings can work well, especially in smaller communities. The property manager or property owner schedules a picnic and invites all of the tenants and their employees in that project. The entire event is devoted to the landlord indicating his appreciation for the tenants. It is possible to get the building's contractors to contribute either money or food to the event with the net result being very little cost to the building. The landlords of one small office building took the tenants and their employees out on a boat for cocktails and a light snack and gave out awards. In another office building, the managers have an annual lighting and decorating of the building's lobby Christmas tree. The property owner provides the tree and the refreshments and the tenants bring gifts for some charitable organization. The event is funded by the landlord and the atmosphere is positive and upbeat.

Several services can be offered to tenants to help "deinstitutionalize" a building. A food drive or toy collection can build community spirit, while a series of monthly luncheon speakers can provide education and entertainment. Speakers are easily obtained. Bankers and stockbrokers

can discuss investment opportunities, specialty retailers can discuss
new products or fashions, and community organizations such as a crisis
clinic can discuss their programs.

(f) BUILDING IMPROVEMENTS

A tenant retention program consists of improvements to the building,
enhancements to the building's tenant mix, added amenities to the
building, and services to the tenant's employees.

Improvement to the building includes modernizing the elevators and
mechanical systems and maintaining the condition of the common areas. The building's tenant mix can be enriched by adding tenants that either provide a service to the other tenants or add prestige to the building.
A deli, card shop, hair salon, health club, bank, title insurance company,
escrow company, real estate office, or other retail service provides conveniences to the existing tenants and their employees. A prestigious law
firm will enhance the image of an office building just as a well-respected
medical practice in a medical building will enhance the image of a medical building. A lunchroom with vending machines, a conference room,
and outdoor patio areas are just a few examples of amenities that can be
incorporated into a building.

(g) TENANT SURVEYS

Periodically surveying the tenants to determine their opinion of the
building management is one of the best and quickest ways to evaluate a
building's tenant retention program.

(h) LEASE RENEWALS

A manager should initiate the discussion of lease renewals with the tenant at least six months prior to expiration. The initial contact should be
used to determine the tenant's desire regarding the lease and to inform
the tenant about current rates and terms. Quite often tenants do not realize how the market has changed since they signed their lease. It may
take a little time for them to realize they will have to pay higher rents or
increased building operating expenses or utilities. This is the time to be
patient and sympathetic and give the tenant a chance to accept and understand the market. If the situation is handled poorly, the tenant may
move, to the detriment of landlord and tenant alike.

Renewing a lease for a little less than that being offered to new tenants shows that the landlord recognizes the value of the tenant to the
project. However, when owners are concerned with capitalization of income to set sales prices and financing levels, that may not be practical.
It is a good idea under these circumstances to strive for the market rate,
but give the tenant a little free rent or some tenant improvements that

may be desired and/or needed. The cost to the building is generally minimal and the tenant will appreciate the added recognition. The landlord
will not have lost rent due to vacancy, typically will not have large tenant improvements for an existing tenant renewing, and the leasing
commission, if there is one, will generally be less than that of the new
tenant. There is generally a real savings when renewing an existing tenant. The cost of keeping an existing tenant can be less than half the cost
of getting a new tenant.

Many landlords, close to the end of the lease, will look for opportunities to help the tenant or perform small favors such as minor repairs that
were not a landlord designated responsibility. Quite often, this approach
will improve otherwise poor relations. The best approach is to keep the
relationship strong throughout the lease, but it is never too late to try to
mend fences.

At one time, a tenant retention program was considered a unique feature to a building's marketing program; today tenant retention is an essential and basic property management service.

§ 5.10   RETAIL TENANTS IN AN OFFICE BUILDING

Retail tenants can provide services to the building's tenants, pay percentage rent, establish an identity for the building, and become an amenity to
be promoted in the building's marketing and leasing program.

A prospective retail or service tenant must be analyzed more carefully
than an office user to ensure compatibility with the other tenants and
with the building. A merchant who sells inferior merchandise or provides
poor service will harm the building's reputation and annoy its tenants.

The office building lease must include provisions found in shopping
center leases such as hours of operation, percentage rent, sales reporting,
sales audit, and a very restrictive use provision. Operational issues that
must be considered are trash removal, deliveries, pest control, janitorial
service, after-hours entry, signage, supplementary HVAC, and overstandard utility usage.

A restaurant, health spa, deli, card and gift shop, and most other retailers will be an asset to an office building. The manager who understands
the impact these tenants will have on the building's operations and addresses that in the lease will have a better relationship with tenants and a
smoother building operation.

§ 5.11   TENANT RELATIONS

The management of an office building doesn't have as direct an impact
on the success of a tenant's business as the management of a shopping
center has on its tenants. However, the property manager still must be

sensitive to the needs of the office tenants. It is easy for the relationship between the manager and the tenant to be damaged during the interval between the signing of the lease and the day the tenant moves in.

The property manager should meet with the tenant soon after the lease is executed to give him or her a copy of the building handbook and emergency procedures. It is a good idea to review these booklets with the tenant.

Once the space is complete and the tenant has moved in, the manager should pay a visit to welcome the new occupant and check that everything is in order. If necessary, a punch list should be prepared and the work completed at the earliest possible time. Delayed response gives the impression of poor management, which can last for the entire lease term. Some property owners will have the manager send a floral arrangement when a tenant opens for business.

Follow-up monthly visits can be a big boost to the relationship. Just a quick visit to see if there are any problems will demonstrate the property manager's concern and facilitate communication. Again, quick response to any problems brought up during these visits will improve the relationship. Taking each tenant out to lunch periodically is an excellent opportunity to develop good rapport. If the manager is unable to visit the tenants on a regular basis, a questionnaire from time to time can be helpful in bringing out problems and demonstrating that management does care.

§ 5.12 PARKING MANAGEMENT

Office building parking will vary from free, open parking for most suburban office buildings to parking for a charge in garages of downtown office buildings and some suburban buildings.

The basic parking policy of all office buildings is to allow convenient parking for tenants' customers and visitors and to eliminate unauthorized parking. This can be achieved by providing twenty-minute and two-hour visitors' parking in stalls close to the building's entrance. Preventing unauthorized parking in a suburban office building's free lot can be difficult. An inexpensive approach is to provide all the employees of the tenants in the building with parking stickers for their car's rear bumper. A more effective but more costly approach is to control employee parking with a card gate. Either approach must be accompanied by signs at the entrance to the lot warning of unauthorized parking.

Most downtown office buildings and some suburban office buildings provide paid parking. Most owners will contract with a parking garage operator to manage the building's parking. The owner receives a percentage of the income, and the operator pays all the expenses from its share of the income. The owner's percentage will vary from 60% to 85%, depending upon potential income. For example, the owner's percentage may start at 60% and increase 5% for every additional $50,000 of income above a fixed base income level. Another approach is to pay the operator a management fee in lieu of a percentage of the income. A third approach is for the building's owner to operate the parking garage.

Paid and permit parking can be controlled by either parking attendants or a card system. Lots that have all-day in and out paid parking generally must be staffed. If employees pay to park, they are generally assigned to a specific area but not to a specific space. This approach allows for more paid parking and reduces the problem of one person parking in the assigned space of another.

When parking is sold on an unassigned basis, 120% of the parking stalls can be sold since all of the building's employees are not in the building at the same time. On any one day, some will be on vacation, ill, or have business out of the building.

If the parking is for tenants only, a card system can be very cost-effective compared with the cost of one or two shifts of attendants each day to cover normal business hours. Typically overnight parking is prohibited, and most free lots are legally posted so that the property manager can tow abandoned or illegally parked cars.

If an office building does not have adequate parking for its employees and visitors, leasing nearby parking can be explored. A church, lodge, or theater might not use its parking lot on weekdays, or a nearby shopping center might have abundant parking.

Parking lot security is discussed in Chapter 10.

§ 5.13   BUILDING STORAGE

As office rents become more expensive, tenants are becoming more cost conscious about how they use their space. It seldom makes sense for a tenant to pay office building rates for dead storage, yet businesses need a place to keep old records. Basements, attics, and dead corners of the building and parking garages are great locations for storage areas in any building. Storage rates can range from 25% to 60% of base rents, with higher rates charged for the convenience of having the storage space in the same building as the tenant's office. The build-out can be as simple as cubicles divided by a two-by-four inch stud open wall with a heavy mesh screen separating the units. Each unit is provided with lights and a door, and the tenant uses its own padlock. Storage can add income and value to the building while offering a convenience to the tenants.

§ 5.14   CONFERENCE ROOMS

A building conference room that is available to the occupants can be an excellent leasing tool. Many occupants do not want to pay monthly rent and costs on a room that is seldom used. However, they are quite willing to pay for the use of the room on an as-needed basis, or it can be factored into the overall rental rate for the building and offered as a service of the building.

Scheduling of the room is coordinated by the management office. The room should be fully equipped with conference tables, chairs, easel, blackboard, plug-in phone, coffee area, and a podium.

Not all buildings benefit by having a conference room for their occupants. If the room is not used regularly or is not perceived as a positive leasing tool, the space should be converted to rentable area.

§ 5.15 LOST AND FOUND

Losing personal items in office buildings is common. A lost-and-found policy should be established and conveyed to the occupants. Generally, the building office is the drop-off and pickup point. Some method of identifying missing property should be established and a record kept of what is found and who claimed it. In large buildings this activity may be handled by security, and in small buildings the management office or the maintenance personnel may handle lost and found.

The tenant kit or handbook should include a section outlining the building's lost and found procedures.

§ 5.16 MEDICAL BUILDINGS

There are many similarities between managing a medical office building and an office building. This section will focus on specific issues that are unique when managing a medical office building.

Medical office buildings (MOBs) may be the most challenging commercial buildings to manage and lease. Because of the nature of their work, medical professionals are very demanding. Many of them have limited business education and experience and some of their requests may seem unreasonable.

Medical office buildings are more expensive to build and operate than traditional office buildings. The physical structure has more complex systems, such as heavier sound proofing, gas and air pumping into medical and dental suites, shielding for X-ray equipment, and considerably more plumbing. Spaces are often divided into small cubicles for use as examining rooms. Tenant improvements and remodeling are generally quite extensive and expensive. Heating and air conditioning are also critical in the medical environment.

Since doctors have smaller suites than office tenants, there are usually more tenants in a medical building than in a similar-sized office building. Most physicians are part of a group practice. This enables the physicians to operate their medical practice more efficiently and cost effectively. They are able to share after-hours on-call duties. A two to four physician group will usually lease between 2,000 and 5,000 square feet. There are group practices that will need in excess of 5,000 or 10,000 square feet and solo practices who will need 1,000 to 1,500 square feet.

A medical professional will have more daily visits by patients than the typical office tenant occupying the same size space will have client visits. As a result, a medical building will have greater use of its common areas.

Operating expenses are greater in a medical building. Janitorial expenses will usually cost 20% to 35% more than in an office building. This is due to the large number of small offices, greater number of sinks and restrooms, and the higher level of janitorial service required by doctors. Depending upon the type of equipment the medical physicians use, the building's utility cost can be appreciably higher than a typical office building's utility cost. Some medical professional's suites, such as radiologists, may require a separate utility meter to monitor their standard utility usage. Additional security and more frequent maintenance may be needed.

An additional janitorial concern is the disposal of medical wastes. Medical professionals are provided with a special container for depositing biohazardous waste, and the building may have a storage room dedicated to its temporary storage. Either each tenant or the building manager contracts with a firm specializing in the pick-up and proper disposal of medical waste. The regular janitorial service usually does not pick up biohazardous waste. Janitors must be provided with special health and safety training to identify articles that may be hazardous. Medical waste cannot be dumped in the building's trash bins. A blood-borne pathogens training program should be developed to educate the maintenance, security, and management on the proper procedures to safely clean blood and other bodily fluids spills.

Because of the amount and variety of drugs in the building, security is an added concern. The medical professional must have a secure place to store drugs in their suite along with a security procedure and access procedures to the drugs. Every building does not need a security guard. The property manager, however, must develop a procedure for securing the building after normal business hours, while providing the medical professional and their patients with after-hours access to the building.

If the building doesn't have a security guard, a card control or similar access system may be provided.

There are special considerations when developing a medical office building's evacuation procedures. A medical building's emergency procedures plan must consider that doctors may be performing outpatient surgery, patients may have medical procedures, such as kidney dialysis or infusion therapy, and many patients will be elderly and non-ambulatory.

The property manager should survey the tenants to determine these and other special issues that need specifically designed procedures. A meeting should be scheduled with the fire department representatives and the business managers of each medical office to review the procedures for evacuations and the special concerns of each tenant. Emergency procedures are thoroughly discussed in Chapter 11.

One of the advantages of medical office buildings is the low turnover of tenants. When a medical professional is happy with its location, he or she is unlikely to relocate to another building. Since they seldom relocate, when a medical practice does relocate the move can be a traumatic experience. Often no one on the staff has experience in relocating an office. The property manager can prove invaluable to the business manager of a medical practice that has just entered into a lease with the building by providing important knowledge and assistance on how to coordinate the move.

Some medical office buildings will have many elderly and sight-impaired patients. It is important that the parking lot be well-signed, and interior signage and building directories be easy to read and also have Braille markings.

Medical buildings are classified as either an on-campus MOB (part of a hospital campus) or an off-campus MOB (freestanding building). An off-campus building may have a tunnel or skywalk connecting the building to the hospital. Managing a medical building is more intense and time consuming than managing most other property types. As a rule of thumb, an on-site manager is needed if the building is in excess of 100,000 square feet. Smaller buildings may be able to justify the cost of an on-site manager if the manager is responsible for other properties and his or her cost is shared by the other properties.

There is limited information available on managing and leasing medical office buildings. Three publications of note are: *Medical and Dental Space Planning for the 1990s,* by Jain Malkin (New York: Van Nostrand Reinhold, 1990); *Health Care Facilities Handbook,* 2nd ed., edited by Burton R. Klein (National Fire Protection Association); and *Managing and Leasing Commercial Properties: Complex Issues,* by Alexander and Muhlebach (New York: John Wiley, 1993), which has a chapter on managing and leasing medical office buildings.

§ 5.17   SICK BUILDING SYNDROME

Sick building syndrome is becoming more familiar to property managers than any of us had ever expected. It may well be the source of considerable future problems and expense to the buildings we manage.

Sick buildings can be caused by a minor incident (for example, many employees smoking in one suite of offices, causing irritation to those in adjacent suites), or a major incident (for example, a full blown outbreak of Legionnaire's disease caused by problems in the air conditioning or water supply systems). In either case, and in all cases that fall in between, the property manager must be aware of and sensitive to the issues involved. The property manager must act quickly to be sure that the employees of the building are protected from health risks caused by problems within the building.

(a)   CIGARETTE SMOKE AND ODORS

In a small West Coast office building, a group of employees complained of headaches, nausea and lack of ability to concentrate. They believed these symptoms were caused by odd odors within their suite. They did some investigation within the suite and were not able to find any source or explanation, but the symptoms continued. The problem was brought to the attention of the property manager and a more thorough investigation was conducted. On-site personnel were unable to determine the source of the odor, but they were able to conclude that the odor was probably caused by cigarette smoke. No one in the complaining office smoked within the suite, in accordance with an existing company policy.

At that point, a general contractor and the building's air conditioning service contractor were brought in. The problem was finally traced to two sources. First, the adjacent tenant, who had recently moved into the building, was an office where almost all employees smoked. The building had an open plenum system above the ceiling grid and the smoke-fouled air, drawn into the open plenum, made its way into the neighboring suite. Second, the affected suite was equipped with two exhaust fans which could be operated by internal switches; however, none of the employees were aware of them and therefore did not put them to use. The solutions to the problem were as follows: (1) An exhaust fan was installed in the offending suite to divert that air to the exterior of the building; (2) a barrier was installed between the two suites so that any foul air that did get into the plenum area would not find its way into the neighboring suite; (3) the employees of the affected area were made fully aware of the exhaust fans. These fans were put on timers to ensure that they began operating each morning when work started and turned off at closing time. The complaints stopped and the problem was solved.

In a similar building, the employees were complaining of a strong pungent odor which was causing headaches and nausea. The employees tried to find the source within the materials that they used on a day-to-day basis. They were unable to trace the source, but the problems continued. Finally, a complaint was made to management and an investigation ensued. An inspection of the air conditioning returns, plumbing fixtures, ceiling tile, electrical outlets, and machinery within the suite provided no answers. An air conditioning contractor was called in to determine if tests were needed. The service man, who had a keen sense of smell, found the source of the problem without the use of sensitive equipment. The tenant had a large plant in the lobby of the suite, located almost directly under the return air duct. The plant was watered liberally and the water which overflowed within the planter became stagnant. Over a period of time, it had become quite foul and pungent. The air conditioning system picked up the odor and recirculated it back through the suite. The plant was removed and replaced with an artificial plant and the problems ceased.

(b) NEW CONSTRUCTION SYMPTOMS

Two years ago, a new mid-rise office building opened in the greater San Francisco Bay Area. Within a few days of opening, several employees complained of unusual odors which caused headaches, nausea and, in some cases, vomiting. The building management conducted an investigation but was unable to identify any source of odors which could be linked to the symptoms.

A consulting company was called in to investigate and the source of the problem was finally determined to lie in the building materials themselves. Problems were traced to synthetic furnishings such as carpets, insulation, and wall coverings. Adhesives and caulking materials were thought to be emitting harmful odors. Copy machines, laser printers, other office machinery and even cleaning compounds may emit similarly harmful odors. The degree of harm depends upon the percentage of these odors in the air. Most new buildings that are being put on line today go through a period of "airing out," "burn out," or "bake off" before opening. "Airing out" refers to a period of time between construction and occupancy that allows the odors to dissipate without harming building occupants. In many cases it has been enough to open the windows and let the odors dissipate over a period of time, thus reducing the offending odors. The more pro-active approach is the "burn off." With the help of a consultant knowledgeable in these areas, the building is sealed off with an exhaust fan installed and the temperature raised above norms for occupancy for a specific period of time. This procedure "bakes" the odors out of the materials thereby reducing the levels of damaging materials in the air. This procedure must be carefully controlled. Temperatures set too high or too low may cause a substantial loss of benefits and may do more harm than good.

Techniques are currently being devised to measure the particles in the air, evaluate their sources and recommend solutions. Philip R. Morey and David E. MacPhaul of Clayton Environmental Consultants performed sampling for volatile organic compounds (VOCs) in 43 buildings with indoor air quality (IAQ) problems and made some of the data available for their report. The objective of the study was to illustrate that rank order assessment is useful in deciding if the indoor VOCs are abnormal and thereby a contributing factor to IAQ problems.

Rank order assessment is a method which evaluates airborne VOCs present in nonindustrial indoor environments. VOCs are collected on Tenax and analyzed by gas chromatograph/mass spectrometry. Specific VOCs are ranked in order of abundance for an indoor site and then compared to the concentrations of the same materials in the outdoor air. This method should reveal if the indoor VOCs are unusually high and possibly contributing to indoor air quality problems. If total indoor and outdoor VOC concentrations are similar, rank order assessment can be used to help determine sources of specific VOCs found in indoor air.

This method is one of several proposed to assess the effects of VOCs on the occupants of nonindustrial indoor environments. Research suggests that a total concentration of VOCs between 160 and 5000 micrograms per cubic meter ($\mu/m3$) may well be levels which will cause annoyance and discomfort among sensitive occupants.

Morey and MacPhaul determined that total concentrations of VOCs in indoor air are typically 2 to 10 times higher than those outdoors. Sick buildings are likely to be those with higher total indoor concentration rates than those of the outside air. Other researchers have called attention to the specific nature of various VOCs, including those emitted from new construction and finishing materials, cleaning materials, combustion processes, and so on.

The authors performed IAQ evaluations in 105 buildings. In 43 of these buildings, air sampling for VOCs was performed in areas where complaints were registered and also in areas that appeared free of irritants, as well as in the outdoor air (most often taken on the roof of the building) to be used as a reference. Complaints usually included offensive odors and irritation of the eyes, nose, and throat. Below are results from one representative VOC sample taken from a building area with a number of occupant complaints compared to outdoor air samples in each building.

Sampling was performed by drawing air at a flowrate of 50 to 75 cc/minute through Tenax for a period of 5 to 8 hours. Tenax was thermally desorbed and analyzed by gas chromatography/mass spectrometry.

We have limited our discussion to one case study for illustrative purposes. Employees in a suburban hospital laboratory complained of inability to concentrate, earaches, and muscle aches. The total concentration of VOCs both indoors and outdoors was approximately 500 $\mu/m3$.

The VOCs outdoors were dominated by methylene chloride, possibly due to ongoing paving or a nearby parking lot. Indoor VOCs were dominated by C_9H_{12} alkylbenzenes and xylene and ethyl benzene, most likely from solvents used in the laboratory. Local exhaust ventilation was recommended for removal of indoor aromatic hydrocarbons.

This paper clearly illustrates the need for professional evaluation of reported symptoms within a commercial building. In most cases, it appears that the sources of the problem are fairly common items within our buildings, but often beyond the ability of the property manager or maintenance personnel to pinpoint and resolve. The use of an outside expert with experience within these types of problems combined with a very timely response is strongly suggested when such problems are brought to the attention of building management.

At the most extreme, the air conditioning system and/or water system may be the source of Legionnaire's disease. This disease was first discovered in the mid 1970s shortly after an American Legion Convention in Philadelphia. Within a very short period of time after the convention, hundreds of attendees fell ill. Eventually over 30 died and well over 200 became seriously ill. The common thread connecting the people who fell ill was their attendance at the American Legion Convention. We now know that the disease was caused by an unknown bacteria that thrives in warm moist places such as cool or tepid water standing in cooling towers and air conditioning systems. This bacteria has since been identified as Legionella Pneumophilia—Legionnaire's disease.

This form of pneumonia can be fairly easy to treat if caught in the early states. Quite often, however, it does not appear to be too serious and may be left untreated, causing the rate of fatality to be around 15%. The bacteria seems to thrive in warm moist places; known outbreaks usually occur between June and November in the Northern Hemisphere and have been traced to cooling towers or evaporative condensers, or to exposure to cleaning such equipment.

Although there are different types of Legionella Pneumophilia, current diagnostic procedures have made it possible to diagnose other epidemics of respiratory illness. An epidemic of a two- to five-day acute febrile illness in Pontiac, Michigan, affecting 144 people who worked in a county health department building was caused by this organism.

Two similar outbreaks, one at St. Elizabeth's Hospital, Washington, DC, and another in Spain, were both later identified as Legionnaire's disease.[3]

In addition to being concerned with air conditioning systems, the building manager must also be concerned with the water supply. At a hospital in South Dakota, there were 26 cases of hospital-acquired Legionnaire's disease over a three and a half year period. Ten of the patients eventually died. Investigation of these cases linked them to use of the showers: patients who took showers were at increased risk for contracting Legionnaire's disease than those that took sponge baths. It was suggested

[3] *Introduction to the Study of Disease*, William Boyd, Huntington Sheldon, Eighth Edition, pp. 176–177.

that the shower heads had been colonized by the bacteria, but replacement of the shower heads did not end the Legionnaire's disease outbreak. It was concluded that persistent colonies of the bacteria survived in the hot water supply for the three and a half year period. It also appeared that amoebae in the water supply helped the bacteria to survive. At this time, research is being conducted to see if disinfection methods that kill the amoebae will be effective in preventing Legionnaires' disease.

The typical property manager may not directly encounter all of the potential sources of Legionnaire's disease, but it is worth noting some of the more unique cases. One such example occurred in Louisiana. Thirty-four people contracted Legionnaire's disease from misters used to freshen vegetables at a supermarket. Of the people who had breathed the infectious mist, eventually two died.

The mist was generated ultrasonically and was unusually fine. The machine had not been cleaned adequately and it drew water from a standing tank which provided a breeding ground for the bacteria. In effect, the machine was discharging dirty water.[4]

In another case, an outbreak of Legionnaires' disease occurred at a Social Security building in Richmond, California. Several employees complained of headaches, dizziness, runny noses, itchy eyes, nausea, lethargy, respiratory infections, scratchy throats and inability to concentrate. More than a dozen employees became ill and at this writing one is still seriously ill and one has died.

The source of the problem was traced to two cooling towers and a sink in the janitor's closet. It was felt that the problem was further compounded by the fact that many older buildings are "sealed" buildings, meaning that the windows cannot be opened and that circulation relies on the ability of the air conditioning system to provide adequate turnover.

To date, the Social Security administration has spent in excess of one million dollars to flush and clean the air conditioning system as well as clean the interior of the building to be sure that there are no lingering traces of Legionnaires' disease bacteria. Additionally, the agency has spent half a million dollars to relocate employees to other work areas; there is no way to calculate the cost of lost time and the personal losses of the employees.

A contributing factor in Richmond was probably the placement of the water towers, which were built in the basement of the building and extended approximately 30 feet above ground. This aspect of the building is currently being studied. Most water towers are placed on the roofs of buildings. While it has not been determined to be a cause of the problem in the Richmond case, it is believed that closing off outside air intakes can contribute to such problems. Tightly sealed buildings can

---

[4] "Health & Fitness," *Changing Times*, April 1990, p. 90.

trap pollutants within the building which create irritants. Additionally, bringing in outside air can dilute the carbon dioxide that occurs when the occupants exhale. On the exterior of the building, outside air intakes can bring in polluted air if not placed properly, (if, for example, they are located in closed alley areas or close to other sources that may pollute the air prior to being taken into the building).

(c) SPECIFIC AREAS OF CONCERN

Turnover of air is a critical factor. The Healthy Office Research Program, National Safe Workplace Institute of Chicago, Illinois, has indicated that a building's heating and air conditioning system should process 20 cubic feet of air per minute per person. Their research shows that the systems in many sick buildings process much less than that, and in some cases as little as 5 cubic feet per minute per person.

Many cleaning compounds can be the source of problems. Labels should be carefully inspected and evaluated for possible harmful effects. If there are doubts, the Occupational Safety and Health Administration or the Environmental Protection Agency can help. Local colleges or universities can also offer assistance.

The type of carpeting can also contribute to the "sick building syndrome." Many carpets are manufactured and/or treated with synthetic materials. Some of these materials emit odors or vapors that may be harmful and are suspected of causing upper respiratory tract irritation. These substances are 4-phenylcyclohexene, toluene and xylenes. Carpeting should be thoroughly researched prior to installation.

Finally, it has been well-documented that second hand smoke is associated with respiratory problems. Even if an office is "smoke free," problems can be caused by other offices within the building, such as in the example given earlier in this section. Many communities are enacting ordinances that either ban smoking in public areas or allow building owners and managers to ban smoking in specific areas.

Several government agencies are studying the Richmond situation and gathering information for further research. Blood tests, air samples and other pertinent information are being studied to see if they can come up with a standard for a safe office environment.

On the national level, some elected officials have already introduced legislation to set standards that will eliminate the "sick building." Joseph Kennedy of Massachusetts and George Mitchell of Maine have sponsored bills entitled "The Indoor Air Quality Act." The bills address expanded research, ventilation standards, product labeling and sick building assessments.

In addition to the human suffering and the time lost from the workplace, sick building syndrome has produced a tremendous amount of litigation. So far, over 12 million dollars of lawsuits have been filed in

the Richmond case alone and that is not likely to be the final amount
sought.

It is imperative that the property manager be aware of and sensitive to
the complaints of employees within a building. It is all too easy to brush
off such complaints as those of unhappy employees or individuals who
find all environments troublesome. Failure to investigate complaints on
a timely basis and to follow up with responsible action may very well
subject the manager and the building employees to illness, discomfort,
loss of wages, and possibly to life-threatening diseases. Sick building
syndrome is preventable, and the consequences of a failure to act are too
great not to take preventive and/or corrective measures at the first indication of a potential threat.

§ 5.18   PROFESSIONAL ASSOCIATIONS

Two professional associations provide education and information to the
office building industry. Building Owners and Managers Association
(BOMA) is dedicated primarily to office buildings and has chapters in
major cities throughout the United States. It awards the Real Property
Administrator (RPA) designation and presents classes in various aspects
of office building operations. It also lobbies on behalf of building owners.

The Institute of Real Estate Management (IREM) has been a leader in
office building management for many years. It awards the Certified
Property Manager designation (CPM) and the Accredited Management
Organization (AMO) designation. IREM sponsors classes in office building management as well as other classes in the areas of commercial and
residential property management.

The services offered by BOMA and IREM are reviewed in Chapter
One, Introduction.

§ 5.19   REFERENCE MATERIALS

An outstanding service that BOMA and IREM provide to the office
building industry is their annual operating expense reports. BOMA publishes the *Experience Exchange Report,* and IREM publishes the *Income/
Expense Analysis, Office Buildings, Downtown and Suburban.*

The BOMA *Experience Exchange Report* is a compilation of information on office buildings of all types throughout the United States. The
report compares buildings by size, age, location, and specific characteristics. Income and expenses are broken down into meaningful categories and then compared on the basis of the highest cost, the lowest
cost, and the median for that item. Costs are also stated on the basis of
cents per square foot.

The Institute of Real Estate Management's *Income/Expense Analysis* is an annual publication analyzing office buildings' income and expenses in every metropolitan area and suburban area. Operating expenses and vacancy trends are analyzed in chart and graph formats.

It is always helpful and enlightening to be able to compare buildings that have similar characteristics. This is a benefit when setting the budget for a proposed or new building, preparing the operating budgets of an existing building, and evaluating expenses at year's end. These reports are helpful in evaluating whether or not the building's property tax assessment is correct as well as in appealing the assessment.

Both BOMA and IREM publish several informative publications. BOMA has produced a two-volume *Management Notes*. This publication, edited by Jack Gringorten, RPA, covers in a concise form over 300 areas of concern to office building management. *Trends* is a five-year income and expense trends profile for office buildings. *Office Tenant Moves and Changes* reviews the space needs of tenants, what they look for in a building, and why they relocate. *Office Building Lease Manual* presents alternative approaches for lease provisions. *Leasing Concepts: A Guide to Leasing Office Space,* written by Ron Simpson, CPM, RPA, explores conducting a market survey, measuring office space, and analyzing lease documents.

IREM has published three office building publications: *Forms for Office Building Management* by Bodie Beard, Jr., CPM, and Cher Zucker, CPM; *Managing the Office Building,* written by several CPM members with office building expertise; and *Office Building Leasing* by Duane Roberts, CPM. Also helpful is the *ODM,* published by the ULI.

The Urban Land Institute has published the *Office Development Handbook.*

Six

Industrial Property Management

§ 6.1   INTRODUCTION

Industrial properties can be more complex than they appear on the surface. Years ago, industrial buildings were located in old or poor parts of town. They were dingy, with little concern for aesthetics. Today the industrial building is often located in a master planned development with strict design, sign, and maintenance controls.

Industrial properties run the gamut from a 1,000-square-foot warehouse area for the local painter to store materials, to incubator buildings with many smaller spaces for start-up business and small operators, to multitenanted industrial parks encompassing hundreds of acres, to large single-tenant buildings.

The industrial industry has identified four types of properties: industrial areas, industrial parks, planned industrial districts, and planned employment centers. Evolution of the industrial industry can be seen in the definition of these four types of industrial properties. The Urban Land Institute's *Industrial Development Handbook* identifies and defines these property types as follows:

In older, heavily urbanized areas, large concentrations of freestanding factories, warehouses, and supply yards are frequently found intermixed with commercial and service establishments. These industrial areas are characterized by multilevel masonry construction and a high level of site coverage.[1]

Properties in these areas are usually triple net leased with limited management requirements.

The next phase in the evolution of industrial properties was the industrial park. Industrial parks were the first assemblage of individual buildings in a planned development. The industrial park has also been known as the business park, the office park, the research park, and research and development park.

> The phrase business park or office park has been introduced in part to indicate a variety of industrial and related service activities, but also to deemphasize the industrial character of many of the occupants. Whatever the name, the presumption is that the industrial park is a project which has been planned and developed as an optimal environment for industrial occupants.[2]

The next stage in the evolution was the master planned development with restrictions on the design, use, and occupancy of the industrial buildings.

> A planned industrial district may be further described as a suitably located tract of land subdivided and promoted for industrial use by a sponsoring managerial organization. In this sense, industrial district connotes a restricted use of improved land over which there is a proprietor who devotes himself to the area's planning and development.[3]

The final stage in the evolution of industrial properties is the planned employment center. The planned employment center includes a variety of office and service uses to serve the industrial businesses in the master planned area and the community at large.

> The planned employment center is a multiuse district to provide for employment needs of urban areas. It should be self-sufficient to the degree that basic employee requirements are provided within its boundaries and carefully designed to provide an optimal environment for a wide range of commercial and industrial needs. It should be fully integrated with the larger community of which it is a part.[4]

---

[1] Urban Land Institute, *Industrial Development Handbook*, (1975).

[2] *Id.*

[3] *Id.*

[4] *Id.*

§ 6.2   MANAGEMENT RESPONSIBILITIES

The typical industrial tenant is more concerned with the physical needs of the space than with aesthetics, even though the appearance of the buildings may have been a strong part of the initial attraction. The industrial tenant will focus on such features as location, labor pool, prevailing wages, zoning of the building, availability of common carriers, loading facilities, floor load capacities, clear span areas within the buildings, utility needs, and other physical requirements. The effective manager will work to meet these needs while maintaining the project in such a way as to present a pleasing appearance to existing tenants, prospective tenants, and the surrounding neighborhood.

The management of industrial properties ranges from limited management services for a single-tenant building with a triple net lease to very intense management services for the multiuse planned industrial development. The management responsibilities for a building with a triple net tenant consist primarily of collecting rent, monitoring the tenant's lease requirements, insuring the building, paying real estate taxes, and maintaining the building and improvements. A long-term triple net lease (see § 6.5), with General Motors, Boeing, or a government agency would require limited property management services.

At the other end of the spectrum of industrial management services is the multiuse planned industrial development. This development, occupied by industrial, office, and retail tenants, is highly management intensive. These projects are staffed with an on-site manager, administrative support person, and possibly maintenance personnel and a construction supervisor. Their responsibilities include lease administration, common area maintenance, limited building maintenance, tenant improvement construction, a tenant-retention program, development of emergency procedures, marketing and public relations, and coordination of leasing activities with the brokerage community.

§ 6.3   INSURANCE

The insurance requirements for industrial tenants will vary, depending on whether the building is single-tenant or multitenant. Most single-tenant buildings are leased on a triple net basis. The tenant is required to obtain an insurance policy with specific, minimum limits of coverage, and the landlord is named insured. Tenants in multitenant buildings will reimburse the landlord for their pro rata cost of the insurance.

While most owners today require at least $1 million in liability coverage by the tenant, there are dangerous industrial uses that warrant a higher limit. An insurance agent can be a valuable resource in setting the proper limits for a tenant with a risky use.

§ 6.4 TAXES

Tenants commonly pay their pro rata share of real estate taxes on the premises. On a single-user building, it is not unusual for the bill to go directly to the tenant although many owners prefer to pay the bills and collect from the tenant to be sure the taxes are paid on time. In multiple occupancy buildings, the landlord pays the bill, allocates it per the leases, and generally collects it with the budget estimates outlined in § 6.5.

§ 6.5 MAINTENANCE

The single-user industrial building is quite often leased to the tenant on an absolutely net basis, known as a triple net lease, with the tenant being fully responsible for repair or replacement of all parts of the building. Even in this situation, some standards should be set, such as quarterly air-conditioning service, periodic painting of the exterior, and annual roof inspection. An inspection should be conducted regularly to be sure the work is being performed.

Maintenance responsibility for buildings with triple net leases falls solely on the tenants. The property manager must periodically visit the properties to ensure that the tenant is fulfilling the lease responsibilities. A thorough inspection of the property should be conducted within six months of the lease expiration, and the tenant should be informed of all maintenance needs. When the tenant vacates, the property manager conducts a final inspection or walk-through with the tenant. The security deposit is not released until all maintenance is completed.

Maintenance responsibility for multitenant buildings is usually divided between the landlord and the tenants. The tenant's lease must be carefully reviewed to identify areas of responsibility. The tenant is usually responsible for the interior and mechanical equipment maintenance. The landlord is usually responsible for the maintenance of the roof, common areas, and the structural components detailed in the lease.

When the property is a planned industrial development with many different uses, the maintenance responsibility will vary depending upon the building and the users. This is evidenced in an industrial development that includes incubator space, office users, retail tenants, and large industrial users. In a park with a combination of uses, the maintenance responsibilities will vary depending upon the needs of the tenants, which are reflected in the maintenance clause of their lease.

Basically, the different users are responsible for the maintenance of the interior of their premises, including janitorial services, although in some situations the landlord is responsible for providing janitorial services. It is prudent for the property manager to assume responsibility for maintenance of the HVAC units and to require tenants to reimburse the

landlord for this expense. The property manager will develop mainte-
nance specifications based on the type of equipment and the tenants' use.
This will ensure that the units are in good condition when tenants vacate.
Tenants are billed quarterly or semiannually for their pro rata cost of the
HVAC maintenance.

Common area maintenance for industrial properties is handled much
like it is in shopping centers; that is, the property manager maintains the
common area and bills the tenants for the cost. The property manager develops an annual budget, bills the tenants monthly for their pro rata
share, and adjusts the billing to the actual expenses at the end of the budgeted period. Depending upon the lease, roof and structural maintenance
are either an expense of the landlord or are included in the common area
maintenance expense.

§ 6.6   TENANT SERVICES

The maintenance management program should help tenants with their
maintenance responsibilities. The property manager interviews and
evaluates several service contractors such as janitorial, window washing, and carpet cleaning and provides a list to the tenants. The list should
include at least three contractors for each area of maintenance with no
preference.

A key-making machine on the premises enables the manager to provide
keys at a charge to the tenants.

Because they have a mix of industrial, service, office, and retail tenants, multitenant industrial developments provide an opportunity to
bring these businesses together to promote themselves within the development. The manager of a 500,000-square-foot multitenant industrial development in the Northwest conducts an annual trade fair at which
tenants display their products and services and the landlord provides refreshments and music. This event gives tenants additional business opportunities and creates an esprit de corps within the development. A
monthly or quarterly open house during the lunch period at the on-site
management office gives the management staff a chance to develop rapport with the tenants and to meet their employees.

§ 6.7   CONSTRUCTION MANAGEMENT

Large industrial developments, especially those with incubator space,
will have considerable ongoing tenant improvement construction. The
property manager should develop a construction management program
to meet the improvement requirements of new tenants and the expansion and remodeling needs of existing tenants.

The first step in developing a construction management program is to obtain the "as built" plans for the development. The next step is to compile a list of the general contractor and all subcontractors who have worked on the project. Space planners are interviewed and one is selected to work with prospective tenants. The space planner will prepare the working drawings for construction of tenant improvements. Several general contractors should be interviewed and at least three selected to bid on tenant improvements. Contractors must provide evidence of worker's compensation and liability insurance and include the landlord and property management company as named insured on their insurance policy.

Each general contractor is requested to bid each job. If the work doesn't require extensive remodeling or build-outs, the property manager may use construction unit pricing. Under unit pricing, the property manager acquires bids that are good for a year on specific construction activities, such as installing an electrical outlet or building a stud wall, and contracting the work based on the unit price. This method is often used when a tenant renews and the landlord is making minor improvements to the premises. Unit pricing eliminates the need to bid small jobs. The property manager or the maintenance supervisor conducts a final walk-through with the contractor and the tenant before the tenant moves into the space.

A construction management program will facilitate the marketing and leasing program, meet the existing tenants' construction needs, and provide a construction supervision or coordination fee for the property management company.

§ 6.8   EXTERIOR SIGNAGE

The control of exterior signs is as important in industrial properties as it is in all other types of commercial properties. The property owner should establish reasonable sign criteria for the property in conjunction with the municipal authorities and require strict adherence. The sign criteria should be included as an exhibit in the lease.

§ 6.9   EXTERIOR STORAGE

Control of exterior storage is critical to the operation of industrial properties. It is not unusual to discover delivery pallets, 55-gallon drums, or even truck trailers being stored outside the tenants' premises. These items are unsightly, often take up valuable parking space, can become a fire hazard. and may contain hazardous materials. The best way to control storage is to include the development's rules and regulations on storage in the lease as part of the overall rules and regulations for the property.

§ 6.10   SECURITY

A security audit and an ongoing security program are integral parts of a property's emergency procedure plan. Most industrial properties have few security problems because of their suburban location, limited tenant activity in the evening, and open-air common areas. Even with these advantages, the manager cannot assume that the property will never have security problems. The manager must conduct a security audit and take preventive measures to minimize or eliminate problems.

Since there are usually no interior common areas, security problems would most likely occur in the parking lot or in the tenant's premises. Parking lot security starts with good lighting to eliminate areas where people can hide. Administrative and maintenance personnel must be constantly alert for loiterers, cars cruising, and anything that appears suspicious. Tenants should be reminded to report suspicious people on or near the development to the management office or the police. In the evenings, a drive-by security patrol can check for unlocked doors, abandoned cars, and loiterers. If a security problem exists, the property manager can hire on-site guards, erect a fence around the project with limited or guarded access, and install surveillance equipment. The police should be encouraged to drive through the development and to meet with tenants to review security procedures for their premises.

§ 6.11   ENVIRONMENTAL CONCERNS

The industrial tenant that manufactures or processes chemicals on the premises may have a potential for polluting the ground, air, or water in the area. The manager must understand how the property is to be used, what environmental concerns that use may present, and how the landlord is to be protected from damage, both during the lease term and after.

§ 6.12   EVALUATING THE NEEDS OF INDUSTRIAL TENANTS

Industrial tenants have a wide variety of space needs ranging from incubator space of under 1,000 square feet with one or two offices to hundreds of thousands of square feet for manufacturing. The property manager needs to assess which space requirements the building can meet.

The first consideration to meeting tenants' needs is zoning. Most municipalities have several zoning classifications ranging from light industrial to heavy industrial. The next consideration is the size and configuration of the building. Outside storage and parking are concerns for trucking companies and central warehouses. The type of construction and the availability of a fire sprinkler system may determine whether a company can obtain insurance for its manufacturing or operations. The utilities capacity is a concern of many large users and heavy manufacturing companies. The amount of floor area, column spacing, floor load capacities, and ceiling heights will determine if a company can lay out its equipment and supplies. The ratio of warehouse space to office space will eliminate some users. However, it usually is relatively easy to build more office space in the warehouse area. Truck loading facilities, rail spur, and access to the airport, freeway, and shipping ports are essential to many firms. The property manager should try to match the building's features to specific users.

§ 6.13   SELF-SERVICE STORAGE/MINIWAREHOUSES

"A self-storage facility is a rental property consisting of individual units of space. For each unit, which has its own door, the tenant normally provides the lock, keeps the key, and handles the goods to be stored."[5]

Miniwarehouses or self-storage facilities were first developed in the 1960s to meet the storage needs of businesses and residents. The concept is to provide storage space at a cost less than expensive office space or less than renting a larger apartment or purchasing a larger home.

Miniwarehouse or self-service storage facilities are developed on industrial-zoned properties. Because of the flexibility of laying out the buildings, they often can accommodate odd shaped parcels, be built under freeways, or used as a buffer between heavier industrial uses and office or residential areas.

Even though miniwarehouses are just over thirty years old, significant changes in their development have occurred. Early ministorage facilities were managed much like apartment buildings. The project included a small apartment, and a live-in manager was hired to manage and lease both day and night. However, no one can work twenty-four hours a day, seven days a week, and problems can occur when a relief person used the manager's home. Today it is much more common to have a small day office for leasing and management activities. After-hours activity is either not permitted or is controlled by an electronic system that is activated by a plastic entry card.

The main fear in ministorage leasing is break-ins. A minimal system of security is a drive-by patrol four to five times a night. Obviously, a burglar will watch the routine and take advantage of the time between visits. An electronic sensing system is one of the most effective, especially when connected to a direct-dial system that alerts a central station or the police. This system can be tied to the card-operated entry

[5] R.E. Cornwell and B. Victor, *Self-Service Storage*, p. 1 (1983).

system to allow for late-hour entry, or the entire system can be closed at a given hour and secured by the system. It is unwise to use security dogs as protection because of the physical harm they can inflict.

Retail and ministorage have proven to be a good combination in some circumstances. If the store is located on a busy street, retail can be a strong income and traffic generator on the front of the property, while storage facilities occupy the less expensive back areas. Shopping centers have used deep lot space for ministorage where retail space would not likely be successful.

§ 6.14   INDUSTRIAL ORGANIZATIONS

Four prominent organizations service the industrial real estate industry. The Society of Industrial and Office Realtors (SIOR), located in Washington, DC, is an affiliate of the National Association of Realtors. Its membership consists primarily of industrial brokers. Most metropolitan areas have a SIOR chapter.

The National Association of Industrial & Office Parks (NAIOP) focuses its activities on multitenant industrial parks and low-rise or garden office parks. This organization consists of developers, brokers, and related professionals and has local chapters. NAIOP's headquarters are located at 1215 Jefferson Davis Highway, Arlington, VA 22202. The American Industrial Real Estate Association (AIR) is an organization of developers, brokers, and related professionals. The association has developed different forms of industrial leases. It is located at Sheraton Grande Office Center, 345 South Figueroa, Suite M-1, Los Angeles, CA 90011. Each organization conducts seminars and addresses concerns of the industry. The Urban Land Institute (ULI), a real estate research institute, has many publications and studies on industrial real estate.

§ 6.15   INDUSTRIAL PUBLICATIONS

The industrial real estate industry has published several excellent books on developing, marketing, and managing industrial properties. Three leading publications are *Industrial Development Handbook*, published by the Urban Land Institute; *Parking For Industrial and Office Parks*, by the National Association of Industrial and Office Parks; and *Self-Service Storage*, formerly *The Miniwarehouse*, by Richard E. Cornwell, CPM®, and Buzz Victor, published by the Institute of Real Estate Management. Additional references include:

Employment and Parking in Suburban Business Parks, Gruen Gruen and Associates, Urban Land Institute (1986).

Business and Industrial Park Development Handbook, Michael D. Beyard, Urban Land Institute (1988).

The NAIOP Industrial Income and Expense Report, NAIOP, The Association for Commercial Real Estate (1992).

Amenities for the 1990s, NAIOP, The Association for Commercial Real Estate (1991).

Marketing Office and Industrial Parks, NAIOP, The Association for Commercial Real Estate (1983).

The Impact of Hazardous Waste Issues on Real Estate Transactions, Karl S. Bourdeau, Stephen L. Gordon, Holly Cannon, Craig B. Kravit, Beveridge & Diamond P C (1989). Available through NAIOP, The Association for Commercial Real Estate.

§ 6.16 CONCLUSION

At first glance, industrial properties do not appear to be very management intensive. However, with the evolution of industrial properties from freestanding masonry buildings with triple net tenants to multi-tenanted developments with multiple uses, industrial property management now entails many of the management responsibilities of office and retail properties.

Seven

Marketing and Leasing

§ 7.1 INTRODUCTION

Leasing space is the critical activity that validates development and management efforts. The success of a commercial development or investment is dependent upon a successful leasing program. Five major factors contribute to a successful leasing program: (1) the building's location, (2) the building's design and features, (3) the owner's understanding of the market, (4) the market conditions, and (5) the development and implementation of an effective leasing program. If any one of these factors is missing, the leasing program will suffer.

The success of these five factors is ultimately apparent in the building's value. Value is created in commercial properties by capitalizing the net operating income (NOI) (see Chapter 3). The components of the NOI are the building's income and expenses. The NOI can be increased by increasing the income or by reducing the expenses, the former providing far greater opportunity for increasing value. Increasing the occupancy and maintaining rent at market rates will have a greater impact on the NOI than will reducing expenses. Once a building's maintenance management program is implemented, an energy audit completed, and an energy-saving program put into place, there are limited opportunities to lower operating expenses. Leasing opportunities that significantly impact the NOI are always present. Maintaining a higher occupancy than the average for the area, maintaining the rental rates at market, and reducing tenant turnover increase the building's income and value.

This chapter will review the elements in developing and implementing an effective marketing and leasing program.

Everyone on the leasing team, especially the owner, must understand the building's position in the market. The economies of each signed lease—the "deal"—must be understood, and this chapter will discuss how to establish the rental rate.

The most important element in the leasing program is the person responsible for leasing. This chapter will discuss the three options for developing a leasing team. Remember, obtaining the cooperation of the brokerage community is a crucial element in a successful leasing program.

Every business is not a potential tenant for a commercial building because each business has its unique space and location requirements, and some tenants have cotenancy requirements. An analysis of the building's market and potential tenant mix is necessary to target an appropriate market for it.

Once the owner and the property manager have determined who can most effectively lease the building, established the building's market rate, and identified potential uses, the leasing team is ready to develop and implement a program to contact potential tenants. After prospects have been located, their financial ability must be evaluated to determine if they can fulfill their lease obligations and if their use is suitable for the building.

If the tenant is a match for the building, a lease is negotiated that includes the rental terms and lease provisions which establish the rights and obligations of the landlord and the tenants. The control the landlord has over the operation of the property is established in the rights and obligations of the lessor and lessee. Each lease provision has a specific purpose, and the property manager or leasing agent must understand the impact each provision has on the operations of the property and the property's NOI. The property manager or leasing agent needs to know which lease concessions can be given to a prospective tenant to make the deal, since an inflexible stand on all provisions will result in deals lost.

An opportunity to make a significant impact on the property's NOI can be enhanced by developing and leasing pads/outlots. This opportunity is most often found in shopping centers, but it can occur in office and industrial sites as well.

The last factor in an effective leasing and marketing program is keeping the building full, consequently the leasing effort should continue even when the building is 100% occupied. Unexpected move-outs or opportunities to replace a tenant with one who is willing to pay higher rents can happen at any time.

Lease renewals, a component of keeping the building fully occupied and the most inexpensive deals in the market, are discussed in Chapter 8.

The leasing team must be able to identify which spaces, if any, are difficult to lease and adjust the leasing program to compensate for these deficiencies.

The marketing and leasing program will receive most of the property owner's attention. An ineffective leasing and marketing program will soon be evident to the property owner and result in a change in leasing agents and possible property managers.

§ 7.2   THE MARKET SURVEY

The greatest effect the property manager has on the value of a property is to influence the income side of the income-expense equation. Opportunities exist to improve the value of property by reducing operating expenses, but more significant opportunities exist to increase the property's income.

An essential element in maximizing the property's income is maintaining the building's rental rates at their market value. To do this, the property manager must be knowledgeable about market conditions. This information can be gathered through a market survey. Trends can be identified when the surveys are conducted on a regular basis.

Market surveys are also used in managing and financing the property and in the acquisition process. The surveys entail projecting rates, concessions, and lease-up or a building's absorption rate—all of which are essential to developing the income components of a budget. Market surveys are needed when developing or refinancing a building. They also are needed to satisfy the due diligence requirement when analyzing a building for purchase.

Accurate information and a correct analysis of the information are essential to meeting the objectives of the market survey.

(a)   DETERMINING THE MARKET

Determining the boundary of the market is not difficult when the property manager is active in the area, but when the manager is new to the area, a more detailed analysis is necessary.

It is impossible to place a mileage ring around the property to determine its market area. The boundaries are formed by man-made barriers such as freeways, change of property use, or location of competing buildings. Natural barriers such as a river will also shape a market area. A rule of thumb for determining market area does not take into consideration the many variables mentioned.

The size of the market is another variable in defining the boundary of a market. For instance, the market for a Class A office building in a city's central business district (CBD) may be a mile or two in each direction, while the market for a regional mall in the same city may encompass the entire county. The boundaries of the shopping center market start with the center's trade area. This is the area in which most customers live.

When determining a neighborhood shopping center's market rates, all shopping centers anchored by one or more major tenants and located in the shopping center's trade area would be surveyed. It would not be necessary to survey the small unanchored strip centers or the enclosed malls because they would not be direct competition to the neighborhood center. If there are not sufficient competing centers to provide a valid comparison, the manager would then survey neighborhood centers outside the subject center's trade area.

Office buildings are classified as Class A, B, or C buildings and are located downtown, in a secondary business district, or in the suburbs. To establish the boundaries of the area to be surveyed, the property manager must first identify the classification of the subject office building and then determine which buildings are competition.

The method used in determining the area to survey for industrial properties is similar to the method used for office building surveys. Suburban buildings do not compete directly with downtown office buildings since most tenants choose between buildings in one particular area.

(b) CONDUCTING THE SURVEY

The only effective means for gathering market information is contacting leasing agents and property managers in the marketplace and inquiring about their "asking" and "deal-making" rates, the concessions they make, and their vacancies. Some leasing agents are reluctant to spend time conducting a market survey because they believe that their ongoing activities already keep them current on market activity. However, these individual activities do not give a comprehensive picture of the market. Even though a broker can be current on the activities of one segment of the market, such as high-rise office buildings in the central business district, general assumptions should not be applied to other segments of the market or other markets.

Conducting the market survey is not a difficult or time-consuming activity. Depending on the size of the market, the initial survey can take between two and three days. Subsequent surveys will take between one and two days. The initial survey takes approximately twice as long because the boundaries of the market must be defined, competing properties within the boundaries must be identified, and the person responsible for leasing the properties must be located.

The best way to locate competing properties is to drive the area within the boundaries of the market area and inspect the competing buildings using a market survey form. Competing properties are marked on a map and updated for subsequent surveys. While inspecting the properties, the manager will find the name and phone number of the leasing agent either on the directory of the office building or mall or on a sign on the property.

The property manager needs to develop a market survey form to record the rental information and features of the subject properties and the competition. The information on the survey form will vary according to property type. Exhibits 7.1, 7.2, and 7.3 are market survey forms for shopping centers, office buildings, and industrial properties, respectively. They request information on location, building features, condition of the property, deal-making rates, tenant charges, concessions, and vacancies. With the form in hand, and the market area identified, the property manager is prepared to conduct the survey.

Each competing property must be visited to understand how it compares with the subject property. The building's leasing agent can provide the rental data, but only a visual inspection will disclose the building's features and the condition of the property. Office building features such as life safety systems, energy conservation features, and security programs may not be observed during a property inspection. These features are obtained by contacting the property manager or leasing agent.

Once the building's features and property conditions are noted, the manager then schedules an appointment with the on-site manager to review the property's rental information. Those properties without an on-site manager will either indicate a contact person on a For Lease sign on the property or list the manager on the building's directory. If this information is not readily available, inquire with one of the tenants.

Although the property manager could acquire the information for the market survey by posing as a prospective tenant, most property managers and leasing agents are willing to share their information with one another. One way to elicit market information from a competitor is to share specific rental information on one's own property. The manager should be prepared to discuss briefly the size of the building, its location, the rental information, and vacancies. He or she should explain the asking rate and deal-making rate and the concessions he or she typically gives. For instance: "My building is asking $19.50 per square foot, but we will make a deal at $18.50 with one month free rent for each year of the lease." It is essential to obtain the deal-making rates. If only the asking rates are requested, the survey data will be distorted and the conclusion will be incorrect.

Free rent, overstandard improvements, moving allowance, and other concessions affect the face rate that is charged. Face rate is the rent paid without deduction for concessions. For instance, a rental rate at $18 per square foot for five years with six months free rent has a face rate of $18 and an effective rate of $16.20 per square foot. The effective rate takes into account the free rent and other concessions.

EXHIBIT 7.1

Market Survey—Shopping Centers

Center	Age	Center Data				Majors						Rental Info										Condition						
		Number Shops	Sq.Ft.	PK Lot		Majors	Vacancy	Asking Rts	Deal-making Rts	%	Tax	Ins	CAM	CPI	HVAC	Other	P/L	Bldg	Area	Access	Tenants	Comments						

EXHIBIT 7.2

Market Survey—Office Buildings

Building Data				Rental Information							Building Services							
Office Bldg	Age	Stories	Sq.Ft.	Vacancy	Asking Rental	Deal-making Rental	Escal	CPI	Other	Parking	On-Site Mgmt.-Maint.	Janitorial	Secur	Elev	HVAC/HR	Life Safety	Other	

	Parking		Bldg Condition		Community Services				
Office Building	Open	Covered	Interior	Exterior	Transp	Restaurants	Shopping	Other	Comments

EXHIBIT 7.3

Market Survey—Industrial Properties

Property	Property Date				Majors		Rental Info									
	Zoning	Age	Sq.Ft.	No. of Bldgs	Major Tenants	Vacarcy	Asking Rates	Deal-making Rates	Tax	Ins	CAM	CPI	HVAC	Other		

	Condition			Features								
Parking Lot	Bldg	Area	Access	Type Const	Sprinklers	Util	Ceiling Heights	% Ofc Space	Truck Loading Facilities	Rail Spur	HVAC	Misc

367

Tenant charges also affect the rental rate. Are the office building esca
lation charges established from a base year? If so, what is the base year?
Is a stop clause used? If so, what is the dollar amount of the expense
stop? Base year and stop clauses are discussed in Chapter 8 (Vol. II),
Lease Administration. If the property is a shopping center, what are the
charges for common area maintenance, real estate taxes, insurance and
merchants' association or marketing . . . fund dues? Does the industrial property have a base year escalation charge or triple net pass-
through?

The last information to obtain is the vacancy rate or the amount of vacant square footage. For some properties, this information can be obtained by walking the property. For others, such as office buildings, the
information must be provided by the property manager or leasing agent.

(c) FREQUENCY OF SURVEY

The frequency of the market survey depends on several variables. A
market survey is essential when drafting the property's annual management plan and when projecting the lease-up or absorption of a new
building. Lenders frequently require a survey when financing a project
to estimate the building's income. A survey is also needed when estimating income for the budget; when assuming a new management
account; and when establishing or adjusting market rental rates.
Whatever the variables, the market survey must be conducted as often
as necessary to remain current with the market. Usually a quarterly or
semiannual survey will suffice.

There are additional sources of information that can be consulted in
developing a market survey. Most major commercial brokerage firms
produce a quarterly or annual market survey that they release to the
newspapers and industry journals. The leading commercial brokerage
firms often hold an annual breakfast or luncheon meeting to report on
the market in their area. Many BOMA chapters produce a quarterly office building market survey, and some IREM chapters hold market forecast miniseminars. The real estate or business section of local business
magazines and newspapers frequently report on the real estate market.

After the market information is obtained and the information placed
on the market survey form, the property manager can compare the subject property with the competition, determine the property's position in
the market, establish market rates and concessions, and project the
property's lease-up.

(d) INACCURATE SURVEYS

Accurate market information is essential for projecting lease-up, vacancies, and building income—key components of the leasing program.

Any error in the market survey will result in inaccurate rental rates and concessions.

If the rental rates obtained during the survey do not accurately reflect the market rates, and the conclusions drawn from the survey are inaccurate, the recommended rates may be above market. This can affect the property's competitive position and obstruct leasing activity. Brokers immediately recognize when a building's rates are above market and will be reluctant to bring deals to the property owner. They will consider that the manager or the owner are not deal makers.

Inaccurate survey conclusions can also cause the recommended rates to be lower than market. As a result, the property will have less income and, consequently, a reduced net operating income and value. Whether the recommended rates are too high or too low, the results are the same— the property's NOI and value are reduced.

The credibility of the property manager is at stake. The relationship between the manager and the owner can be jeopardized if the building's rental rates are not maintained at their market rates at all times.

(e) EVALUATING THE MARKET SURVEY

Properly evaluated, the market survey will clarify the position of the subject property in the market and rank the property within its specific classification. The survey will compare building features and indicate areas in which the subject building excels and those in which it is deficient. This information can be used to identify areas of the building that need better maintenance or capital improvements. These improvements may be necessary to maintain or upgrade the building's position in the market.

In evaluating the information from the market survey, it is important to recognize that there isn't just one market rate for a classification of properties, but a range of rates. For instance, the Class A office space in a major city's CBD may range from $24 to $30 per square foot.

The variance in the range will depend on several factors. One factor is the building's location. A Class A building adjacent to a rapid transit station may command a higher rate than a building several blocks away. Another variable is location within the building. A space with a view will command higher rents than one without a view. A corner location in a mall will rent for considerably more than an in-line location with less exposure and foot traffic.

The size of the space is a third variable. Small spaces will rent for more per square foot than larger spaces when everything else is equal. In a shopping center, deep spaces usually lease for less per square foot than shallow spaces.

Other variables include: an office building with a prestigious address, a shopping center with a strong major tenant, an office building with a unique design, the cost of the pass-through expenses to the tenants, the building's immediate neighborhood, the quality of the building's management, the condition of the property, the services the tenants receive, and the features or amenities of the building.

When determining the subject property's position in the range of market rental rates, all of these variables are compared with the competitions'. The Institute of Real Estate Management recommends using a grid chart that assigns a number rating to the subject property in comparison with the competition.

Another method calls for the property manager to rate each building based on a visit to the buildings and general knowledge of the area. Even though evaluating buildings is more of an art than a science, an accurate analysis of the market and the market rates for each building are essential for the property manager to establish the building's position in the market and its rental rates and concessions.

Formal Market Survey Analysis

The market survey analysis (Exhibit 7.4) provides a complete picture of the market area in a standardized format. It is used to compare the subject property to its competition in order to establish the property's market rental rate. The purpose and scope section of the analysis is critical as it defines the objective and sets parameters. The recommendations section must be responsive to the purpose of the analysis and may include more than one alternative.

The market analysis will include general information on competition, demographics, traffic patterns, and other items that have a direct impact on the subject property. The survey will also include an objective analysis of the property so it can easily be measured in the market place. An analysis of comparables includes all comparable centers either in the trade area of having an impact on the subject property.

Shopping Center Market Survey

The shopping center market survey form (Exhibit 7.1) includes information on the property, the major tenants, rental information, and the physical condition of the property. The following is an explanation of the items in the shopping center survey. Some of the information cannot fit on the form and should be attached to it.

☐ *Center*—List names of each shopping center survey with the name of the subject property first.
 Age—Estimated age of property.
 Number of shops—Number of all shop spaces (occupied or vacant).
 Sq. Ft.—Number of square feet of the gross leasable area (GLA).

PK Lot—Number of parking stalls. This is only important if the center doesn't have sufficient parking, making it difficult for the tenant's customers to park.

Majors—List of the major tenants.

Vacancy—Number and size of each vacancy, i.e., one 1,200 sq. ft., two 1,800 sq. ft., one 2,800 sq. ft.

Asking Rate—The rental rate the leasing agent is quoting.

Deal-making Rate—The negotiated rental rate. If only the asking rate is included, the incorrect conclusions will be drawn.

%—Do tenants have a percentage rent clause? Yes or no?

Taxes—The cost per square foot for real estate taxes.

Ins.—The cost per square foot for insurance.

CAM—The cost per square foot for common area maintenance.

CPI—Is a Consumer Price Index adjustment in the tenant's lease? Yes or no?

HVAC—Does the tenant pay for the maintenance of the heating, ventilating and air conditioning unit? Yes or no.

Other—Any other tenant charges such as merchants' association or marketing funds dues or mandatory advertising.

Bldg.—Comment on the physical condition of the building. Good or poor.

P/L—Comment on the physical condition of the parking lot. Good or poor.

Area—Comment on the surrounding area.

Access—Comment on access to the shopping center.

Tenants—A list of the tenants. Attach to form.

Comments—General comments.

Office Building Market Survey

Many of the above items are included in the office building survey. Additional items are discussed below. The industrial park market survey is similar to the other two forms and self-explanatory.

☐ *Janitorial*—Number of nights janitorial service is provided.

Escal—Escalation charges or tenant charges.

Secur—Security on site; full or part time; drive-by; none.

Elev—Number of elevators.

HVAC/HR—Is after hours HVAC available and at what rate?

Life Safety—Does the building have life safety features?

Transp—Is convenient public transportation close by?

Restaurants—Are restaurants close by?

Shopping—Is shopping close by?

Other—Other community amenities.

EXHIBIT 7 4
Market Survey Form

MARKET SURVEY

OF

_____

(Subject Property Name)

Prepared for:

_____

Submitted by:

_____

Date: _____

EXHIBIT 7.4 *(Continued)*

TABLE OF CONTENTS

EXHIBIT 7.4 *(Continued)*

Assignment, Purpose and Scope

A statement clarifying the area(s) that the market survey constitutes. Include where, how and from whom you obtained the information you have compiled for this report.

State the property's name, address, the individual that the survey was requested by or company name (if applicable) and the general purpose and reasoning for preparation of this survey.

Recommendations and Conclusions

Based on the analysis of the subject property and comparable properties in the market area, the following recommendations for the subject property should be presented:

   A. Recommended square foot rate
   B. Price each space based on its location and desirability
   C. Concession (free rent, tenant allowance, etc.)
   D. Tenant mix
   E. Possible improvements to the property
   F. Cost of living provision (CPI adjustments)
   G. Overage rent provision
   H. Square footage rolling over in the next 12 months
   I. Specific marketing and leasing plan for releasing
   J. Timing of recommended actions

Also, the conclusions should include a summary comparison of comparables to the subject property in relationship to tenant mix, specific location and traffic counts.

Summarize anticipated results of actions you recommend be taken (i.e. vacancy factor, "return to full occupancy timing," etc.). Discuss the property's future upside potential and recommendations for a future sale.

Market Analysis

Define the market area within which you compiled the data for your survey. In *general terms*, describe the subject property's competition whether they be direct or indirect, such as location, range of square foot rates, general description of types of buildings (commercial or shopping centers) and landscaping, age of properties, occupancy, acreage, etc. Include a copy of the Urban Decision System, Inc. (213) 820-8931 demographic data for your market area and any additional pertinent data and entities that would effect the market.

Describe the economy in your defined area, where the work force is coming from, the population and predicted future growth. Discuss the drawbacks and positive aspects of the area as they would relate to the specific type of commercial property being analyzed.

EXHIBIT 7.4 *(Continued)*

Subject Property

A narrative description of the subject property. Include in this description rental rate history, past performance, location and access, capability of further development, potential maintenance and landscaping problems, parking, tenant mix, on-site management (if any), and any other problems and recommendations. Discuss the advantages and disadvantages of the property's location, tenant mix, size, etc. Include any other important information about this property which is relevant to your market analysis.

In general, describe the property's status as it would compare to other comparables in the market area.

List all the property's tenants, approximate square footage and a brief description of each tenant's business.

Do not include information in this section that will be shown on the Commercial Market Survey Analysis Form.

Commercial Market Survey Analysis

Shopping Centers

1. *The subject property.* Should be included in the first column of this form.
2. *Type of center.* Should be specified, such as service center, neighborhood center or fashion center.
3. *Property name and address.* Include full name and address of all properties.
4. *Contact name and telephone number.* Identify the person, company and telephone number through which you obtained the information on each property.
5. *Age.* Approximate age of properties.
6. *G.L.A.* Gross leasable area in square feet.
7. *Size of spaces available/range.* Provide the square foot range of spaces available in the shopping center—i.e. 500 sq. ft.—2,800 sq. ft.
8. *Current vacancy percentage/how long?* Provide the percentage of leasable square feet available on the property and approximately how long it has been available.
9. *Rent per square foot.* Provide the current rent per square foot—"street quote."
10. *Concession.* (free rent, tenant improvement allowance, etc.)
11. *C.A.M. billbacks/structure.* State what the common area maintenance billback structure is.
12. *C.O.L. provision.* Cost of living provision (CPI rent adjustment). Yes or No.
13. *Shop depth range.* Specify the range of shop depths at the shopping center.

EXHIBIT 7.4 *(Continued)*

14. *Overage rents/percentage rents.* Specify what the overage rent provisions are for the tenants.
15. *Date last lease signed/rate.* Provide the date of the last lease that was signed and the rate given to the tenant.
16. *Finish out.* Yes or No.
17. *Condition.* Rate the condition of the property overall—exc., good, fair, poor.
18. *Visibility.* Rate the visibility of the property—exc., good, fair, poor.
19. *Parking/ratio.* State the parking ratio at the shopping center.
20. *Ingress/egress.* Rate the ingress and egress at the property—exc., good, fair, poor.
21. *Location.* Rate the location of the shopping center—exc., good, fair, poor.
22. *Rating.* Rate the property against the other shopping centers analyzed on a scale of 1-5, 1 being the highest and 5 the lowest.

A similar analysis is conducted for office buildings and industrial properties except that the features discussed are property type specific.

APPENDIX

1. Regional or area map
2. Photograph of subject property
3. Photographs of comparable properties
4. Pertinent newspaper ads and articles

(f)   USING MARKET SURVEY INFORMATION

Market survey information must be shared with the property owner as soon as possible to determine the building's rental rates and concessions. Rental rates must be adjusted to reflect current market conditions and to maintain the competitiveness of the building.

Although property owners are usually aware of market conditions, they may have a misconception of their property's position in the range of market rates. They inevitably err on the high side and perceive their building's rates as higher than justified. The market survey will keep the owner aware of the property's correct position in the range of market rates.

Ideally the property manager would arrange for a meeting with the owner to review the survey and establish the rental rates and concessions. If the owner is out of the area, the survey can either be included with a monthly management report or sent as a separate report. Exhibit 7.5 illustrates another market survey analysis format suitable for either purpose. The property manager should include recommended rental rates and concessions. An owner who is aware of market conditions and deals being made in the market is in a better position to evaluate the deals the manager presents.

The market survey can also be used to promote the property management company. The survey and a brief summary can be sent to potential clients. This gives the manager an opportunity to request a meeting to discuss market conditions.

The survey can be used as background for an article on market conditions written for one of the local newspapers or business journals. In addition, the property manager can be a resource person on a panel discussion held by BOMA or IREM, or other real estate organizations on market conditions. The information can also be shared with appraisers and investment salespeople who might in turn refer their clients to the manager. In house, the survey makes an excellent topic for discussion at leasing meetings.

§ 7.3   PRO FORMA RATE VS. MARKET RATE

The correct rental rate is a critical component in the marketing and leasing plan. Leasing agents are reluctant to work on a property whose rental rate is above the market rate because they have little chance of making a deal. The property manager must work with the property owner in establishing the building's market rental rates or pro forma rate.

The pro forma rental rate is derived from the income projection in the property's pro forma. The pro forma is the financial analysis of a property for a specific time period, such as one year or five years, and includes

EXHIBIT 7.5

Commercial Market Survey Analysis Format

1. Cover page
2. Table of contents
3. Recommendations and conclusions

   Based on the analysis of the subject property and comparable properties, make recommendations for the subject property and timing of recommended actions. Make a recommendation for the optimum market rentals for the property, compare with current rents, and show the gross potential monthly income and increases. Include in the conclusions the status of the overall vacancy factor in the market, including inventory levels and absorption rates. Summarize anticipated results of the actions recommended to be taken at the property (i.e., move-outs and existing tenants, vacancy factor, "return to full occupancy" timing). Include a summary of the marketing and promotional program, listing possible alterations or plans of action needed to maintain high occupancy levels. Discuss the property's future upside potential and recommend future property sale.

4. Assignment and purpose of survey

   State the area that the market survey constitutes, the subject property's name and address, the individual or company that requested the survey (if applicable), and the general purpose and reasoning for preparing this survey.

5. Trade area analysis

   Starting with a demographic report from a service such as Urban Decisions, determine the characteristics of the surrounding population as to age, family makeup, income levels, and home ownership. Plot the competition on a map and determine the trade area for the shopping center. Obtain traffic counts in the area and evaluate the center's traffic as compared with other locations.

6. Subject property

   Prepare an objective analysis of the subject property, including major tenants, overall tenant mix, ingress, egress, visibility, management, parking ratios, amenities, landscaping, security, maintenance, sales comparisons, and compatibility with population in trade area.

7. Analysis of comparables

   Compare subject property with all other competitive properties. Compare properties using the market survey evaluating each property in relationship to subject property.

8. Commercial market survey analysis

   In narrative form, compare the subject property with the competition, making recommendations about property tenant mix, rental levels, probably lease terms, physical changes or improvements, management considerations, and advertising and promotional recommendations.

9. Attach all supporting materials such as demographic reports, traffic maps, area maps, photos, newspaper articles, zoning maps, zoning decisions, an/or other supporting materials.

projections for income, the vacancy factor, operating expenses, and debt service (loan payment). A pro forma is prepared for new developments, for refinancing properties, and for the sale or purchase of a property. If the pro forma is being developed for a new or remodel project, it will include an anticipated lease-up, which is a projection of different occupancy levels during different periods of the pro forma until the building reaches a stabilized occupancy.

No commercial property is ever leased at the pro forma rate simply because it is the pro forma rate. Space is leased only at market rate. When a developer's or owner's pro forma rate is the same as the market rate, it is either a coincidence or the result of a thorough analysis of market conditions.

When pro forma rates have no relationship to market rates, value is robbed from the property by a longer lease-up time and higher vacancy rate, resulting in less income. A pro forma rate that is below the market rate will result in a faster lease-up and a higher occupancy, but the building's overall income during the initial lease up and in subsequent years will be less because of the lower rental rates, and the building's value will be correspondingly less. When the property owner's rental rates are not at market, the error is usually on the high side of the market rental rate.

Frequently the developer or the owner becomes blinded to market conditions because of emotional involvement with the property or a lack of understanding of the market conditions. Sometimes the property must produce a certain income level to be financed or to achieve a desired sale price, and the pro forma rate is selected solely to achieve this income "on paper." This is known as "backing into the rental rates."

The manager has the responsibility to keep the owner aware of the market conditions and the property's market rental rate. This responsibility is especially important when rates are experiencing a rapid decline or increase. An example of a rapid change in market rates occurred in the oil-producing states in 1986 when the price of a barrel of oil dropped from above $30 to $10. In Anchorage, the rates for Class B office space and neighborhood strip center space dropped 30 to 50 percent in less than nine months. During the same period, Class A office space and enclosed mall space dropped 10 to 15 percent. The market rates in Anchorage continued to drop through 1988. Within two years, Class A office rents dropped by 50 percent. The prudent manager surveyed this market every two to three months and communicated any market changes to the owner. When leasing agents or property managers did not keep current with market conditions, their buildings were not competitive and suffered from less leasing activity, a higher vacancy rate, and lower income.

It is important to note that rental rates for different property types do not increase or decrease at the same rate. Even within a property type, the market rental rates for the different classifications of property do not change at the same rate. For example, in a soft office market, Class A office space may experience a small drop in its market rates, while Class B office space will probably experience a greater reduction in rates. This is often the result of tenants in Class B space upgrading to Class A space at the same or slightly higher rates. Since rental rates do not change at the same rate for all property types, no rule of thumb for determining the percent of increase or decrease in market rates can be applied to each property type or each classification of property.

Occasionally a property owner who has experienced slow leasing activity in a building for an extended period may respond by slashing rental rates below market and adding concessions not required in the market. This panic is usually the result of the property owner's having established a rental rate higher than the market rate for an extended period and then overreacting by lowering rates below what is necessary to be competitive.

The manager has several opportunities to keep the owner current on market conditions. The best opportunity is by reviewing the market survey with the property owner. The monthly management report is another means to communicate market conditions to the property owner. A statement on the market conditions and leasing activities in the monthly management report, along with copies of articles on the market conditions, will provide the property owner with a regular review and understanding of the market. The monthly management report is thoroughly reviewed in Chapter 12, Reports to Owners.

Few issues are more important to a property owner than the building's leasing activity. The property manager can provide the owner with the necessary information to analyze the market and arrive at a realistic market rental rate. Combining market information with an effective marketing and leasing program will enable the property to achieve and maintain its highest value.

§ 7.4   BREAKEVEN ANALYSIS

How will a property manager, leasing agent, or property owner know if a proposed lease is a good deal or a bad deal? The economics of a lease are determined when a breakeven analysis is performed. When a deal is presented to the property owner, an analysis should be included showing the proposed lease profit or loss. The manager can determine the breakeven rental rate for the property and then compare it with the proposal.

The breakeven analysis amortizes the income, commission, and tenant improvements over the life of the lease and includes the building's operating expenses. These figures are then converted to a dollar per square foot per year amount to arrive at the dollar per square foot profit or loss before and after debt service. Depreciation and amortization of the loan and time value of money are not considered.

The following is an example of a breakeven analysis: A lease is proposed for 2,000 square feet of space in an office building for five years, with three months' free rent one year and nine months at $15 per square foot, two years at $17 per square foot, and the fifth year at $19 per square foot. The landlord contribution towards tenant improvements (TI) is $15,000. The building has an operating expense stop clause of $5 per square foot. The lease commission is 5 percent of the base rental income over the term of the lease, payable one half on lease execution and one half when the tenant takes occupancy and commences paying base rent.

Terms:
   Space: 2,000 sq. ft.
   Rent: 3 months free, 1 year 9 months at $15/sq. ft.,
                   2 years at $17/sq. ft., and 1 year at $19/sq. ft.
   TI: $15,000
   Stop expense: $5/sq. ft.
   Commission: 5% of gross income

1. Determine rent over 5 years, average annual rent, and average annual rent per square foot.
   Rent:
      Year 1
         Three months free   = $ 0
         Nine months (2,000 sq. ft. × $15/sq. ft. =   30,000
           ÷ 12 mo. = $2,500/mo. × 9mo.)   =   22,500
      Year 2 2,000 sq. ft. × $15   =   30,000
      Year 3 2,000 sq. ft. × $17   =   34,000
      Year 4 2,000 sq. ft. × $17   =   34,000
      Year 5 2,000 sq. ft. × $19   =   38,000
                                  $158,500

   $158,500 ÷ 5 years   = $31,700 (avg. annual rent)
   $31,700 ÷ 2,000 sq. ft. = $15.85/sq. ft. (avg. annual rent/sq. ft.)

2. Determine owner's nonreimbursable operating expenses. The lease states that the owners will pay the first $5 per square foot of operating expenses over the life of the lease. All increases in operating expenses will be paid by the tenant.

3. Determine base commission, annual commission averaged over five years, and the commission per square foot per year.

Gross income	$158,500
Commission rate	× .05
Commission	$ 7,925
Divided by five years	÷ 5
Avg. annual commission	$ 1,585
Divided by 2,000 sq. ft.	÷ 2,000
Commission/sq. ft./yr.	$ .79

4. Determine tenant improvement cost per square foot per year.

TI	$ 15,000
Divided by five years	÷ 5
TI cost/yr.	$ 3,000
Divided by sq. ft.	÷ 2,000
Cost/sq. ft./yr.	$1.50

5. Determine debt service.

Obtain annual debt service from the owner and divide this amount by the square footage of the rentable or usable area of the building, depending upon how the building is being leased. Assuming the debt service in this example is $400,000/year, and the rentable area of the building is 55,000 square feet, compute the following:

$$\frac{\text{Debt service}}{\text{Rentable sq. ft}} \quad \frac{\$400,000}{55,000} = 7.27 \text{ debt service/sq. ft.}$$

	Annual Rate/Sq. Ft.
Base income	$15.85/sq. ft.
Less: Operating expenses	(5.00)
Lease commission	(.79)
Tenant improvements	(1.50)
Profit (or loss) before debt service	$ 8.56
Less: Debt service	(7.27)
Net profit (or loss)	$ 1.29/sq. ft.

Breakeven Analysis

The profit of $1.29 per square foot times the 2,000 square feet provides a total dollar profit of $2,580 per year or $12,900 for five years.

Armed with this information, the property manager can determine whether this is a good or bad deal. Each time a lease is presented to the owner, a breakeven analysis should accompany the deal. If the net amount is a loss, the property manager then compares the loss with the cost of not making this deal. The cost of not making the deal is the cost of additional lost rent added to the breakeven analysis that is projected for the next deal. The next deal is a best estimate of how long the space will remain vacant, how much rent can be collected, and how much tenant improvements will cost. During a soft market, the owner is sometimes better off accepting either a low net profit or even a small loss than gambling on finding another tenant for the space at a higher rate. Giving four months' free rent may be better than waiting for a more lucrative deal. If there is no backup prospective tenant and another deal is unlikely in the next few months, giving free rent is losing nothing since the space would be vacant and nonproductive anyway. The phrase "it is better to collect rent than dust" was common during the soft office building market of the mid-1980s. This phrase suggests that it is often better to accept a lease with a net loss than to allow the space to sit vacant for an extended period and incur a greater loss.

§ 7.5   THE LEASING TEAM

An effective leasing program must have a team that understands market conditions, has common objectives, and exhibits a willingness to work together.

The property owner selects and monitors the leasing team. If the property is held under a joint venture partnership with more than one general partner, an owner's representative must be selected among the partners. The balance of the team includes a leasing agent, who may or may not be the property manager, and administrative support persons. The advertising agency is included initially while the leasing package is being developed and continues if an ongoing public relations program is implemented.

Competition is keen in leasing space, and the leasing team must work as a cohesive unit with one objective—to lease the property at market rates as quickly as possible.

(a)   WHO SHOULD LEASE THE PROPERTY?

One of the owner's most critical decisions is who should lease the property. In making this decision the owner must recognize that the choice will vary according to the circumstances. The owner first needs to clarify the leasing objectives, which are to lease the property as quickly as possible at the best rental rate to the best tenants. The property owner then needs to ask, What is the best way to achieve my leasing objectives? Who is best qualified to accomplish these objectives? Should the leasing be the responsibility of a leasing broker, an in-house leasing agent who is the employee of the owner, or the property manager? Each of these alternatives—the leasing broker, the in-house leasing agent, and the property manager—has advantages and disadvantages depending on the leasing situation.

Leasing Broker

The leasing broker working for a local or national commercial brokerage firm can offer the services of an organization geared solely to leasing or leasing and selling commercial property. The organization will have several people actively involved in commercial leasing who share ideas and regularly brainstorm leasing situations.

Since the leasing broker has one responsibility, leasing space, the total focus of his or her working day will be on leasing. The leasing broker will develop contacts with other leasing brokers in the community and will co-broker many deals. Unless a leasing broker is the exclusive agent for a major project such as a high-rise office building or a regional mall, the broker will be leasing several properties simultaneously. Even when the leasing agent has an exclusive on a major building, he or she may be leasing other properties. The broker is always in the "market" and is aware of tenant movements and new tenants in the area, and may develop a clientele who will call the broker when they need space. The broker may become a tenant's exclusive broker for locating space.

On larger projects, the leasing broker may develop a team to lease a project. For instance, in a regional mall, three or four leasing brokers will divide the leasing responsibilities, basing their leasing assignments on categories of tenants. One broker will work with the restaurant and specialty food tenants; another broker will be responsible for the gifts, speciality, and service stores; while a third broker will be responsible for the fashion stores.

A seasoned leasing broker may employ an inexperienced leasing broker, sometimes referred to as a "runner," to canvass the area.

Using a leasing broker offers a further advantage. Since the broker is active in the market, he or she may know more about the types of deals that are being made in the market. The leasing broker also has negotiating experience and the support of an entire organization experienced in leasing commercial properties.

There are some concerns, however, that must be addressed when using a leasing broker. Leasing brokers work for commission only. If a 50,000-square-foot office building has only two vacancies totaling 1,800 square feet, will the broker spend adequate time and effort leasing the space? Along this line, when deals are slow at one property, will the broker give attention to more promising properties and neglect the difficult ones? In both of these situations, the property owner may end up with an exclusive leasing agreement, a broker's sign on the property, and little else.

Many brokers are reluctant to go to the property owner and suggest the leasing agreement be terminated or not renewed. There are several reasons for this: First, the broker may be concerned that the relationship with the property owner will be severed if he or she gives up on leasing a property. Second, since one rule of real estate is, "The one who controls the property gets paid," even though the broker may not be actively working the property, if another broker brings in a tenant, the broker with the exclusive will receive a co-broker's commission. Even though these motives may be understandable in the eyes of the broker, most property owners would prefer that the broker terminate the leasing agreement rather than let an unsuccessful leasing situation continue. Owners will respect brokers who consider the good of the project as their number one priority.

In-House Leasing Agent

The in-house leasing agent is an employee of the property owner and is usually paid a salary with an incentive bonus based on leasing results. This person will devote 100 percent of his or her time and effort to the owner's properties. The in-house leasing agent is able to become completely familiar with the owner's property and to spend full time working (leasing) the property. If the owner has properties at which leasing is slow, the in-house leasing agent can afford to continue to work the property because he or she has a base salary to cover the lean periods when few leases are being made. The in-house leasing agent also has the same opportunity to network in the leasing market as does the outside broker.

The disadvantage of in-house agents is that they may not work as hard to make a deal because they have a base salary available and may rely too heavily on outside brokers to bring in deals. In addition, frequently the in-house agent is working *alone* and can't benefit from the creative synergy that results when several leasing brokers work together. Because of a lack of support staff, the in-house leasing agent may not be able to use his or her time effectively.

Property Manager as Leasing Agent

The property manager as leasing agent also has distinct advantages and disadvantages. One obvious advantage is that the property manager is more familiar with the area, the property, the tenants, and the goals of the owner. The property manager is either on site or visits the property regularly and is motivated to devote time to leasing even when only one or two vacancies exist. If the property manager has been conducting market surveys regularly, he or she knows the market better than anyone else. One disadvantage of using the property manager to lease space is that the manager may not have sufficient time or expertise. And because the manager may not be active in the leasing market, he or she may be unaware of new tenants coming into the area or tenants who are considering expanding or relocating. The property manager's leasing time can be diluted by pressing management responsibilities. Further, prospective tenants often prefer to work with a broker who represents several properties.

Deciding whether to use a leasing broker or a property manager to handle lease renewals is sometimes difficult. A leasing broker may be more familiar with the market and better able to obtain the best deal, but the leasing commission, especially if it is for a small space, may not be worth the time spent negotiating the renewal. Another disadvantage is that the leasing broker is not familiar with the tenant's contributions to the property and may approach the negotiations in an impersonal manner that offends the tenant.

The property manager offers the advantage of knowing tenants' backgrounds and concerns. If the renewal rate is a significant increase over the existing rate, the property manager can provide information on market rates prior to negotiating the renewal, thereby avoiding an unpleasant shock when the higher rate is discussed. On the other hand, the property manager may have too much sympathy for the tenant and not negotiate a market rate deal.

None of the advantages or disadvantages apply to all brokers, all in-house leasing agents, or all property managers, nor do they apply to every leasing situation. However, the property owner must consider these factors when evaluating who should lease the property. Remember, the objectives are to lease the space as quickly as possible to the best tenants at the market rate. If the property manager believes someone else can best accomplish this objective, he or she should state this to the owner and recommend the best leasing broker for the property.

(b) WORKING WITH THE BROKERAGE COMMUNITY

When leasing is handled by the property manager or an in-house leasing agent, the brokerage community should become part of the leasing and marketing plan.

Many tenants will appoint a broker as their leasing representative for locating space and negotiating the lease. Brokers more often represent office and industrial tenants than shopping center tenants for two reasons. First, most office and industrial space users lease larger spaces than do small shop users in shopping centers. Seldom does a local retailer's space exceed 2,500 square feet, while office and industrial tenants requirements range from a few thousand square feet to in excess of one hundred thousand square feet. There are a few large national and regional tenants that occupy large spaces called "Big Boxes." Hence, the commission to be earned representing an office or industrial user is usually much greater than the commission earned representing a retail user. Usually a retail broker must lease more retail spaces to equal the commission earned by an office or industrial broker. In addition, the opportunity to represent a large or major user is greater when representing office and industrial users.

Second, many of the small shop tenants are independent (mom and pop) tenants who are not familiar with the services of a broker. Many of these tenants look for space on their own and either hire an attorney or negotiate the lease themselves.

The property manager must recognize that brokers have tremendous influence over the tenants they represent. In some situations, they can even influence which buildings the tenant will visit and, of course, they have a major influence over which building the tenant selects. Alienating a broker or the brokerage community will result in some prospective tenants not being shown your property and lost deals. The property manager should emphasize that the broker's role is important throughout the lease negotiations.

The property manager can communicate in many ways to the brokerage community that broker cooperation is encouraged. First, the For Lease sign on the property should state, "Broker Cooperation Welcome." Personal contact with the brokers is the best method to communicate information concerning available space. Regularly taking brokers to breakfast or lunch is an excellent way to develop a working relationship. Membership in professional organizations provides another opportunity to meet with brokers. Some areas have multiple listing services for commercial properties, and ads in this service should be considered.

The property manager should inform the broker that he or she is more than willing to share property operating information. Escalation charges and common area costs, operating expenses, and vacancy factors are a few items that may be helpful to brokers when they are listing a property for sale or comparing lease proposals. If the property management company doesn't have a large leasing staff or leasing capacity, it may team up with a brokerage firm for joint proposals to manage and lease a property. This can result in cross-referrals.

Next, the property manager can arrange to make presentations to leasing agents at brokerage firms that have weekly sales and leasing meetings. Either the brokerage firm will specialize in leasing one type of property, such as office buildings, or it will have several divisions with each division specializing in a property type. When making a presentation to a brokerage firm with several divisions, the manager should request a meeting with the division that leases the property type he or she is representing. The manager should provide marketing materials, brochures, plot plans, photos, and aerials as handouts.

Continuous follow-up with the brokers is necessary to keep properties in front of the brokerage community. The property manager can develop a mailing to brokers listing on one side all of the properties to be leased and a collage of photos on the reverse side. The one-page mailer can be preprinted in large quantity on card stock, with the collage on one side and the other side left blank. For each broker's mailing, the list of properties with vacancies can be added to the blank side and reproduced by a quick print process. Commercial brokers should receive these mailings at least quarterly and as often as monthly.

A list of brokers can be developed by contacting the local board of realtors and requesting a list of its commercial brokers; by reviewing the multiple listing books and noting the brokers with commercial buildings for sale or lease; by developing a list from the commercial For Lease signs on buildings; by reviewing the membership list of the real estate professional organizations; and by checking the Yellow Pages. Many areas will have an organization for commercial brokers, which is an excellent source for a commercial broker's mailing list. Every commercial broker has an operating network, and no broker, regardless of experience or size of the company, should be overlooked.

The broker wants to believe the property manager as the landlord's representative is a deal maker not a deal breaker. A property manager who is not flexible in negotiating the lease terms and lease clauses will be perceived as a deal breaker. The property manager doesn't have to give in on every point but should be willing to compromise when appropriate. For instance, national tenants will request several changes to the lease, and the property manager must be willing, able, and available to review the lease with the broker and negotiate many of the tenant's concerns.

Once the deal is executed, the broker's next concern is payment of the commission. Most brokers earn a commission, not a salary with a regular paycheck, and the property manager should see that the broker is paid on time per the commission agreement. If a commission payment— for example, the second half—could be paid a little early, the broker will be even more grateful.

Another means of showing appreciation for brokerage cooperation is to give Christmas gifts to brokers who brought tenants to the property. A small gift can be presented to brokers who cooperated in one or two deals and a larger gift to those who cooperated in several leases or a major lease. Gifts can be wine, fruit, or cheese assortments, which are packaged in several sizes.

A broker's open house at a new development or a remodeled property is another means to present the property to the brokerage community. Refreshments and possibly musical entertainment can be part of the event as well as a supply of materials on other properties that might be of interest to the broker.

An open house for the business community is another means to market a property. The property manager should be careful not to mix guests from the brokerage community and the business community so that the brokers will not solicit the business community for other properties.

When the broker does register a tenant and negotiations commence, the property manager should coordinate with the broker, providing information early in the negotiations. Information such as tenant charges, construction schedules, and other items that the broker must know to analyze and compare the property with other properties being considered are essential for the broker to present a proposal. The property manager should respond quickly to the broker's questions. The old saying, "Time is money," is a fitting statement for someone whose income is earned from commissions.

After a lease is executed, give the broker recognition in the community. Some major developers will annually place a half-page or full-page ad in the newspaper expressing appreciation to those brokers who have brought in leases. A list of leases executed and the names of the leasing agents can also be given to local newspapers and business journals as public relations articles about the property and for recognition for the brokers.

A major concern of the broker is that his or her position in the deal will be protected. All brokers can tell stories about how they were shut out of a commission by a landlord or another leasing agent. Since most brokers act as independent contractors whose income is from commissions, creating and protecting this income is of great interest to them. The broker wants to be protected in the deal; a written commission agreement will provide this protection. Equally important, the property manager must assure the broker that he or she will be paid a commission if the broker brings the property manager a tenant, follows the manager's requirements for registering tenants, and a lease is executed. It is obvious that the cooperation of the leasing brokers is an essential element in a marketing and leasing plan, and the property manager should consider the broker as an additional marketing tool.

(c) BROKER'S AND LEASING AGENT'S RECOGNITION

Leasing commercial property is very competitive. There are scores of leasing agents either seeking to represent the same tenants or soliciting their interests in occupying space in buildings they control. Agents have control of a space or building when they have the exclusive right to lease the space or the building.

Since most leasing agents' compensation comes entirely from commissions, with no salary, they are careful that their position in the transaction—often called the "deal"—is protected. The landlord and property manager are concerned that after a lease is executed, no one claims commissions they are not owed.

Another concern is that only one leasing agent claims to represent the tenant. For instance, a tenant selects a leasing agent as his or her exclusive broker and that agent representing the tenant contacts the landlord. A deal is not executed, and later the tenant terminates the agreement with its leasing agent and appoints another leasing agent. A lease is eventually executed with the tenant, and both the former agent and the current agent claim that they are owed a full commission. In this case, a costly legal suit could occur and a second commission, unearned but paid.

To assist in preventing potential disagreements about representation, the landlord or property manager must clarify who represents the tenant and acknowledge the tenant's authorized agent by using a letter of recognition. The process for recognizing a leasing agent's position in the deal starts by requesting that the leasing agent have the tenant prepare a letter of representation on the tenant's letterhead and signed by an officer of the tenant stating that the leasing agent is the sole person authorized to represent the tenant. In lieu of a letter, some landlords will accept the leasing agent bringing the tenant to the property and introducing the tenant as the agent's client (Exhibit 7.6).

After either a recognition letter or a personal introduction, the landlord or property manager sends the leasing agent a letter of recognition. This letter limits the time period the leasing agent has to complete the deal, evidenced by an executed lease between the landlord and the tenant. This period is usually between 30 and 120 days, depending upon the complexity of the lease negotiations. The letter of recognition also requires the tenant's leasing agent to sign the landlord's brokerage agreement. The brokerage agreement is specific regarding what the leasing agent must do to earn a commission, how the commission is calculated and paid, and the leasing agent's obligations.

(d) BROKER'S AND LEASING AGENT'S LETTER OF NONRECOGNITION

Unfortunately, in commercial real estate there are leasing agents who will try to back into a deal. This happens when a leasing agent who didn't represent either the landlord or the tenant and played no part in facilitating the deal claims a commission. This can happen in several ways. One instance is when a leasing agent calls a landlord and tells the landlord that a tenant, not represented by the agent, is looking for space. The leasing agent has no other part in the deal, and if a lease is executed then claims a commission has been earned. A problem can also develop when a leasing agent discovers that a landlord is looking for a particular tenant or use for a space, say a pad or outlot, and calls the landlord claiming to represent one or several tenants. Later, another broker who is authorized to represent the tenant that the other agent falsely claimed to represent brings the tenant to the landlord, negotiates the lease, and expects a

EXHIBIT 7.6

Recognition of Broker's Status Letter

RE:

Gentlemen:

We are in receipt of your letter dated _____ regarding the above referenced company.

As you know, we are pleased to cooperate with brokers in securing tenants. We will present to you for your signature, prior to the execution of any lease documents, our standard form of brokerage agreement.

If a lease between said prospective tenant and this company is executed within thirty (30) days from the date hereof, wherein you are designated by them as the sole procuring broker, and if you have executed and delivered to us our standard form of brokerage agreement, we shall be pleased to recognize your status in this matter.

Sincerely,

XYZ Management Company

As Agent for _____

By: _____

commission for being the producing leasing agent. Now two leasing agents are claiming a full commission.

When a leasing agent is unable to provide evidence that he or she represents a prospective tenant, a letter of nonrecognition is sent to the leasing agent (Exhibit 7.7).

(e) EXCLUSIVE LEASING AGREEMENT

The intent of an exclusive leasing agreement is to protect the leasing agent's position in a deal and to come to an agreement between the leasing agent and the property owner on how a commission is earned, the commission schedule, and the rights and obligations of both parties. The leasing agent wants his or her position in a deal protected if the lease is executed within a reasonable time after the agreement is terminated. The property owner wants to have the right to terminate

EXHIBIT 7.7

Nonrecognition of Broker's Status Letter

RE:

Gentlemen:

We are in receipt of your letter dated _____ regarding the above referenced company.

We cannot consider your status in this matter unless and until you deliver to us a letter from said prospective tenant which designates you as the sole broker with whom they have and will deal in such proposed lease transaction. It is imperative that such a letter be executed by an officer or other representative of the prospective tenant who is duly authorized to bind the tenant in such matters.

Sincerely,

XYZ Management Company

As Agent For _____

By: _____

the agreement if the leasing agent is not actively working the property. Several other issues are also addressed in the exclusive leasing agreement. (See Exhibit 7.8.)

(f) LEASING AGREEMENT

The leasing agreement sets forth the understanding between the property owner and the leasing broker. Several items must be negotiated in the agreement.

The first term discussed is the commission rate. The agreement must state how the commission will be calculated—a percentage of the rents, a fixed fee, a dollar amount per square foot, or any formula agreed upon by the owner and broker. It also should state how the commission will be shared on a co-broker deal.

The payment schedule is the next concern. Will the commission be paid entirely when the lease is executed or will it be divided over time?

The agreement should state whether a commission is paid when the tenant renews, expands, or exercises an option. Brokers often believe that they should be paid each time a tenant renews and expands because they introduced the tenant to the property. However, many property owners refuse to pay a commission on renewals and expansions because they paid the broker for bringing the tenant to the building, and any changes to the tenants occupancy are negotiated by the owner or property manager.

The property owner and broker now need to negotiate the length of the agreement. A broker will need a year or two to market a proposed building and six months to one year for an existing building. An agreement must be reached on who pays for the marketing materials, publicity, signs, and brochures. The owner will want a right to cancel the agreement if the broker's marketing and leasing program is ineffective. The agreement will state that the broker is an independent contractor and not an employee of the owner.

The property owner will want to be held harmless and indemnified for gross negligence and misconduct of the broker. The broker will want to be held harmless for any inaccurate information provided by the owner. The agreement should state that neither party will discriminate based on race, color, creed, nationality, gender, age, or handicap. There will be other clauses generic to all contracts.

(g) NON-EXCLUSIVE BROKERAGE AGREEMENT

Occasionally, the property manager will find a party interested in purchasing one of the properties he or she manages. The property owner may be interested in considering the sale of the property but is not willing to give the property manager an exclusive listing. Property

EXHIBIT 7.8

Sample Exclusive Leasing Commission Agreement

THIS EXCLUSIVE LEASING COMMISSION AGREEMENT (hereinafter referred to as the "Agreement") is made and entered into this _____ day of _____, 19___, by and between _____ (hereinafter referred to as "Landlord") and _____ (hereinafter referred to as the "Broker").

WITNESSETH:

WHEREAS, Landlord is the owner of _____ _____ _____ _____ _____ (the "Project"); and

WHEREAS, Landlord desires to delegate certain exclusive leasing responsibilities to Broker subject to the terms and conditions of this Agreement, and Broker agrees to accept such responsibilities and to perform them according to the terms and conditions contained herein; and

WHEREAS, pursuant to this Agreement, Broker is or may be, engaged in certain negotiations between Landlord and certain prospective tenants (hereinafter collectively referred to as the "Prospective Tenant") for one or more leases covering space in the Project; and

WHEREAS, Landlord and Broker desire to set forth the terms and conditions which must be fulfilled prior to any commission due from Landlord being deemed to have been earned by Broker to confirm and reduce to writing their entire understanding and agreement with respect to said negotiations, commissions, and fees;

NOW, THEREFORE, in consideration of the mutual terms, covenants, and agreements herein contained, together with other good and valuable consideration, the receipt and sufficiency of which is hereby acknowledged, the parties hereto hereby agree as follows:

I. TERM; TERMINATION

A. **Commencement Date and Termination Date.** The term of this Agreement shall commence as of _____, 19___, which shall be the "Commencement Date." It shall continue until midnight on _____, 19___, unless sooner terminated pursuant to the terms hereof, which shall be the "Termination Date" of this Agreement.

B. **Termination.** It is understood and agreed that this Agreement may be terminated by Landlord or Broker on not less than thirty (30) days written notice. In the event of such termination, Broker shall receive from Landlord any commissions earned and which are then due and payable, according to the terms of Section II below.

II. RATE OF COMMISSION AND TIME OF PAYMENT

Lease Commission Calculation. In the event, prior to the Termination Date of this Agreement or earlier termination, the Broker delivers to Landlord written leases, validly executed and acknowledged by the Prospective Tenant and executed by Landlord (hereinafter referred to as a "Lease"), Landlord will pay to Broker one (1) leasing commission based upon the following formula:

_____
_____
_____
_____
_____
_____
_____
_____

EXHIBIT 7.8 *(Continued)*

III. LIMITATIONS ON COMMISSIONS

A. Exclusions. In computing the rental upon which the aforesaid commission is based, the following shall be excluded and no commission shall be earned thereon:

(1) **Increase In Rent.** Increase(s) in rent pursuant to any escalation provision of said Lease.

(2) **Subletting by Landlord from Tenant.** Rental upon any portion of the demised premises payable or credited by Landlord to Prospective Tenant by reason of the subletting of all or any portion of the demised premises by Landlord or Tenant.

(3) **Percentage Rent.** Percentage rentals.

(4) **Tenant's Extras.** Rentals or any compensation payable by the Prospective Tenant for parking, leasehold improvements, decorations, utilities over standard utilities or services or other tenant extras furnished or paid for by Landlord or Tenant.

(5) **Security Deposits.** Any security deposits whenever paid.

(6) **Termination Payments.** Any payment made by Tenant in connection with a termination or cancellation of the Lease.

B. Exclusions Based on Renewal and Additional Space. No commission shall be earned or paid to Broker as a result of any renewal, option, or extension of the Lease between Landlord and the Prospective Tenant. No such commission shall be earned or paid as a result of the exercise of an option by or other right of the Prospective Tenant for additional space.

C. Exclusions Based on Cancellation. If the Lease shall provide that the Lease may be cancelled by either party at any time prior to the commencement of the term thereof, then in the event that the Lease shall in fact be so cancelled, no commission shall be deemed due or earned by Broker, and Broker shall credit against future commissions earned by Broker pursuant to this Agreement any sums which may have been theretofore paid or advanced by Landlord, to Broker with respect to said Lease.

IV. REGISTRATION

Landlord agrees that it shall pay any commissions earned by Broker pursuant to the requirements of Section II above, if within ninety (90) days following termination of this Agreement by either Landlord or Broker, the Project or any portion thereof is leased to any person or entity to whom Broker has submitted the Project and with whom Broker has entered into substantial negotiations for the Project prior to the expiration of the term or termination of the Agreement, the identity of whom has been provided to and approved by Landlord. Broker agrees to submit a list to Landlord of all persons or entities satisfying the foregoing conditions of submittal and substantial negotiation not later than fifteen (15) days following the expiration of the Term or earlier termination of the Agreement. Landlord shall have an additional fifteen (15) days from its receipt of said list to approve it.

V. LANDLORD'S RIGHT TO REJECT LEASE

It is expressly agreed that Landlord shall have the unqualified right, in its sole and absolute discretion, to refuse to enter into the Lease for any reason whatsoever without Landlord incurring any obligation to Broker for the payment of a commission, or otherwise.

VI. INDEMNITY

Broker warrants and represents to Landlord that Broker is a licensed broker in good standing under the laws of the State of _____. Broker's Real Estate License Number is _____.

Broker shall indemnify Landlord, its partners (collectively referred to as "Indemnitees") and the agents, servants, and employees of each of said Indemnitee, from any and all claims, demands, losses, causes of action, arbitrations, attorney's fees, expert witness fees and costs of defense to the extent that they are based upon any negligent, reckless, unlawful or intentionally wrongful act or

EXHIBIT 7.8 *(Continued)*

omission by Broker, its agents, servants or employees, including, but not limited to, representations, concealments, nondisclosures, claims for personal injury or death, or injury to or destruction of tangible property, related to or arising out of performance of the services of this Agreement to be performed by Broker.

VII. ASSIGNMENT AND BINDING EFFECT

This Agreement shall be binding upon and inure to the benefit of the heirs, administrators, executors, personal representatives and assigns of the respective parties hereto, provided, that this Agreement is a contract for provision of personal services by Broker pursuant to the delegations contained herein, and may not be assigned or transferred, nor may the rights, obligations, and duties of the Broker herein contained, be delegated to any other party or individual, without the prior written approval of Landlord, which approval may be withheld or conditioned as Landlord may deem appropriate.

VIII. EXCLUSIVE LEASING

The Broker and Landlord agree that until the Termination Date, or earlier termination of this Agreement, the Broker shall be the exclusive leasing agent with respect to Leases covering all or any part of the Project.

IX. INDEPENDENT CONTRACTOR RELATIONSHIP

A.   Independent Contractor. It is understood and agreed that Broker's relationship to the Landlord is that of an independent contractor and not an employee and that Landlord will not be held responsible for the collection and payment of taxes or contributions of any nature on behalf of the Broker.

B.   Representations and Concessions. The Broker, its agents, employees, or affiliates, shall make no representations, misrepresentations, warranties, concessions, or agreements pertaining to the Lease or the Project without the prior written approval of Landlord, and Landlord shall not be responsible for any representations, misrepresentations, warranties, concessions, or agreements, which Landlord does not expressly so approve and authorize.

X. BROKER'S WARRANTIES

Broker agrees to abide by all laws, ethical practices, standards, and regulations promulgated by the State of _____ Real Estate Commission, or equivalent thereto, as now exists or may be established from time to time. Broker further warrants and represents that it will devote sufficient time and services to secure Prospective Tenants for the Project in order to accomplish the purposes of Broker and Landlord.

XI. ENTIRE AGREEMENT AND ATTORNEY'S FEES

This Agreement contains the entire agreement of the parties respecting the delegation to Broker by Landlord, and no representations, promises, or agreements, oral or otherwise, between the parties not embodied herein shall be of any force or effect. In the event that at any time during the term of this Agreement either Landlord or Broker shall institute any action or proceeding against the other relating to the provisions of this Agreement, or any default hereunder, then, and in that event, the unsuccessful party in such action or proceeding agrees to reimburse the prevailing party for the reasonable costs, expenses, attorneys' fees and disbursements incurred therein by the prevailing party.

XII. NO DISCRIMINATION

It is understood that Landlord does not discriminate against any tenant or Prospective Tenant including, but not limited to, discrimination by reason of race, color, creed, national origin, handicap, religion, sex, age or any other protected class of persons.

XIII. BROKER'S EXPENSES

A.   Broker will be responsible for all its expenses.

B.   At Landlord's request, Broker will develop a Project brochure for the Project pursuant to the Landlord's specifications.

EXHIBIT 7.8 *(Continued)*

XIV. NOTICES

All notices and communications required under this Agreement shall be mailed certified mail, return receipt requested, or shall be delivered personally, to the addresses set forth below:

Landlord:

_____

_____

_____

To:

_____

_____

_____

Broker:

_____

_____

_____

The foregoing addresses may be changed by giving written notice to the other party. All notices shall be deemed delivered when personally served or when actually received through the mails as evidenced by the return receipt, whichever first occurs.

XV. MISCELLANEOUS

A. Time. Time is of the essence of this Agreement.

B. Law. This Agreement shall be interpreted under, and governed by, the laws of the State of Washington.

C. No Third Party Rights. Nothing herein shall create, or give rise to, any rights, claims, benefits, or preferences in any person, corporation, partnership, or other entity whatsoever.

D. Survival. The provisions of this Agreement shall survive the execution and delivery of any Lease.

E. Captions. The captions of this Agreement are for convenience and reference only and in no way define, limit, or describe the scope or intent of this Agreement, nor in any way affect this Agreement.

F. Amendment and Waiver. No agreement hereafter made shall be effective to change, modify, or discharge this Agreement or constitute a waiver of any of the provisions hereof, in whole or in part, unless such agreement is in writing and signed by the party against whom the enforcement of the change, modification, or discharge or waiver is sought.

IN WITNESS WHEREOF, the parties have entered into this Agreement as of the day and year first above written.

LANDLORD:

BROKER:

managers wishing to have their position protected if their investor purchases the property may use a non-exclusive brokerage agreement for this purpose. The agreement is between the property owner and the property management firm for the purpose of representing a particular buyer (Exhibit 7.9).

(h) LEASING COMMISSIONS

Commissions are the driving force behind all leasing activities, mainly because the leasing agent's livelihood comes solely from commission income. Therefore, structuring the commission schedule is one of the most critical elements in a marketing and leasing program. The commission schedule must be carefully thought out to provide the proper incentives to the leasing agent and to be a fair expense of the project.

Commissions are negotiable; there are no standard commission rates. The rate of commission is dependent upon several factors: the size of the space being leased, the length of the lease, the gross or net income the landlord earned during part or all of the lease term, the expertise of the property manager or leasing agent, the condition of the market, the difficulty of the leasing assignment, the property management or leasing company's cost of doing business, and what the property owner is willing to pay.

Frequently there is a difference of opinion between the property owner and the person responsible for leasing over what is a fair compensation for marketing the property and negotiating the leases. The difference of opinion is usually resolved after carefully negotiating the terms of the leasing agreement. Items that are negotiated are: amount of the commission, incentive commissions, and the timing of the payment of the commission. Other business terms are also negotiated as shown in Exhibit 7.9.

Commissions may be calculated according to different formulas. They can be based on a percentage of the gross or net rents. This method requires first determining which income will be used to calculate the commission. When the commission is based on the gross income, a percentage rate is applied to all the income and tenant charges the tenant will pay during a specific period of the lease. For instance, for a commission for a three-year lease with an industrial tenant who pays base rent and the real estate taxes and insurance on the building, the property owner would calculate the base rent collected during the three years and add to this amount the tenant's estimated reimbursement for real estate taxes and insurance for calculating the commission. If the commission is paid annually, the property owner would calculate the actual reimbursement of the tenant charges for determining the commission. Another method is calculating the commission as a percentage of the base rent only (known as *net income*).

EXHIBIT 7.9

Sample Non Exclusive Brokerage and Commission Agreement
Sale of Commercial Property
(Co-Broker)

THIS NON-EXCLUSIVE BROKERAGE AND COMMISSION AGREEMENT (hereinafter referred to as the "Agreement") is made and entered into this _____ day of _____, 19___, by and between _____ a _____ (hereinafter referred to as the "Owner") and _____ (hereinafter referred to as the "Broker").

W I T N E S S E T H:

WHEREAS, Broker is, or may be, engaged in certain negotiations between Owner and certain prospective purchasers (hereinafter collectively referred to as the "Prospective Purchaser") for the sale of the building or other improvements (hereinafter referred to as the "Project") known as _____ _____ and located in _____; and

WHEREAS, such sale negotiations have not been concluded; and

WHEREAS, Owner and Broker desire to set forth the terms and conditions which must be fulfilled before any commission or brokerage fee will be deemed earned by Broker or due from Owner by reason of the sale of the Project; and

WHEREAS, Owner and Broker desire to confirm and reduce to writing their entire understanding and agreement with respect to said sale negotiations, commissions and fees;

NOW, THEREFORE, in consideration of the mutual terms, covenants and agreements herein contained, together with other good and valuable consideration, the receipt and sufficiency of which is hereby acknowledged, the parties hereto hereby agree as follows:

1.   **Rate of Commission and Time of Payment**

(a)   As more fully set forth in Section 7 below, the Broker understands and agrees that _____ is the Owner's exclusive sales agent with respect to the sale of the Project. The Broker further understands and agrees that Broker shall earn a commission (the "Commission") with respect to the negotiations for and the sale of the Project only in the event all of the following conditions (the "Conditions") are fully satisfied. The Conditions set forth in Sections 1(a)(i), (ii) and (iii) must be fully satisfied prior to the Termination Date, as defined below, or the earlier termination of this Agreement. The Conditions are as follows:

(i)   The Broker shall deliver to Owner a written offer to purchase the Project as signed by the Prospective Purchaser.

(ii)   The Owner accepts and signs such written offer to purchase the Project in the form as presented by the Broker or, within the exercise of the Owner's sole discretion and judgment, modifies and signs such written offer to purchase, which modified offer to purchase is signed by the Prospective Purchaser (the written offer to purchase the Project signed by both Owner and the Prospective Purchaser shall be referred to herein as the "Offer").

EXHIBIT 7.9 *(Continued)*

(iii)   The Broker has delivered to Owner the written verification signed by the Prospective Purchaser as required under Section 4(b) below.

(iv)   The sale of the Project shall occur at the time and in the manner set forth in the Offer.

(b)   In the event all of the Conditions are fully satisfied at the times and in the manner specified in Section 1(a) above, then the Broker will have earned a Commission equal to _____% of the final sales price of the Project as set forth in the Offer (subject to the provisions of Section 2 below), which Commission shall be in the total amount of compensation, fees, brokerage and/or salesman's fees or other consideration due Broker by reason of its involvement in or with respect to the negotiation for or sale of the Project. The Broker agrees that the Commission shall be payable solely and exclusively from funds available to Owner from and at the closing of the sale of the Project pursuant to the Offer and from no other source. The Commission shall be payable through the escrow established for the closing of the sale of the Project pursuant to the Offer or by the Owner's check, as Owner may determine.

(c)   Broker understands and agrees that _____, as Owner's exclusive sales agent with respect to the Project, will earn a real estate brokerage commission upon the closing of the sale of the Project pursuant to the Offer. Broker hereby waives any right, title or interest in, to or under all or any portion of the real estate brokerage commission earned by ____ _____ by reason of the closing of the sale of the Project pursuant to the Offer or otherwise.

2. Limitations of Commissions.

(a)   **Exclusions.** In computing the final sales price upon which the aforesaid Commission is based, the following shall be excluded and no Commission shall be payable thereon:

(1)   **Lease Deposit:**. Any security, cleaning or other deposits, repayments or replenishments thereof, or prepayment of rent under any leases affecting the Project.

(2)   **Personal Property.** Any personal property transferred through or in conjunction with the Offer or the sale of the Project.

(3)   **Earnest Money Deposits.** Any earnest money or good faith deposits, extension fees, option fees or other such consideration, unless such fees and/or deposits are given as a credit toward the purchase price at the closing of the sale of the Project.

3. **No Commission if Offer to Purchase not Executed or Closed.** If, for any reason whatsoever, including but not limited to the acts, omissions, negligence or the willful default of Owner, its agents, employees or representatives, such Offer shall not be executed by and between Owner and the Prospective Purchaser and/or the transaction evidenced by the Offer shall fail to close for any reason, then no Commission or other brokerage or finders fee, or any portion thereof, shall be deemed due to or earned by Broker, nor shall the same be paid to Broker by Owner, and Owner is and shall be relieved from liability for the payment of any and all Commissions, fees, claims or charges whatsoever. It is expressly agreed that Owner shall have the unqualified right, in its sole and absolute discretion, to refuse to enter into and/or to modify and/or terminate the Offer and/or refuse to close the sale of the Project for any reason whatsoever without incurring any obligation to Broker for the payment of a Commission, brokerage or finders fee or otherwise.

EXHIBIT 7.9 *(Continued)*

4.   **Broker's Representations and Covenants.**

(a)   **General.** Broker warrants and represents to Owner that Broker is a licensed real estate broker in good standing under the laws of the State of _____, having Real Estate License No. _____ , and, except for _____ , is and shall be, the sole real estate broker, salesman, and/or finder involved in procuring the Offer; that no other broker, finder or person other than _____ and legal counsel for the Owner and the Prospective Purchaser have or has participated or shall participate in said negotiations for the Offer; that no other broker, finder or other person or entity is or will be entitled to any commission, brokerage fee, or finder's fee in connection with the Offer; that the Broker represents _____ _____ in the negotiations with respect to the Offer; and that Broker will fully comply with all laws, statutes, ordinances, rules and regulations by all applicable governmental authorities having jurisdiction over Broker.

(b)   **Verification by Purchaser.** In the event the Broker represents the Prospective Purchaser in the negotiations with respect to said Offer, then and in such event Broker shall, upon execution of this Agreement, deliver to Owner written evidence acceptable to Owner of such exclusive representation signed by the Prospective Purchaser. In the event the Broker shall fail or refuse to deliver such written evidence to Owner at the time and in the manner set forth above, then the Owner shall have no obligation to sign this Agreement, or if signed by Owner this Agreement shall not take effect until such written evidence is delivered to the Owner and Broker shall not be deemed to have earned a commission or fee, regardless of Broker's activities, until such evidence is delivered to Owner.

5.   **Assignment and Binding Effect.** This Agreement shall be binding upon and inure to the benefit of the heirs, administrators, executors, and personal representatives of Owner. This Agreement is a personal services contract on behalf of the Broker and neither (a) the Broker's Commission, if any, rights, obligations and/or benefits under this Agreement may be assigned or transferred nor (b) may the rights, obligations and duties of the Broker herein contained, be delegated, without the prior written approval of the Owner, which approval may be withheld or conditioned as the Landlord may deem appropriate.

6.   **Expiration and Termination.**

(a)   **Expiration Date.** Subject to the provisions of Section 6(c) below, the Commission, if any, to be paid under this Agreement will become due and payable only if the written Offer referred to herein is fully executed and acknowledged by all necessary parties prior to _____ , 19___, which shall be the Expiration Date hereof.

(b)   **Termination.** It is understood and agreed that this Agreement may be terminated by Owner on not less than ten (10) days' written notice. In the event of such termination, Broker shall receive a Commission for the sale of the Project only upon the terms and provisions set forth herein. In the event this Agreement is terminated prior to the Expiration Date as set forth above, then Broker shall immediately cease all negotiations with Prospective Purchasers except those Prospective Purchasers which Broker represents as described in Section 4(a) above.

(c)   **Registration Period.** Not later than the Expiration Date and within five (5) days after an earlier termination of this Agreement pursuant to Section 6(b) above, the Broker shall deliver to Owner a true and complete list (the "Registration List") of all Prospective Purchasers represented by Broker, all Prospective Purchasers with whom Broker has negotiated for the sale of the Project, and/or to whom the Broker has presented the Project as a viable purchase opportunity. In the event the Owner shall enter into an Offer with any Prospective Purchaser on the Registration List within ninety (90) days (the "Registration Period") after the Expiration Date or date of earlier termination of this Agreement, then and in such event the Owner shall pay the Commission to Broker at the time, in the amount and upon

EXHIBIT 7.9 *(Continued)*

the satisfaction of the conditions imposed upon the payment of the Commission above as if the Offer was entered into prior to the Expiration Date or prior to the earlier termination date.

(d)   No Commission after Registration Period. If no Offer is fully executed between Owner and the Prospective Purchaser, and if the conditions to payment of a Commission are not satisfied by the Expiration Date or date of earlier termination (as said dates are extended for the Registration Period with respect to Prospective Purchasers on the Registration List), then no Commission or other brokerage fee or compensation of any sort shall be payable by Owner to Broker under any circumstances even if a sale of the Project is thereafter consummated between Owner and the Prospective Purchaser, and even if such sale is consummated with a Prospective Purchaser with whom Broker has negotiated for the sale of the Project.

7.   **Non-Exclusive Sale Agreement.** Broker understands and agrees that _____ _____ is the Owner's exclusive sales agent with respect to the negotiations for and sale of the Project with the Prospective Purchaser presented to Owner by Broker. The Broker further understands and agrees that this is an open listing agreement, and that Owner reserves the right to offer the Project for sale through any other broker without payment to Broker of any Commission. Broker shall be entitled to a Commission only in the event that Broker procures a Prospective Purchaser who purchases the Project in accordance with the terms and conditions of this Agreement and if the Broker otherwise fully performs all of the Broker's obligations under this Agreement.

8.   **Independent Contractor Relationship.**

(a)   Independent Contractor. It is understood and agreed that Broker's relationship to Owner is that of an independent contractor and not an employee and that the Owner will not be held responsible for the collection and payment of taxes or contributions of any nature on behalf of the Broker.

(b)   Representations and Concessions. The Broker shall make no representations, warranties, concessions or agreements pertaining to the Project without the prior written approval of the Owner and the Owner shall not be responsible for or with respect to, and Broker shall indemnify, defend and hold Owner harmless from and against any loss, damage, injury, judgment, cost or expense (including attorneys' fees) incurred or charged by or against Owner by reason of any representations, warranties, concessions or agreements which Owner does not so approve in writing.

9.   **Broker's Warranties.** Broker agrees to abide by all laws, ethical practices standards and regulations promulgated by the State of _____ Real Estate Commission, or equivalent thereto, as now exists or may be established from time to time.

10.   **Entire Agreement and Attorney's Fees.** This Agreement contains the entire agreement of the parties respecting the engagement of Broker by Owner, and no representations, promises, or agreements, oral or otherwise, between the parties not embodied herein shall be of any force and effect. In the event that at any time during the term of this Agreement either Owner or Broker shall institute any action or proceeding against the other relating to the provisions of this Agreement, or any default hereunder (including court actions or mandatory arbitrations), then, and in that event, the unsuccessful party in such action or proceeding agrees to reimburse the prevailing party for the reasonable costs, expenses, attorneys' fees and disbursements incurred therein by the prevailing party.

11.   **No Discrimination.** It is understood that the Owner shall not discriminate against any Prospective Purchaser including, but not limited to, discrimination by reason of race, color, creed, national origin, sex, or age.

EXHIBIT 7.9 *(Continued)*

12.   **Miscellaneous.**

(a)   **Time.** Time is of the essence of this Agreement.

(b)   **Law.** This Agreement shall be interpreted under, and governed by, the laws of the State of _____.

(c)   **No Third Party Rights.** Nothing herein shall create, or give rise to, any rights, claims, benefits or preferences in any person, corporation, partnership or other entity whatsoever.

(d)   **Survival.** The provisions of this Agreement shall survive the execution and delivery of the Agreement and the sale of the Project.

(e)   **Captions.** The captions of this Agreement are for convenience and reference only and in no way define, limit or describe the scope or intent of this Agreement nor in any way affect this Agreement.

(f)   **Amendment and Waiver.** No agreement hereafter made shall be effective to change, modify or discharge this Agreement or constitute a waiver of any of the provisions hereof, in whole or in part, unless such agreement is in writing and signed by the party against whom enforcement of the change, modification or discharge or waiver is sought.

IN WITNESS WHEREOF, the parties have entered into this Agreement as of the day and year first above written.

OWNER   BROKER

_____   _____

By.   _____   By: _____
       Its: _____   Its: _____

Co-Broker

EXHIBIT 7.10

Exclusive Leasing Commission Agreement

THIS EXCLUSIVE LEASING COMMISSION AGREEMENT (hereinafter referred to as the "Agreement") is made and entered into this _____ day of _____, 19 , by and between _____ (hereinafter referred to as "Landlord"), and _____ (hereinafter referred to as the "Broker").

W I T N E S S E T H:

WHEREAS, Landlord is the owner of _____
_____
_____

WHEREAS, Landlord desires to delegate certain leasing responsibilities to Broker subject to the terms and conditions of this Agreement, and Broker agrees to accept such responsibilities and to perform them according to the terms and conditions contained herein; and

WHEREAS, pursuant to this Agreement, Broker is or may be engaged in certain negotiations between Landlord and certain prospective tenants (hereinafter collectively referred to as the "Prospective Tenant") for one or more leases covering space in the Project; and

WHEREAS, such negotiations have not been concluded; and

WHEREAS, Landlord and Broker desire to set forth the terms and conditions which must be fulfilled prior to any commission due from Landlord being deemed to have been earned by Broker; and

WHEREAS, Landlord and Broker desire to confirm and reduce to writing their entire understanding and agreement with respect to said negotiations, commissions, and fees;

NOW, THEREFORE, in consideration of the mutual terms, covenants, and agreements herein contained, together with other good and valuable consideration, the receipt and sufficiency of which is hereby acknowledged, the parties hereto hereby agree as follows:

I.   RATE OF COMMISSION AND TIME OF PAYMENT

Lease Commission Calculation. In the event, prior to the Termination Date of this Agreement as defined below or earlier termination, the Broker delivers to Landlord written leases, executed and acknowledged by the Prospective Tenant and acceptable to Landlord as evidenced by its execution thereof (hereinafter referred to as a "Lease"), Landlord will pay to Broker one (1) leasing commission based upon the following formula:

_____
_____
_____
_____
_____
_____
_____
_____

II.   LIMITATIONS ON COMMISSIONS

A.   Exclusions. In computing the rental upon which the aforesaid commission is based, the following shall be excluded and no commission shall be earned thereon:

(1) Increase in Rent. Increase(s) in rent pursuant to any escalation provision of said Lease whereby the Prospective Tenant is obligated to pay an increased rental based upon any escalator provision or index, or pay a share of Landlord's costs over the term of the Lease, including, but not limited to, taxes, assessments, insurance premiums, common area maintenance charges, and/or other expenses.

(2) Subletting by Landlord from Tenant. Rental upon any portion of the demised premises payable or credited by Landlord

EXHIBIT 7.10 *(Continued)*

to Prospective Tenant by reason of Landlord's retaining, as subtenant or otherwise, any portion of the demised premises.

(3) <u>Percentage Rent</u>. Percentage rentals.

(4) <u>Tenant's Extras</u>. Rentals or any compensation payable by the Prospective Tenant for parking, leasehold improvements, decorations, or Tenant's extras furnished or paid for by Landlord, or utilities or equipment charges where such equipment charges are identified as such in the Lease or where the cost for the same is a part of the rent charged the Prospective Tenant under the Lease.

(5) <u>Security Deposits</u>. Any security deposits, and repayments or replenishments thereof.

(6) <u>Termination Payments</u>. Any payment made or to be made by Tenant in connection with a termination or cancellation of the Lease.

B. <u>Exclusions Based on Renewal and Additional Space</u>. No commission shall be earned or paid to Broker as a result of any renewal or extension of the Lease between Landlord and the Prospective Tenant, whether or not such renewal, or extension, is the result of an option for renewal, or extension contained in the Lease. No such commission shall be earned or paid as a result of the exercise of an option by or other right of the Prospective Tenant for additional space.

C. <u>Exclusions Based on Cancellation</u>. If the Lease shall provide that the Lease may be cancelled by either party at any time prior to the commencement of the term thereof, then in the event that the Lease shall in fact be so cancelled, no commission shall be deemed due or earned by Broker, and Broker shall credit against future commissions earned by Broker pursuant to this Agreement any sums which may have been theretofore paid or advanced by Landlord, to Broker with respect to said Lease.

III. <u>REGISTRATION</u>.

Landlord agrees that it shall pay any commissions earned by Broker pursuant to the requirements of Sections I.A and I.C above, if within ninety (90) days following termination of this Agreement by either Landlord or Broker, the Project or any portion thereof is leased to any person or entity to whom Broker has submitted the Project and with whom Broker has entered into substantial negotiations for the Project prior to the expiration of the term or termination of the Agreement, the identity of whom has been provided to and approved by Landlord. Broker agrees to submit a list to Landlord of all persons or entities satisfying the foregoing conditions of submittal and substantial negotiation not later than fifteen (15) days following the expiration of the Term or termination of the Agreement. Landlord shall have an additional fifteen (15) days from its receipt of said list to approve it.

IV. <u>NO COMMISSION IF LEASE NOT EXECUTED</u>.

If, for any reason whatsoever, including, but not limited to, the acts, omissions, negligence or the willful default of Landlord, its agents, employees, or representatives, any Lease shall not be entered into between Landlord and a Prospective Tenant, then no commission, shall be deemed to be due or earned, nor shall the same be paid to Broker by Landlord, and Landlord is and shall be relieved from liability for the payment of any and all commissions, claims, or charges whatsoever. It is expressly agreed that Landlord shall have the unqualified right, in its sole and absolute discretion, to refuse to enter into the Lease for any reason whatsoever without Landlord incurring any obligation to Broker for the payment of a commission, or otherwise. It is further agreed that for any commission to be deemed due or earned, Broker must satisfy the requirements set forth in Section I.A and III above.

V. <u>INDEMNITY</u>.

Broker warrants and represents to Landlord that Broker is a licensed broker in good standing under the laws of the State of _____. Broker's Real Estate License No. in _____, is _____.

EXHIBIT 7.10 *(Continued)*

Broker shall indemnify Landlord, its partners (collectively referred to as "indemnitees") and the agents, servants, and employees of each of said Indemnitee, from any and all claims, demands, losses, causes of action, arbitrations, attorney's fees, expert witness fees and costs of defense to the extent that they are based upon any negligent, reckless or intentional wrongful act or failure to act by Broker, its agents, servants or employees, including, but not limited to, representations, concealments, nondisclosures, claims for personal injury, sickness, disease or death, or injury to or destruction of tangible property, related to or arising out of performance of the services of this Agreement to be performed by Broker.

VI.   ASSIGNMENT AND BINDING EFFECT.

This Agreement shall be binding upon and inure to the benefit of the heirs, administrators, executors, personal representatives and assigns of the respective parties hereto, provided, that this Agreement is a contract for provision of personal services by Broker pursuant to the delegations contained herein, and may not be assigned or tranferred, nor may the rights, obligations, and duties of the Broker herein contained, be delegated to any other party or individual, without the prior written approval of Landlord, which approval may be withheld or conditioned as Landlord may deem appropriate.

VII.   TERM; TERMINATION.

A.   Commencement Date and Termination Date. The term of this Agreement shall commence as of _____, which shall be the "Commencement Date." It shall continue until midnight, Seattle, Washington, time on _____ unless sooner terminated pursuant to the terms hereof, which shall be the "Termination Date" of this Agreement.

B.   Termination. It is understood and agreed that this Agreement may be terminated by Landlord or Broker on not less than thirty (30) days written notice. In the event of such termination, Broker shall receive from Landlord any commissions earned and which are then due and payable, according to the terms of Section I above.

VIII.   EXCLUSIVE LEASING.

The Broker and Landlord agree that until the Termination Date, or earlier termination of this Agreement, the Broker shall be the exclusive Leasing Agent with respect to Leases covering all or any part of the Project.

IX.   INDEPENDENT CONTRACTOR RELATIONSHIP.

A.   Independent Contractor. It is understood and agreed that Broker's relationship to the Landlord is that of an independent contractor and not an employee and that Landlord will not be held responsible for the collection and payment of taxes or contributions of any nature on behalf of the Broker.

B.   Representations and Concessions. The Broker, its agents, employees, or affiliates, shall make no representations, misrepresentations, warranties, concessions, or agreements pertaining to the Lease or the Project without the prior written approval of Landlord, and Landlord shall not be responsbile for any representations, misrepresentations, warranties, concessions, or agreements, which Landlord does not expressly so approve and authorize.

X.   BROKER'S WARRANTIES.

Broker agrees to abide by all laws, ethical practices, standards, and regulations promulgated by the State of Washington Real Estate Commission, or equivalent thereto, as now exists or may be established from time to time. Broker further warrants and represents that it will devote sufficient time and services to secure Prospective Tenants for the Project in order to accomplish the purposes of Broker and Landlord. Broker further warrants not to make any representations, misrepresentations, concessions or agreements regarding any Lease with a Prospective Tenant, the Project, or any other Prospective Tenant, which has not been approved expressly by Landlord.

EXHIBIT 7.10 *(Continued)*
XI.   LEASING AGREEMENT.

Broker agrees and acknowledges that is is subject to all terms and conditions of the Leasing Agreement, in addition to the terms and conditions set forth herein.

XII.   ENTIRE AGREEMENT AND ATTORNEY'S FEES.

This Agreement contains the entire agreement of the parties respecting the delegation to Broker by Landlord, and no representations, promises, or agreements, oral or otherwise, between the parties not embodied herein shall be of any force or effect. In the event that at any time during the term of this Agreement either Landlord or Broker shall institute any action or proceeding against the other relating to the provisions of this Agreement, or any default hereunder, then, and in that event, the unsuccessful party in such action or proceeding agrees to reimburse the prevailing party for the reasonable costs, expenses, attorneys' fees and disbursements incurred therein by the prevailing party.

XIII.   NO DISCRIMINATION.

It is understood that Landlord does not discriminate against any tenant or Prospective Tenant including, but not limited to, discrimination by reason of race, color, creed, national origin, handicap, religion, sex, or age.

XIV.   BROKER'S EXPENSES.

A.   Broker will be responsible for all its expenses.

B.   Broker will, at Broker's expense pay for a Project brochure which was developed by Broker and Landlord.

XV.   NOTICES

All notices and communications required under this Agreement shall be mailed certified mail, return receipt requested, or shall be delivered personally to the addresses set forth below:

Landlord:

_____

_____

To: _____

_____

_____

_____

And to: _____

_____

_____

_____

Broker:

_____

_____

_____

The foregoing addresses may be changed by giving written notice to the other party. All notices shall be deemed delivered when personally served or when actually received through the mails as evidenced by the return receipt, whichever first occurs.

XVI.   MISCELLANEOUS.

A.   Time.   Time is of the essence of this Agreement.

B.   Law.   This Agreement shall be interpreted under, and governed by, the laws of the State of Washington.

EXHIBIT 7.10 *(Continued)*

C.   <u>No Third Party Rights</u>. Nothing herein shall create, or give rise to, any rights, claims, benefits, or preferences in any person, corporation, partnership, or other entity whatsoever.

D.   <u>Survival</u>. The provisions of this Agreement shall survive the execution and delivery of any Lease.

E.   <u>Captions</u>. The captions of this Agreement are for convenience and reference only and in no way define, limit, or describe the scope or intent of this Agreement, nor in any way affect this Agreement.

F.   <u>Amendment and Waiver</u>. No agreement hereafter made shall be effective to change, modify, or discharge this Agreement or constitute a waiver of any of the provisions hereof, in whole or in part, unless such agreement is in writing and signed by the party against whom the enforcement of the change, modification, or discharge or waiver is sought.

IN WITNESS WHEREOF, the parties have entered into this Agreement as of the day and year first above written.

LANDLORD:

_____
_____

By: _____
_____
_____

By: _____
Its: _____
_____
_____

By: _____
Its: _____
_____
_____

Broker:

_____
_____
_____

NOTARY

STATE OF WASHINGTON   )
                      :   ss.
COUNTY OF KING   )

I certify that I know or have satisfactory evidence that
_____ signed this instrument, on oath stated that
he/she was authorized to execute the instrument, and acknowledged it as the
_____ of _____ to be the free and
voluntary act of such party for the uses and purposes mentioned in the
instrument.

DATED: _____,

_____
Notary Public in and for the
State of Washington, residing
at _____. My
commission expires _____

TABLE 7.1

Calculation of Commission Based on Percentage of Income

Lease Year	Space (Sq. Ft.)	Rental Rate	Annual Income
1	2,000	$15	$ 30,000
2	2,000	15	30,000
3	2,000	15	30,000
4	2,000	17	34,000
5	2,000	17	34,000
		Total Base Income	$158,000

Total Base Income	$158,000
Percentage Rate (5%)	× .05
Commission	$ 7,900

Next, determine what period of time during the lease term is used to calculate the commission. For instance, the agreement may state that the income during the entire lease term is used to calculate the commission. If the lease term is for fifty years, possibly only the income during the first ten years is used to calculate the commission. Finally, determine which percentage rate will be used and whether it will be a fixed or a sliding percentage rate for the term of the lease the commission is being paid.

An example of a commission based on a percentage of the income is shown in Table 7.1. A lease for 2,000 square feet of space in an office building for five years at $15 per square feet for three years and $17 per square feet for two years. The commission is based on 5 percent of the base rent received during the entire term of the lease.

A shopping center space of 1,400 square feet is leased for four years at a base rent of $16.50 per square foot. Table 7.2 shows a commission

TABLE 7.2

Calculation of Commission Based on Base Rent

Lease Year	Space (Sq. Ft.)	Rental Rate	Base Income	Commission Rate (%)	Commission
1	1,400	× $16.50	$23,100 ×	.06 =	$1,386
2	1,400	× 16.50	23,100 ×	.05 =	1,155
3	1,400	× 16.50	23,100 ×	.04 =	924
4	1,400	× 16.50	23,100 ×	.03 =	693
				Total Commission	$4,158

calculated on the base rent as follows: 6 percent the first year, 5 percent the second year, 4 percent the third year, and 3 percent the fourth year.

Another method for calculating commissions is based on a dollar amount per square foot leased. The shopping center industry first adopted this method in the late 1970s. Some developers believed that a conflict could arise over the length of the lease if the commission were based on the income over the term of the lease. The developers preferred shorter leases, ranging from three to five years. This enabled them to roll the leases over, increase the rents, and improve other terms more frequently than they could with longer term leases. If commissions were based on a percentage of the income over the life of the lease, the leasing agent might be encouraged to negotiate longer term leases because the commission would be greater. These developers negotiated a fixed dollar amount per square foot for leases beyond a certain length, say, three years. If the lease term were less than this, the commission would be pro rated.

Examples of commissions based on a fixed dollar amount per square foot:

Example 1

Lease terms:	A shopping center lease on 2,000 square feet for four years at $15 per square foot
Commission terms:	$3 per square foot on leases of three years or longer and pro rata for less than three years.
Formula:	Space square footage × commission rate = commission, or
	2,000-sq.-ft. space × $3/sq. ft. commission rate = $6,000 commission

Example 2

Lease term:	A lease on an industrial space of 5,000 square feet for two years at $12 per square foot
Commission terms:	$3.50 per square foot on leases three years or longer and prorated for less than three years
Formula:	Space square footage × commission rate = commission, or
	5,000-sq.-ft. space × $2.35 prorated (.67 × $3.50) commission rate = $11,750 commission

Commissions can be negotiated as a fixed amount for a specific space. For example, a commission of $10,000 will be paid for a sublease of 4,000 square feet for 2½ years at a rate in excess of $11 per square foot.

A commission may be paid based on an hourly basis to negotiate a lease. For example, a property owner has a prospective tenant and hires a property manager or leasing agent to negotiate the terms and pays the broker $200 per hour.

How commissions are to be paid is another negotiable item. One method is to pay the commission in its entirety when the lease is executed. Most landlords do not favor this method because the tenant may never move into the space.

Another method is to pay one half when the lease is executed and one half when the tenant opens for business. Some property owners will extend the second half commission to the time the tenant opens for business and commences to pay base rent. This extension is to encourage the leasing agent to give as little free rent as possible. If the tenant is financially weak, the owner may wish to delay paying a portion of the commission until the tenant has paid a few month's rent. For instance, the commission may be paid in thirds: at the time of lease execution, when the tenant opens for business and commences paying base rent, and when the twelfth monthly rent payment is received. Commissions may be paid monthly during the term of the lease. When the tenant pays its monthly rent, a commission is paid for that portion of the income from that lease. The commission on a five-year lease is paid at a rate of one sixtieth each month. When this is the agreement, the property owner may be willing to pay the entire commission on a discounted basis when the tenant moves in.

Commissions for a pad or ground lease could be based on a percentage of the gross or net income, an amount per square foot of building or pad area, the first year's rent or a fixed amount, or any other method left up to the imagination of the property owner and the property manager or leasing agent.

Incentive Commissions

Incentive commissions are offered by the property owner when the leasing market is soft or as an incentive to achieve a specific leasing goal. They can be an effective method of obtaining either the attention of the brokerage community or the additional effort of the exclusive leasing agent. A simple incentive is a commission and a half or a double commission.

In a soft market, a property owner may offer a double commission for making a deal on the property. Some owners will offer an expensive gift, a car, or a trip to the Caribbean or Hawaii if a leasing agent or property manager leases a minimum amount of space. A word of caution: All states require commissions to be paid to the broker, not the real estate salesperson or leasing agent. Most property managers and leasing agents are not brokers but associate brokers or real estate salespeople. When a commission is paid to the broker, it is shared with the person making the lease based on a formula the brokerage firm has agreed on. If an expensive gift is all or part of the commission, it must be given to the broker, not the leasing agent. The broker and the leasing agent then decide who will receive the gift.

Most incentive commissions are additional monies paid to the broker and can be based on a number of situations—for example, leasing a particular space that has been vacant for a long time. On a new development, incentive commissions can be based on a percentage of the space leased by the grand opening of the building or a specific period of time after the grand opening. For instance, an additional $1 per square foot can be paid on all spaces leased if the office building is 75 percent leased at grand opening, and an additional 50 cents per square foot on all spaces leased if the office building is 90 percent leased one year after the grand opening.

Incentive commissions can also be based on an average rental rate. For example, an additional 2 percent commission can be paid on all space leased within 12 months of the date the new building receiving its certificate of occupancy if the average rental rate exceeds $30 per square foot and 80 percent of the building is leased.

Renewals

Renewals are another source of commission income. Renewal commissions can be determined any number of ways, including a fixed dollar amount, a percentage of the commission for a new lease, the same commission as for a new lease, or an hourly rate. Lease renewals may be one of the responsibilities of the management company and compensation is included in the management fee. The management fee may include lease renewals, with the property manager being responsible for the renewals, or it may be an additional fee to the property management company.

Options

Most property owners prefer not to pay a commission when a tenant exercises an option. If the commission on the original terms of the lease was based on a dollar amount per square foot, an agreed upon fixed dollar amount, or an hourly basis, there would be no additional commission if the tenant exercised an option. If the commission was based on a percentage of the gross or net income, the option period would become an issue to negotiate. The property owner would probably maintain that the commission paid on the original term of the lease completed the agreement between the owner and the leasing agent. The leasing agent would argue that another commission is due because the option was included in the lease negotiations. This is yet another issue to negotiate in the commission agreement or management agreement.

If the commission agreement excludes payment on options, and the property manager receives a commission on renewals, the question is,

Should the leasing agent or the property manager be paid a commission when the tenant exercises an option right? Most property owners will argue that if the terms of the option were prenegotiated, and the tenant only has to notify the owner or manager in writing that the option will be exercised, a commission has not been earned by the manager. The manager will reason that if the option states that the rental rate must be negotiated or is adjusted to market rate, then the rental rate must be negotiated, and this is similar to negotiating a lease renewal.

Should a commission be reimbursed to the property owner if the tenant does not fulfill the terms of the lease? This is an issue that should be addressed in the leasing agreement. This situation usually arises when a tenant files bankruptcy or vacates without notice before the lease expires. The leasing agent or property manager presents a prospective tenant to the property owner who has the responsibility of deciding whether or not to accept the tenant. If the tenant files bankruptcy and stops paying rent, or vacates the premises and stops paying rent during the first year of the lease, the property manager or leasing agent would be prudent to maintain a good relationship with the property owner and either refuse the portion of the commission yet to be earned or find a replacement tenant at no additional fee or a partial fee to the owner.

Commissions have traditionally been paid by the property owner, but more and more tenants are hiring and paying brokers to find them space and to negotiate on their behalf. Commissions can be a major expense of the property owner and a major source of income for the property manager and leasing agent. All the terms of the commission agreement are negotiable, and care must be exercised when negotiating the terms, especially the commission amount and payment schedule. The property owner must always remember that commissions are the driving force behind leasing deals, and these deals create the building's value.

Leasing Meetings and Reports

There is no issue more important to a property owner than leasing. Value is created by the income stream, and the income stream starts with leasing. A property owner who is not aware of the activities of the leasing and marketing program can easily become discouraged with the leasing team and may eventually change leasing personnel.

Regular leasing meetings and reports can accomplish several objectives:

1. Keep the property owner informed of the leasing team's activities
2. Keep the property owner aware of changes in the market rental rates

3. Enable the property owner and leasing team to adjust the property's rental rates and concessions to reflect changes in the market
4. Review the marketing and leasing activities since the previous ʹleasing meeting
5. Review the prospects listed in the leasing report
6. Review proposals and counterproposals

A leasing report is provided by the leasing personnel at the beginning of the meeting. The report needs to be tailored to the property. The leasing prospect report in Exhibit 7.11 outlines the state of each prospect. A supplementary report may be included to show: the amount of space available, leases out for signature, spaces occupied and vacant, tenants' move-in and move-out during the past month, the amount of tenant improvements, the commission paid and budgeted to date, and the average rent per square foot achieved to date. A map or floor plan of the property is color coded for spaces leased but not occupied, occupied, leases out for signature, and leases in serious negotiations.

Meetings should not be held too often or be too lengthy to avoid taking up the leasing personnel's valuable leasing time. Yet, if the meetings are held too infrequently, communication breaks down. A one- to two-hour meeting every two to four weeks is usually sufficient to accomplish the objectives. During these meetings, the property owner or representative will be able to judge whether or not the leasing personnel are motivated to continue to lease the property and whether they are devoting sufficient time to marketing and leasing the property.

If the property owner is an absentee owner or asset manager who visits the property only two to four times a year, the property manager needs to include a thorough leasing report in the monthly management report. In addition, the property manager and leasing personnel should call the owner or asset manager at least monthly to review the leasing status of the property (Exhibit 7.11).

§ 7.6 LEASING PACKAGE

The leasing package is helpful for both brokers and prospective tenants. Brokers use it to keep current on the property. Prospective tenants most often become aware of a property either by driving the area and visiting the property or by receiving a leasing package.

There are three approaches to presenting a prospective tenant with a leasing package. The first approach is to provide sufficient but limited information to pique the prospect's interest. If the prospect shows continued interest, then the full leasing package is provided. This approach is used when the leasing package is too expensive to be mailed

EXHIBIT 7.11

Leasing Prospects Report

PROJECT NAME: College Plaza

MONTH: March/1993

DATE PREPARED: March 30, 1993

PREPARED BY: Joan Jones

Suite #	Usable Sq.Ft.	Date Shown Space	Prospective Tenant (Company)	Type of Business	Name of Contact	Current Location	Phone #	Source	Term yrs	Rent Quoted	TI Work (cost)	Free Rent	Broker Comm.	Status/Remarks
A-12	1,400	3-23	Anita Cross	Health Fc	Anita	Highland St	786-5321	C	5	$12.00	?	?	$4200	4
A-14	1,400	3-23	Little Nickel Ads	Ads	Sandy	6th Avenue	381-4646	A	5	$12.00	?	?	$4200	4
B-2	1,500	2-3	Crystal Jewelers	Jewelry	George	None	385-3568	A	7	$13.50	$2,000	2 mos	$4500	0
B-4	2,800	2-15	Cards Galore	Cards/Gifts	Mary	West Mall	773-7766	C	10	$11.75	0	1 mo	$8400	1
B-6	1,400	1-6	Tanning/Toning	Tone/Tan	Karen	Main St	398-6868	B	3	$12.00	0	1 mo	$4200	2
B-10	2,800	12-10	Pizza/Pizza/Pizza	Restaurant	Mario	Broadway	589-6896	D	10	$11.75	0	2 mos	$8400	3
A-16	1,800	2-15	Sandwich Shop	"	Jim	None	785-1234	E	7	$12.00	0	1 mo	$5400	6

STATUS LEGEND
0 - Lease Completed   4 - Preliminary Project Talks
1 - Lease Out For Signatures   5 - Problem in Talks
2 - Lease Under Negotiations   6 - Dead Deal
3 - General Terms Discussion

SOURCE LEGEND
(How prospect found out about Building)
A. Drive-by   D. Direct Mailing
B. Newspaper Advertising   E. Broker
C. Cold Call by Property Staff   F. Other

Page _____ of _____

to thousands of prospects. The other approach is to provide the entire package to each prospect. A hybrid approach is to send the complete package to those prospects who have a high probability of leasing space, with all other prospects receiving the limited package.

All materials should be professionally prepared to reflect the quality of operation. An expensive four-color brochure is not required, but all materials should be complete, attractive, and easily understood.

The leasing package is designed to present the property in its best light and to answer as many questions as possible. An incomplete leasing package can misinform the prospect.

A discussion of items to include in a shopping center, office building, and industrial leasing package follows.

(a) THE LEASING PACKAGE: SHOPPING CENTERS

The leasing package for a retail tenant should include general information of interest to all retailers but should also be tailored to the specific retailer. There must be a balance between sending too much material, which will likely go unread, and sending too little information, which keeps the prospect from reaching any conclusions. The basic leasing package should contain a transmittal letter, a list of tenants, a plot plan, an area map, an aerial photograph of the site, if available, a demographic profile of the trade area, comments on the shopping center's sales and, if available, a merchants' association or marketing/promotional fund activity calendar.

Transmittal Letter

The letter of transmittal is a critical part of the leasing package. Neither leasing agents, especially for large chains who receive a great number of leasing packages, nor prospective tenants have the time to read long complicated packages. Therefore, the letter should be brief, professionally prepared, and addressed to an individual by name, telling the benefits of leasing space in the shopping center. Letters can be easily personalized through computer technology to address the specific features of the location and the specific requirements of the tenant. For example, a cover letter sent to ice cream parlors could mention the number of schools within walking distance of the shopping center. A letter sent to auto supply stores could emphasize the large percentage of blue-collar workers in the area.

Tenant List

Prospective tenants are most often interested in the center's existing and future tenants. Some merchants follow other merchants into new locations, as their past experience tells them they will do well next to a given merchant. It is helpful to list the merchant's trade name as well as what is sold: for example, "Lucky Market, a discount grocer."

It is also very important that the list of tenants not imply that a tenant has signed a lease for the subject center when the tenant is only in the negotiating stages. Should those negotiations fail, the leasing agent is open to possible liability from a tenant who was counting on a specific tenant for cross-traffic. Prudent owners will not reveal the name of a tenant if the lease has not been executed. The list should have a disclaimer stating that there is no assurance that tenants will not vacate the shopping center.

Plot Plan

The plot plan should be prepared specifically for leasing or modified for inclusion in the leasing package. The engineering plot plan may suffice, but it is not attractive. It is helpful to show trees and automobiles as well as tenants' names in the locations they occupy. A prospect may want to be next to the dress store or, conversely, may not want to be next to the pet store or the record shop. A disclaimer stating that the landlord does not guarantee the information, and that the information is subject to change, may protect the landlord from a lawsuit if the layout of the center changes, a tenant is replaced, or a major tenant moves out.

Map of the Area

The area map should show freeways and major roads. Important items should be clearly labeled for quick identification by the reader. If the location is not in an area readily known to many retailers, an area map is helpful in orienting the reader.

Aerial Photograph

Sophisticated retailers are interested in the immediate trade area. An aerial photograph very quickly tells the retailers the housing density in the area, the road patterns, and the shopping center's proximity to its competition. These photographs can be obtained rather inexpensively from companies that specialize in aerial photography. Many are shelf items.

Demographics/Psychographics

Complete demographic/psychographic packages can be obtained from any one of several companies specializing in demographic information. The demographic company is informed of the shopping center's cross streets and the area of demographic interest, such as a two- or four-mile radius. The information is usually prepared and delivered within 48 hours. This provides the prospect with a quick look at the area to help decide if the population in the area represents the store's customer base. See §§ 2.2 and 7.2 for more detail.

Center's Sales

An experienced tenant views any retail location on the basis of its probable sales potential. Rent is a function of sales. For this reason, it is important to show the tenant a strong sales potential, if it really exists. Care must be taken to keep the confidentiality of an individual merchant's sales, unless that merchant gives specific approval to reveal them. However, general indications can be given, such as: the shopping center sales are averaging $310 per square foot; sales are up 11 percent for the most recent twelve-month period; the fashion merchants are averaging sales of $325 per square foot; the market share of the shopping center is increasing steadily; the supermarket is number one in its division.

Any positive sales information is of interest to the knowledgeable merchant. Comparing a center's merchant sales with those in the *Dollars and Cents of Shopping Centers* will provide the basis for a meaningful evaluation.

Traffic Counts

Traffic passing the shopping center is very important. Absolutely accurate car counts are not required for any center, but traffic volume can be reported relative to other locations in town and by comparing current traffic counts with past counts. Traffic counts are measured on the basis of average daily automobile traffic passing the center. These figures are generally available from city, county, or state traffic agencies for little or no cost.

It is important to compare the automobile traffic counts on the shopping center's street with other streets in the area, as their relative counts are significant, but it is also important to measure the increase or decrease in traffic counts because it may affect the shopping center's location. At times the street with the second-best traffic count may be a better location because of less congestion at peak hours. It is possible that the automobile traffic on a street travels too fast to be of help to the shopping center. If traffic is one way and in the direction of work, many retailers, such as liquor stores, prefer homebound traffic. Many regional shopping centers have car counters built in at each entrance to provide daily traffic counts into the mall. Multiplying this number by the average number of persons in the car will provide daily customer traffic counts.

Merchants' Association or Marketing Fund's Calendar of Events

While some major tenants do not want any involvement with a merchants' association or marketing fund, it is still a positive aspect to any shopping center to have a coordinated advertising and promotion program. A professionally prepared calendar of events will show the prospect that there is a concern for the tenants' success and that there is a coordinated, ongoing effort to generate traffic, which should translate into higher sales for everyone. Photographs of successful merchandising, sales, or promotional events can create interest in a prospective tenant.

(b) THE LEASING PACKAGE: OFFICE BUILDINGS AND INDUSTRIAL PROPERTIES

Leasing packages for office buildings and industrial properties are very similar. Following is a review of information that can be included for either of these properties.

Brochure

Brochures can be a simple one-page, two-color handout or an elaborate, multicolor presentation. They may include a photo or rendering of the building, a location map, list of the building's features, and the leasing agent's name and phone number.

Building Photo

Color photos of the exterior and interior features of the building are of great assistance to an out-of-town company or prospects who must convince their headquarters of their building selection.

View Photo

Views are a desirable feature of an office building, especially water views. Photos taken from several floors will give different view perspectives. If the building is proposed or under construction, aerial photos are useful.

Floor Plan

A large floor plan showing common areas and window modules is used for office buildings. A plan showing office and warehouse space is used for industrial properties.

Transportation

A map indicating public transportation routes, freeways, and major arterials is useful for prospective tenants of both industrial and office properties. The industrial user may need additional information on air, water, and bus transportation.

Employment

The cost and availability of skilled and unskilled, union and nonunion labor are a major concern to industrial users and major service office users.

Housing

The cost of rental housing and the price of homes is a concern of some businesses.

Building Services

A list of tenants in the building who provide a service to other tenants, such as a stockbroker, restaurant, post office, or escrow company, is a helpful part of the leasing package.

Building Features

Special features, such as life safety, common area, and covered parking, are excellent selling points.

List of Tenants

Fortune 500 companies, well-known law firms, restaurants, and health clubs can add prestige to the building. Their names should be included in the leasing package.

Any information that will convey the message of service and quality and distinguish the building from the competition should be included in the leasing package.

§ 7.7   MEASURING TENANT SPACE

The method of measuring space in a building will have an impact on the building in many ways. Since rent is usually calculated on a dollar-per-square-foot basis, a tenant's rent is determined by multiplying this rate times the number of square feet leased. If a building is being measured by a method that is confusing or uncommon in the area, the building may develop a reputation for charging more for space than is common in the industry.

The property manager should contact other property managers, leasing agents, and property owners to investigate the accepted methods of measuring space in the geographic area in which the building is located. Managers who wish to pioneer a new method for measuring space in an area should proceed with caution, for the marketability of the building may be affected.

The only recognized standard for measuring office space is the one established in 1915 and revised in the early 1980s by BOMA and the American National Standard (Exhibit 7.12). However, there are regional differences that vary from this method, and some property owners prefer to use their own method.

Usable and rentable square footage, two commonly used methods to measure office building space, can be misleading to a tenant. Usable square footage is the space the tenant has within the demised premises. It is measured from the center of the demising walls (the walls between tenants) and from the inside surface of the dominant exterior wall and common area walls. The square footage is approximately the amount of square footage the tenant occupies. The slight difference is in the square footage lost by measuring to the center of the stud in the demising wall. For many years space was measured in this way. Tenants understood this measurement and knew that if they leased 1,000 square feet they had approximately 1,000 square feet to use; hence the term *usable square footage*. A 1,000-square-foot space at $20 per square foot rented for $20,000 annually.

New buildings usually must be leased at a higher rental rate than older buildings because of the increased costs of land, materials, and labor. In the late 1970s, some office building developers, wanting to have their rental rates sound competitive, switched to a rentable method of measuring space. For example, a developer needs a rent of $22,000 for 1,000 square feet of space but might not want to quote a rate of $22 per square foot when existing buildings are leasing for $20. The additional rent may be difficult to achieve in a soft leasing market. So the developer added on a "load factor" to the 1,000 square feet of usable area. The load factor is the percentage of the square footage of the common area on the tenant's floor and, in some cases, of the common areas in the building's entrance lobby. If the common area was 1,500 square feet and the tenant occupied 1,000 square feet on a 15,000-square-foot floor, the tenant is occupying 7.41 percent of the usable space on the floor (15,000 sq. ft. − 1,500 sq. ft. = 13,500 sq. ft. of usable area; 1,000 sq. ft. ÷ 13,500 sq. ft. = 7.41%); 7.41 percent of the 1,500 square feet of common area is 111 square feet of common area that will be added to the tenant's usable space of 1,000 square feet, giving the tenant 1,111 rentable square feet.

EXHIBIT 7.12

Standards for Measuring Office Space

American National Standard Z65.1-1980

Usable Area

The Usable Area of an office shall be computed by measuring to the finished surface of the office side of corridor and other permanent walls, to the center of partitions that separate the office from adjoining Usable Areas, and to the inside finished surface of the dominant portion of the permanent outer building walls.

No deductions shall be made for columns and projections necessary to the building.

The Usable Area of a floor shall be equal to the sum of all Usable Areas on that floor.

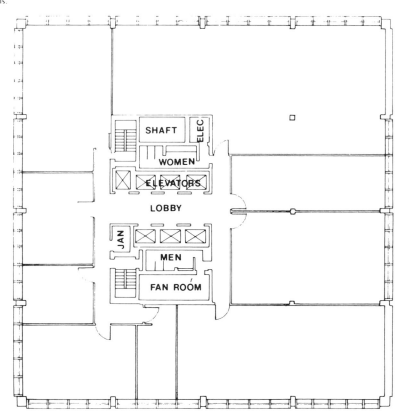

*Note: Assumes glass line as illustrated is the dominant portion. See illustrations "A" through "D".

Page six of a ten page document. *To avoid misinterpretation, this page should not be used without the complete document.*

Reprinted with permission of Building Owners and Managers Association (BOMA) International, Washington, DC.

EXHIBIT 7.12 *(Continued)*

Rentable Area

American National Standard 265.1-1980

The Rentable Area of a floor shall be computed by measuring to the inside finished surface of the dominant portion of the permanent outer building walls, excluding any major vertical penetrations of the floor.

No deductions shall be made for columns and projections necessary to the building.

The Rentable Area of an office on the floor shall be computed by multiplying the Usable Area of that office by the quotient of the division of the Rentable Area of the floor by the Usable Area of the floor resulting in the "R/U Ratio" described herein.

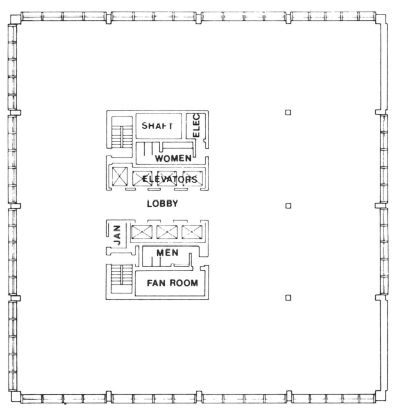

*Note: Assumes glass line as illustrated is the dominant portion. See illustrations "A" through "D".

Page seven of a ten page document. *To avoid misinterpretation, this page should not be used without the complete document.*

Reprinted with permission of Building Owners and Managers Association (BOMA) International, Washington, DC.

EXHIBIT 7.12 *(Continued)*

American National Standard Z65.1-1980

Construction Area

The Construction Area of a floor shall be computed by measuring to the outside finished surface of permanent outer building walls. The Construction Area of a building shall be the sum of the Construction Area of all enclosed floors of the building, including basements, mechanical equipment floors, penthouses, and the like.

Store Area

The number of square feet in a ground floor Store Area shall be computed by measuring from the building line in the case of street frontages, and from the inner surface of other outer building walls and from the inner surface of corridor and other permanent partitons and to the center of partitions that separate the premises from adjoining rentable areas.

No deduction shall be made for vestibules inside the building line or for columns or projections necessary to the building.

No addition should be made for bay windows extending outside the building line.

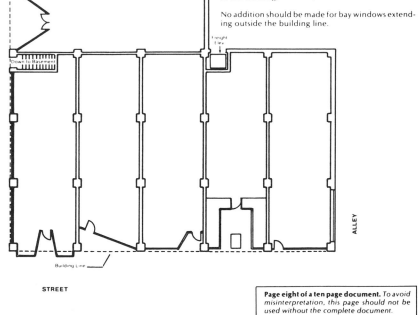

Page eight of a ten page document. *To avoid misinterpretation, this page should not be used without the complete document.*

Reprinted with permission of Building Owners and Managers Association (BOMA) International, Washington, DC.

The developer must get $19.80 per square foot on 1,111 square feet to achieve $22,000. This space of 1,111 square feet rentable, which includes 1,000 square feet usable and 111 square feet of common area, generates $22,000 of income when it is leased at $19.80. The $19.80 rentable rate appears to be more competitive than the $22 usable rate.

Another method of determining the load factor is to measure all common areas, including the building's lobby, and divide this number by the square footage of usable area to arrive at a percentage load factor.

Some owners believe they are generating additional rent by leasing a building on a rentable basis instead of a usable basis, but it is difficult to believe that tenants would be fooled by the different methods of quoting rent per square foot. A building can only achieve market rents, regardless of how space is calculated. Tenants know that they need a certain amount of usable space; when leasing agents are comparing rents for several buildings, they will determine the monthly or annual rental cost for the amount of the space actually occupied regardless of how the landlord measures the space.

Developers are conscious of the tenant's concerns regarding the cost of space and are responding by attempting to minimize inefficient common areas and decrease the load factor. The exception to this is buildings that have a special common area feature such as a spacious and elegant lobby or atrium to create a prestigious ambience.

Neither the shopping center industry nor the industrial building industry has adopted a standard method of measuring space, so the property manager will need to conduct a survey of how space is measured in the area. While measuring usable space from the center of the demising walls to either the interior surface or exterior surface of outer walls is a common method, few property owners would go so far as to measure to the outside of the overhang in front of the building, known as the drip line. This aggressive method could earn a landlord a shady reputation when tenants realize that the landlord did not explain that rent is being paid on the sidewalk or the area under the building's overhang.

Whatever method is used for measuring space, the person responsible for leasing should explain the method to the prospective tenant to avoid any misunderstandings or ill will.

§ 7.8 PROSPECTING FOR TENANTS

Prospecting for commercial tenants is one of those never-ending responsibilities that takes the leasing agent down many paths, quite often with uncertain results. However, most leasing agents indicate that in spite of the uncertainties, they are most successful when they are actively prospecting, no matter the particular activity.

(a) PROSPECTING TECHNIQUES

Following is a review of prospecting techniques for shopping centers, office and medical buildings, and industrial properties.

The Leasing Sign

It is generally agreed that one of the most effective leasing tools is a sign on the property. The sign should be in good condition and professionally designed and fabricated to reflect well on the project. It should be easily read from the street, with the leasing agent's name and phone number in large print, the name of the developer, particularly if the developer is known for quality projects, major tenants and, where applicable, an indication of broker cooperation. Some leasing agents like to indicate the square footage of space available, but that can limit the inquiries, and quite often tenants are not sure of their space needs.

Direct Mail

A direct-mail program to selected prospects can be very effective. The mailer should be professionally prepared and should have all necessary information without being too cluttered. An 8½-by-11-inch sheet folded three ways can be sent out without an envelope or placed in an envelope with a letter. The mailing can be targeted to a specific use or to tenants in a specific area. Even those who are not in the market for space become aware of the project and may discuss it with someone who does have an interest. Those who do extensive direct mailings indicate a better response if the mailing includes a postage-paid response card. An overall response of 1 to 2 percent is considered good in direct-mail campaigns.

Cold Canvass

Calling on tenants in their place of business can be very time consuming, but it is still considered to be a very productive prospecting activity. The leasing agent can canvass for specific uses or for overall knowledge of an area and can find prospects for other properties as an additional benefit. For each canvassing trip, a goal of a specific number of calls should be determined. Business cards and information sheets should be handed out freely. It is wise not to try to accomplish too much in the first visit. If the decision maker is not in, the astute leasing agent will speak with the manager, clerk, or receptionist; leave the information; and request that the information be passed on to the decision maker.

Telephone Canvass

From the point of view of time, the telephone can be a very effective leasing tool because it allows one to contact many prospects in a single day. As in canvassing, specific goals are necessary. The purpose of the call is to find out if the business owner is in the market for additional space and to obtain permission to send a brochure or schedule a follow-up visit.

Billboards

Larger centers, specialty centers, and major commercial projects with a large trade area can often benefit from a "coming soon" billboard campaign. It is difficult to measure the impact of billboards, but there are many situations where they can be a useful marketing tool.

Project Signs

New projects will often have a large project sign with a color rendering, with the names of the developer, leasing agent, architect, general contractor, and lender. The leasing agent's phone number including area code is placed strategically on the sign.

Trade Journal Ads

Every profession has a trade organization with a trade journal. Advertising property in a trade journal—for example, advertising a shopping center in *Women's Wear Daily* or a restaurant pad in *Restaurant News*—is an effective way to reach a specific category of tenants.

Classified Ads

It is generally agreed that in most major cities classified ads for the renting of commercial space do not work well. Quite often they are effective in smaller cities, but heavy reliance should not be placed on this source for tenant prospects.

Display Ads

These larger box-shaped ads are used to announce the grand opening or remodeling of major buildings, major lease-up activities, or major tenants who have just executed leases in the building.

Ads in Business Magazines

Ads in the weekly business newspaper or business magazine in the community are a direct way to reach businesses.

Radio and TV Advertising

These sources are almost never used for leasing. If the shopping center is using radio or TV for merchants' association or marketing fund advertising, it may make sense to add a "space available" trailer, but as a primary source it is not effective in most markets.

Publicity

Publicity has a credibility well beyond that of advertising. The leasing agent should develop a publicity program to cover the entire leasing effort. A creative leasing agent can find many legitimate opportunities for publicity. These include: unique building features, energy-saving features, design features, ground breaking, placing of the corner store, topping off, signing of well-known tenants, signing of anchor tenants, impressive levels of lease-up, naming a building or center manager, assigning a new store manager, and the grand opening. A public relations agency can assure maximum coverage of the property's news. If public relations are handled in-house, a rapport with the media should be developed in advance.

Civic and Business Meetings

Being active in local civic and business organizations offers another means of broadcasting the leasing message and of meeting prospective tenants. These meetings offer an opportunity to tell your story and to listen to what others are doing in the business and civic areas.

Open House

Hosting an open house for the brokerage community and another for the business community to show off a new or remodeled building is a means to bring prospects to the site. Events for an open house include ground breaking, topping off, grand opening, and remodeling.

Employment Ads

Employment ads can indicate which companies are expanding and in need of additional space.

Business Directories

Business and trade associations such as the chamber of commerce, the local economic development council, and the downtown business association have directories that include excellent leasing leads.

Community Charitable Events

Encouraging a community organization such as the metropolitan cultural arts association to hold a benefit black-tie party at the mall or on one of the top floors of an office building will bring community and business leaders to the property and generate excellent publicity for the building.

Monitoring Government Contracts

When the government awards a contract to a manufacturer, the Boeing Company for example, the manufacturer and its suppliers may need additional office or industrial space.

Government's Space Requirements

The General Services Administration sends out mailers for its space requirements. Property owners can be included on the mailing list by contacting the local GSA office. State and local municipalities may have similar mailings for their space needs.

Model Office

Furnishing a model office and inviting brokers to tour the building can help them market the unique features of the building.

Developing Contacts at a Hospital

Medical buildings and office buildings with medical space should be marketed to hospital administrators. Hospitals are encouraging doctors to affiliate with them, and these doctors often need medical office space.

Medical Building Mailing List

The mailing list of the county's medical society is usually available for purchase.

Medical Journal Ads

Another means of direct contact with the medical profession is to advertise in local and regional medical journals. In the Seattle area, the local journal is the King County Medical Society *Bulletin,* and the regional journal is the *Western Journal of Medicine.* The best position for the ads would be the back cover or inside cover pages.

Luncheon for Medical Business Manager

Host a luncheon for the business managers of medical practices to present a new medical building.

Networking

The buzz word in the early 1980s was networking. Networking is simply developing and sharing contacts. It is important to stay active with real estate and business organizations and to have a finger on the pulse of the market.

Brokers' Tours

Scheduling a tour of the building with individual brokerage companies is an excellent opportunity to develop a rapport with a brokerage company and to discuss the building with small groups of leasing agents.

Managers and Leasing Agents of Other Projects

It is worthwhile to build a network with managers and leasing agents of competitive projects. Sharing can produce valuable information on prospective tenants for everyone.

Suppliers

Suppliers of goods or services often have a vested interest in new tenants who could be their new customers. For example, a supplier of restaurant equipment would suggest prospects who would be interested in purchasing equipment from that supplier. A manufacturer of ice cream could be helpful in locating an operator who would then provide another retail outlet for the ice cream. Suppliers can suggest many uses, such as laundromats, dry cleaners, and gift stores.

Building Tenants

Existing tenants are a good source of new tenants. Keep tenants aware of vacancies, as they may be in need of expansion space or know of prospects who would be interested in the building. Remember, the competition is canvassing your building's tenants and so should you.

(b) SOURCES OF RETAIL PROSPECTS

There are several useful prospecting resources for leasing shopping centers and retail properties.

1. The Yellow Pages. The telephone directory in every city has a list of retailers by category.

2. Polk's Directory and Contacts Influential. These companies and other mailing list suppliers will, for a fee, provide a list of retailers by category in almost any area. For example, a list of all men's wear stores in a given city, county, zip code, or state can be purchased from this resource.

3. Annual Franchise Handbook Directory. Not only does this source list hundreds of franchise opportunities, but the franchisor provides the novice merchant with business backup and a plan. While all franchise opportunities are not top-notch, the responsible franchisor can be of great help to the leasing agent in providing recognized businesses to inexperienced operators.

4. ICSC Leasing Opportunities (Annual). This annual publication lists retailers nationwide that have specific expansion plans for the coming year. This is one of the best sources of tenants because the retailers are definitely interested in expanding. The publication provides such information as required size, location, and type of center desired.

5. Directory of Leading Chain Stores. This directory lists all leading chain stores in the country with five or more locations. The tenants are listed by category and by state. Information includes the company name, address and phone, the number of stores, area of activity, and the names of responsible parties in that company.

6. The Book on Value Retailing. This book lists the off-price and outlet discount tenants throughout the country, showing their existing locations and providing information on contacting those merchants. These tenants are now going into more traditional centers, making them likely prospects for leasing all types of centers.

7. Retail Tenant Directory. This directory, published by the *National Mall Monitor*, lists tenants in the major centers in the United States plus many tenants in smaller shopping centers.
MacLean Hunter Media, Inc.
Four Stamford Forum
Stamford, CT 06901
(203) 325-3500

8. Retail Lease Trac. A new publication that publishes tenant prospects by areas of the country, by size, category, and needs.
National Excess Property Exchange
1140 Hammond Dr., Suite 4255
Atlanta, GA 30328
(404) 394-5449

9. Deal Maker's Weekly and Retail Leasing Reporter. These two biweekly publications list tenants around the country who are actively seeking space. They also cover what is happening in various chains, areas of the country, and segments of the business.

10. Shopping Center Digest. This publication covers many of the same areas of the previously mentioned publications but concentrates on centers of 500,000 square feet or more.

11. Factory Outlet World. This publication lists outlet centers and outlet tenants by category.

12. Chamber of Commerce. Prospective tenants sometimes stop by the chamber office to see what's going on, and they will note any leasing opportunities that are registered at the chamber.

13. Redevelopment Agencies. One of the most active sources of tenants today is the redevelopment agency. Its function is to market the benefits of its area to create interest.

14. Other Shopping Centers. The leasing agent should regularly visit other shopping centers and shopping areas with an eye to new tenants, new uses, and new ideas.

15. Monitoring Tenants' Ads. Advertisements on radio and television or in the magazines and newspapers provides a viable list of desirable tenants. Those who advertise warrant special attention in leasing efforts.

16. Classified Ads. Read the classified ads for retailers looking for managers or additional help because they could be in the market for expansion space.

17. Local and Area Directories and Newsletters. Many local directories and newsletters supply excellent information. A call to the leasing leaders in your area should turn up specific publications for a given area.

18. Shopping Center Conventions. The International Council of Shopping Centers' (ICSC) annual convention in May includes a leasing mall. During this three-day event, developers, brokers, and retailers rent booths to display their products. It is not necessary to have a booth to attend, however. The leasing agent can make many contacts with retailers by visiting their booths and scheduling meetings with them during the convention.

19. Deal-Making Sessions and Idea Exchanges. ICSC conducts a deal-making session in the fall similar to the leasing mall activity during its May convention. These trade shows are an excellent place to talk with many tenants in a short period of time. Idea exchanges are two-day conferences attended by brokers, developers, managers, and retailers held in every region of the country.

20. Shopping Center Trade Journals. The following journals are good sources of prospects:

- *Shopping Centers Today,* published monthly by the International Council of Shopping Centers, contains news of the industry, feature stories about retailers, and advertisements.
  665 Fifth Avenue
  New York, NY 10022
  (212) 421-8181
- *Shopping Center World* is published by Communication Channels and includes information and advertisements related to retailers.
  Shopping Center World
  6151 Powers Ferry Road
  Atlanta, GA 30339
  (404) 955-2500
- *Chain Store Age Executive* is published by Lebhar-Friedman, Inc. and carries in-depth information on retailers and the latest trends in retailing.
  Chain Store Age
  P.O. Box 31182
  Tampa, FL 33631-3182
  (813) 664-6707
- *Monitor* focuses on malls but contains general information on shopping centers as well as retailer's ads and news.
  Monitor
  Four Stamford Forum
  Stamford, CN 06901
  (203) 325 3500

Techniques for prospecting are limited only by the property manager's and leasing agent's imagination.

§ 7.9 APPRAISING PROSPECTIVE TENANTS

Proper evaluation of prospective tenants is almost as important as setting the rents at the right levels. If qualifications are too restrictive, some excellent tenant prospects will be lost. On the other hand, if care is not taken, the property manager will be faced with rent collection problems and needless evictions. In very tough leasing markets when tenants are hard to come by, financial requirements can often be relaxed and a chance taken on a weak tenant.

In all properties the leasing agent should ascertain if the prospect has a good history of paying bills and sufficient capital to fulfill the lease obligations. A credit check should be made on the entity that will sign the lease. It is not uncommon for individuals to present themselves as tenant prospects, produce an excellent credit history and financial statement, and then ask that the lease be in the name of a corporation that has poor credit or no credit history at all.

It is not necessary that a tenant prospect have a perfect credit history, but it is a disadvantage if the tenant is burdened with many delinquent accounts. Some tenants pay their bills promptly even in the worst of times, and some pay their bills late even in the best of times. There are no hard and fast rules to determine a good or bad credit report, but it is essential to review each credit and financial report.

A financial statement is always helpful. It should be a signed statement and reasonably current. The building owner is looking for the tenant to have sufficient capital to meet the lease obligations even in difficult times. It is always reassuring to see ownership of real estate on the financial statement since a tenant is less likely to leave without notice if he or she owns property. It must also be remembered, however, that the home is often protected against claims of creditors.

Liquidity commensurate with the obligation being undertaken and a reasonable debt-to-equity ratio is another plus factor. It is not productive to set a minimum net worth. It is better to evaluate each prospect in light of the space being leased, the history of the tenant, the probable investment by the landlord, the risk involved, and the condition of the building in the marketplace. In some cases, small or start-up prospects are asked to prepare a qualification package to help them think through the process and costs of a new business (Exhibit 7.13).

In offices and industrial spaces, the use of the space is seldom the reason a tenant is turned down. Sometimes a prospective tenant may want to employ too many people in the space or will generate too much noise but, generally, office and industrial tenants are evaluated with emphasis on their financial statement rather than on their use.

In shopping centers, the property manager not only will review a tenant's financial statement and credit checks, but also will look at the tenant as a merchant and analyze how the business fits the shopping center's intended tenant mix. In most uses, these considerations are equal to the financial considerations. While property managers should not discriminate in commercial properties based on a tenant's race, color, creed, national origin, age, or gender, a tenant can be turned down if its use does not fit the tenant mix.

The tenant's ability as a merchant must be evaluated. What are the tenant's current sales? Does the tenant have a good reputation in the

EXHIBIT 7.13

Prospective Lessee Qualifications

Complete in full and submit to:

This form does not obligate either party to the performance of a contract for leasehold property. It is purely for information and does not constitute an offer to lease property or any negotiation for such a purpose.

Name: _____ Home Phone: _____

Residence Address: _____ Business Phone: _____

_____ Social Security #: _____

_____

Own ____ or Rent ____ If rented, monthly rent: _____

Name and address of landlord: _____

_____

_____

Which shopping center are you interested in? _____

What kind of business do you propose to run there? _____

_____

Present business or profession: _____

     Salary (annual) _____ Will this income continue? _____

     Other income (annual) _____

May we contact your present employer? Yes ____ No ____

Shall we contact you first?: Yes ____ No ____

Employer's name and address _____

_____

                Phone number: _____

Business Experience— Retail: Describe fully the business operations and your roles; indicate dates:

_____

_____

_____

_____

EXHIBIT 7.13 *(Continued)*

<u>Other Work Experience</u>: Describe fully the business operations and your roles; indicate dates:

_____

_____

_____

_____

_____

_____

_____

If you have other businesses, please provide pertinent operating statements for the last twenty-four months where possible.

Will you have a continuing role in these businesses? If so, what will that role be?

_____

_____

_____

_____

_____

_____

How will you operate your new business at our property? Who will manage? How many employees will you need?

_____

_____

_____

_____

_____

_____

_____

_____

_____

_____

EXHIBIT 7.13 *(Continued)*

If your business is a partnership or a joint venture, describe its legal and financial structure and submit copies of all appropriate legal documents.

_____   _____

_____   _____

_____   _____

_____   _____

_____   _____

_____   _____

If your business involves a franchise, supply a copy of the agreement, information on how the purchase is being financed and financial and business report on the franchisor.

What improvements do you plan to make to the premises (fixtures, carpet, etc.) and at what cost? How will improvements be financed?

_____   _____

_____   _____

_____   _____

_____   _____

_____   _____

_____   _____

_____   _____

Describe your anticipated start-up operating expenses at the new location and list amounts (include inventory, supplies, initial payroll costs, insurance, etc.)

_____ $_____

_____ $_____

_____ $_____

_____ $_____

_____ $_____

_____ $_____

_____ $_____

_____ $_____

EXHIBIT 7.13 *(Continued)*

How will you finance your start-up expenses?

_____

_____

_____

Analysis of projected income from operations at the new location for the first two years (complete where applicable).

Revenues

Gross sales	$_____	$_____
Cost of goods sold	_____	_____
Gross margin	_____	_____
Other revenues (specify)	_____	_____
TOTAL REVENUES	$_____	$_____

Expenses

Salaries and wages	$_____	$_____
Payroll taxes	_____	_____
Compensation insurance	_____	_____
Utilities (PG&E, water, telephone)	_____	_____
Repairs and maintenance	_____	_____
Janitorial services, laundry	_____	_____
Supplies	_____	_____
Advertising and promotion	_____	_____
Rent and related costs	_____	_____
Insurance (fire, liability, plate glass)	_____	_____
Management fee	_____	_____
Real estate taxes	_____	_____
Personal property taxes	_____	_____
Financial expenses (include principal payments)	_____	_____
Total expenses	$_____	$_____
Net Operating Income (cash)	$_____	$_____

EXHIBIT 7.13 *(Continued)*

If you project a loss in net operating income, explain how it will be financed and supply supporting material.

_____

_____

_____

_____

_____

_____

_____

_____

_____

Current Financial Statement

I   Personal: Where a partnership, joint venture or corporation is involved, the appropriate financial statement should be supplied.

II. Business: If several businesses are involved, supply separate individual financial statements where possible.

Indicate sources and amounts of income other than that from business described herein

_____

_____

_____

_____

_____

_____

_____

_____

_____

Please include a means of verification of all items on the attached financial statement: i.e., account number, tax bills and returns, inventories, etc.

EXHIBIT 7.13 *(Continued)*

FINANCIAL CONDITION AS OF _____, 19 ____

Name(s)	
Residence Address	Telephone Number
Business Address	Telephone Number

MARITAL STATUS:

☐ MARRIED   ☐ SEPARATED   ☐ UNMARRIED

If you check either of the first two boxes, are any of the assets listed community property?   ☐ Yes ☐ No

If the answer is "Yes," list spouse's name if not listed above: _____

	ASSETS	AMOUNT			LIABILITIES	AMOUNT	
CASH				NOTES PAYABLE TO BANKS			
					(Itemize, Schedule 6)		
STOCKS AND BONDS	Listed (Schedule 1)			OTHER NOTES AND ACCOUNTS PAYABLE	Real Estate Loans (Schedule 2)		
	Unlisted (Schedule 1)				Sales Contracts & Sec. Agrmts. (Sch. 5)		
					Loans on Life Insurance Policies (Sch. 4)		
REAL ESTATE	Improved (Schedule 2)						
	Unimproved (Schedule 2)			TAXES PAYABLE	Current Year's Income Taxes Unpaid		
	Trust Deeds & Mortgages (Schedule 3)				Prior Year's Income Taxes Unpaid		
					Real Estate Taxes Unpaid		
LIFE INSURANCE	Cash Surrender Value (Schedule 4)						
					Unpaid Interest		
ACCOUNTS AND NOTES RECEIVABLE	Relatives and Friends (Schedule 5)			OTHER LIABILITIES	Others (Itemize, Schedule 5)		
	Collectible (Schedule 5)						
	Doubtful (Schedule 5)						
OTHER PERSONAL PROPERTY	Automobile				TOTAL LIABILITIES		
	Other (Itemize, Schedule 5)				NET WORTH		
	TOTAL				TOTAL		

ANNUAL INCOME	(REFER TO FEDERAL INCOME TAX RETURNS FOR PREVIOUS YEAR)		ANNUAL EXPENDITURES	(REFER TO FEDERAL INCOME TAX RETURNS FOR PREVIOUS YEAR)	
SALARY OR WAGES			PROPERTY TAXES AND ASSESSMENTS		
DIVIDENDS AND INTEREST			FEDERAL AND STATE INCOME TAXES		
RENTALS (GROSS)			REAL ESTATE LOAN PAYMENTS		
BUSINESS OR PROFESSIONAL INCOME (NET)			PAYMENTS ON CONTRACTS AND OTHER NOTES		
OTHER INCOME (DESCRIBE) (Income from alimony,			INSURANCE PREMIUMS		
child support, or maintenance payments need not			ESTIMATED LIVING EXPENSES		
be disclosed)			OTHER		
TOTAL INCOME			TOTAL EXPENDITURES		

Give details of any contingent liability as endorser or guarantor, or on suits or judgments pending. (If necessary, use separate sheet.)

_____

_____

HAVE YOUR INCOME TAX RETURNS EVER BEEN QUESTIONED BY ANY GOVERNMENTAL AUTHORITY? _____ (If so, explain) _____

_____

HAVE YOU EVER GONE THROUGH BANKRUPTCY? (Explain)

_____

HAVE YOU FILED HOMESTEAD? (Explain)

_____

EXHIBIT 7.13 *(Continued)*

Additional Bank References

Name: _____   Acct # _____

Bank: _____   Phone: _____

Address: _____

_____

I hereby authorize the bank to release information confirming my account to .
Company.

          Signature: _____

. . . .

Name: _____   Acct # _____

Bank: _____   Phone: _____

Address: _____

_____

I hereby authorize the bank to release information confirming my account to .
Company.

          Signature: _____

. . . .

Name: _____   Acct # _____

Bank: _____   Phone: _____

Address: _____

_____

I hereby authorize the bank to release information confirming my account to .
Company.

          Signature: _____

. . . .

EXHIBIT 7.13 *(Continued)*

II   Bank managers and loan officers: (include phone numbers)

_____

_____

_____

_____

_____

III   Landlords (business): (include phone numbers)

_____

_____

_____

_____

_____

IV   Suppliers: (include addresses, phone numbers and account numbers)

_____

_____

_____

_____

_____

_____

community? It can be harmful to the other merchants if a tenant does not maintain the center's hours, sells shoddy merchandise, offers misleading sales, has an unreasonable return policy, or has rude help. On the other hand, the well-respected, high-volume merchant is highly desirable and is often granted concessions because he or she will attract other good merchants and create traffic for the center.

Sales in shopping centers are stated, for comparison purposes, in sales per square foot. By using *The Dollars and Cents of Shopping Centers* as a guide, the property manager can evaluate how a tenant measures up to similar merchants in the area. If, for instance, a prospective boutique tenant plans to generate sales of $100 per square foot, and *Dollars and Cents* indicates that an independent women's shop will generally gross about $178 per square foot, this prospect is probably not a successful operator and will generate less traffic than a typical women's shop. If the rent is more than 15 percent of its sales, the tenant may have problems paying the rent. While the lease may still make sense, the situation requires clarification. The manager needs to know the sales trend for the merchant, the merchandise line, and the industry's performance as a whole.

Each tenant's merchandise must be viewed in light of the type of customers it will attract to the center. An auto parts store does not fit into a fashion center because it draws the wrong type of customer and will not generate traffic for the other merchants. The appearance of the store is another factor in evaluating a prospect. Is the tenant's present store attractive, well stocked, modern, inviting, and clean? If the prospect falls short in any of these areas, it may create a poor image for the center.

Does the merchant advertise? Many small tenants mistakenly assume that the center will provide their traffic and they will not have to advertise. Retail tenants should expect to spend 3% to 4% of their projected gross sales on advertising.

In evaluating retail tenants it is necessary to talk with them about their business plan, their philosophy, and how they work with other tenants and center management. Making inquiries of other merchants, suppliers, and former landlords can provide valuable information.

If a merchant is opening his or her first store, the property manager might want to locate a similar shop and visit it to be able to discuss likes and dislikes and suggestions for adapting to the prospect's new operation. A business plan with an operating budget and sales projection is essential in evaluating a first-time operator. The new merchants needs to be aware that most retail businesses do not generate a profit during its first year of operations.

The appraising process is more of an art than a science. The final decision will be based on many factors, including the financial strength of the tenant, the tenant's ability as a merchant, how much the landlord has to spend on improvements, how crucial it is to have that particular use, how many vacancies are available on this property, and how many vacancies are available in the general marketing area. The goal is to obtain the best possible merchant under the existing circumstances, thus minimizing the risks of tenant failure and maximizing the potential for percentage rent.

§ 7.10   TENANT MIX

Tenant mix is the synergism created by the right grouping of tenants. Webster defines synergism as "the simultaneous action of separate agencies which, together, have greater total effect than the sum of their individual effect." In other words, with the right mix, the whole is greater than the sum of its parts.

In a shopping center, the strength of the synergism created by several merchants in close proximity is dependent upon which merchants are grouped together. The correct tenant mix in a shopping center will maximize each tenant's sales potential and the center's percentage rent potential. For instance, regional malls are tenanted primarily by fashion department stores and fashion and gift shops. A neighborhood center anchored by a supermarket and drugstore will be occupied primarily by service and food tenants who service the customer's daily needs.

Another aspect of tenant mix is the placement of tenants. Some businesses will thrive in a space with high traffic and high visibility. For instance, a jewelry store is an ideal center court tenant in a mall. A pharmacy should be on the ground floor of a medical building and have street-level exposure.

When a leasing plan is developed, the leasing team compiles a list of ideal tenants and assigns each a location in the building. When negotiating a lease with these tenants, the agent attempts to sell them on a particular location. The leasing agent's success depends primarily upon the strength of the negotiating parties. Seldom is every tenant located on the first proposed leasing plan, but this plan is the starting place for locating tenants.

(a)   SHOPPING CENTERS

Once the property manager has completed an in-depth market survey, the elements of the shopping center's tenant mix start to form. The purpose of the tenant mix is to provide the broadest range of goods and services consistent with the customers within the trade area and within the center itself.

Each type of shopping center will have a different tenant mix because it is meeting or serving different customer needs and different trade areas. A neighborhood shopping center anchored by a supermarket and drugstore provides the daily household needs for its customers and must fit the neighborhood. You would not place a gourmet supermarket in a low- or middle-income neighborhood, nor would you place a discount drugstore in an affluent suburb. If the market and drugstore are properly selected for the trade area and the other stores are consistent with these anchors, the tenant mix will be compatible with the purpose of the center and the trade area.

Restaurants are usually a good draw to a shopping center, but again, they must be in keeping with the residents in the trade area. Fast-food restaurants might be very successful in younger markets but are not likely to do as well in the affluent, older market. A community of retired persons is not likely to support a pizza parlor or a jeans shop; a small college town is not likely to support a guild jeweler or a Gucci store.

Typical tenants for a neighborhood shopping center include cleaners, laundromat, shoe repair, florist, bank, savings and loan, real estate office, card and gift shop, travel agent, video rental, fast food, restaurant, delicatessen, pizza, books, ice cream, yogurt, hobby shop, liquor store, records, film developer, health spa, hardware, variety store and, to a very small degree, fashion.

The community center generally has a fashion focus in addition to the service tenants found in the neighborhood center. It is usually anchored by two or three major tenants, including a junior department store or discount fashion store, and draws from a wider trade area than a neighborhood center. Because of the fashion draw of the community center, it is not unusual to see several men's and women's apparel, jewelry, and shoe stores in this type of center. Community centers also provide for the daily needs of its trade area, so supermarkets, drugstores, variety stores, and home improvement stores are additional anchors.

The regional and super-regional centers are heavily fashion oriented because of the fashion orientation of the anchors—the department stores. You would probably find Saks or Neiman Marcus as an anchor in a regional center serving a high-income area and Sears or Wal-Mart in a middle-income area. The emphasis in regional and superregional centers is on fashion, with upwards of 20% of the square footage of the small shops leased to fashion stores.

Food is always a good draw, and because of the traffic generated, small specialty shops can do very well. Generally, supermarkets are not compatible with mall tenants. If a supermarket is part of a very large center, it is generally located on the perimeter of the parking lot rather than on the mall.

The festival or theme center is oriented to the tourist and, to a lesser degree, to nearby workers. The center itself is a draw, and the merchandise is more "one of a kind" than in traditional shops. For example, music box shops, teddy bear shops, or kite shops will not usually survive in a neighborhood or community center but will thrive in a specialty center.

Restaurants are the traditional anchors for festival or theme centers. Some smaller theme centers specialize in very specific uses such as restaurants only, automobile service and support, home decorating and furnishings. A very large trade area is usually required to support these types of centers.

Discount, outlet, and off-price centers are now referred to as "value centers" and have tenants selling in all three areas. It is important to maintain the value image, but it is also difficult to ensure that merchants will actually sell at a discount. "Fashion for less" is the main attraction of this type of center, with other merchandise lines filling out the balance of the mix. Restaurants, again, are an important part of the tenant mix, as are linens, shoes, jewelry, children's wear, and gifts.

Sources like *Sales and Marketing Management* magazine, *Dollars and Cents of Shopping Centers,* and other trade publications reveal how customers generally spend their money. This information can be measured against what is actually being spent in the area, and why, to determine the probable market support available for new retail ventures in the area. This is not a science, as many factors must be evaluated, but such an exercise can help the leasing agent or owner direct the leasing effort to uses that have the greatest probability of success.

(b) OFFICE AND MEDICAL BUILDINGS

The tenant mix is not as critical to the success of an office or medical building as it is to the success of a shopping center. However, office building tenants can enhance or impair the reputation of the building and its marketing and leasing program.

In marketing the building, the property manager can use the presence of respected and established tenants to great advantage. For example, an office building tenanted primarily by Fortune 500 companies will provide a reputation of success and prosperity to the building, as will a building with leading law firms. An office building located in the state capital may have several government agencies as tenants, lending a sense of stability and strength to the tenant mix. A building's tenant mix may include services to the business community. A restaurant, bank, escrow office, stockbroker, printer, health club, business club, and gift shop are amenities that should be marketed as additional services in the building.

A building's tenant mix will be reflected in its population level. A building with mostly professional offices usually has a low population count, while one tenanted mostly with service companies will have a high density. In a heavily populated building, everything from paper supplies to elevators will receive greater use. This is a consideration in estimating the operating expenses for a building.

The tenant mix or tenant profile of a medical building can be a positive feature in marketing and leasing. A pharmacist is a convenience to physicians and their patients. A coffee shop is a convenience to the doctors and their staff. A general practitioner may use specialists such as cardiologists or obstetricians for consultation and referral. Medical groups such as radiology labs and physical therapy departments are draws for other doctors to locate in the building. All of these services should be used in marketing and leasing the building.

(c) INDUSTRIAL PARKS

The industrial park is least affected by the tenant mix but, like the office building, it does benefit from prestigious tenants and supporting uses within the park. Larger industrial parks will develop pads or outlots for restaurants and market space to tenants that will provide services to other tenants in the park. If an industrial park is near a major manufacturer or can attract a major manufacturer, this tenant may attract its suppliers to locate in the park.

Planned industrial developments will include areas for businesses that service the employees of the industrial tenants. The Irvine Industrial Park in southern California includes fast-food facilities, full-service restaurants, a medical facility, business services, hotels, and retail facilities. Smaller industrial parks frequently develop a similar tenant mix on a smaller scale. Supporting uses within or adjacent to an industrial park provide important services to the park's tenants and their employees.

The tenant mix in an industrial park or area should be one of the features in the marketing materials for the project.